社会转型与教师教育改革

——第三届教师教育国际研讨会文集

SHEHUI ZHUANXING YU JIAOSHI JIAOYU GAIGE

——DISANJIE JIAOSHI JIAOYU GUOJI YANTAOHUI WENJI

主　编　汪青松　徐书业　张　群

副主编　曹长德　梁　庆　包琼就

中国科学技术大学出版社

内容简介

本书是第三届教师教育国际研讨会文集，由全国教师教育研究会和全国师范学院协作委员会结集出版。

文集共分三大部分。第一部分，社会转型与教师教育策略的变革（共收录论文13篇）；第二部分，教师专业发展研究（共收录论文10篇）；第三部分，师范院校教师培养的探索与研究（共收录论文29篇）。

图书在版编目(CIP)数据

社会转型与教师教育改革：第三届教师教育国际研讨会文集/汪青松，徐书业，张群主编. —合肥：中国科学技术大学出版社，2010.6

ISBN 978-7-312-02710-9

Ⅰ. 社… Ⅱ. ①汪… ②徐… ③张… Ⅲ. 教育改革-国际学术会议-文集 Ⅳ. G511-53

中国版本图书馆CIP数据核字（2010）第102980号

出版 中国科学技术大学出版社
地址：安徽省合肥市金寨路96号，邮政编码：230026
网址：http://press.ustc.edu.cn

印刷 合肥学苑印务有限公司

发行 中国科学技术大学出版社

经销 全国新华书店

开本 787 mm×1092 mm 1/16

印张 21.25

字数 544千

版次 2010年6月第1版

印次 2010年6月第1次印刷

定价 50.00元

序

把握社会转型契机，深化教师教育改革

王宏凯
（全国教师教育课程资源专家委员会秘书长）

百年大计，教育为本。教育大计，教师为本。经历百年历史的我国教师教育正处于一个历史性转折和重要的发展时期。教师教育作为教育事业的工作母机，关系到教育改革发展的全局和建设更高水平小康社会的目标。中国教师教育的发展伴随着中国社会的变革和转型，在教师教育改革与发展的新的历史时期，我们应该从社会转型与教师教育改革的高度认识教师教育优先发展的战略地位。

改革开放以来，中国社会政治、经济、文化等各个方面都发生了深刻变化，从农业的、乡村的、相对封闭的传统型社会，向工业的、城镇的、开放的现代型社会转型。由此而带来了社会结构转换、机制转轨、利益调整和观念转变，甚至人们的行为方式、生活方式、价值体系都会发生明显的变化。社会转型具有整体性、复杂性和渐进性的特征，社会转型长期积累而带来的社会变化是巨大的和深层次的，其中必然包含对教育的影响。在中国教育体系中，教师教育具有非常重要的地位。党和国家高度重视教师队伍建设，党的十七大报告中明确指出：加强教师队伍建设，重点提高农村教师素质。《国家中长期教育改革和发展规划纲要》专章阐述“加强教师队伍建设”问题，提出了教师队伍建设和教师教育发展的目标和任务。近年来，国家在教师教育领域采取了一系列的举措，加大对教师教育领域的投入，提升教师素质，促进教师队伍的专业化发展，先后启动教师教育网络联盟计划，教师教育创新平台项目计划，农村学校教育硕士师资培养计划，农村义务教育阶段学校教师特设岗位计划，中小学教师国家级培训计划，农村中小学教师特岗计划，实行师范生免费教育，研制《国家教师教育课程标准》，成立全国教师教育专家委员会、全国教师教育课程资源专家委员会，高校学前、小学、中学教育教学指导委员会等有力措施。中国教师教育的改革与发展无不是在中国社会转型的大背景下展开的。

为了探讨社会转型与教师培养和专业发展的问题，全国教师教育学会师范学院协作委员会于2009年10月23日至25日，在广西钦州学院围绕着“社会转型与教师教育改革”这一主题，召开了第三届教师教育国际研讨会暨第二届全国教师教育学会师范院校协作委员会年会。会议的主题引起了国内外专家学者的高度关注，正如马立会长给大会发来的贺词中所言：“‘社会转型与教师教育改革’这一主题非常具有前瞻性，是教师教育必须面对的问题，必须解决的问题。”来自美国、澳大利亚、泰国、越南、韩国等国家的教师教育专家、学者以及全国教师教育学会师范院校协作委员会各理事单位、国内各师范院校等共200多名代表参加了会议。

大会分为专家主题报告、代表发言、代表讨论等程序，陈永明教授题目为“社会变革与教师作用”、汪青松教授题为“社会转型与教师教育的改革与创新”、美国 Douglas DeWitt 博士题

为“21世纪的师资培训——使教师有能力指导学生为适应新兴国际社会做准备”等报告，让人耳目一新，并引起了与会代表热烈的讨论。会议强化了世界范围内的学术交流；传递了国内外的研究信息，学术动态；展示了新思路、新成果；深化了与会者对“社会转型与教师教育改革”这一个主题的认识；分享了世界各地、各学校教师教育改革的成果和经验。

会上的交流固然精彩纷呈，但却是短暂的；研究论文的汇集虽然不是轰轰烈烈的，但却是研讨者智慧的结晶，是研讨会成果的固化和积淀。全国教师教育学会师范学院协作委员会已经分别于2008、2009年出版了两本国际研讨会的论文集，在国内外赢得了良好的声誉。从第一届教师教育国际研讨会的主题“科学人文融合与复合型教师能力培养”、第二届研讨会的“科学人文艺术教育的融合与教师综合素质和实践能力培养”，到本届“社会转型与教师教育改革”，关注的问题层次越来越高，对教师教育研讨越来越深入，为推动教师改革产生了重要作用。

《国家中长期教育改革和发展规划纲要》明确指出：“加强教师教育，深化教师教育改革，创新培养模式，增强实习实践环节，强化师德修养和教学能力训练，提高教师培养质量。”中国教师教育已进入从规模发展转向质量提升的新阶段。随着社会结构和劳动力市场的变化，教师的供求关系和队伍建设的制度环境正发生较大变化，教师培养数量和规模问题基本解决，质量和结构问题成为突出矛盾。可以这样认为，中国教师教育的总体发展思路已明确。一是教师教育在教育事业中处于优先发展的战略地位。二是教师教育是国家的事业和政府的责任。三是教师教育需要一个开放灵活的体系。四是教师教育是大学的使命，职前职后一体化势在必然。

在中国教师教育体系中，师范院校的改革与发展扮演着重要的角色，全国教师教育学会师范学院协作委员会以其卓有成效的工作，在教师教育理论研究、教育教学实践、师范院校之间互相交流、取长补短和资源整合等方面，有力地推进了地方师范学院的共同发展。

在论文集出版之际，借此序言祝愿全国教师教育学会师范学院协作委员会越办越好，为中国教师教育事业做出更大的贡献。

2010年5月于北京

目 录

第一部分 社会转型与教师教育策略的变革

第二部分 教师专业发展研究

第三部分 师范院校教师培养的探索与研究

第一部分
社会转型与教师教育策略的变革

社会转型与教师教育的改革与创新

汪青松*

（安庆师范学院，安徽 安庆 246011）

摘 要：社会转型要求教师教育随之转型。教师教育发展的三个阶段，正好与从农业社会向工业社会再向信息社会的双重转型相对应。大众化教育要求师范院校从封闭向开放、从定向培养向非定向培养转变。教师教育改革适应社会转型，高师教育面向、适应、服务、引领基础教育。

当代中国社会正处于深刻的转型过程之中。社会转型要求教育随之而转型，要求教师教育呈现崭新的面貌。研究社会转型的内涵与特点，并根据社会转型的要求开展教师教育改革创新，对于高师院校的发展具有重要的现实意义。

一

社会转型是社会从较低社会发展形态向较高社会发展形态的转变过程。关于社会转型的基本定义，学界看法不尽一致。有人认为，社会转型是社会形态类型的转换；有人认为，社会转型是技术形态类型的转换，从经济全球化视角看，社会转型是世界范围内社会开放与交流的过程；还有人认为，人类社会是一部社会变迁的进步史，社会变迁是一个缓慢的过程，而转型是社会变迁中的“惊险一跳”。我们认为，社会转型是社会经济结构、发展方式、文化形态等发生的深刻变化；当前我国的社会转型是经济、政治、文化、社会结构的重组与跃迁，是整个社会由僵滞走向变革、由封闭走向开放、由落后走向文明的现代化过程。邓小平把1978年以来中国社会转型概括为从以阶级斗争为纲转到以发展生产力为中心，从封闭转到开放，从固守成规转到各方面的改革。

从社会转型的内容看，当代我国的社会转型表现为从农业社会向工业社会、从计划经济向市场经济、从乡村社会向城镇社会、从封闭半封闭社会向开放社会转变的现代型变革，胡锦涛在党的十七大报告中将其表述为以工业化、市场化、城镇化、国际化等为内容的“四化”驱动现代化的进程。从社会转型的特点看，21世纪初我国正处于第二次社会转型。党的十一届三中全会启动的第一次社会转型是从以阶级斗争为纲转向以经济建设为中心；第二次社会转型是科学发展观指导下的从经济建设为中心转向经济社会发展为中心，即经济增长从出口与投资

---

* 汪青松，男，安庆师范学院教授，管理学博士，安徽行政学院常务副院长，全国教师教育学会师范学院协作委员会会长，安徽省高教学会副会长；主要从事高等教育发展、马克思主义中国化研究。

主导转向消费主导，经济社会发展从经济与社会失衡转向经济与社会协调，城乡二元结构转向城乡一体化。

社会转型不可避免地带来文化教育的变化，教师教育必须改革创新才能与社会转型相适应。有学者认为，教师教育发展将历经三个阶段：第一阶段是经验模仿的非专业化阶段，第二阶段是封闭式定向培养阶段，第三阶段是开放式非定向培养阶段。教师教育发展的三个阶段，正好与农业社会向工业社会再向信息社会的双重转型相对应。

过去，高校存在中央级、省级、市级三个层次，现在把高校分为学术型、教学型、应用型、技能型。地方性教学型高校应培养通识型、应用型人才。按就业划分，可把人才分为金领、白领、蓝领，职业院校培养蓝领人才，一般本科培养白领人才。按功能、学科、就业划分高校，我们地方师范院校就可以找到自己的发展空间和位置。

二

传统社会只需要精英治理，所以是精英教育；工业社会需要大量人才和成批技术劳动者，学校教育应适应工业化需要，象牙塔小规模已不适应，大众化教育要求师范院校从封闭向开放、从定向培养向非定向培养转变。

教师教育从精英教育转到大众化教育，这是两种不同的教师教育形态。精英化教育注重少而精，强调学术性、学科性、实践性，是培养专家的；大众化教育不过分强调学科与学术，而要强调面向与适应社会。学校是工业化的产物，靠私塾、学堂教育培养不出工业化需要的流水作业式的人才。不要把一门课从大一开到大四，大众化教育是培养劳动者，知识要实，适应社会需要，有些课可开专题，少而精，面宽些，要求不能过高。

过去是学历型社会，强调学历，现在是终身教育，终身学习。建设学习型社会，建设学习型企业，起点重要但不是唯一的，可不断学习，是为了适应不断转型不是要我学，而是我要学，大众教育培养学生养成爱学习的习惯，就是成功；如果学生讨厌害怕学习，一门课结束时把教材卖掉、扔掉或烧掉，那就是失败。

信息化社会要求学校不能关门办学，而应是开放的、拓展的、延伸的，应是学校与社会高度联结，相互配合，相互推动，工作后可以再培训学习。不仅要重视职前培养，而且要重视职后培训，把教师培养的师范教育与教师职后培训打通。

为什么要成立师范学院协作会，师范大学、师专和师范学院各有特殊使命，应正确定位，所以自己组织起来，明确自己的发展空间与层次。从高校人才培养、科学研究、社会服务功能看，全国重点大学重点在科技创新，最基层的服务型师范教育高校，人才培养应注重通识性、应用性。正如安庆师范学院倡导通识为基、人文为魂、能力为本、服务为重的办学理念。

三

教师教育改革要适应社会转型，高师教育面向、适应、服务、引领基础教育。第一要面向，“三个面向”；第二要适应，还要服务，服务才是深度面向与适应；最后是引领。我们有资格引领基础教育了吗？我们正适应社会转型的变化，师范生到农村、企业、地方，顶岗支教、社会实践，服务社会的发展；高师院校还存在与社会脱节，对社会转型视而不见，听而不闻的现象。有一次我听一位教师上课，她始终站在讲台上，满堂灌，一言堂，从书本到书本，从概念到概念，概念讲完了课也讲结束了，很抽象，不管用。少数教师只顾自己讲，教师授课从上课讲到下课，学生记笔记从上课记到下课，学生坐立不安，没有师生互动，那种课堂用两句话概括：老师累死了，学生烦死了。

我们要学习陶行知的教育观。陶行知教育理念是草根教育，从民间来到民间去，解放学生，社会大课堂，陶行知教育观是教学做合一，以做为中心，做决定学，学决定教。有的教师还是以教学为中心，不知教是干什么、学是干什么。教师教育适应基础教育并不容易，要创新、适应社会转型，要大量投入精力，大量调研，要有强烈的事业心、责任感。要从教育哲学的高度，经济基础与上层建筑关系的高度看待适应社会转型，否则就要落伍被淘汰。

创新型国家建设对教师教育是一个挑战，师范学校长期存在师范性与学术性的争论，实质上是教育性与创新性的争论，综合高校是 4 年制，师范学校是 4 年本科加 1 年师范。教育观、学生观、课堂观、质量观上都要创新。比如，教师上课不能照本宣科，应脱稿教学，如拿着讲稿教学，一是胆小，放不开，怕讲错；二是对教学内容未搞懂，记不熟；三是不尊重学生，盯着讲稿，眼中就没学生，无法互动，脱稿教学有利于师生互动，师生共享共建课堂，例如教育发达国家的课堂非常活跃，是快乐学习。

课堂应是讨论式、启发式的，对学生发言应给予鼓励。信息化社会师生关系已不是一桶水与一滴水的关系，学生可能是一桶水老师却只是一滴水，所以尊重学生十分重要。有一次我搞课堂调查，让学生发表对课堂教学的看法，有一位学生的体会文章是："老师，您第一次让我在课堂上站起来说话，读书这么多年，没哪位老师让我站起来发言。"可见，我们高师院校一般化地要求启发式和互动往往没有实效，而要在教学设计时作出明确规定划出互动、讨论的时间与内容比例，比如一堂课 40 分钟，20 分钟讲课，20 分钟互动。教育创新无所不在，内容、理念、方法、评价等方面都可以创新，关键是要落到实处。

我们把人才培养方案设计为四个模式，知识课、能力课、人文课、服务课，这就把能力培养落到实处了。师范院校仅靠教育学、心理学、实习课培养教师能力是不够的，要把能力培养落实到每个专业课程中去。

素质教育对教师教育提出了挑战。什么叫素质教育？有人说，就是知识、能力、素质协调发展，这里就存在大素质与小素质的重复。有人认为知识、能力、品德协调发展，这还不够，胡锦涛 2009 年五四青年节在中国农业大学的讲话要求培养大学生执著的信念、高尚的品德、丰富的知识、过硬的本领，把素质教育四大要素讲全了，信念、品德，是做人的问题，知识、本领，是做事的问题。这四条对教师教育创新是重大指导。2009 年 8 月，在大连全国教师教育学会年会上，国家总督学柳斌呼吁学习陶行知，解放小学生的手和脚，解放学生大脑。听后感慨万千，陶行知讲话这么多年了，为什么还未解决？就是未当真、未落实、未纳入评价。素质教育不纳入学生考核，教师评价，都无法落实。

教师教育面对全体学生发展素质教育，就要评价标准"四多"即多层次、多元化、多样化、多维度。多维度，是德智体美；多元化，是创新、升学、就业；多层次，是不求全优，而求合格与少数特长；多样化，是面试、笔试、技能测试、顶岗，分流培养。

有人概括素质教育是三位一体，面对全体学生让学生全面发展，从而适应工业化建设；一技之长是有特长、有特殊能力。这还比较抽象，如何面向全体学生，这要有一个评价。教师教育要面向基层，服务社会，培养师范生服务基础教育的能力。

社会转型期地方本科师范院校人才培养的策略
——云南玉溪师范学院师范生培养的探索及实践

熊术新*

(云南玉溪师范学院,云南 玉溪 653100)

摘 要:本文阐述了玉溪师范学院在学校办学定位及人才培养理念下,以学生能力形成为核心修订人才培养方案,以"四个改变"指导课程建设和课堂教学改革以及优化教师教育课程体系,培养适应社会转型人才的教学改革及实践。

关键词:地方本科师范院校;师范生培养;教师教育课程体系

我国目前正面临着前所未有的社会系统整体性变革,在高等教育改革发展中突出表现为学校定位以及人才培养质量规格的多样化。玉溪师范学院属于中国西部边疆地方新建本科师范院校,在社会转型及高等教育改革的背景下,努力探索及实践适合学校改革发展并具有特色的师范生培养办学理念、定位及模式。

一、学校办学定位及人才培养理念

在近十年的本科办学过程中,学校确立了"地方性、教学型、应用型人才培养"的发展定位,确立了"以人为本、能力本位、融入地方、服务区域"的办学理念。为区别于高职高专强调学生的岗位技能培养以及研究型大学强调学生研究开发能力的培养,将应用型人才培养定位于:培养适应基础教育改革发展需要的专业化教师和适应经济社会发展需求的应用型人才。

(一) 以学生能力形成为核心修订人才培养方案

"玉溪师范学院'十一五'改革发展纲要"提出的教育哲学思想是:现代大学的核心内涵是构建主动适应社会对职业能力需要的人才培养模式。据此,学校组织开展了"以学生能力形成和培养为核心的应用型人才培养方案"的研讨和制定工作,新制定的27个本科专业人才培养方案基于应用型人才培养的定位,通过融入现代教育教学理念下的人才观、质量观和课程观,明确了人才培养的规格质量、素质能力要求以及专业能力的内涵、标准、实现方式与途径;以学生能力形成和培养为核心,以实践教学体系构建为重点;实现了人才培养在能力内涵、课程体系、实践体系、教学方法与手段、考核方式等方面的构建和完善,增强了各专业人才培养方案的

---

* 熊术新,男,教授,文化传播学博士,玉溪师范学院院长;主要从事高等教育发展、文化传播及民族文化的研究。

系统性和可操作性,使学校应用型人才培养的目标和任务得到具体落实。

案　例:学前教育专业人才培养方案

人才规格:学前教育专业学生必须具有扎实的专业基本素质,良好的幼儿教育教学活动能力,初步的专业发展能力,现代社会合格公民必备的思想文化素质和身心素质,即现代公民素质。本专业人才规格在"素质"与"能力"两个维度的四个项目上体现,并以能力为核心,其具体表述与解释见下表。

学前教育专业人才培养规格一览表

项目	要素	内涵与要求	培养途径	支撑课程	考核方式
现代公民素质	政治思想道德素质	有正确的政治态度、政治立场,能正确处理个人与他人、集体、国家、民族之间的关系;有合理的世界观、人生观、价值观,学会理性、辩证地分析问题;有求实、创新、参与、合作、竞争等时代精神。有良好的社会公德,能遵纪守法,行为文明;有初步的职业道德,懂得依法执教,喜爱本专业并严谨治学	课程教学;教育见习、实习;班级管理;第二课堂活动	毛泽东、邓小平思想概论与"三个代表";中国近代史纲要;思想品德修养与法律基础;马克思主义基本原理;形式与政策;教育法规与政策	学科课程考试;各学期操行评定及综合素质测评;实习成绩综合评价
	社会适应性	正确理解社会关系、社会精神风貌,积极地接纳现实的社会,使自己的需要切合社会的实际,行为符合社会的共同规范;角色行为恰当,能够适应不同阶段的学习生活;能够识别、接受良好的社会生活方式,生活态度乐观,不断适应变化与发展的社会生活	课程教学;班级管理;第二课堂活动;心理辅导;社会实践	思想品德修养与法律基础;马克思主义基本原理;教育概论;形式与政策;普通心理学	学科课程考试;各学期操行评定及综合素质测评
	自我意识	对自己进行分析、判断和评价,进而准确定位,恰当地自我设计,有效地自我调控	课程教学;班级管理;第二课堂活动;心理辅导	思想道德修养与法律基础;普通心理学;教育概论;人文科学概论	学科课程考试;各学期综合素质测评;实习成绩综合评价
	人际交往能力	以语言等各种象征符号与他人进行思想交流、情感沟通,正确处理人际关系。掌握礼貌、诚恳、谦虚、信任、宽容、有分寸等基本的交往法则	课程教学;班级管理;第二课堂活动;心理辅导;社会实践	思想品德修养与法律基础;马克思主义基本原理;教育概论;普通心理学;大学语文	学科课程考试;各学期综合素质测评;实习成绩综合评价

续表

项目	要素	内涵与要求	培养途径	支撑课程	考核方式
专业基本素质	爱心为主的职业情感	能够悦纳大部分人(特别是幼儿)、事、物,给予关心和爱护;能够得到他人认同,赢得喜爱与支持;喜欢教师职业,在职业训练中有成功感、荣誉感;能给幼儿爱的呵护	课程教学;班级管理;第二课堂活动;教育见习、实习;社会实践	普通心理学;学前心理学;教育概论;学前教育学;中外学前教育史;思想品德修养与法律基础	学科课程考试;各学期综合素质测评;专业素质考核;实习成绩综合评价
	合理的专业知识结构	一定深度的学前心理学、学前教育学、幼儿保育与保健知识;懂得幼儿园教育活动及家园联系的基本原则与方法;有从事幼儿园教育必需的语言文学、音乐、舞蹈、美术、手工、体育的知识及基本的自然科学、人文科学知识	课程教学;第二课堂活动;教育见习、实习	本专业所开设的各类专业课程都为学生合理的知识结构提供了支持	学科课程考试;各学期综合素质测评;实习成绩综合评价
	专业合作意识	能在幼儿教育活动中与同事、幼儿、家长及其他社会成员通力合作,有机配合以完成教育教学活动,实现各种活动目的。(现阶段能与老师、同学通力合作,很好地完成各种学习任务)	课程教学;第二课堂活动;教育见习、实习;社会实践;专业素质训练	幼儿游戏理论;幼儿社会性发展;学前教育学;幼儿园管理与幼教法规;学前心理学;普通心理学	学科课程考试;各学期综合素质测评;专业素质考核;实习成绩综合评价
教育教学能力	语言表达能力	以清晰、简练、生动的儿童可接受语言清楚地表达思想、交流情感、讲述故事、朗诵其他文学作品;教学用语准确、简练、生动	课程教学;第二课堂活动;专业素质训练;教育见习、实习	大学语文;教师口语训练;儿童文学;幼儿园语言活动设计;幼儿游戏理论	学科课程考试;专业素质考核;实习成绩综合评价
	艺术活动能力	包括音乐欣赏、唱歌、合唱指挥、钢琴弹奏与伴奏能力;舞蹈欣赏能力,民族民间舞蹈和幼儿舞蹈的表演、编排能力;美术作品欣赏创作,指导幼儿绘画的能力,制作工艺作品、幼儿活动玩具、教学用具的能力;组织幼儿艺术活动的能力	课程教学;第二课堂活动;教育见习、实习;社会实践;专业素质训练	乐理与视唱;琴法Ⅰ、Ⅱ、Ⅲ;声乐Ⅰ、Ⅱ;合唱与指挥;民族民间舞蹈;书法Ⅰ、Ⅱ;幼儿舞蹈技法与创编Ⅰ、Ⅱ;幼儿美术Ⅰ、Ⅱ、Ⅲ;幼儿手工Ⅰ、Ⅱ、Ⅲ;幼儿玩教具设计与制作	学科课程考试;各学期综合素质测评;专业素质考核;实习成绩综合评价
	保育与保健能力	开展养育膳食、物质环境、卫生、安全等方面保育工作;进行心理健康教育、疾病防治、常见护理等	课程教学;第二课堂活动;教育见习、实习	人体解剖生理学;幼儿游戏理论;幼儿园管理与幼教法规;幼儿园五大领域活动设计	学科课程考试;专业素质考核;实习成绩综合评价

续表

项目	要素	内涵与要求	培养途径	支撑课程	考核方式
专业发展能力	幼儿园教育活动的设计、实施能力	准确领会“纲要”，整合教学活动的目标与内容，选择恰当的教学模式与方法来筹划、设计幼儿园五大教育活动；通过语言、行为、特定组织形式和教育手段，以一定的进程把设计好的活动方案实现于自己与幼儿所进行的各类活动之中；并在教学活动中（课堂）有效调控各种要素，使活动有序实施，教学目标得以实现的能力	课程教学；第二课堂活动；教育见习、实习；社会实践；专业素质训练	学前教育学；幼儿园课程；幼儿语言活动设计；幼儿艺术活动设计；幼儿社会活动设计；幼儿科学活动设计；幼儿健康活动设计；幼儿游戏理论	学科课程考试；专业素质考核；实习成绩综合评价
	现代教育技术应用能力	根据幼儿思维发展特点、教育活动类型及目标任务，恰当选择、熟练使用多媒体等设备来提高教育教学质量的能力	课程教学；教育见习、实习	课件设计与制作；计算机文化基础；幼儿园五大领域活动设计	学科课程考试；实习成绩综合评价
	学习能力	自觉、能动地获取各种知识经验，继而不断地调整意识观念和行为方式；提取所需知识进入已有知识体系中并使之发生多项联系，建构新的知识结构以维持自我与社会的平衡的能力	课程教学；第二课堂活动；教育实习；专业素质训练	以“教育概论”、“普通心理学”为基础的本专业众多的学科	学科课程考试；专业素质考核；实习成绩综合评价等
	教育科研能力	能在教育教学中发现问题，对自己的教育教学决策与行为进行反思，并以基本的教育科研方法进行探究；及时获取信息，能动、有效地应用教育信息，以提高对问题的认识和解决水平；能将发现的问题、探究的结果及解决问题的办法撰写为教育科研论文	课程教学；第二课堂活动；教育见习、实习；社会实践；专业素质训练	幼儿卫生与保健；教育社会学；学前教育学；学前心理学；幼儿园管理与幼教法规；幼儿园课程；教育科研方法；教育测量与评价；幼儿游戏理论	学科课程考试；专业素质考核；实习成绩综合评价，调查报告与毕业论文评价

（二）以“四个改变”指导课程建设及课堂教学改革

提出了“四个改变”的教学改革的观点和理念，即：改变传统的以学科课程为中心的模式，转向采取以学生职业能力形成为中心的新模式，重新审视或构建现有的课程体系；改变认为学生学习了某些课程就能达到教育要求的认知理念，转向以学生职业能力形成作为教学活动的首要目的，课程体系是实现这一目标的终极保障；改变形式上的德、智、体全面发展的模糊性概念，将德、智、体全面发展的内涵具体化到每一门课程中；改变课程导致能力的不合理认知，采取能力要求课程的构建理念。从以学生职业能力形成为中心的角度探讨课程体系的构建框架，主要由四个部分组成，一是职业能力培养模块化；二是课程体系框架化；三是课程标准能力化；四是考核形式多样化。据此进行“公共基础课、专业基础课、专业课、专业选修课和公共选修课”的课程体系和课程方案建设，初步构建了以学生能力形成为主线的课程体系。

二、优化教师教育课程体系

借鉴国内同类院校的经验与方法，结合实际情况，我校教师教育改革和发展的基本设想是：第一阶段(1～3年)，通过整合、调整相关专业，建构并优化教师教育课程体系，强化能力本位理念下的师范生教师素质培养；第二阶段(4～5年)，形成有多学科专业支撑的教师教育学院。

(一)提出基于新课程理念的教师教育课程体系优化目标

“玉溪师范学院教师教育课程体系”由7门课程构成，即“心理学”、“教育学”、“走进新课程”、“现代教育技术”、“普通话与教师口语”、“黑板板书训练”和“学科教学论”。

培养适应我国基础教育课程改革需要的新型教师是教师教育改革发展的“应然”选择。新世纪之初，我国正在开展建国以来规模最大的第8次基础教育课程改革运动，此次课程改革确立了新的基本理念，如：确立以学生发展为本的课程目标，倡导自主、合作与探究的教学方式，探索有利于学生、教师和学校发展的课程评价制度，实现教育观念的重建等。让师范生了解新课程、理解新课程，掌握新课程的理念和实施方法，提升其“从教素质”，为今后从事教育工作做好观念、知识和能力上的准备，这是我校教师教育课程体系中各类课程要承担的共同任务。其中，“教育学”课程要解决学生教育观念以及多元智能、建构主义等教育理论问题，“学科教学论”要解决新课程理念下确定教学目标、教学设计以及教学组织实施等方面的问题。

(二)课程优化要解决的主要问题

1. 新建地方本科师范学院在传统的人才培养模式下，如何完善和优化教师教育课程体系。要求强化“应用型”、“专业化”、“能力本位”下“准教师”教育的途径和方法；改变教师教育课程之间“各自为阵”的现状，构建基于共同教育理念及目标、定位及职责明确的课程体系。

2. 在思想和理念层面，实现“一体化”落实学校教学改革的目标要求。落实学校“‘十一五’改革发展纲要”中提出的“学生能力培养目标符合社会的职业要求，并以此建构实现目标的课程解决方案”，“以学生能力培养为核心成为教师教学设计的核心理念”。

3. 实践层面实现在课程设计、课堂教学组织形式和教学方法、学生学习评价、实践训练等方面的改革及新突破。

4. 师范生教师基本素质和教学能力有明显提升。学生对新课程的理解，以及体现新课程理念及要求的教学能力得到增强；学生课堂教学技能明显提高，在学校组织的抽查评价中优良率达90%以上；学生能够独立完成教学设计、组织课堂教学、说课、评课，并且达到相关要求。

Teacher Training in the 21st Century: Equipping Teachers to Prepare Students for the Emerging Global Society

Douglas DeWitt*
(International Council for Education Development)

The world for which we are preparing students is in a state of rapid change. "Here is a stark reality. Growing numbers of people will live outside their home country, hold a job with a multinational organization, have their lives affected by social or economic conditions in another part of the world, or realize they can only be successful by working with people who hail from many different cultures and are different from themselves" (Marx, 2006). It is this new Global Society that our current and future students will be entering. China is in the enviable position of having the potential for "leapfrogging" to the top of the new Global Society as a major economic and technological leader. For this to happen, though, Chinese teachers will have to be equipped with the skills to prepare their students to meet this challenge and participate on the world stage as major players.

Since the publication of his landmark work *Frames of Mind: The Theory of Multiple Intelligences*, Howard Gardner (1983) has been the inspiration for much innovation and inspiration in American education. Gardner argued that there is not one way to measure intelligence, but rather seven. In his subsequent work, *Intelligence Reframed: Multiple Intelligences for the 21st Century*, Gardner (1999) expanded the number to nine. Nine ways to measure student learning and student success!

This paper will explore the ways in which Gardner's nine intelligences can be used to help teachers transform an educational system and prepare their students for leadership roles in the current global society. By identifying various ways to tap the potential of each of the nine intelligences, teachers can expand the critical thinking and creativity of each student. Innovation and inventiveness can be developed at an early age by understanding the strengths of each student and helping them to develop their gifts and talents. As students develop, they will then be in a position to contribute to the greater good and help China achieve a substantial position of leadership and influence. These developed skills and talents will then

* Douglas Dewitt, Ph. D. and Chairman Board of Directors of International Council for Education Development.

mature and develop even further on into adulthood.

A convergence of theory, practical application, and forward systems thinking will be presented to illustrate the potential for using these ideas as China "leapfrogs" to its inevitable position of influence and leadership in the 21st Century. Gardner's *Five Minds for the Future* (2007) will provide a catalyst for this discussion.

21 世纪的师资培训:使教师有能力指导学生为适应新兴国际社会做准备

道格拉斯·德威特
(国际教育发展委员会)

我们正在帮助学生为适应当今世界做准备。然而,当今世界无时无刻不在发生着巨大的变化。"人们都不得不面对这样一个不争的事实:越来越多的人不是生活在他们的祖国,而是客居异国他乡,在某个国际组织供职,他们的生活也正被世界上其他地方的社会状况或经济状况所影响,甚至发现他们只有通过和来自与自己祖国文化迥异的其他文化圈的人们合作,才能取得成功。"(马克思,2006)这样的一个社会,就是我们现在和将来的学生要踏入的社会。中国的大好形势令人羡慕,因为中国潜力巨大,可以实现跨越式发展并跻身于世界前列,在国际社会扮演经济和技术主要领导者的角色。然而,这一切要发生,中国教师必须具备相应的能力以培养学生迎接上述挑战并在世界大舞台上扮演主要角色。

霍华德·加德纳的具有里程碑意义的作品《智能的结构:多元智能理论》于 1983 年出版以后,加德纳的作品就成为美国教育革新和灵感的源泉。他认为,人的智能不只是一种,而是区分为七种。在 1999 年的著作《智能重组:21 世纪的多元智能》中,他又将人的智能分类由七种增加到九种。通过这九种智能来衡量学生的学习情况和学生获得成功的可能性。

本文将探讨加德纳的九种智能如何被用来帮助教师改变教育制度和帮助教师在当今国际社会中培养学生的领导才能。通过不同的途径来开发学生的九种智能的潜力,教师可以培养学生的批判性思维和创造性。当老师了解每一个学生的长处之后,就可以帮助学生发展天赋和才能,这样,学生的创新能力在学生的幼年时期就能得到发展。随着学生的成长,他们对社会的贡献逐渐增大,这有助于中国在世界上获得稳固的领导地位进而向全世界发挥她的影响力。这些与日增长的技能和才能变得成熟起来,甚至于在成年期也在发展。

当中国正以势不可挡的态势跨越式发展,并逐渐成为 21 世纪极具影响力的世界领导者时,笔者将理论、实际应用和系统思维这三者结合起来,用以更好地说明上述思想的潜力。另外,加德纳的著作《关于未来的五个创意》将会用来帮助这个探讨的进行。

References

[1] GARDNER H. Frames of mind: The theory of multiple intelligences[M]. New York: Basic Books, 1983.
[2] GARDNER H. Intelligence reframed: Multiple intelligences for the 21st century[M]. New York: Basic Books, 1999.
[3] GARDNER H. Five minds for the future[M]. Boston: Harvard Business School Press, 2007.
[4] MARX G. Sixteen trends: Their profound impact on our future: Implications for students, education, communities, and the whole of society[J]. Alexandria, VA: Educational Research Service, 2006.

Learning from the past, changing for the future: Salisbury University's history and current practices in Liberal Arts Education

Maarten Pereboom* Lori DeWitt**
Salisbury University

The liberal arts tradition has been the defining characteristic of higher undergraduate education in the United States, and it has helped to distinguish its colleges and universities as among the world's best. It evolved in a country that held extraordinary promise and opportunity for its people, rooted in economic growth and prosperity. While today students and parents alike often focus on the narrower objective of securing gainful employment upon graduation, it remains very much in their best interest to develop a wide range of knowledge, skills and ability that will equip them for lifelong learning and careers that enable them to realize their full potential as human beings. In the face of pressure from professional and pre-professional programs, organizations such as the American Association of Higher Education have asserted the enduring value of the liberal arts philosophy in such programs as Liberal Education, America's Promise (LEAP). An investigation of the past and current practices at this institution can provide useful information to fledgling liberal arts programs and all programs that share its vision of rigorous and meaningful liberal arts instruction.

Salisbury University reflects this evolution and debate in its own history and identity. In 1963, Maryland State Teachers College became Salisbury State College and began offering a liberal arts education with the goal of producing well-rounded, civic-minded citizens. Since that time Salisbury University, as it is now known, has grown to house four schools: The Fulton School of Liberal Arts, the Henson School of Science, the Purdue School of Business, and the Seidel School of Education. Throughout the past four decades there has been agreement at SU that the best liberal education involves a deep level of understanding of a variety of content, the ability to reflect upon and apply that information, and engagement in activities that not only enrich the students but ultimately the community at large. What constitutes a rigorous liberal education and how best to achieve these goals has been a subject of much debate at Salisbury over this time and in the past four years in particular. This

* Maarten Pereboom, Dr., Dean of the School of Liberal Arts, Salisbury University.
** Lori Dewitt, Dr., Professor, Department of Commanication Arts, Salisbury University.

debate has culminated in the Fulton Curriculum Reform movement. At the foundation of this movement is the belief that students and faculty need the time and opportunity to explore course content in a deeper, more active and sustained fashion than they had been doing.

Starting with pilot programs in the departments of Art, Philosophy and Political Science in academic year 2007～2008 and encompassing all Fulton departments in 2008～2009, the reform has reconfigured its 3 credit per course structure to a 4 credit per course structure. This has resulted in a reduction in the total number of courses that students take and that professors teach. However, the content of the courses has been made much more rigorous, requiring a larger investment of time and engagement for both parties. "The main purpose of this reform is to engage students more in the individual courses they take and, as a result, provide students with a deeper-and often more active-learning experience and encounter with the subject at hand." Throughout this process there have been many challenges to both the implementation and enactment of this new system. While the reform movement is an active process, continually being refined, early feedback from both students and faculty has been overwhelmingly positive. Through an examination of the process and reactions to these reform efforts, we can gain insight into the keys to building a strong liberal arts education.

Salisbury University is a very selective regional comprehensive university that is gaining in stature and reputation nationally. It is of a size that both enables and requires its four schools to collaborate to provide a liberal arts foundation for all students, including those in professional and pre-professional programs. Our experience with curriculum reform is therefore of considerable national and international interest as it continues to reshape and improve the undergraduate experience of its students.

吸取前车之鉴，为未来而改变

——索尔兹伯里大学人文科学教育的历史和现行实践

马尔腾·佩雷布姆　罗依·德维特

（索尔兹伯里大学）

人文科学传统一直是美国大学教育的一个显著特征，它使美国众多的学院和大学称雄世界，声名远播。这个传统在充满希望、人民有很多机遇的美国逐渐形成；同时，这个传统也植根于经济的快速发展和繁荣。当下，学生和他们的父母都一样，通常目光专注于一个狭隘的目标——在毕业后谋到一份有报酬的工作。然而，掌握多种知识、技能和能力对学生是非常有益的，因为它能够促使学生进行终身学习，也能使学生在他们的工作中发挥他们作为人的全部潜能。面对来自专业课程和（为专业课程做准备的）基础课程的压力，诸如美国高等教育协会的一些机构肯定了人文科学教育在许多培养方案中(比如,人文教育和美国的希望,LEAP)持久的重要性。对索尔兹伯里大学的过去和现在的实践的研究对所有的人文科学培养方案都有借鉴意义,无论这些方案是新推出的与否,只要它们提供严格的、有意义的人文科学教育。

索尔兹伯里大学(各学派)曾经对人文科学教育争论不休,以致后来连自己的身份都起了变化。索尔兹伯里大学本身就是对人文科学教育形成过程的最好明证。1963 年,马里兰州立师范学院更名为索尔兹伯里州立学院。自此,以培养全面发展的、有公德心的公民为目标,它开始开设人文科学教育课程。从那时起,索尔兹伯里大学(更名前的索尔兹伯里州立学院)成长为由 4 个学院组成的大学:富尔顿人文科学学院、亨森科学院、普度商学院、赛德尔教育学院。经过 40 年的探讨,索尔兹伯里大学一致认为,对各种各样的内容深层次的理解、对信息的思考和运用、对既能充实学生亦能有益整个团体的活动的参与,是最好的人文教育的组成要素。什么是真正的人文教育和怎样才能更好地达到人文科学教育的目标,这一直是索尔兹伯里大学里争论不休的话题,尤其是在过去的 40 年里。今天,这些争论终于以富尔顿课程改革运动告终。这项运动有一个支撑性理念:学生和院系要有时间和机会以一种比以往更积极、更持续的姿态去更深入地探索课程的内容。

2007~2008 学年,艺术系、哲学系和政治学系进行试点课程改革;2008~2009 学年,富尔顿人文科学学院的所有系都参与改革。这样,每个科目由 3 个学分变为每个科目 4 个学分。这种变化导致学生需要学习的课程和教师教授的课程的总量减少。然而,课程变得比以前更加严格,所以教学双方都必须花更多的时间。“这项改革的主要目标是促使学生在他们的课程上花更多的时间,进而为学生提供更深刻更主动的学习经历,这样他们就能经常和手边的科目不期而遇。”在这个过程中,无论是新体制的制定还是新体制的实行,都会碰到很多挑战。改革运动是一个积极的过程,不断地进行修改,来自学生和院系的早期反馈也都是正面的。通过对这个过程和改革效果的反应的研究,我们可以洞察到成功进行人文科学教育的关键。

索尔兹伯里大学是一所优秀的区域性综合大学,现在它在全美的声望正在上升。它有能力也要求 4 个学院通力合作,为正在攻读专业课程或基础课程的所有学生的人文科学教育夯实基础。因此,在索尔兹伯里大学继续重塑和提高大学本科学生的过程中,我们的课程改革经验对全美和全世界都是很有意义的。

Leapfrog Learning via Transdisciplinarity

Arthur M. Harkins*
(University of Minnesota, Minneapolis)

Framework

The goal of this paper is to explore future "leapfrog" learning contributions to emerging knowledge societies and economies through perspectives and processes of transdisciplinarity. Leapfrogging refers to leadership in overcoming barriers to knowledge production and innovation. Transdisciplinarity refers to the production of knowledge through continuously creative syntheses. What can transdisciplinary educational and leapfrogging skills offer students in the year 2015 and beyond?

The author believes that successful innovators in academic and commercial contexts will require knowledge and skills developed through transdisciplinarity, or syntheses beyond interdisciplinarity. Leapfrog-supportive skills provide students with transdisciplinary approaches to the development of knowledge ideally suited for innovation.

Leapfrog-supportive skills (communication, critical and multi-paradigmatic thinking, literacy, focused imagination, developed intuition, innovation, and emotional and design intelligence) are core cognitive competencies which students can develop in strategically oriented education programs. Both before and after graduation, leapfrog-supportive programs can satisfy emerging student needs for "tool box" learning applications in economy and society.

Practical Applications

The futures of educational and leapfrog-supportive skills depend on the ability of faculty to anticipate the needs of student populations within diverse and emerging social and economic contexts. Many such needs will be driven by the requirements of communities and businesses for innovative, self-organized, and highly skilled knowledge and innovation workers. Yet the ability to anticipate, adapt to, and create productive futures necessitates continuous imaginative and creative responses by leapfrog-supportive skills programs.

This paper explores the implications of blended educational and leapfrog-supportive

* Arthur M. Harkins, Ph. D., University of Minnesota.

skills programs through five lenses:

—The liberal skills, or the perspectives and tools associated with the intellectual core of praxis-based thinking appropriate for the 21st Century.

—Transdisciplinarity, or the capability of the liberal skills to help students develop continuously creative syntheses.

—The individualizing effects of transdisciplinarity that help students become high-functioning, practical, and unique innovators.

—The roles of formal, informal, non-formal, and experiential pedagogies in realizing practical results from programs created with these perspectives in mind.

—The critical dynamic role to be played by advanced learning, simulation, and gaming technologies.

通过跨学科进行跨越式学习

阿瑟·哈金斯*

(明尼苏达大学,美国 明尼阿波利斯)

框架

本文的目的是通过跨学科学习的观点和过程,探索未来"跨越式"学习对新兴的社会和经济知识的贡献。跨越指的是知识生产和创新中克服障碍的领导能力。跨学科是指通过不断综合创新产生新的知识。跨学科教育和跨越性技巧在 2015 年及以后能给学生带来些什么呢?

笔者认为,在学术和商业环境中成功的创新者,需要通过跨学科或者超出跨学科综合能力来提高知识和技能。而辅助的跨越式技能为学生拓展知识提供了交叉学科学习的理想方法。

跨越辅助技能(沟通,批判式和多范式思维,阅读能力,重点想象力,开发直觉,创新,情感和设计能力)是学生发展战略导向教育课程的核心认知能力。毕业之前和毕业之后,跨越辅助项目能够满足学生在经济和社会中新兴的"工具箱"学习应用的需要。

实际应用

未来教育和跨越技能依靠全体教师在新兴化和多样化的社会经济环境中有能力预测对学生人数的需求。很多这样的需求会由于团体和企业为培养创新的自我组织和高技能的创新工人的要求所推动。然而,预测、调试和创造未来需求的能力需要跨越辅助技能项目不断的想象和创造来作出反应。

本文通过五方面探讨了混合教育和跨越辅助技能的影响:

---

* 阿瑟·哈金斯,博士,明尼苏达大学。

——自由技能,或是适合 21 世纪的与知识为核心的实际思想相联系的观点和工具。

——跨学科,或是帮助学生不断提高创新合成的自由技能。

——帮助学生成为全面、踏实以及独特的创新者的跨学科个性化的影响。

——项目中正式的、非正式、非正规的和体验性的教学法的实际成果创造了这些观点。

——能动作用的关键是发挥先进的学习、模拟和游戏技术。

Changing Roles of Teacher Education in the Process of Social Transformation

Song Hong-zhuan*

(International Council for Education Development, USA)

Abstract:

Purpose To explore how well Chinese teacher education position itself in preparing qualified teachers for its vast k-12 education system, especially in the transition from examination-oriented education to that of future-oriented.

Method This paper looks at literatures discussing background, strengths and weakness of current Chinese teacher training programs. It also employs Delphi-based scenario research method to explore plausible futures of curriculum design for teacher education.

Findings In order to ensure its astonishing economic development and present itself a constructive force to the world betterment, it is crucial for China to carry on its on-going educational reform, especially in the area of curriculum for its teacher training programs.

Conclusions The disciplinary curriculum currently employed in Chinese teacher education should be shifted to trans-disciplinary curriculum to produce future-oriented, internationally-prepared, and ICT savvy raduates with high moral standards. The country demands in its effort to play an important role on the international stage.

Implications This research, while meriting the structured instruction displayed by the Chinese education system, argues that the system should strive to provide students with such skills as creativity, flexibility, initiative, leadership, all necessary in the globally connected future world. The second part of this paper will focus on four scenarios as a result of his recent research among Chinese educators and administrators.

Key words: Scenario of BEACON; 3H+i Model; ICT; exemplary; participatory; emancipatory reflective; experiential learning; systems thinking; adaptive; coherent; innovation; collaboration; lifelong learning; service-based learning

* Song Hong-zhuan, Ph. D., President/CEO International Council for Education Development.

社会转型过程中教师教育的角色转变

宋红专*

（国际教育发展委员会，美国）

摘　要：

目　的　探讨中国在基础教育体制下培养合格教师过程中教师教育的定位，特别是从应试教育过渡到面向未来的教育过程中的教育定位。

方　法　本文着重探讨目前中国教师培训的优势、劣势和背景，并以“德尔法-景象规划研究法”(Delphi-based scenario planning research method)来探究未完全成熟的教师教育的课程设置。

成　果　为适应经济快速增长及显示其改造世界的建设性作用，中国必须继续实施教育改革，尤其是教师培训项目课程改革。

总　结　目前适用于教师培训的课程标准应从分学科课程向跨学科课程转变。以培养出面向未来，面向国际的，通晓信息科技和具有崇高品质的毕业生，能在国际舞台担当重要角色。

意　义　本文在呈现中国教育系统结构的同时提出培养学生与世界接轨的能力的必要性。其能力主要包括：创造力、灵活性、能动性、领导能力等。本文的第二部分以作者最近对中国教育家和相关管理人员的调查为依据着重从四个方面进行了论证。

关键词：情景信标；3H＋I 模式；信息通信技术；典范；参与；解放反思；经验学习；系统思维；适应；连贯；创新；协作；终身学习；在职学习

Four Alternative Future(s)

As discussed in the first part of this paper, for the last decade and a half, Chinese teacher education has been facing a lot of challenges both from inside the education system and from the larger society. Therefore, there has been an increasing demand for reform in order for the teacher preparation system to position itself better serving the basic education system and thus meeting the demands from the larger society. As a part of the effort to look for the direction of reform and to provide the policy maker with some sense of what possible futures look like, the author has spent a substantial amount of time conducting a Delphi-based scenario planning study on curriculum reform for teacher education in China by inviting

* 宋红专，博士，国际教育发展委员会总裁。

a group of key stakeholders related to the system with a specific focus on the curriculum for teacher education (a detail description of the research process and methodology employed can be found in Song, 2007). The rest of this paper is a result of the research findings, what the author terms "Four Scenarios" which in some sense represent the future of Chinese teacher education system. Since these scenarios are constructed on the basis of the shared and agreed-upon mental models of the external world*, they are created as internally consistent and challenging descriptions of possible futures.

As the facilitator of the entire research process, I present the following four scenarios constructed on the basis of the findings from the first two phases of data gathered throughout the course of this study. These four scenarios include "HOARDER" (1-H Model), "EXPERT" (2-H Model), "LEADER" (3-H Model), and "BEACON" (3-H + i Model). The names for each scenario are derived from acronyms of English words that stand for underlying principles or characteristics of the curriculum design each symbolizes.

For example, "HOARDER" stands for homogeneous, objective, assimilative, reactive, departmentalized, ethnocentric, and redundant, elements considered resilient markers for this type of curriculum; "EXPERT" stands for elaborative, exclusive, pedagogical/psychological, experiential, rigorous, and thoroughbred, all essential requirements for teacher education curriculum design to train an "EXPERT"; "BEACON" stands for the basic/fundamental, exemplary, adaptive, coherent, open and navigating elements of teacher education curriculum, and "LEADER" presents such characteristics as liberal, engaging, applicable, dialogical, emancipatory, and reflective.

As shown in the matrix (see Figure 1), EXPERT and BEACON scenarios have one structural characteristic in common: they both place emphasis on the importance of the personal development of learners, though they differ in that "BEACON" falls in the category of systems thinking, while "EXPERT" fall in the category of the disciplinary thinking paradigm. On the other hand, scenarios "HOARDER" and "LEADER" both share the commonality of emphasizing the importance of social betterment. However, "HOARDER" belongs to the category of the disciplinary thinking paradigm, and "LEADER" is a product of a systems thinking framework.

As shown in the four-quadrant structure (Figure 1), the HOARDER and EXPERT scenarios fall in the area that indicates a low degree of impact while the LEADER and BEACON scenarios are categorized in the area of a high degree of impact. BEACON is considered the scenario with a high degree of impact and a high degree of uncertainty. Though a wide range of areas exists within which the scenarios can be elaborated, the discussion of each scenario focused on five key areas: purposes, learners, contents,

* Mental models are conceptual structures in the mind that drive cognitive processes of understanding (Senge, 1990). Mental models are assumptions made by participants and lodged in place which are considered as obstruction to change (Ackoff).

processes, and assessments. In other words, after a brief introduction regarding how each scenario was constructed and a general description of the scenario, its response to the following questions will be discussed within the framework of this research: What to accomplish, how the learners should be viewed, what should be taught, how to accomplish the goal(s), and how to evaluate the outcome(s).

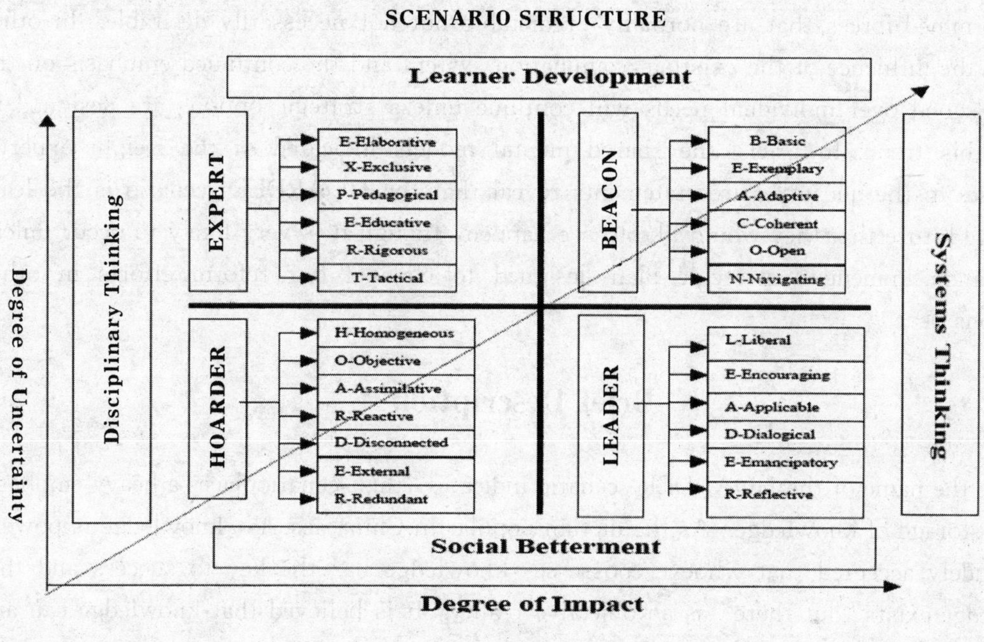

Figure 1 Four Scenario Structure(Song, 2007)

Scenario of HOARDER (1-H Model)

Basis of Delphi Findings

As reflected in the third round of the Delphi survey (Song, 2007), regrouped categories Ⅱ and Ⅲ (e. g. those rated as unlikely or both undesirable and unlikely) indicate that there was a high percentage of Delphi experts who rated the statements (items ＃3, 4, 8, 11, 24) as "unlikely" and rated statement ＃12 as "somewhat undesirable." For example, more than 60 per cent of the panel members did not believe that the existing rigid national examination system would be replaced by an integrated and authentic assessment system (e. g. statements ＃3 and ＃8: both rated as highly unlikely with a mean score of 1.93 and 1.80 respectively) even though the majority of them believed that the transformation was highly significant and highly desirable. Similarly, over 33 per cent of the participating experts disagreed that the needs of individuals should be placed above the needs of the nation (e. g. statement ＃12), and more than 46 per cent believed that this would not happen.

Also, as briefly discussed in Song's research (2007), the expressed pessimism among the experts about likelihood (e. g. the transformation of the assessment system) or resentment over the desirability (e. g. individual interests over those of the nation) brings to light the emerging clash between the deep-rooted traditional Chinese culture and beliefs and the emerging trends that result from the macro-environment (e. g. STEEP*) and from pedagogy/psychology theories. Based on discussions in the previous chapters (e. g. the literature review and methodology chapters), traditional cultures belong to the predetermined forces that are normally predictable but not necessarily desirable. In other words, the influence of the existing examination system and the continued emphasis on the national good over individual needs will continue unless strategic options are designed to divert this trend. In brief, the shared mental models indicated in the Delphi experts' responses to the questionnaire statements reveal that the HOARDER scenario is the least desirable future that they would like to see happen, though it is very likely to occur unless there is an immediate strategic plan designed to channel our reform efforts in other directions.

Brief Description

As the name of the HOARDER scenario indicates, this scenarioplaces a heavy emphasis on the storage of knowledge. As the dictum popular in China asserts, knowledge is power. It is widely accepted that whoever possesses knowledge has the key to success and that knowledge exists "out there" as an objective reality. It is believed that knowledge can and should be broken down and reorganized so that people can assimilate and grasp it in the most cost effective manner. Generally speaking, this scenario represents an inertial trend of the current curriculum mode that predominates Chinese teacher training programs.

Underpinning society, the Confucian emphasis on the intellectualism pervades the Chinese culture. An individual's success is largely determined by the years of his or her schooling, and by the amount of knowledge s/he stores. The sacred tradition of the national examination system is enshrined everywhere. Test results are held as the most important hallmark and measure of success for both a teacher and the school. High paying, prestigious positions in government or in universities still prefer those "book worms" whose heads are filled with factual knowledge. Though it is widely recognized that teachers play an important role in the entire education system, teaching as a profession is still held in low esteem as if anyone is qualified to teach as long as s/he has knowledge. Political, business and media commentaries frequently criticize about the inability of teachers to adequately prepare students for the many challenges that result from the rapid changes the society experiences.

---

* This acronym refers to social, technological, economic, environmental and political influences (Morrison and Wilson, 1997).

The realities of the centralization of the educational administration, the dictates of the national college examination system, and the culturally customized expectation of parents (that their children do well on tests), all combine to create a powerful system immune to any major curriculum change(s).

In terms of the increasing process of globalization, there is a group of intellectuals and other influential figures in society who still retain a close-minded nationalism with the guise of protecting native characteristics against foreign infiltration. This blocks any potential influence(s) from the outside and only serves to perpetuate problems.

As a result, the HOARDER scenario idolizes knowledge and requires future teachers to code an store information within a certain subject matter area. The resilient markers of this curriculum scenario include homogeneous, objective, assimilative, reactive, departmentalized (or disconnected), ethnocentric and redundant. The need for an efficient method of acquiring an adequate level of knowledge that the future teachers are expected to master makes it necessary to reorganize the content and the learners in a homogeneous way. In other words, students are grouped by age and learning level and are enrolled directly into a set of departmentalized courses that allow for little freedom to select courses, or to transfer to other majors of interest.

Also, knowledge in this scenario is treated as something objective rather than subjective (or personal); it is departmentalized into subject matter areas and learners are grouped as English or mathematics majors, wherein no synergetic relationship exists between them. In this scenario, it is the norm to maintain a practice where learners assimilate knowledge in a reactive way* (e. g. teacher centric, to proactive way of learning (Dodani, 1999). lecture oriented, rote learning, etc.). Everything students absorb appears to be disconnected from their personal life experiences and knowledge taught in courses is more often isolated and redundant. In brief, the scenario of HOARDER is essentially deep-rooted in a traditional training that emphasizes the head of learners, which I term the "1-H Model".

Purposes, Learners, Contents, Processes, and Assessments

Purposes. This scenario is built on the continuation of a powerful "memory based paradigm**" (Harkins, 2003). Teacher training programs are expected to produce future teachers with solid subject atter content knowledge. The larger society (media, k-12

---

* This is a way of learning characterized by teacher-centric, lecture-oriented, rote learning. This approach of learning is as opposed . This is a way of learning characterized by teacher-centric, lecture-oriented, rote learning. This approach of learning is as opposed.

** "The memory based paradigm is the sine qua non of conventional education, which requires the use of student time to code and store information and present the results on demand, as though they were living disk drives" (Harkins, 2003, p. 17).

schools, and the local community) determine whether or not a teacher training institutes are successful by how well their graduates can "support efficient downloads of information" (Harkins, 2003, p. 17). This efficiency is often based on how well students do on various tests of facts learned in textbooks.

Learners. In this scenario, learners (e. g. prospective teachers) are treated as passive knowledge recipients whose prior knowledge or experiences are often down-played or neglected in the course of learning. They are required throughout their training programs to absorb as much knowledge in their respective majors as they can retain in order to become masters of their subject matter areas. In the process of learning, future teachers are not valued in and of themselves, but rather they are viewed as means to an end. They do not have their own lives, and they are not yet considered contributors to society. Naturally, future teachers in this scenario are anything but active participants in the community or in society at large.

Contents. As for what future teachers should learn, a great portion of their training hours are focused on the subject matter content knowledge coupled with some general (common) courses and a few required pedagogical and psychological courses that are taught by faculty members from other isolated departments. After an intensive academic training, student teachers are expected to look for a grade school to gain some pre-career "practical" teaching experience for a period no greater than three months. In short, everything included in the curriculum seems to be independent from one another.

Processes. Since much attention within the curriculum is given to the intake of the subject matter content knowledge, there is not much time and space remaining for other co-curricular activities wherein student teachers are supposed to utilize their knowledge but also generate new knowledge with their peers. On the contrary, such activities are generally regarded by "disciplined" students as either a distraction or burden, rather than as an integral part of their training process. Even though student teachers have an easy access to ICTs* that are already widely used in other sectors of society, such information technologies are mainly employed to enhance classroom instruction. In this scenario ICTs are not used as an inter-disciplinary tool or as an effective way to connect the learning/research activities with future teachers' professional development andother actual social activities.

Assessments. As for the evaluation system, assessing the outcomes of the training programs is always determined by the set purpose of the programs. In this scenario, the main purpose of teacher training programs is to guarantee that the graduates are able to teach their subject matters with confidence. As a result, content knowledge is considered the most important part of the training programs. How well future teachers are prepared to "present the results [of their information storage] on demand" (Harkins, 2003, p. 17) is determined by how well they do on their final written exams. This kind of rigid exam system continues

---

* ICTs refers to Informatoin and Communication Technologies.

to function as the "fairest" way to evaluate how well the prospective teachers are prepared though far from authentic. As Anne Hulbert puts it, "In a country so huge-and in a culture so steeped in cronyism — the fear is that no other process could work as fairly" (2007).

Scenario of EXPERT (2-H Model) Basis of Delphi Findings

As indicated in the findings after three rounds of Delphi study (Song, 2007), the ratings on the possibility of occurrence for the statements #3, 4, 8, 11, and 24 (e. g. those listed under Category Ⅱ) were either somewhat unlikely or highly unlikely even though these statements were all rated as highly significant and highly desirable. On the other hand, most of the Delphi experts demonstrated a high level of confidence that curriculum for teacher education would emphasize the importance of individual development, teaching as a profession, ICT, and globalization. For example, those statements listed under Category I (such as # 5, 6, and 9) were all rated as highly significant, highly desirable, and highly (or somewhat) likely. Statement # 5 (e. g. "Development in learning theory and student development theory will demand future teachers to focus on the importance of knowing their students in addition to their mastery of subject matter knowledge.") was rated as highly significant, highly desirable, and highly likely.

On the other hand, findings of those statements listed under CategoryII (e. g. those rated as highly significant, highly desirable, but highly unlikely or somewhat unlikely) indicated that Delphi experts were not optimistic about some of the futures (e. g. statements # 11 and 24). In other words, according to the experts, unless strategic plans are designed to dramatically change the present mindset that has been heavily influenced by the two-thousand-plus-year Confucian tradition, teacher education in China will most likely continue its "disciplinary thinking" paradigm.

These combined findings resulted in the construction of the EXPERT scenario, which is characterized as a future where, unlike in the previous scenario, teaching is considered a profession, and the learner's personal development begins to receive recognition.

Brief Description

The EXPERT scenario results from a growing resentment among political and business leaders against the failure of current teacher training programs to effectively fulfill their tasks, especially in terms of how little these programs prepared students for their development as complete human beings.

This scenario is in response to an outcry for the need for the professionalism of teaching, requiring every interested candidate to go through rigorous professional training before entering into the school system as a teacher. This scenario, therefore, treats teaching as a profession that is supposed to have its own distinctive characteristics or traits.

Because of the high expectation of society and because of its much-improved social status, teaching as a profession for the first time starts to form its own autonomousunion which has rights to determine a shared vision, goals, strategies, and best practices for the professional development of every practitioner.

Also, there is an increasing demand within society to produce student are fully developed as human beings possessing qualities necessary for sustainable development of the nation's economy that is comparable to that of other developed countries. In addition, the increased exposure of Chinese educators to updated learning theories and to theories about child and adolescence development in a social context (Darling-Hammond, 2006b) makes it possible and necessary for Chinese educators to place greater emphasis on the development of students' "individualization and teamwork [capabilities]" (Harkins, 2003); ICTs are widely employed in the training process to enhance student teachers' learning and research. Overall, curriculum in this scenario signifies what the EXPERT acronym represents: elaborative, exclusive, pedagogical/psychological, experiential, rigorous, and thoroughbred. In other words, the curriculum for future teachers is carefully planned (e. g. elaborative) according to a high standard, includes rigorous training programs that are not able to be emulated (e. g. exclusive) by competitors (as do other professional training institutes, such as medical and law schools), and gives importance to pedagogical /psychological training to equip student teachers with knowledge about student learning (e. g. experiential learning*). In this manner program graduates are experts who are thoroughbred and prepared.

In the learning process, attention is given to the balance between intellectual and emotional components (Rogers and Freiberg, 1994). Since this scenario places an emphasis on the performance of teaching and learning, I characterize this scenario the "2-H Model" (e. g. a combined training of both head and hand, or knowledge and performance).

Purposes, Learners, Contents, Processes, and Assessments

Purposes. There would be, in this scenario, a great shift from the reactive learning mode of current teacher training programs toward a mode that begins to give attention to an experiential style of learning. This EXPERT scenario somewhat resonates with what Harkins calls the "performance based paradigm" (2003). The main purpose of this scenario is to prepare future teachers for a task that only professionally trained individuals are entitled to perform. Put differently, the curriculum for teacher training programs is charged with the mission to make education programs so distinctive that no one is qualified to apply for a teaching position in a school system without first going through the school of education,

---

* Experiential learning refers to a type of learning where students' needs and wants are addressed; it emphasizes applied knowledge.

exactly as an applicant to be a medical doctor or a lawyer has to go through in medical or law school.

Learners. Consequently, not everyone is qualified for admission in a school of education. Applicants must first pass a test designed to select the most promising and committed job candidates, an exam that is expected to lay the foundation for the future of society. Unlike in the HOARDER scenario wherein learners are considered merely as passive knowledge receivers, learners in this scenario are perceived as individuals who bring their prior knowledge, experiences and background to influence their learning outcomes. Even though knowledge is still organized into different subject matter areas and instructional arrangement is departmentalized, a more learner-centered experiential learning process emerges where student teachers are actively engaged in the learning process.

Contents. In order to become a contingent of thoroughbred professionals, future teachers in this scenario are required to go through a well-designed curriculum that includes rigorous subject matter content knowledge, pedagogical/psychological theories, content teaching methodology, and also embodies experience(s) essential for student teachers to become effective in the real classroom setting. In addition, all core courses "are taught in the context of practice and grounded in the knowledge of child and adolescent development and learning, an understanding of social and cultural contexts, curriculum, assessment, and subject matter pedagogy" (Darling-Hammond, 2006b, p. 305). Knowledge that is included in this curriculum is not once-for-all or one-size-fits-all type of information; rather, the information is continually updated and expanded. This situation requires that qualified teachers, like medical doctors and lawyers, not only learn basic conceptualized knowledge but also learn to become lifelong learners.

Processes. In this scenario, influence of theories about child and adolescent development and learning is evident in every aspect of curriculum design. In addition to subject matter content knowledge, student teachers are required to familiarize themselves with how future students learn and develop in their various social economic, cultural and language contexts, examining how to best help all individuals succeed in maximizing their potentialities. As an essential part of the training process for future teachers, each teacher candidate must be immersed in activities including classroom visitation/observation and guided practice teaching. A year-long practicum is mandatory for all future teachers prior to entering their teaching profession.

Scenario of LEADER (3-H+i Model) Basis of Delphi Findings

This scenario was constructed on the basis of findings (Song, 2007) from Category I (e.g. those rated as highly significant, highly or somewhat desirable, and highly or somewhat likely). 14 out of 26 Delphi statements were included in this category. One of the most significant observations was that 9 out of 12 Harkins' liberal skills (Harkins, 2007) were rated as highly significant, highly (or somewhat) desirable, and highly (or somewhat) likely. According to Harkins, "[The liberal skills] offer a definite set of guidelines for structuring pre-k/16 education to take maximum advantage of the imaginations, knowledge production problem solving, and opportunity generating potentials of children and youth, together with their adult collaborators" (p. 6). These liberal skills signify systems thinking and proactive leadership in the training of future citizens.

It is also worth noting that statements # 20 and 23 (e. g. "Future educated people are expected to tunderstand and effectively utilize existing information: accessing and selectively employing information in pursuit of opportunities and problem resolutions." And "Future educated people are expected to effectively utilize current and emerging ICT systems: staying atop the technologies that permit modern learning and economies; being first in the adoption and effective use of hardware, software, and net-working technologies.") were both rated as highly significant, highly desirable, and highly likely. This indicates that ICTs were recognized as important factors for the future of society in general and for teacher education in particular.

In other words, taken together, these findings send a clear message that not only is a paradigm shift from disciplinary thinking to systems thinking necessary, but also that the application of ICTs in teacher education (and thus in the entire school system) is a must if the country desires to "become [one of the] human capital development leaders among global knowledge and innovation economies" (Harkins, 2007, p. 1).

Brief Description

As China aspires to become a global leader in the political, cultural, and economic sectors, there is an increasing demand for reform in education, in particular, teacher education, in particular. Government and business leaders "have grown concerned that too many students have become the sort of stressed-out, test-acing drone who fails to acquire the skills-creativity, flexibility, initiative, leadership-said to be necessary in the global marketplace" (Hulbert, 2007). As a response to this challenge, the LEADER scenario finds favor within society.

In this scenario, education is widely esteemed as one of the most important factors in shaping the future of the nation; teacher education is regarded as "the engine" or "carrier" of the entire education system. In the media, among those every day expressions include innovative leadership, systems thinking, critical thinking, knowledge workers, ICT, collaboration, and simulation.

In China, teacher training institutes in particular are charged with the primary mission of turning the world's most populous country into a nation with a well-developed reservoir of human capital. As Harkins (2007) asserts, future educated citizens are expected to have 12 basic liberal arts skills (e. g. those embodied in the Delphi instrument statements 15-26). We live in a society where ICTs are literally used in every aspect of daily life. Therefore, it is no longer a question of whether or not information technologies should be included in the curriculum, but rather how these technologies can best be employed to prepare individuals for a society that experiences changes at such an exponential rate, thanks to the wide application of ICTs.

As a result, teacher education curriculum in the LEADER scenario should embody liberal arts courses and simultaneously include courses that are engaging in instruction and applicable in content; both content and pedagogy of teacher training programs should also take into account the following key qualities: dialogical, emancipatory, and reflective. As Eugene Allen (1993) eloquently argues: "the liberal arts and general education requirements of the curriculum…[are] ways that truly enhance the intellectual growth of the individual" (p190-191). In order to prepare future teachers to produce knowledge workers and innovative leaders, it is essential to include elements that help to promote qualities compatible with the requirements of a society that is dominated by ICTs and characterized by an exponentially changing pace.

In the future where this scenario demonstrates its robustness, the entire society is a big learning community where team learning is highly valued as one of the chief characteristics. In this scenario, citizens are required to be expert in two types of communication: discussion and dialogue to promote team learning among community members. Similarly, citizens are expected to challenge their own thinking while actively contributing to the creation of new knowledge in the society. This is what Senge refers to as the two types of openness: participatory and reflective (Senge, 1990).

Since this scenario focuses on the development of the head, hand, and heart of individual learners, I call this the "3-H model". This scenario appears to fit into what Harkins (2003) terms the "innovative paradigm" which places a great importance on the creation of new knowledge. The interdependence of the nation's economy with other parts of the world makes it vital for future citizens to develop a global vision and corresponding competencies, these include cultural awareness, and language proficiency, and an attitude to accept and respect differences between countries in terms of cultures and value systems.

Purposes, Learners, Contents, Processes, and Assessments

Purposes. In order to ensure that schools produce these desired citizens, the teacher training programs in this scenario are expected to prepare future teachers as forward-looking professionals who are well grounded in their own academic areas, expert at the application of the existing ICTs in teaching, and trained to possess reflective thinking about their profession, community and large society (including the global community).

Learners. Applicants are those who are promising and demonstrate a strong passion for the education of younger generations. Chosen from an elite group of young people, future teachers are academically well prepared, proactive, and hold systems thinking perspectives. They are actively engaged in all aspects of the process of the training programs in which they are learner, participants, and contributors of new knowledge.

Contents. A contingent of forward-looking professionals is the chief outcome of a specially designed curriculum. This curriculum must embody a large range of interconnected theories and practices. This list includes (but is not limited to) liberal arts/general education courses that are naturally interwoven with core courses, pedagogical/psychological courses, the application of ICTs in education, communication skills, and content knowledge teaching methodology.

Processes. Since the main purpose of teacher training programs in this scenario is to prepare future teachers for an increasingly changing world, the development of creativity is deemed so crucial that all activities throughout the programs are designed with this chief concern in mind. Furthermore, ICTs are used extensively in every possible way to assist future teachers in "accessing and selectively employing information in pursuit of opportunities and problem resolutions" (Harkins, 2007, p. 6).

Professional Development Schools (PDS). PDS are created to partner with a college or university to accomplish common educational goals that develop exemplary practice to maximize student outcomes. These PDSs provide optimum sites for pre-service teacher training programs, offering connected in-service teacher professional development and implementing reflectiveinquiry to enhance teacher and student learning and development. Such partnerships between teacher training institutes and schools are collaborative relationships built on mutual trust, respect, and a shared belief that together they may better prepare students for the world of tomorrow.

Assessments. In the LERDER scenario, in addition to the traditional cognitive tests, it is required that a more integrated, holistic and authentic examination be instituted to assess abilities of future teachers as leaders of learning communities, including schools. For example, in order to enable student teachers to "produce teaching actions and analyses" (Darling-Hammond,2006a. p. 113), each of them is asked throughout the training programs to demonstrate their ability to conduct cases studies, analyze and reflect on examples of teaching and products of student learning, and keep long-term portfolios of her/his practice as evidence of their thinking, learning, and performance (Darling-Hammond, 2006a, p. 138). A national assembly of teacher educators is responsible for developing the standards that beginning teachers should know and be able to accomplish. These standards take many qualities into consideration, assessing knowledge, skills, and dispositions acquired by each candidate teacher throughout their training programs. Among those key qualities are abilities to use ICTs to promote learning and independent inquiry, to promote the values and practices of citizenship, and to work collaboratively with others, etc.

Scenario of BEACON (3-H +i Model)
Basis of Delphi Findings

This scenario was constructed on the basis of the combined findings (Song, 2007) of all five categories. As described in the previous section, Category I indicated that experts were confident that Chinese teacher education will go through a transformation that will lead to a paradigm shift and to the wide spread application of ICTs in teacher training programs. Category II revealed that experts found that urgent changes are needed in the current education system, including teacher education, and the rigid examination system, yet they found it too challenging to implement change. The society as a whole still has the fear that no other process could work as fairly as the national examination system (Hulbert, 2007). Category III implied that the long history of Confucian tradition would constitute a huge road-block for a dramatic change (e. g. individual needs should be subjected to those of the nation), which requires a convergence of individual desires and national interests. Categories IV and V suggested that the impact of Confucian cultural tradition and the disciplinary thinking paradigm was so deep-rooted that any fundamental change entails a concerted effort by all walks of life. Change also requires the support of the government, an issue that is particularly important since China remains a politically centralized country (Song, 2007).

As revealed in the results of Category I, all findings combined reflected the fact that whereas Chinese might intellectually desire a paradigm shift that will enable the country to sustain rapid growth in a healthy way (e. g. contributive to the common good of the entire human race), the nation is still culturally hindered by the mindset that is the result of a two-thousand-year long tradition, as shown in the findings of Categories Ⅱ, Ⅲ, Ⅳ and Ⅴ.

Also, this projected dramatic change will lead to a chaotic world that leaves little room for routines. This means that future educators are charged with the important role of guide or "beacon" to help students navigate and "thrive in the midst of changes, challenges, and unknowns" (Harkins, 2007, p. 5).

Brief Description

As China moves rapidly to the center stage of international politics and economics, a new generation of Chinese with less influence from the traditional Confucian culture is emerging. This has produced a greater demand for school education to produce citizens who will serve their country (or the world community) and fulfill their own life purposes. In addition to forging a national allegiance, citizens are required to develop a strong sense of global community, exhibiting a "willingness and ability to participate in politics at local, national, and international levels" (Cogan, 1997, p. 9). All walks of life are undergoing rapid changes thanks to easy access to ICTs. This reality completely changes the conventional concept of knowledge and education in a manner similar to what the industrial revolution did to that of the agricultural tradition. In this scenario, books are no longer the exclusive or even a chief means of acquiring knowledge. This requires that every educator stay abreast of the existing technologies (Harkins, 2007) they use to deal with their own concerns and to help enhance students' learning. Under this situation, ICTs make it almost impossible for learning to take place without using emerging new technologies to meet the demand from the ever quickening change in the external world. They simultaneously make it very convenient for everyone to study at his/her own pace to maximize his/her potentials. Everything in the external world appears pretty much like a chaos where routines are no longer the norm; instead, in order to thrive in the midst of challenges (Harkins, 2007), everyone has to think, plan, and implement according to a systemic way.

We are not only connected between races and between past and future, but we are also connected with the environment. This means that we can never look at any event or activity in an isolation. Rather, whenever something happens here or now, these events should be considered in relation to other parts of the world in the future and with regard to the environment. Living in this changing world is exactly like sailing in the vast ocean at night, without knowing what lies ahead.

As a result, in this scenario, the entire process of education is regarded as "navigating" through a chaotic sea of information. As the title of this scenario indicates, future teachers should be trained to function as beacons for learners to safely navigate in the midst of "dark" and uncertain world into which their students are "tossed". This scenario also embodies the key characteristics of a curriculum a successful teacher training programs should have: curricularly basic or fundamental, coherent, exemplary, pedagogically encouraging future teachers to be adaptive, open and competent to navigate their future students. Since this scenario emphasizes the intelligence training (e. g. multiple intelligence*), problem solving skills, emotions, and innovative creation (e. g. head, hand, heart, and innovation), I also call this scenario the "3-H + i Model".

Purposes, Learners, Contents, Processes, and Assessments

Purposes. Teacher education in this scenario is aimed to equip future teachers with qualities, enabling them to help optimize human capital development, by guiding their navigation through the rough seas of chaotic information world, so that teachers can become both innovative knowledge workers for the world where they are living and creators of a

* Multiple Intelligence theory was first proposed by Howard Gardener (1983). According to him, there are eight different kinds of intelligences: Linguistic intelligence, Logical-mathematical intelligence, Spatial intelligence, Bodily-Kinesthetic intelligence, Musical intelligence, Interpersonal intelligence, Intrapersonal intelligence, and Naturalist intelligence (1983).

meaningful and peaceful human society.

Learners. This scenario is within the framework of systems thinking and constructivist learning theories. Here learners are no longer students who sit on their hands listening to their professors; instead, they are all survivors of "sailing through rough seas" and they must each share stories about their pasts and create simulations of their futures. In other words, student teachers are contributors to the world they are entering under the guidance of teacher educators along with professionals from other fields, all through interdisciplinary training.

Contents. Each student teacher must take courses that include those important aspects that directly relate to the discipline, the humanities, pedagogy/psychology, content knowledge teaching method, and interdisciplinary courses that address major social and/or world issues. It is necessary "to involve faculty from professional and liberal arts colleges in jointly taught interdisciplinary classes" (Allen, 1992, p. 191). Also, in order for future teachers to function as reliable "beacons" in the midst of a chaotic world, human relationship (the central part of which is mutual love and respect) will hold a center-place in the curriculum. This relationship signifies a common vision, motivates a passionate action, and sustains a joint effort to fulfill one's life purpose. In addition, ICTs constitute an integral part of teacher education curriculum since they are inseparable in our daily lives.

Processes. In this scenario the entire training process is regarded as a part of the career of the future teachers, meaning that their identity, ability, passion, and ethics as teachers begins to develop from their very first day in the training programs. Therefore, activities are carefully designed to help teacher candidates to grow professionally, academically, and socially. Activities throughout the programs include building human relationships, awakening cultural and political awareness, honing communication skills, and employing technologies into their academic research and learning development. Each prospective teacher is required to go through at least two years of practicum teaching before s/he becomes a full time teacher.

Assessments. As in the LEADER scenario, the rigid written examination does not exist as the only form of evaluating the outcome of an individual's learning activities. A list of integrated and effective ways of examining student teachers' knowledge, skills, competence, and other qualities is required for all qualified teachers. Just like a driver license test where a combination of a written test and a road test is used to ensure a result of a knowledgeable and safe driver on the road, an authentic assessment that places importance on the development of creative leadership and moral characters is needed to create a reliable "BEACON" for young people in the midst of a chaotic world. This assessment must include tests of knowledge, skills, and dispositions (e. g. vision, passion, and wisdom, etc.).

Concluding Remarks

Though, as indicated, it is not the purpose of the researcher to pinpoint or tell the education policy makers what scenario(s) would and should be the most desirable future(s) for the Chinese teacher education training programs, this research does give us a picture of how the four alternative futures unfold in the next two decades or so. These are the futures Chinese education policy makers (and maybe those of other parts of the world as well) should be aware of and get themselves prepared for. The researcher may take one step further in predicting that it would be in the interest of Chinese education authorities to take measures as a response to the four scenarios if they don't want to be caught unprepared when time comes. In other words, a sooner and firmer decision about what scenario into which Chinese education leaders want to direct their teacher training programs would position China as a leader in designing the best teacher education programs which will in turn produce highly qualified teachers for the humongous school system. It becomes more evident that education in general and teacher education in particular needs to go through paradigm shift as discussed in this paper to embrace innovation which includes emphasis on education of competence via service-based learning and global collaboration via the connectivity made possible by Internet. It would not be presumptuous to conclude that, if China's teacher education system takes heed to how the future(s) unfold and plans ahead of time accordingly, this sleeping giant will reshape the world's education system.

走向实践生存
——教师教育变革的人学路径

赵复查*

(韩山师范学院,广东 潮州 521041)

摘 要:实践生存是马克思主义关于人的本质研究的重要理论,是教育人学研究的基础。从实践生存的理论探讨教育属性,对回归属人的教育具有重要意义。实践生存教育是理性与非理性统一的教育,是对象性与非对象性相互转化的教育,是主体性与主体间性相融合的教育。走向实践生存的教师教育要以人的生存境遇为背景展开,要从人学的视野进行教育转换,要关怀现实、具体和历史生成的人。

关键词:教育人学;实践生存;教育选择;人文关怀

Walking Toward Practical Existence: Humanities Approach of Education Reforming

Abstract: Practical existence is the important theory of Marxism on the hypostasis of human and the basis for the research of educational humanities. It has great significance for the regression of humanities education to discuss the educational attribute from the practical existence theory. The practical existence education is the education uniting ration and non-ration, the education inverting from objectivity to non-objectivity reciprocally and the education integrating subjectivity and Inter-subjectivity. The education walking toward practical existence shall be developed under the background of people's existence circumstance, shall make the educational conversion from the visual field of humanities and shall concern for the real, idiographic and historic people.

Key words: Educational Humanities; Practical Existence; Education Selection; Humanities Concern

---

* 赵复查,男,湖北嘉鱼人,韩山师范学院教师教育研究所教授,主要从事教育理论研究。

一、何谓实践生存

实践生存是蕴涵于马克思实践哲学中的具有自我批判与超越精神的人学理论，它以人的生存为基础，以人的实践活动的展开为主旨，围绕人自由自觉的生存目标，把人的研究置于生活境遇之中，从人的感性、超越与现实的结合上理解、确立人性，使人真正走向自己，回归人的实践的属人本性。

生存意味着生命存在的展现、开拓与创新，意味着人性异化的真切呼唤，同时也意味着人对自身境遇及活动的追问与反思。人的生存境遇既不是预定的、凝固的，也不是永恒的，它是人在现实的感性活动和历史过程中生成的。不同的生活方式、不同的存在境遇、不同的生存结构，形成并造就不同属性的人。“人是一个特殊的个体，并且正是他的特殊性使他成为一个个体和现实的、单个的社会存在物，那么，同样地，他也是总体、观念的总体、可以被思考和被感知的社会之主体、自为的存在，正如在现实中，他既作为社会存在的直观和对这种存在的现实享受而存在，又作为属人的生命表现的总体而存在一样。”[1]人的生存活动既具有个体性，又具有整体性，它是主体与类主体两个生存维度不可分割的统一体。人对自身生存的高度自觉集中体现在生命活动的理论阐释与自我批判的活动中。人的个体生命，人的自我生存，以及人的自我实现，都是人自由自觉的自我超越结果。人类社会对自身生存观念的重大转变是从对动物性的生存观念的批判开始的，通过对绝对占有的物欲生存观、片面发展的异化生存观的批判，逐步发展到升华生命存在的意义与质量，协调人、社会、自然全面和谐发展的属人的生存观。现实中的人始终是未完成的、不断变化的、“在路上”的人。人的生存境遇是人之自我实践的结果。

实践是人存在的方式。在实践活动中，人成了一种实践性存在物，实践构成了人的整体性。在人与物的关系上，人“是能动的自然存在物”；在人与人的关系上，人“是社会存在物”；在人与己的关系上，人“是有意识的类存在物”。[2]实践又是人改造世界的方式，实践是人之为人的根本属性，离开实践，人类将不复存在。历史上一切关于人的本性的超验学说都抽掉了人的“实践”这一根本问题，使人的生存堕入了纯生物的自然主义泥坑。马克思认为，“社会生活在本质上是实践的，凡是把理论导致神秘主义方面去的神秘的东西，都能在人的实践中以及对这个实践的理解中得到合理的解决。”[3]人的实践是为了人的生存，人的生存也是为了人能更好地进行实践。人类对生存的理解并不完全定位在已有的存在物上，人通过自身的历史实践活动造就一个属于自己且更赋予其生存意义的属人世界。改造世界，就是通过实践构建一个更加完美的、更加富有人性的生活世界。实践还是人自身价值的一种确证。人本质力量的丰富性、完整性、发展性主要体现在生命活动的历程中，人生价值的张扬，人自身价值的确证，只有通过实践才能得以展现，人自身的本质、特性、能力和力量，只有在实践中才能表现。实践具有感性、对象性和目的性的特征。实践是人的感性活动，它具有直接现实的品格，它是人真实的、可靠的感知觉过程，它与思辨和假设具有本质的区别；实践是人的对象性活动，它是人作为对象性存在物的最基本的特征，人通过活动的对象意识自己、确认自己、展现自己；实践又是人有目的的主观见之于客观的活动，目的性把人的实践活动和动物的本能活动区别开来，实践的目的性决定人实践活动的方式与方法，体现人自由自觉的超越本性。

实践与生存是互为的。一方面它要求主体实践融入生存活动的自觉与反省之中；另一方面它又要求生存活动必须以人的实践作为对象和基础,通过生活世界展现实践生存中的主体,并通过类主体的追求达到实践生存的最高目的。

实践生存是关于"自然、人、社会"通过人的感性的历史性的实践及社会化活动所实现的三位一体的自为生存理论。在这一理论体系中,"自然、人、社会"不再以自在的实体形式存在。自然是活生生的自然,是社会化的人生存于其中的自然,马克思称之为"自然界的生活",自为性、现实性、开放性、历史性是人化自然的基本特征;人不再是抽象的自我意识,而是以全面发展与人类解放为旨归并处于具体历史活动中的人,自觉追求类生存是人的所有历史实践活动的最高标准;社会则是正在历史性地生成的人类共同体,生活世界的自由自觉活动是类主体生命意义的现实性展现。实践生存理论强调人的实践活动必须体现生存主体的感性、现实性、历史性和超越性,通过自身的历史实践活动生成或创造具有与世界统一的合人性的生存主体,在创生中做到个体与整体的统一、超越与责任的统一、自由与自然的统一。[4]实践生存理论揭示了人生存的全面丰富的内涵,把人的生存定位于现实性与历史性的实践活动中,把人对自由自觉的类本质追求看成是人类解放的终极目标。

二、实践生存的教育属性

实践生存是人的本质及其生活的确认,是人接受教育的前提和基础。离开人的实践生存属性的教育是缘木求鱼的教育。教育是引导人参与社会实践的复杂性活动,教育的存在与人的生存实践密不可分,教育只有依据实践生存的属人本性展开才具有现实意义。

(一)理性与非理性的统一

在人的本质及其生存的哲学理论中,曾出现过理性和非理性的论争。黑格尔认为,人是"理性的存在物",理性是人的灵魂、理性是世界的主宰,自然和人类的历史都是人的绝对观念自身展开和实现的结果。理性是世界上一切事物的内在本质,是世界发展的动力。理性是人的精神力量的自决,当理性表现为自由时,则对人具有内在的规定性。人的自由本质是在绝对理性中自我生成、实现和发展的,世界上的一切,包括人在内,都是理性的工具。理性的"自决力量"是人的本质生成的唯一途径。海德格尔认为,人是一种"非理性的存在物",理性不能揭示人的本质,人只有在畏惧、烦怒、死亡等边缘性体验中才能意识到自己的真实存在。人的本质是在人的神秘的自我体验和论证中,在非理性的自我反思活动中生成的。理性只能分析现实的存在者,而不能洞察人的生命,因为人的存在是一种非理性的生命领悟。柏格森把生命的流变看成世界的本质。他认为世界是一种盲目的、非理性的、永不停息的生命冲动,"是一条无底、无岸的河流,它不借可以标出的力量而流向一个不能确定的方向。"[5]在生命之流统治的世界里,自我是不能凭借理性的力量来认识复杂多样的物质世界的,人只有凭借直觉才能体察到自然、把握人的存在、感悟人性的真实。

马克思主义认为,人是一种"实践的存在物",实践是人的本质的内在本源,是人得以真正诞生的园地。人的本质是在现实的社会实践中,自我生成和发展的,实践生存是人成为人,人作为人的唯一途径。理性与非理性,是人类实践生存不可分割的两个方面。在实践生存活动中,理性与非理性只有和谐统一,才能促使人充分自由地发展。没有理性,人的生存实践只会处于低能的动物性阶段,没有非理性,人的实践也不可能真实地展现生命特质,正是理性和非理性的统一,才真正生成了人的本质。理性和非理性是人在实践生存中的具体展现。理性是实践生存的重要组成部分,是人类超越自我,追求价值,探索生命意义,改善生存境遇的一种自由与自觉。人的理性本质是在实践中不断走向完善的。非理性是人通过自身的活动展示生命的存在与价值,体现生命欲望与冲动,表现生命感性、流变及其有限特性的多样性生命本质。"人作为自然的、肉体的、感性的、对象性的存在物,和动植物一样,是受动的、受制约的和受限制的存在物。"[6]"因为它感到自己是受动的,所以是一个有激情的存在物。激情、热情是人强烈地追求自己的对象的本质力量。"[7]在实践生存中,人要摆脱困境,就必须在理性和非理性之间寻找均衡,保持张力,实现认识世界和改造世界的统一。

理性与非理性的统一,是类主体自我创造、自我生成、自我发展和自我完善的实践生存过程。在生存实践活动中,理性和非理性是互相作用、互相渗透的。非理性的激情、热情、欲望与冲动是主体确立活动对象的原动力,而理性则引导非理性构建或迎合人类文化、道德、规范、习俗与社会理想,实现人生的意义与价值。没有非理性的生命激情与冲动,人类自身的活动难以实现超越,没有理性的智慧与创造,人类的自我超越只会处于短暂或较低的水平上。人类理性思维中的概念、判断与推理,具有自觉性、抽象性、逻辑性、连续性、过程性的特点,它是在批判非理性的基础上发展起来的,而非理性思维中的灵感、直觉、顿悟又是在具有一定知识理性和智慧的基础上发生的。在实践生存领域,理性与非理性表现为两种相异的思维方式。这两种思维都是人类生存所必需的,没有任何一方,人类的实践生存活动都难以展开。实践生存教育要围绕人的本质进行。人的理性本质展现了知识智慧的属性,人的非理性本质揭示了生命的激情、欲望与冲动,教育活动如果忽视人的任何一面,都是对人性的亵渎,都是对生命的漠视!实践生存教育是理性和非理性统一的注重人的本质的教育。

(二) 对象性与非对象性的转化

马克思主义实践生存论认为,人既是对象性的存在物,又是非对象性的存在物。对象性揭示的是人的自然,或物化的属性,非对象性揭示的是人的异化,或非物化的精神性。人的生存所体现的对象和非对象性,正是人的生命特性和本质力量的内在与外化的象征。人类的生存首先是对象性的实践活动,对象性是人存在的基本特征。人要意识到自己的存在,就必须具有对象意识,"人是肉体的、有自然力的、有生命的、现实的、感性的、对象性的存在物。""人只有凭借现实的、感性的对象才能表现自己的生命。"[8]感性的、对象性的实践活动,是人的生命存在,及自我确证的基本方式,离开了对象性活动人就成了非人或异化的人。人的对象性活动在物化过程中同时也体现着非物质的精神性创造活动,这种非物质的创造,就是劳动的非对象化。正是人的劳动的非对象性,人才回到人自身,使人"真正占有自己的本质",[9]体现人的生命精神。马克思认为黑格尔的"伟大之处"正在于发现了"劳动的非对象性","黑格尔把人的自我产生看作一个过程,把对象化看作失去对象,看作外化和这种外化的扬弃;因而他抓住了劳动的本质,把对象性的人、现实的因而是真正的人理解为自己的劳动的结果。"[10]

对象性和非对象性的转化,是人类实践生存活动得以可能的最基本的条件,没有对象性活动,人就无法确认自己,没有非对象性活动,人就难以理解生命存在的价值与意义。对象性和非对象性从两个不同的侧面呈现了人的本质,体现了人生存发展的实践特征。对象性强化了人对自然,以及其它客体的改造,把人的主观能动性发展到较高的境地,使主体赋予生命力量,为人的自由自觉活动提供前提。非对象性则相反,它使主体转化为客体或形成主体间关系,使人的生存活动受制于对象的客观规律,促使人与自然、人与社会、人与自身的和谐发展,从而更充分自由地发挥人的创造性。在人的实践生存活动中,对象性与非对象性之间是相互逆转的,人改变对象,对象也改变人。当人改变对象时,主体所获得的是生命存在的物质条件与社会关系。当对象改变人时,主体所获得的是更富生命意义与价值的物质条件与社会关系,使人的生命存在及其发展达到真善美结合的理想高度。教育是改变人的活动,教育要在人的实践生存中充分体现对象性与非对象性,使教育真正成为促使人全面自由发展的活动。

实践生存教育的对象性与非对象性是人接受教育的出发点,是教育适应人的身心发展的前提,也是教育回归人性的觉醒。教育要顺乎人性,就必须遵循人的实践生存发展的规律,从人的实践活动中寻找答案。我们要体悟教育的真正内涵,就必须进入人的生存境遇,了解人的真正生活。对象性提供了人生存的条件,非对象性开启了人的智慧,对象与非对象的相互转化则创造了人的主体意识和自由自觉的本性。教育活动首先要使人认识自己的对象,使人在物化的过程中理解人与对象的关系,把人的理性本质物化在对象中。其次,要充分认识自己的非对象本质,使人具有非物化的精神,要在批判、扬弃和超越外部自然,以及物化的生存活动、生活现实、直观感性的基础上实现自我肯定,使生命的意义与价值凝聚在主体升华的实践活动中。再次,要认识对象性和非对象性的相互转化,使教育成为引导人进入生存自觉的活动。只重视对象性的教育,人的发展就会停留在自在、自发的片面阶段,只重视非对象性的教育,人的发展就会失去生存的根基。只有将对象性和非对象性整合在教育中,并形成创造性的转化,人的发展才能真正进入自由自觉的全面发展状态。

(三) 主体性与主体间性的融合

主体性源于笛卡儿"我思故我在"的哲学命题。它以人的自我意识为核心,通过对主体的探讨展现人的认识运动。康德认为人的理性是世界的主体,外部世界的一切都是人的思维表象,提出要以"人的理性为自然界立法",从而夸大了主体的作用。黑格尔从劳动实践出发,构造了主体的实践对象,赋予主体能动的内涵;但他只是从精神领域确立主体和主体性,因而忽视了主体和主体性的客观存在。主体性是人的生命活动及其表现形式中所体现的自我认识、自我创造和自我超越,是人实践生存的能动反映。人是物质世界的一部分,自然性是人的感性的物质存在,社会性是人的能动的物质存在。自由自觉、自主自为是人特有的本性。在实践活动中,人将自身的本质力量外化或释放在客体身上而表现出一种能动的属性,体现出"对象性的本质力量的主体性"。[11]人的主体能动性,是人通过实践和反思而达到的存在状态和生命境界,是人生命的深度与广度不间断的选择、创造,是生命运动的自觉意识。主体能动性展现了主体性的丰富内涵,闪耀着多彩的生命智慧之光,使人类社会充满了勃勃生机。

在人类的意义活动中,主体间性客观地存在于不同主体之间,人的生命只有处在主体间性的共生、共在的和谐生态文化中才有可能生存、发展,从而实现自我价值。主体间性试图把人与人、人与自然、人与自身的对立、分裂结合起来,通过视界融合、主体统觉、移情等整合生命存在的价值,使生命主体走向类主体。海德格尔从个体生存的联系论述了主体间性,他把个体当作"此在"。他认为,"此在"中渗透了世界和他人,"此在世界是共同的世界。'在之中'就是与他人共同存在。他人的在世界之内的自在存在就是共同此在","此在自己本来就是共同存在。此在本质上是共在",所以,"此在"不可能单独、孤立地存在,"共在在生存论上规定着此在。此在之独在也是在世界中共在。"[12]主体间性是对现实生活世界中人的重新认识,是对人的主体性进行更准确、更具价值的关系性定位。在实践生存中，任何个体都是一种处在由他人共同构成的主体间性的生活世界，类主体的共生、共在与自由发展是主体间性的价值追求。

主体间性是对主体性的扬弃与超越，是主体性合理的、适度的发挥与发展，它强调主体在尊重人性的前提下实施生命价值的弘扬。它把主体性从过去仅涉及主客之间的关系，扩展为包含主体之间的关系。在弘扬主体性上，将只关注主客二元的工具理性改造为以交往为核心的并蕴涵有自由、民主、平等精神的主体间性，使主体从认识世界的"手段——目的"等工具性占有的线性思维窠臼中跳出；在交往实践上，以理解、对话、视界融合、多元渗透、意义建构、同感、移情、交互主体的可涉性等理念，摆脱"自我"走向"他人"，从单数的"我"走向复数的"我们"，从而实现主体间性的哲学认识。主体间性是主体间关系的规定性，是主体与主体之间的理解、通融与共识。实践生存教育是主体性与主体间性相融合的教育。教育生命的深不可测，充分展示了主体性的丰富内涵；教育心灵的情感碰撞、智慧生发、创造交往，以及生命感受的体验与人生价值的升华，更需要主体间性的关照。实践生存教育是主体之间的交往活动，是主体性得以充分施展的生命体验，离开主体性就不可能有教育的主体间性。

三、实践生存教育的人学路径

实践生存的人学是"系统研究人的本质、存在和历史发展规律的理论"，[13]是从整体上研究人之存在、人性和人的本质、人的活动和发展的一般规律，以及人生价值、目的、道路等基本原则的学问。[14]实践生存教育以人为出发点，把人的生存、发展放在教育的重要位置，把关注"整体的人"作为教育活动的目的，把提升人的生命意义与价值作为教育活动的内容，把引导人自由自觉地发展作为教育活动的手段。通过教育这一富有生命意义的特定活动，使人性得到彰显，使人更具丰富多彩的个性，使自由自觉的发展成为现实。

（一）生存境遇的教育选择

人的一切都是在实践生存的历史活动中展开的，离开生存环境，离开人类的历史，人的发展变化是不可能实现的。教育是引导人适应、超越和创造生存环境的复杂性活动。教育要引导人追求美好的人生，实现生命的意义与价值，就要依据人的生存状态进行合理地选择。人的生存状态决定人接受教育的程度、类型与方式，处于不同生存境遇的人对教育的态度与要求也是不一样的。马克思主义实践生存论从人类发展的历史反观人类的生存状态，认为人的存在具有三种不同的形态。一是自在自发的存在，二是异化受动的存在，三是自由自觉的存在。[15]实践生存教育以人的生存状态透视教育现象，解读教育类型，分析人的生存境遇，要求教育从自在自发、异化受动走向自由自觉。

1. 自在自发的教育。这是人的生存实践所需要的最低层次的教育，它满足人类生存的基本需要，如衣食住行、社会规范和谋生的基本知识与技能等。自在自发的教育是一种被动、复制型的教育，它受自在自发思想的支配，强调知识技能的背诵、记忆与重现，注重知识、技能的机械训练、重复叠加，忽视教育的主动性、创造性和个体发展的全面性。它要求受教育者被动接受现成的知识与技能，以适应社会生活的需要。自在自发的教育是理性、对象性和工具性的集中体现，它以理性知识取代人的非理性情感，忽视人的多种需要；一味追求知识的占有，把知识看成对象性的客体，忽视了非对象性的知识与技能的创造；学习目的只是为了个体的简单的生存与基本的物质占有,缺乏自由自觉的类主体精神,具有明显的工具理性特征。自在自发的教育是人类社会发展中不可缺少的教育阶段,也是个人发展不可逾越的基础,它是人生存境遇发展的一种必然,此阶段在人生发展过程中是必需的。但这种教育不是人的终极目标,教育必须超越这种羁绊,到达理想的自由自觉教育阶段。

2. 异化受动的教育。这是人的生存实践依据社会发展的本质被动发展的教育阶段,它最基本的特征是教育与人的自由发展严重脱离,教育受制于外来的本质力量,教育的目的是为了满足社会的政治、经济、文化的需要,教育的动机只是顺应或接纳社会的权威、物质和文化。教育与个人的发展已成为社会发展的必须与必然,个人自由自觉的全面发展被淹没在异化受动的劳动需要中。异化受动的教育是自在自发教育的超越与发展,是人的本质力量得以实现的前提条件,是对原生态自发教育的扬弃。它使人的主体性、个性和创造性得到社会的认可,使人的生存实践进入更高的发展阶段;但社会劳动的异化,社会竞争的现实,社会发展的物质欲望与工具理性,以及制度化的劳动选择或社会化教育力量的分层,迫使异化教育的持续运作。当今社会各种类型的应试教育、考试教育、升学教育、证书与护照教育,甚至专业化教育都是异化受动教育的表现。它充满了工具理性的意味,无视教育的精神享受,使教育蜕变为生存实践的工具和手段,偏离了教育的本真意义;但这是必需的,它是人类生存发展状态的回应,是社会发展的必由之路。

3. 自由自觉的教育。这是理想的教育模式,它是建立在人类生存实践的自由自觉状态下的教育活动。这种教育模式摆脱了日常生活的羁绊,挣脱了名利欲望的束缚,规避了工具理性的要求,实现了人的全面而自由的发展,使教育真正成了人的精神享受与需要。自由自觉的教育是与人的自由自觉生存状态紧密相联的。人类社会发展史和人的成长历史都表明,自由自觉的生存是人类追求的美好目标,是人的主体精神上升为类主体精神的人的本质力量的终极体现。人的生存发展是否处于这一状态,要从社会发展的客观实际和个体主观的认同去整合。历史上出现的伟大人物,如政治、军事、经济、科学、哲学、艺术等精英,都是将自己置于自由自觉生存境遇下的英雄人物,他们置个人的日常生存状态而不顾,完全献身于人类的解放事业,为人类的发展奠定了坚实的基础,为类主体的发展树立了光辉的榜样。自由自觉的教育是一种献身于人类事业的全面发展教育,也是受教育者享受社会生活,充分展示个体人格力量的自由发展教育。它强调教育的全面性、完整性、多样和谐性和个体发展性,要求受教育者自由发展独特的个性,自觉形成独立的创造性人格,自然展现高雅厚重的文化品位,自主发挥人类的文化精神。

根据人类实践生存的境遇把教育划分为三种对应的状态,并不意味着三种教育是决然分开的。在人的发展中,自在自发、异化受动和自由自觉的教育是相互联系的开放生成过程,自由自觉教育所体现的全面性、完整性、个体性、独特性和创造性,在自由自发状态下已潜在于教育活动中,在异化受动状态下已得到开发和认可,只是被生存境遇的选择所淹没、扭曲、泯灭,或扼杀。教育要达到自由自觉的程度必须对传统教育进行改造。

(二) 人学视界的教育转换

实践生存是人的本质力量的体现,是人接受教育的出发点。教育要回归真正属人的教育,体现人的本质,实现人自由自觉的发展,就必须以实践生存的人学去改变传统的教育。

1. 教育目的的人学转换。教育是以人为出发点的教育,离开人的实践生存目的,离开人性的真善美追求，教育就失去了本真的内涵与意义。传统教育最大的弊端是剥离人的本性，以极端的功利主义为目的，把本属于人的教育变成了机械或物化的动物训练，使教育失去了人性的光芒。实践生存教育把人的发展视为最高目标，把人的创造个性的生成视为基本目的，把人的类主体共生共展视为教育的终极目标。实践生存的人学教育通过对人性的反思，要求我们在教育目的上做到两个转换。一是从极端功利主义的教育目的转换到以人为本，通过培养"完整的人"实现教育目的。马克思认为"人是人的最高目的"，培养人的教育要以人为根本，如果脱离人的本性去追求人性之外的附加值，教育就会坠入功利主义的陷阱。教育的功利主义使人的发展限于片面，使人的本性遭到误读。人要全面发展就必须追求自由自觉的本性，把人的尊严、人的意义、人的价值、人的本真内涵凝聚在实践生存的教育活动中。二是从追求知识考试的升学教育转换到以培养人的实践生存能力的智慧教育，通过对人的生存能力的培养达到学会生存的教育目的。教育是人的灵魂塑造与智慧生成的社会实践活动，生存能力是人之存在的前提，只关注升学的知识训练，是一种表层的知识堆集，它忽视了人的生存智慧的生成，是对人性的漠视，也是对本真教育的亵渎。实践生存教育要以人的生存能力的生成来确立教育目的，要围绕生存智慧的生成来规划教育，它不是物化的简单的升学考试，它是对人性的一种理解与追求。

2. 教育内容的人学转换。实践生存教育是促使人全面自由发展的教育，它以提升人的实践生存能力、生命意义、生命价值为目的，通过人性化、个性化、创造性和类主体的教育，让受教育者真正成为"完整的人"。传统教育以理性主义的知识观作为教育的全部内容，使教育在理性的知识、智能、技术训练中斡旋，它忽视了生命发展中的非理性，使人的激情、热情、奔放的灵性坠入深渊，使人处于片面发展境地。实践生存教育从理性与非理性的结合上重新审视属人的教育内容，用人性化的教育取代片面的理性知识训练，使人性得以回归，使人的个性充分自由地发展，使类主体的教育成为现实。教育的人性化要以生命的成长为目的，要把对生命的珍惜、敬畏、舒展放在最重要的位置，使生命在人性的观照下自由地生长。教育的个性化要以尊重生命价值的多样性为前提，通过生命价值与意义的提升，促使个体生命形成各具特色的第二生命。类主体是生命得以生存、发展的重要基础，类主体教育要以类主体生存的需要，引导生命个体为类主体的发展创造条件，并为类主体的生存而充分自由地发展个体生命。实践生存教育的内容围绕人的本质特性展开，以生成"完整的人"为出发点，将人性化教育、个性化教育和类主体教育完满结合，在实践中形成统一的生存教育模式。

3. 教育策略的人学转换。实践生存教育以孕育自由自觉的人性为出发点，以促进人的生成发展为支撑，通过教育的情境转化与智慧生成策略，达到润泽生命的教育目的。传统的教育策略以知识的占有为目的，以知识的获得为终点，只见知识不见人，看重的只是机械重复的智力训练和知识堆集的升学、"应试"，它忽视生命的意义与价值，使人生长在荒芜的精神沙漠中，从而迷失人性。真正的教育是人之生命意义的建构，是对人的生命价值的生成与拓展，是对生命意义的提升。"训练是一种心灵隔离的活动。"[16]"教育过程首先是一个精神成长过程，然后才成为科学获知过程的一部分。"[17]教育要把知识与人的生存境遇、命运和幸福联系起来，让人去追求生命存在的价值。实践生存教育是以主体间性为前提的教育，在师生关系上强调主体性与主体间性的融合，在学习内容的处理上强调对象性与非对象性的转化，在教育理想上强调预期性与非预期性的统一，在教育评价上强调个体生命生成与发展的多样性与多元化。总之，教育策略要以引导生命的自由自觉发展为目的，要以弘扬生命的主体意识为主旋律，通过人对人的教育焕发出生命的活力,让人的知识、智慧与生命意义一起自由地放飞。

(三) 实践生存的教育关怀

实践生存教育以人的生存境遇的改变为目的,以对人的生命关怀为终极目标。它与传统教育最大的区别就在于从关心抽象人,转到关心现实、具体和历史生成的人。

1. 关怀具体感性的人。马克思主义实践生存论认为,人既不是预定、假设的,也不是永恒不变的,人是在现实的感性活动中生成的。离开感性活动,人就脱离了自身的特性。在现实生活中,世界是感性的世界,人也是感性的人。当我们把"感性世界理解为构成这一世界的个人的、共同的、活生生的、感性的活动"[18]时,人的感性生活就成了联结自然与社会、自我与他人、自觉与自身的生存因素,人便成了感性活动的人。传统教育忽视人的感性,认为情感、情绪等非理性因素是知识、智慧学习的干扰因素,只关注知识理性,不关心现实生活中的感性人。实践生存教育将感性活动与理性活动统一于教育过程中,强调感性对理性的调控,强调激情、热情对知识、智慧的启迪,重视教育主体情感作用的发挥,以人的感性活动建构生命的智慧与意义。关怀教育活动中的感性人,要从教育主体的情感因素关照生命体的感受,以生命的激情、热情去碰撞生命,以生命的体验去感悟生命,以尊重、敬畏、珍惜生命的情怀去引导生命!要了解教育对象的生命感受,要把学生的感性活动放在与理性活动同等重要的位置上,通过对生命意识的情感关怀,激发生命的主体意识,调动生命的激情与热情,从而实现具有生命意义的真正属人的教育。

2. 关怀现实理性的人。教育活动的理性与非理性的统一是实践生存教育的重要属性;但在人的实践生存活动中,由于生存境遇的不同,或受社会异化劳动、异化受动教育的影响,于是有人便偏向知识,崇尚理性,成为现实理性的人。现实理性的人缺乏人文的关怀,认为知识是改变命运的唯一选择,"知识是命运的主宰"、"知识就是力量"、"知识就是财富"。现实理性的人用一只眼看世界,忽视了非理性在人的发展中的重要性,把理性与非理性对立起来,使自己陷入科学主义的泥坑。人是理性和非理性的统一,非理性是人本质力量的源泉与动力,理性是人本质力量的工具。在人的发展中理性与非理性都是不可缺少的。实践生存教育要关怀现实理性的人,首先要从人发展的整体素质出发,把人的全面发展,特别是把人心灵情感、健康人格的发展放在重要的位置,正确处理好知识与情感、技术与人格、升学与做人的关系。把人的品格观照,把人与自然的和谐相处,把类主体的实践生存与生态共创作为人发展的前提;其次是要从实践生存的角度引导,把教育主体的生命意义与价值的提升作为教育活动的根本目的。人生意义的升华,人生价值的提升,是实践生存教育对现实理性人关怀的具有文化意蕴的举措,要通过生命意义的内涵培植,引导教育主体将理性与非理性融合,从而阐释生命的价值,达到人与自然、人与社会、人与自身的生态和谐。

3. 关怀历史生成的人。实践生存论认为人是历史生成的人,人的历史就是人的生长史。要了解、认识、把握教育活动中人的本质或特性,就必须从"抽象的人转到现实的、活生生的人,就必须把这些人当作在历史中行动的人去考察"。[19]要把人的生存与实践紧密联系起来,要从人的生活历史、生活环境、生存境遇去考察人,只有把人的思想观念与人的生存选择统一起来,才能真正了解、认识历史生成的人。实践生存教育不是从抽象的角度去理解人,不是用一般人的抽象理念去对待具有不同生成历史的受教育的人,要从现实的活生生的教育主体的历史去关怀人。要关怀教育活动中历史生成的人,就必须了解受教育者的生长史。要从实践生存的环境关心人的成长，引导人走出宗教命运崇拜的误区，走向自我决定、自我创造和自我实现的历史生成的人的过程；要从人的生存境遇关心人的发展，理解人对教育方式的选择与追求，从教育关怀中引导人走出生存困境，到达理想生存的彼岸；要从历史生成的渐进发展、逐步成熟的过程去理解鲜活的、富有朝气的在实践生存中接受教育的人，要把对人的关怀提升到对生命的生成与敬重的高度来认识，通过教育关怀人的生命价值与生存质量，通过教育关怀人的未来，使教育主体在历史生成中不断提升生命的意义。

参考文献

[1] 马克思. 1844年经济学哲学手稿[M]. 北京：人民出版社，1979：76.

[2][6][7][8][9][10][11] 马克思恩格斯全集：第42卷[M]. 北京：人民出版社，1979：167，167，169，168，170，163，167.

[3][18] 马克思恩格斯选集：第1卷[M]. 北京：人民出版社，1972：18，50.

[4] 周诗鹏. 生存论研究[M]. 上海：上海人民出版社，2005：15.

[5] 柏格森. 形而上学导言[M]. 北京：商务印书馆，1963：68.

[12] 海德格尔. 存在与时间[M]. 北京：三联书店，1999：136-140.

[13] 韩庆祥，邹诗鹏. 人学[M]. 昆明：云南人民出版社，2001：12.

[14] 陈志尚. 再论人学的对象和方法[J]. 社会科学辑刊，2001(2).

[15] 衣俊卿. 论人的存在：人学研究的前提性问题[J]. 学习与探索，1999(3).

[16][17] 雅斯贝尔斯. 什么是教育[M]. 北京：三联书店，1991：12，30.

[19] 马克思恩格斯选集：第4卷[M]. 北京：人民出版社，1972：236-237.

教育史的教师教育价值及教学问题刍议

朱镜人　韦立君　张珍珍*

(合肥师范学院,安徽　合肥　230061)

摘　要:本文研究了作为教育学科中的基础学科——教育史在教师教育中的作用长期被忽略的原因,探讨了教育史的教师教育价值以及教师教育中教育史课程的教学原则、内容和方法等问题。笔者认为:教育史是教师教育专业课程中不可或缺的组成部分;教育史学科应当在教学原则、内容和方法上深入革新,以胜任其承担的教师教育任务。

关键词:教育史;教师教育;价值

一、问题的提出

教育史(history of education)在教师教育中的作用问题长期以来没有受到应有的重视。这一现象突出地表现在教师教育课程设置上。直到目前为止,除了教育学专业和公共事业管理专业(教育)之外,我国师范院校只为师范生开设《教育学》和《心理学》两门公共课课程。目前实施的教师资格考试制度中规定的考试科目也只有《教育学》、《心理学》两门教育理论课程。在这样的背景下,教育史学科也就没有机会发挥它在教师教育中应当发挥的作用了。那么,为什么教育史学科在教师教育中没有受到应有的重视呢?教育史学科在教师教育中能不能发挥作用或到底能够发挥哪些作用?教师教育中教育史课程应当如何开设等问题便成了高等院校教育史工作者回避不了的问题。认真思考和回答这些问题对于发挥教育史学科在教师教育中的作用是十分必要的。

二、教育史的教师教育价值

价值一般是事物的积极作用的体现。教育史在教师教育中的作用为什么会被忽略?笔者认为,原因主要来自两个方面,一是来自学科外部的原因,非教育史专业的人士,包括教育行政部门工作人员,甚至包括教师和一些教育专业工作者,对学科的价值判断和取向往往倾向于“实用”,教育史学科由于它的基础性特点而显得“无用”,因此不受重视;二是来自教育史学科内部的原因,除了史学本身“实用性不强”之外,更多的恐怕要从教育史工作者(教师)自身去寻找原因:为什么没有能通过自己的教学和研究,让人们感受到教育史的价值,激起人们学习教

* 朱镜人,韦立君,张珍珍,合肥师范学院教育系教师。

育史的兴趣呢？分析这两个原因的形成是展开讨论的前提。

首先，人们在教育史价值判断上所形成的教育史“无用”的观点，是建立在急功近利的价值取向上的。“任何事物都是有用的”[1]（Everything has its uses）。英国学者的这一观点是有道理的。如果仅从表层的立竿见影的效果来看，教育史学科的实用性确实不强。但是，从长远观点来看，教育史的作用却是不容忽略的。美国新史学倡导人鲁滨逊（J. H. Robinson）认为，历史“可以帮助我们了解我们自己、我们的同类以及人类的种种问题和前景。这是历史最主要的功能，但一般人所忽略的恰恰就是历史所产生的这种最大效用。”[2]对这一问题，我国著名外国教育史学家滕大春先生也曾有过一段关于外国教育史作用的精彩论述：“外国教育史如何对待‘用’的问题是值得思考的。要求一种教育基本理论学科给当前某些具体教育业务工作提供切实可行的实施方案，是难以胜任的。但在另一方面，教育史却能培养人们较为远大的教育眼光和对教育课题的领悟能力，而这种眼光和能力每每能产生人们意识不到的威力。所以教育史对实际工作的效能常常是迂回的，而不是直线进行的，是须经过较长时期才能显明其伟效的。”[3]滕先生这段话中的“用”包括两个层面的意思，第一个层面，即宏观的层面，懂得教育的历史有利于今天的教育改革，一是吸取历史经验推动今天的教育改革，二是以历史教训为鉴，避免重蹈历史覆辙。历史上重蹈历史覆辙的现象并不鲜见，其重要原因之一是不懂得历史造成的。第二个层面是微观层面，表现在两方面：一方面，学习教育史可以丰富和完善教师的教育理论知识，提升教师的专业修养，包括教师的素养和能力的提升，但这是一个需要较长时间的过程；另一方面，通过对教育史的学习，教师可以从中获得教育和教学方法的启示。然而，对历史上的教育教学方法的理解、领悟、移植并赋予时代特点也需要一个较长的时间。因此，教育史的功能在短期内不能显现。

其次，从教育史学科内部来看，可能是我们在教育史的教学指导思想和教学原则的确定上，在教材内容的处理上、在教学方法的使用上没有凸现其在教师教育中的作用，没有凸现教育史的学科魅力。

尽管由于种种原因，教育史学科在教师教育中没有受到应有的重视。但还是有相当多的教育工作者和在校师范生对教育史的作用和意义有一定的认识。我们围绕“学习教育史对教师专业发展具有怎样的作用和意义”作了一次问卷调查（见表1）。

表1　学习教育史对教师专业发展具有怎样的作用和意义的调查

<table>
<tr><th>问　题</th><th colspan="6">回 答（以百分比计算）</th></tr>
<tr><td>你曾经接触过中外教育史吗？</td><td colspan="3">是（69.4%）</td><td colspan="3">否（30.6%）</td></tr>
<tr><td>你对中外教育史感兴趣吗？</td><td colspan="2">很感兴趣（30.4%）</td><td colspan="2">比较感兴趣（56.3%）</td><td colspan="2">不感兴趣（13.3%）</td></tr>
<tr><td>你读过中外教育名著吗？</td><td colspan="3">是（60%）</td><td colspan="3">否（40%）</td></tr>
<tr><td>你认为学习教育史有助于其他学科学习吗？</td><td colspan="3">是（90%）</td><td colspan="3">否（10%）</td></tr>
<tr><td>学习教育史有助于丰富教育理论知识，提升教师专业修养吗？</td><td colspan="3">是（98.6%）</td><td colspan="3">否（1.4%）</td></tr>
<tr><td>学习教育史对教育教学实践有帮助吗？</td><td colspan="2">很有帮助（30%）</td><td colspan="2">有帮助（69.8%）</td><td colspan="2">没有帮助（0.2%）</td></tr>
<tr><td>你如何看待教育史在教育学科中的地位？</td><td colspan="3">基础地位（90.3%）</td><td colspan="3">辅助地位（9.7%）</td></tr>
<tr><td>学习教育史对教学工作有借鉴意义吗？</td><td colspan="3">是（83%）</td><td colspan="3">否（17%）</td></tr>
<tr><td>学习教育史有助于今天的教育创新吗？</td><td colspan="3">是（92.3%）</td><td colspan="3">否（7.7%）</td></tr>
</table>

调查对象选取的是安徽某高校教育系的学生、进修的教师和培训的校长三个不同群体(最终获得有效问卷160份)。从调查数据可以看出,98.6%的人认为通过学习教育史可以丰富教育理论知识,拓宽视野,提升教师专业修养;99.8%的人认为教育史对教育教学实践是有帮助的,其中认为很有帮助的占问卷总数的30%;92.3%的人认为学习教育史有助于今天的教育创新;另有超过半数受调查者认为通过了解中外教育家的生平及其教育实践活动有助于树立正确的教师职业观以及献身教育事业的精神。但是也有少部分教师和学生未能认识到教育史学科的重要性及其价值所在,其中有13.3%的人对中外教育史不感兴趣,9.7%的人认为教育史在教育理论课程中的地位并不重要。

问卷结果反映的是人们对教育史学科的看法,那么在实际工作中教育史的作用如何呢?由于无法对教育史在日常教育教学工作中的运用情况作定量调查。因此笔者选择研究的是教育史在教育教学研究中的运用情况,即教育和教学理论文章中涉及到教育史的注释、参考文献情况。笔者对2003年的《教育研究》、《教育理论与实践》,2004年的《中国教育学刊》、《教师教育研究》、《教育评论》、《教育研究与实验》以及《现代中小学教育》等教育理论刊物的文章作了一次统计研究(见表2)。从表中的数据可以看出,教育史知识在教育理论研究中发挥了一定的作用,但十分有限。引用最多的刊物的文章中也只有31.3%,不到1/3。引用最少的只有4.3%,不到1/20。这一现象说明了两种可能,一是历史法在当前的教育理论研究中未受到重视,二是人们对教育史遗产的熟悉程度不够。这第二种可能反映了我国教师教育中的教育史课程的缺位所产生的影响。

表2　教育教学理论文章中引用教育史文献的情况统计

期刊名	年份	总篇数	参考文献/注释中引用与教育史内容有关的文章篇数	占总篇数比例约为
教育研究	2003	207	45	21.7%
教育理论与实践	2003	182	44	24.2%
中国教育学刊	2004	217	48	22.1%
教师教育研究	2004	97	15	15.5%
教育评论	2004	287	47	16.4%
教育研究与实验	2004	64	20	31.3%
现代中小学教育	2004	299	13	4.3%

将上面的问卷结果和统计结果放在一起研究,就会发现一个矛盾的现象:在观念上,人们也承认历史的价值;但在实际运用方面,历史的使用价值未能体现。造成这种现象的原因,笔者认为,主要是教师教育中教育史知识普及的不够。当人们对教育史缺乏了解,对教育史价值的认识就会受到局限,更谈不上运用了。为了改变这一状况,笔者建议在教师教育课程体系中增加教育史的课程。其理由,即教育史课程在教师教育中的价值如下:

1. 学习教育史有助于教师专业思想和素养的提升

"读史使人明智"。教育史学科一个最大特点即内容是建立在大量的史实基础之上,读教育史可以让人们了解教育的真实发展历程,掌握教育发展的规律,这些都是教育领域最基础也是最根本的知识,因而也是每一位教师应该了解的。尤其当"教师"这一古老的职业在历经了漫长的发展历程后成为部分社会成员所专门从事的职业时,社会对教师提出的要求也逐步提高了,不仅要求教师须具备良好的学科知识,还要具备良好的教育专业修养,其中包括了解教育发展的历史轨迹:教育作为人类特有的一种社会现象是何时出现的?在不同的历史时期,不同的国家和地区有哪些著名的教育思想家?他们提出了哪些教育思想和教育理论?这些关于教育发展的基本问题,应是每一位教师所知晓的。但是在我们的160份调查问卷中,知道孔子教育思想以及阅读过《论语》的人数分别是106人和5人,而知道苏格拉底及其教育思想的仅有43人。这两位教育家堪称教育史上的大家,但还有这么多受调查者不了解他们的教育思想。在教师教育中开设教育史课程的必要性就不言自明了。

2. 学习教育史有助于教师专业知识的完善

肖尔曼提出,教师要促进学生学习,应具备七种知识和能力,其中一种便要求教师应对教育历史有一定的认识。[4]为什么要了解教育的历史?从教育史的内容组织来看,一直以两根线贯穿始终,即制度史和思想史。教育制度史以各国的学校体系作为其主要研究对象,探讨教育管理制度、学前教育、初等教育、中等教育、高等教育、师范教育等方面的历史发展;教育思想史则主要探讨各个历史时期各国著名教育家的教育理论与教育实践。目前很多教育学科都是对教育史中某个或某些内容的延伸与扩展,因而教育史的知识是教育理论中的基础知识,而教育史学科则是教育学科中的基础学科,"是教育科学的重要源泉"。[5]从这个角度来看,学习教育史有助于其他教育学科的学习。例如教育学,作为教师教育中的教育基础理论课程,其知识体系中有很多内容都是以教育史作为基础的。有了教育史的知识基础,对教育基本问题的理解和领悟就会容易得多。在此次问卷调查中,这一观点得到近90%的受调查者的认同。

3. 学习教育史有助于教师专业技能的培养

对于大多数教师而言,学习教育史的最终目的在于指导实践工作以提高教育教学效果。中外教育史中许多教育家关于教学方法、教学原则、教学内容的论述,对今天的教师依然有强烈的指导意义。对于教育史的这一作用,学习过教育史的人多数是予以肯定的。从本次问卷调查的结果来看,83%的受调查者认为中外教育家关于教学方法、教学原则的探讨对于今天的教学工作仍具有非常重要的指导意义。

4. 学习教育史有助于教师的教育创新

我们今天的教育事业能否长久健康地发展,取决于我们在教育思想、教育理论上能否有所创新。而教育的创新并非在空中建造楼阁,是需要站在前人的肩膀上的。这就需要懂得教育的历史。美国教育史学家布里克曼(W. W. Brickman)说,教育史教学所要达到的目标之一就是减少无知。[6]这话的确有道理,如果缺乏教育史的修养,就很有可能夜郎自大地"创造"一个个别人早已抛弃的想法和尝试,走一些不该走的弯路,尝试一些不该尝试的失败和经验。审视我们今天正在经历的种种教育改革,有些教育理念、教育观点和方法不是还在重写历史吗?因此可以说,不了解教育史,是谈不上教师的教育创新的。我们欣喜地看到,越来越多的教育工作者认识到教育史的"话语权"在教育改革中举足轻重的作用,开始强调教育史的学习。例如许多中小学,如深圳南华中学和成都市龙泉驿区实验小学等已将诸多中外教育名著列入中小学教师的必读书目。上海、江苏、浙江等地还成立了教师读书俱乐部,如上海外国语大学嘉定外国语实验学校青年教师读书俱乐部、张家港市泗港小学读书俱乐部和杭州和睦小学教师"激情飞扬"读书俱乐部等,诸多教育史著作也在推荐的阅读书目之中。

三、教师教育中教育史课程开设的问题

不久的将来,随着我国教师教育理论研究和实践方面的新的拓展,师范院校的教师教育课程将打破原先的“老三门”(教育学、心理学和学科教学法)格局,而增设更多的教育学科的选修课程,这无疑为其他教育学科包括教育史学科的建设提供了契机。高校教育史学者应当把握好这难得的机遇。为了使教育史学科发挥其在教师教育中不可替代的作用,我们认为需要重新思考教育史课程教学的目标、原则、内容、方法等问题。

(一) 教育史教学的目标、原则和内容

教师教育中的教育史课程教学的目标不是培养大批的教育史学工作者,而是为各级学校教师(主要是中小学教师)素养的提高补充历史的营养。因此,在确定教学原则和内容时应当有以下几点考虑。

1. 溯清源头,厚古不薄今

人类教育的进程总体上呈螺旋式上升,前进中有反复,在反复中又有前进。因而,历史上很多教育现象、教育问题对于今天的教育仍具有启示意义。例如外国教育思想史中有许多教育理论和观点都可以追溯到古希腊时代。又如,中国近现代的教育思想同样可以回溯到古代教育思想家那里。因而教育史的内容组织应适当突出古代史部分,这是教育发展的源头,没有源就不会有流,不了解源头便不可能完整地了解各种教育思想的发展脉络,更不可能对今天的教育问题及现象产生多大的领悟能力。但厚古不薄今,近现代教育与今天教育的联系相比古代教育更为紧密,也不能忽略。

2. 脉络清晰,详略有致

教师教育中的教育史课程由于其教学目标的限定,课时不会太多;此外,学生也不会愿意花费太多的时间来学习教育史。这样就对教育史教学内容的安排提出了要求:教学内容必须脉络清晰,详略有致。反映在教材编写上,首先应体现出教育史的制度史和思想史“两根线”的历史发展轨迹,要反映制度史和思想史的历史继承性特点。其次,要重点突出。这样,学习者通过教育史的学习获取的就不会是一些零碎的信息,而是一种系统的了解和有重点的领悟。

3. 突出实践性知识

当前教师教育中所开设的教育史课程,存在一个很大的问题,即让学习者觉得教育史的内容无论从时间上还是空间上都离自己太遥远了。这反映了教育史的内容设置还存在问题,没有做到贴近教师的实际工作与生活。17 世纪捷克著名教育家夸美纽斯在论述如何激发学生求知欲时就曾谈过,如果学生知道所学习的内容对他们将来是有用的,那么他们会对知识的学习充满热情与渴望。同样,学习教育史也是如此。应当增加一些对教师的教学有直接指导意义的内容。但是从目前的教育史教材内容来看,侧重于理论的部分多,对于众多教育家的实践活动只是在介绍人物生平时,或介绍其理论观点时附带谈一些,似乎只是理论的陪衬。因此,应当适当地增加有关教育教学实践的内容,介绍一些教育者在实践领域的探讨与研究,比如历史上的教学案例研究。

4. 突出教育的社会背景。教育史上任何教育事件、教育问题和教育思想的出现都有着深刻的社会背景因素。这些背景因素包括政治、经济、宗教、民族、文化、传统、历史、地理、国外影

响,等等。如果不了解这些因素对教育的影响,仅从教育的角度来探讨教育史现象或问题,视野便会显得狭隘,也难以理解历史上的教育问题和教育思想,更难以获得对今天教育的启示。对于这一点,英国有过教训。20 世纪五六十年代,英国“旧”教育史学(“old ”history of education)受到的批评之一,就是因为没有把教育史的问题放到历史的社会背景中研究。[7]

(二) 教育史的教学方法

长期以来,许多学校的教育史课程教学都是以讲授为主,方法比较单一。如果教师口才不好,讲课没有激情,很容易使学生感到枯燥乏味,失去学习的兴趣。因此需要改革教学方法,比如在讲授的同时,伴以研讨(seminar)、课程小论文(问题研究),课外教育经典阅读(例如中国的《学记》、《论语》、《大学》,西方的《理想国》、《爱弥尔》和《民主主义与教育》等)方法,并利用现代教育技术手段,为学生自学提供充足的电子资源(背景资料)。这样,就可能调动学生学习的积极性和热情。当然,无论采用什么方法,其效果如何是在一定程度上取决于教师的教学态度的,这就是教育史教师对教育史学科的热爱和强烈的专业精神。否则,什么方法都不会产生效果。

四、结论

“懂得历史价值的人便会渴望学习历史”。[8]教育史记述了教育的昨天,没有教育的昨天就不可能有教育的今天,更不可能有教育的明天。作为现代社会的教师,如果要想成为一个真正的教育者(educator),一个真正的教育上的创新者,他就不能不知道教育的历史。教师教育是不能忽略教育史学科和课程的存在的,教育史课程在教师教育中具有不可替代的重要性。同时,教育史学科和课程自身也需要在原则、内容和方法上革新,以便充分发挥其在教师教育中的不可替代的作用。

参考文献

[1][7][8] PETER GORDON, RICHARD SZRETER. History of Education: The Making of a Discipline [M]. The Woburn Press, 1989: 134,6,47.

[2] 何兆武,陈启能. 当代西方史学理论[M]. 上海:上海社会科学院出版社,2003:20.

[3] 滕大春. 外国教育通史:第一卷[M]. 济南:山东教育出版社,1989:5.

[4] 陈永明. 国际师范教育改革比较研究[M]. 北京:人民教育出版社,1998:385.

[5] 孙培青. 中国教育史 [M]. 上海:华东师范大学出版社, 2000:1.

[6] 杜成宪,邓明言. 教育史学[M]. 北京:人民教育出版社, 2004:395.

转型期师生文化冲突的和谐之道

谈儒强*
（合肥师范学院，安徽 合肥 230061）

摘 要：在社会转型、文化多元的当下中国，教师与学生文化冲突呈现诸多新的形态和特点。文化对话可能是一条比较适恰的解决文化冲突的途径，其策略包括悬置偏见、宽容异见、文化理解。文化理解既是手段也是目的，悬置偏见和宽容异见是为了增进文化理解，“和而不同”应奉为文化对话之圭臬。

关键词：文化；师生；文化对话；文化理解

基金项目：安徽省高等学校教学研究项目“教师教育转型与地方本科师范院校师范性重建”(2008jyxm466)。

How to Harmonize Cultural Conflicts Between Teachers and Students During the Transformation Period

Tan Ru-qiang
(Hefei Normal Institute, Hefei 230061)

Abstract: In current China, there is undergoing a multicultural and societal transformation. Cultural conflicts between teachers and students present many new forms and characteristics. Cultural dialog may be a proper way to solve cultural conflicts, whose strategy includes ignorance of biases, toleration of disagreements and understanding of cultural differences. Understanding of cultural differences is both the means and ends. Ignorance of biases and toleration of disagreements aims at fostering cultural understanding, while "harmonization with tolerance of disagreements" should be treated as the principle of cultural dialog.

* 谈儒强，男，安徽舒城人，合肥师范学院教育系副教授。

Key words: culture; teachers and students; cultural dialog; understanding of cultural differences

师生的文化冲突是指持不同文化的教师与学生在价值观念和行为方式上的对抗。当前我国正处于社会转型期,师生文化冲突呈现形态多样、错综复杂且激烈速变等诸特点,主要表现为:代言主流文化的教师与价值多元的学生冲突,强调学科知识传授的教师与兴趣多样的学生冲突,实行统一标准的教师与渴望尊重差异的学生冲突,采用家长式管理的教师与崇尚平等自由的学生冲突,等等。在应对师生文化冲突时,压制或妥协皆不可取,师生都要秉持"和而不同"的原则,以"悬置偏见,宽容异端,增进理解"的立场与方法开展文化对话。教师和学生要尽可能地悬置自己的文化偏见,在表达自己的文化观点的同时,更要以宽容的心态来理解对方的文化主张,共同建设不同质文化和谐共处的师生文化生态。

一、悬置偏见

通常人们选择体验文化的方式以及如何解释所体验的文化,部分地依赖于他们的利益、先前的知识经验,在观察世界的时候总是有意无意地戴上"文化"的镜片。文化的这一特性导致人们的"文化偏见",形成了不同的"价值标准",左右着人们的"思维路线"和"行为方式"。文化对话的开展,要求对话的师生尽可能认识和正视自己的文化偏见,并通过悬置偏见这一策略,发现那些容易被忽略的意义来寻找共识,以破除文化偏见所带来的思想束缚。

(一) 为何要悬置文化偏见

一般来说,小到个人,大到民族都有自己"固执"的文化观念,并成为他们习以为常的生活规范,成为他们文化判断的尺度甚至是文化偏见。尽管可能认识到保持某种偏见是不明智的,但仍把自己蒙蔽在文化的幻象中,无法对自己和他人的文化做客观地认知。

教师和学生也会习惯于以自己文化规范来思维,而且自身很难意识到这一点。当师生文化发生冲突时,双方都会不由自主地维护自己的文化观念。教师可能倾向于借助管理上的权威压制学生文化,学生则可能通过言语争辩和行为反抗来申明他们的文化价值。如果教师和学生都强调自己的意见,那么即便有民主自由的表达机制,也不会有真正意义上的文化对话发生。结果可能是文化强势的一方取得表面上胜利,弱势的一方被迫妥协或转入消极的文化抗争之中。然而,胜出的无论是教师文化还是学生文化,其坚持的文化观念未必全是正确的,这样的文化交往过程很难促进师生文化共同发展。因此悬置文化偏见显得十分必要。

(二) 如何悬置文化偏见

在师生文化对话中悬置文化偏见,就是要清醒认识并虚心检讨自己文化的缺点,不试图将自己的文化强加给对方。并随时准备倾听不同的文化观点,在必要时有勇气抛弃旧的思想和观念,悦纳他人提出的不同观点。反之,固执己见,力图将自己的想法灌输给别人,不愿悬置文化偏见,师生文化对话之路便发生阻滞。

1. 保持开放的文化心态

悬置文化偏见要求师生不要有通过文化对话一定要解决问题,或达成某种共识的思想负担。否则，在文化对话过程中，作为平等主体的教师和学生都难以敞开心扉，对话时也不会感到自由宽松。“在文化对话过程中，重要的不在于答案本身，而在于人们放弃自己固执的思维模式，做到开放思想，兼收并蓄。”“我们并非武断地认为对话没有一定的目的——它只是没有绝对的目的。如果一定要对对话找出一个目的的话，那么我们的目的乃是真正地、流畅地对真理进行交流。”

因此，在师生文化对话中，悬置文化偏见要求从善如流不固执己见。如果在文化对话中发现自己的文化观点不正确，那么还要在“悬置”基础上“放弃”它。但也并非要把他人的观念强加于己。否则，就违背了悬置文化偏见的要求和文化对话的精神。

2. 进行必要的文化自省

在文化对话中真正做到悬置己见，并非只是简单地将文化偏见暂时束之高阁，还需对自己的文化做必要的省思。当与不同群体进行文化对话，自己的文化偏见浮出水面后，就要有意识地控制，做到既不影响判断，也不刻意地去压制。然后努力去厘清文化偏见对自己言行和判断的影响，明白放任可能产生的后果。要做到这一点，则需要把“自己放在自己面前进行审视——就像在镜子前观察自己一样”。同时，也可以“以别人为镜，以群体为镜”来反观、省察自己的文化偏见。这样“群体就成为每个人用于反照自身的一面镜子。别人对你的反应就是你的镜子，同样地，你对别人的反应也是一面镜子。”因此，师生只有悬置自己的文化偏见，并经过认真观察反思，才能越来越熟悉文化偏见的作用方式，才能真正体会到文化对话的精髓所在。值得注意的是，在文化对话中，教师和学生都不应抱有一定要改变什么的心态，但要了解文化偏见是如何产生并发挥作用的。教师要用批判性的思维方法，清醒地认识到不论是师生文化交往中的冲突，还是文化对话中严重争执，都与他们各自坚持的文化偏见有着天然的联系。而且，教师还要知道如何去悬置文化偏见，如何去分析自己和他人的文化，达成师生关系之和谐。

二、宽容异见

文化对话需要宽容并促进了宽容，而宽容的氛围又会促进文化的对话。在多元文化的社会背景下开展文化对话，必须要允许性质和强弱不同的文化自由地表达，与其他文化进行接触、沟通、辩论。因此，各种不同性质文化的持有者，要宽容与己相异的价值与行为。这样做不仅是文化对话所需要的，而且对待与己文化千差万别的不同文化，坚持一种极大的宽容本身就是一种明智的做法。

在师生文化对话中，教师尤其要宽容不同性质学生文化的存在，容忍用与己相异的文化表达其观点，甚至有时候允许学生文化带来的竞争和冲突。这是因为师生文化对话，只有在宽容的文化氛围中才能真正有效地开展。在我国，师生关系不平等并不鲜见，长期受到压抑的学生即便有民主对话的机会，也可能因为害怕说错被罚而不能积极主动提出自己的文化主张。而在宽容的文化对话氛围中，文化上处于弱势的学生就愿意与教师讨论交流一些以前不敢说的话题。而且，学生在师生文化冲突中存在的问题，有一些是他们成长过程中与社会接触所必须经历的问题。随着身心的不断成长，他们将会最终从这些问题中走出来。对于这样的问题，教师可以在文化对话过程中宽容学生，那么这些文化问题将会随着学生的不断成熟而自然而然地消解。

(一)宽容的界定

1. 什么是宽容

宽容乃是一种建立在对人与世界的多样性、真理的相对性与人性的多元性自觉意识基础上的理性和明智的思维方式、行为方式与人生态度;是处理人际关系时面对存在的差异、矛盾和冲突所表现出的一种成熟通达的美德和境界。宽容精神的基本内涵——对不守成规的言行的容忍;对他人的反对意见哪怕是愚蠢和带有偏见的反对意见的容忍;以及对人性弱点的容忍。根据对宽容内涵的这一界定,教师在文化对话中要做到不仅容忍不同意见和甚至错误的观点,而且在平常的学校与课堂中都要做到宽容学生。

2. 宽容学生什么

(1) 宽容学生某些"不守成规"的言行

在教育教学过程中,破除对所有学生整齐划一的追求,给学生"怪异"言行以存在的空间,是教育宽容应有之义。"真正的宽容不是对种种观念的漠不关心或被普遍化的怀疑主义。宽容意味着接受消极的或根据我们的观点看起来是有害的观念的表达所引起的痛苦,以及伴随这种痛苦的意志。"在学校的学习与生活中,要允许每个学生表达不同的声音、不同的意见,要包容学生某些与众不同的行为。秉着宽容的精神,教师还要清醒地认识到学生们如有正当的理由,如人格受到侮辱、自尊心受到打击时所表现出来的愤怒,即使你不赞赏,至少亦应容忍。因为这种情绪如果受到过分抑制,可能会扼杀他们的正义感和是非心。即使没有正当的理由,孩子们发发情绪,也是常见的现象。

(2) 宽容学生的反对意见和错误言行

学生不守成规的言行还不至于对教师权威构成威胁,至多有些刺眼和不快。而学生直接提出反对意见,在某种程度上和教师对着干,常常会使教师难堪。然而真正的宽容也是对学生反对意见的容忍和尊重。且不说学生的反对意见中很可能有正确的成分,即便是错误的,也会促使正确的东西得以彰显,因为"科学的发展不仅是由于反抗它内部的非科学的东西,而且也是依靠着它内部的非科学的东西"。

(3) 宽容学生人性的弱点

教师应容忍学生中存在诸如愚钝、懦弱、庸俗、自卑等人性弱点。人性是多元的,正如每个人都具有优点一样,每个人也同时或多或少带有一些人性的弱点,时常会暴露出愚蠢的思想、懦弱的行为、庸俗的一面和自卑的心理。宽容这些,实质上是宽容人的本性,宽容人自己。而处于成长中的学生,其人性弱点不仅是可以理解的,更应得到教师的宽容。

(二)如何实施宽容

1. 确立"真正的教育始于宽容"的理念

文化对话中宽容的基本理念主要包括:以宽容为表征的师生关系观、照顾差异的教学观、对话生成的课程观以及富有人情味的学校制度观,等等。简言之,宽容应该成为教育的一种基本品性,真正的教育始于宽容。尊重他人的差异性,认同真理的相对性,正视人性的多元性是宽容的哲学根据。在一定意义上,宽容可视为教育的价值标准和动力源泉,它不仅是一种教育境界,也是一种教育的智慧。考察教师宽容的教育理念确立与否,一看是否认识到"教育宽容"的重要性,二看是否相信"教育宽容"的力量,三看是否落实到教育教学实践之中。

2. 采取适当的宽容教育方式

走向宽容教育，关键在于教师在课堂内外要将宽容精神融入教育教学，渗透到日常的教育行为。教师在处理课堂偶发事件时，先要控制自己的情绪，沉着冷静，秉持宽容态度，运用教育机智，对学生的错误，能不公开的就不公开，能事后处理的就事后处理。

鼓励学生提出不同见解，甚至允许学生对教师提出质疑。教师要将这一理念真正落实到课堂教学中，尽力弄清自身文化与学生文化之间的差异，并在一定情况下适应这种差异，利用这种差异，鼓励学生的差异，学生才会愿意追求有个性的多样性的见解，才会敢于呈现自己的真实想法，才会有可能在真理面前与教师平等，甚至有可能为了真理而不惜向教师叫板。这样，学生才会从"知识的奴隶"、"思想的懒汉"转化为"知识的主人"、"创造的主体"，学生的主体性才能得以尊重和发挥。

宽容的教育方式，既要求教师"有所为"，也要求教师"有所不为"。"不作为"在这里并非放任自流，可视为一种特殊的"作为"，我国古代教育家孟子便发现了"不教之教"的教学辩证法，"好为人师"往往事与愿违。

宽容的教育方式，是教师宽容的专业修养和耐心、热情、诚恳、善良等专业品质的外在显现。宽容是教师必须具备的德行。有了宽容，才会有教育之爱，因为教育就是一种爱；有了宽容才谈得上保护；有了宽容，才能等待，教育其实就是等待，要怀有台湾文化学者龙应台所说的"孩子不要急，慢慢来"的耐心，等待是教育的一种至高境界。宽容不单是一种师爱的具体体现，宽容还是一种重要的精神素质和实践策略，它能使教师敞开自己的心扉走进学生的心灵世界，能使教师尊重学生的权利，爱护学生的个性，生发教育机智。教师宽容地对待学生，昭示着他的教育思想更加深刻，进行文化对话的行为更加成熟，对话的方式将更加富有圆融的智慧。

3. 营造宽容的对话氛围

师生文化对话的开展，要求师生在学校中共同营造一个宽松的教育生态环境，创设宽松的文化对话空间。宽容的存在需要一定的空间，需要一种渗透在学校文化之中的宽容精神。在富有宽容精神的学校文化中，宽容的教育理念不仅仅为个别教师所拥有，而且是一所学校教师群体的共同信念。唯有如此，教师们才会自觉不自觉地用宽容的方式教育学生，学生在处理同学之间矛盾时也会有意无意地采用宽容的方式。教师能坦然面对流行时尚文化的冲击，学生追星、求异、反叛也不会被看成洪水猛兽。

办学其实办的就是一种氛围，使师生之间、同事之间、同学之间能够实现多元一体、和而不同、其乐融融。营造宽容的对话氛围，不能毕其功于一役。从学校角度看，应该避免求全责备，尊重教师的专业自主，对教师予以理解与宽容；应该摒弃严苛的"规训"，给学生自由发展的空间。从教师角度看，必须改变心态，做学校的主人；把学生当作朋友，善于倾听、善于等待、善于理解学生。从学生角度看，应该尊重教师的劳动，辩证地看待自由和差异，理性地处理个性化与社会化的关系。

4. 建立宽容的对话机制

文化对话的开展需要宽容，但宽容能否贯彻实施却需要相应的制度支持，以保证那些不习惯宽容的师生尽快融入宽容的氛围之中。"民主政治的可贵，是它把宽容异端形成一项制度，这项制度使双方都能受惠，一方面保障人有权利公开表示一种异见，一方面也可使权势者免于不义。"[9]况且，宽容的实施也不能杜绝对话中可能出现的激烈冲突。这也需要靠制度来控制，以期把矛盾和对抗维持在对话的层面上，避免出现过激的行为或有人借宽容制造事端。因此，在师生文化对话中贯彻宽容精神，不仅要求教师在管理时采用宽容的方式，还要求学校管理者在制定制度时，努力将宽容“常规化”和“常态化”，建立更具人性空间的宽容的学校管理制度。宽容的制度化，为师生文化对话开展提供一个稳定可靠的平台。

此外，还要注意宽容的限度。滥施宽容就可能会走向反面——“泛宽容”以致“非宽容”。当我们倡导宽容，在谈文化对话中宽容“是什么”的时候，必须追问宽容“不是什么”。至少对教师来说，宽容并不是对学生无原则的消极退让，对学生错误的放纵姑息而放弃批评教育之责。总之，在文化对话中要避免表面的做作的“宽容”，而是要确立“有限宽容原则”，“应当超越宽容的简单概念，去促进以尊重和赞赏其他文化为基础的多元化教育”。

三、理解文化

理解就是把握认识对象的意义，它包括对事物理解和对人的理解两种类型。师生文化对话的开展，除了悬置文化偏见、宽容异见外，对话参与者还要理解和体察不同的文化价值，持开放、同情和宽宏的态度进行主体间的文化对话，避免由于理解失偏而行为失范。

（一）理解学生亚文化特点

概括地说，大学生亚文化具有一定的空想性；表现出较为鲜明的个性化；易受大众传媒和流行时尚影响的敏感性；业余生活方式和风格的独特性，等等。教师应深入到学生中间，接触、体察、理解学生感兴趣的文化信息和信奉的文化理念，勤于与学生切磋、交流，力求像学生那样去感知、体验和思考。

（二）理解学生文化的要求

文化对话中的理解，与悬置偏见和宽容异见互为条件。教师在文化对话中除了要理解自己的文化外，更重要的是要理解学生的文化需求，了解他们的日常生活世界，关注他们的生活内容、生活方式、生存状态以及人生理想，才能有的放矢、教育得法。大学生的文化需求主要表现在以下四个方面。

1. 形象

形象是由服装、发型、饰物等的表现构成的。多数青年学生热衷于此，因为这是其有别于成人世界和他人世界的最鲜明的符号。他们常常运用形象这一符号来表达对成人世界和世俗社会的反叛或妥协。

2. 休闲

青年学生钟情于学习以外的休闲时光，在休闲的世界里他们可以忽视成人世界的束缚和限制。他们有着很强的表演欲，“动”远多于“静”，既不“休”也没“闲”。他们热衷于偶像崇拜、醉心于动漫游戏、舞蹈和运动等，尤喜即兴发挥。

3. 语言

青年学生的语言是从主流文化中吸收并转化而来的。一方面，他们模仿成人世界里流行的生活方式和说话方式，来获得成人世界的认同；另一方面，他们还要表明自己对成人世界的不服从，而所谓的新潮时髦的语言能引起他人注意，以此表现自己的个性和社会身份。

4. 价值观

青年亚文化群体的价值观体系是一个过渡性的体系，青年学生在接触和学习成人价值观的过程中，不断尝试同化顺应、改组重构自己的价值图式；处在过渡期的价值观表现出很强的颠覆性，用以树立自己独特的形象来引人注目，这是他们的目的。

（三）祛除文化理解障碍

理解的困难主要是由于师生生活经验的差异而产生的理解障碍。理解的障碍可分为个人内部障碍和外部障碍。内部障碍表现为：一是不理解自我，二是把复杂的文化简单化。前者是竭力掩饰自己的缺陷和弱点，攻讦别人的缺陷和弱点；后者是把复杂事物化约为简单的问题要素，或者把多元价值简单一元化，从而造成文化上的不理解。外部障碍多种多样，主要表现为理解他人的话语、思想、世界观以及价值规范时误解或失听。

老子曰："自知者曰明，知人者曰智。""明"且"智"则无往而不利。对理解障碍的认识和反省，是理解的需要，是祛除障碍达成理解的重要方法，也是畅通师生文化对话的津梁。

文化对话是一条比较合适的解决文化冲突的途径，其策略包括悬置偏见、宽容异见、文化理解。文化理解既是手段也是目的，悬置偏见和宽容异见是为了增进文化理解，"和而不同"应奉为文化对话之圭臬。我们可以相信并满怀希望——师生不同文化间相互理解之时，便是从文化冲突走向文化和谐之日。

参考文献

[1] 约翰·R·霍尔，玛丽·乔·尼兹. 文化：社会学的视野[M]. 周晓虹，徐彬，译. 北京：商务印书馆，2002：320.

[2] 戴维·伯姆. 论对话[M]. 王松涛，译. 北京：教育科学出版社，2004：19-20，55.

[3] 戴维·伯姆. 论对话[M]. 王松涛，译. 北京：教育科学出版社，2004：23，30.

[4] R·本尼迪克特. 文化模式[M]. 王炜，等，译. 北京：生活·读书·新知三联书店，1988：39.

[5] 贺来. 宽容意识[M]. 长春：吉林教育出版社，2001：7.

[6] 埃德加·莫兰. 复杂性理论与教育问题[M]. 陈一壮，译. 北京：北京大学出版社，1999：81-82.

[7] 韦政通. 中国文化与现代生活[M]. 北京：中国人民大学出版社，2005：77

[8] 埃德加·莫兰. 复杂思想：自觉的科学[M]. 陈一壮，译. 北京：北京大学出版社，2001：146.

[9] 韦政通. 中国文化与现代生活[M]. 北京：中国人民大学出版社，2005：172.

[10] 联合国教科文组织. 教育：财富蕴藏其中[M]. 北京：教育科学出版社，1996：46.

[11] 高亚萍. "亚文化"视野中的青年流行文化[J]. 中国青年研究. 2003(5).

谈谈教师教育的"软环境"

徐 杰*

（肇庆学院，广东 肇庆 526061）

摘　要：高师院校的"学术性"和"师范性"之争以及教育学术界重学科理论研究，轻学科教学研究的现实，使教师教育的"软环境"有诸多学术评价机制上的问题。本文就目前教师教育发展中在"软环境"方面存在的不足，针对在部分师范院校，特别是在综合大学和综合学院中，高师教学研究不受重视这个影响高师教师发展的瓶颈问题，阐述自己的观点。重视和加强高师教学理论研究，加强应用和实践研究，从广义上讲是改善教师教育"软环境"的思想基础及提高高师人才培养质量的方法之一，从狭义上看是促进高师教师队伍中每个教师个体全面发展的重要措施。

关键词：教师教育；软环境；学术评价机制；学术性-学科理论研究；师范性-学科教学研究

A Discussion about "Soft Environment" for Teacher Education

Abstract: Teacher education is a task of paramount importance for education. The dispute between "academic education" and "teacher training education" in Teachers College and Universities, and the status of valuing research of discipline theory while neglecting study of teaching of school subjects in educational and academic communities result in many issues about evaluation mechanism on the "soft environment" for teacher education. This article expresses its own views, based on weaknesses existed in "soft environment" on the development of teacher education, especially the neglecting of teaching research which negatively influence college teachers' talent development. It is considered to stress on research of teaching theory and to strengthen and apply in practice. Broadly speaking, it is one

* 徐杰，广东肇庆学院教育学院党委书记，副教授。

of methods to improve teacher education and ideological education in the “soft environment” and to improve college teachers’ quality of talents cultivation; in a narrow sense, it is an important measure of accelerating all-round development in individual college teacher’s competence.

Key words: teacher education; soft environment; evaluation mechanism; academic education-research of discipline theory; teacher training education-study of teaching of school subjects

“振兴民族的希望在教育,振兴教育的希望在教师”。改革开放30年来,随着高等教育发展大众化的浪潮,教师教育(即师范教育,下同)也得到了长足的发展,成绩有目共睹。然而,在教师教育的“软环境”方面,还存在有不少的问题。其中,影响高师教师队伍健康成长的一个瓶颈,就是教学研究不受重视的问题,甚至在一些综合大学和综合学院中,把教学研究排除在科研范围以外的现象也较为普遍地存在着。从大的环境上看,教育学术界目前存在的重视学科专业理论研究,忽视学科教学理论研究的现状,是影响高校学术评价机制的理论基础之一。多数关于教师专业发展的讨论是针对中小学教师的,而本文则主要针对高师和开办教师教育的综合大学或综合学院,以及在“教育母机”任教的教师们专业发展所处的“软环境”的分析和思考。

“软环境”是相对“硬环境”而言的一个概念,它是指物质条件以外的诸如政策、文化、制度、法规及思想观念等外部因素和条件的总和。就教师教育目前的情况看,这些因素又集中体现在科研体制和学术评价机制上。

“硬环境”是面镜子,观察、分析“硬环境”的现状有利于认清现实,从现实的例子中能更清晰地折射出教师教育的“软环境”。我们来看教师教育的“硬环境”的设置情况,20世纪90年代以来,以教育部直属六所师范大学为首,积极改革,开办非师范专业,使传统的师范院校走上了综合化的道路。到2006年前后,已经有一半以上的师范院校转变为综合大学,包括原师专升本以后的综合学院也不例外(从全国来看各省的具体情况有差别)。“从2006年的招生简章和招生计划看,原来的六所部属师范大学的非师范专业已经平均达到66.3%……而就全国省属师范大学的平均值来看,非师范专业占全部专业的62.07%。”全国师范院校综合化最明显的变化是师范专业的大幅减少,到2006年只占全部专业30%多。与之相反的是,原来没有教师教育的综合大学,甚至是理科、工科、农科、海洋、体育、艺术等院校逐步参与教师教育。至2007年,全国培养师范生的综合大学有70所之多(综合学院未计算在内)。综合大学参与教师教育,有其有利的一面。比如,能使师范教育分享综合大学在大学文化、教学质量、科学水平方面的优质资源,为基础教育教师队伍建设提供高质量的、多元化的师资渠道。“但是,综合大学在教师教育中存在着需要研究和解决的问题。如综合大学往往没有认真考虑师范教育的特殊性,把师范生的培养和其他专业的学生同样对待,缺少认真研究和相关的政策支持……在综合大学内,教师教育有被边缘化的倾向。”(源自北京师范大学教师教育研究中心资料,2007)另外,“教师的专业化发展始终未被作为学校管理的一项重要任务来抓,没有充分认识到教师发展是一个全局性、根本性、终身性的概念……”从上述实际情况分析,在影响教师教育“软环境”的不利因素方面,主要与综合大学开办教师教育中存在的问题以及师范院校综合化发展的“利多弊少”中的“弊”有关,同时也凸显出各级教育主管部门以及学校的管理层应负有一定的责任。那么分析问题以及“弊”的成因而达到“驱弊存利”是我们的愿望和初衷。

在上述情况背景下，随着举办教师教育专业的各类院校的增多，就出现了以下两种典型的情况：一是综合大学（包括理科、工科等院校）中增办相关教师教育专业，因为是新办专业，师资、设备等均不够完善，成绩、名气也没有老牌专业那么多、那么大，当然，在学术地位及学校发展的棋盘上的位置也就可想而知。因此，在教学研究不受重视甚至是不被认同的大环境下，这些新办专业的教师在自己的科研方面也只有“随波逐流”了。二是师范院校转为综合大学或综合学院，大量的师资引进是必需的，而引进的多是高职称、高学历的教师，这些教师有相当一部分是从我国中、西部地区的综合大学或理工科院校引进的，他们没有教师教育的经历，在他们的教学理念和学术研究范围中很少或根本不存在“教学研究”这项内容，他们以前培养的学生多是要做技术员、工程师，少数要做科学家的，他们越是优秀，越是固执地认为教学研究不能算是科研。

以上两种重“学科理论研究”、轻“学科教学研究”的典型情况，对教师教育理论研究，特别是高师教学研究的不利影响，起到了雪上加霜的作用。对高师教师来讲，特别是对在综合大学或综合学院中任教的高师教师来讲，“软环境”形成的现实就是教学研究不算科研，科研就是去研究本身的学科专业理论。也就是说，在高师学术界长期存在的“学术性”和“师范性”之争，实际是教育学术界重学科理论研究、轻教学实践研究的流弊在高师院校中的现实反映而已。这严重影响了广大教师从事教学研究的积极性，客观造成了高师教师只做本学科专业理论研究、只重视写论文、发论文，而对于学科教学研究以及如何提高教学水平和教学质量，却成了“吃力不讨好”的事情。只要论文写得多，教学好坏一个样，老教师心痛、中年教师无奈、青年教师“随波逐流”。更重要的是，在参与不同环节评价各学科高师教师学术水平和能力的专家中，有许多是没有教师教育背景的，而在他们看来，教学研究层次太低，没有什么学术性，与科学研究有较大距离。这些事实均体现出教师教育学术评价机制上存在的严重问题。

“教师的专业包括学科专业和教育专业，具有双专业的属性……”笔者认为：作为高师教师，上述属性更为明显，教学实践研究和学科理论研究是同等重要的，过分强调其中一面或以偏概全都是错误的，应该将学术性和师范性有机地结合在一起。而作为非教育学专业的任何其它专业的高师教师，教师教育理论研究实际主要体现在自己的学科教学实践研究上，而这些研究则是可以影响到整体的教师教育理论研究的。缺少教学实践研究的教师教育论文，像无根的浮萍，不可能有深度，这也是教师教育理论研究跟不上现实需要的重要原因。据笔者了解，在不久前“全国师范院校协作会校长论坛”上，就当前教师教育发展中的某些问题，校长们讨论热烈但也一筹莫展。显现出校长们的治学智慧缺少先进的、科学的、符合现实需要的教师教育理论的支撑和支持。很明显，只重视理论研究，不重视应用和实践的研究，是造成上述情况的主要原因之一。

为什么说在教师教育中，教学研究能够影响整体的理论研究呢？笔者认为：非师范各学科的教学研究，其目的大多只是起到提高“传道授业”的技艺，即平时所说的“教学艺术”而已，并不能对该学科基础理论的研究和发展有多大贡献。而在教师教育中，所有专业的教学研究都具有相同的重要性，其原因在于它不仅仅属于一般的应用性研究，而且在素质教育的大背景下，教学研究中所产生的创造性成果，不仅可以充实教师教育的基础理论，而且有些成果将直接形成教师教育基础理论新的一部分，起到填补空白的作用。所谓涓涓小溪终将汇聚成大江大河，我想，从高等教育理论的角度去分析和思考也恰好反映出教师教育的特殊性吧。

笔者认为:改善和建设符合新形势要求的教师教育的“软环境”,是需要政府(教育主管)部门、院校管理层(包括教育学术界)和广大高师教职员工的共同努力才能够逐步达到的。因此笔者斗胆建议如下:

首先,政府(教育主管)部门应在三个方面努力推进。

1. 教师教育体系在向灵活开放转变的同时,应进一步加强教师教育的法制化建设,应将教师教育标准体系内的教师资格标准、教师教育课程标准、教师教育机构鉴定标准等内容写入法律法规之中,明确它们的主要法律功能,建立宏观导向和监督保障的机制,以适应教师教育从独立封闭向灵活开放转型的改革需求。

2. 要改革和完善教师资格证书制度。要修订和提高教师标准,改革教师资格考试制度,教师资格证书制度与教师教育的其它鉴定制度相联系,以促进教师教育专业化和确保教师教育质量。

3. 在以上两条的基础上,建立新的教师教育学术评价机制并逐步建立我国的教师教育标准体系。

其次,院校管理层(包括教育学术界)应在以下三方面努力改善:

1. 思想上树立“教育大计,教师为本”的观念,充分理解国家对教师教育“优先发展、适度超前”的战略意图,充分认识教师教育的特殊性,并在此基础上明确本校的发展思路,调整和修订出既有利于教师教育,又有利于其它各学科全面可持续发展的整体发展规划。

2. 明确所有教师都应具有学科专业和教育专业的双重属性,改变以往把专业知识水平的高低单一地、直接地与师资质量等同起来的错误观念,在褒奖学科专业理论研究的同时,也要肯定和鼓励教师的教学实践研究,引导广大教师把“学术性”和“师范性”有机地融合在一起,逐步建设一支21世纪合格的教师教育师资队伍。

3. 了解基础教育改革现状,特别是新课程标准的主旨和内容,根据国家素质教育的要求,引导院系(二级单位)的师范生人才培养计划的调整和修订,并给予政策和资源等方面的支持。在开办教师教育的院系,对于不了解也不愿了解教师教育特殊性和办学规律的院系领导人予以职务岗位的调整,以确保学校办学理念的贯彻和教师教育在本校调整改革的顺利实施。

第三,从事教师教育的广大教职员工,特别是高师教师,应积极学习国家有关素质教育以及基础教育改革的诸多文献,了解基础教育的现状,熟悉国家试行的基础教育课程标准,主动投身教师教育改革。在不断提升学科专业水平和理论研究的基础上,努力提升教育专业水平和教学研究的能力,将学科专业和教学实践有机地联系起来,将“学术性”和“师范性”很好地融合起来,理论联系实际,大力加强自身的教学实践研究,“聚沙成塔、集腋成裘”,为教师教育的改革和理论研究提供大量的、各专业“一线”的、第一手的资料,为本校的教学质量的提高和新的师范生人才培养方案的落实做出贡献,为国家培养新世纪合格的基础教育师资而努力。

综上所述,目前,教师教育的发展从整体上来看,“硬环境”方面统一性不足而松散性明显,“软环境”方面则存在着理论研究有脱离应用和实践的危险,学术评价机制亟待改善,教师教育已经走到了一个十字路口。教师教育是整个教育体系的“母机”,它的健康成长有赖于各级政府主管部门、院校领导及广大教职员工的共同努力。而对于高师教师们的成长和发展来说,“软环境”的改善是促进科学研究、提高教学质量、提高荣誉感和责任感的重要一环。新中国成立以来,对于广大高师教师来说,“软环境”比起“硬环境”来显得更为重要,在几十年的经历和经验中,这样的感受很真实也很深切。让我们共同努力,用实际行动来改善和建设21世纪清新的教师教育"软环境"。若因此能对教师教育的发展走上康庄大道而稍有启发和"蚁力"之用,则是笔者的希望所在。

参考文献

[1] 中共中央国务院. 中国教育改革和发展纲要. 1993.

[2] 百度百科. [DB/OL]http://baike.baidu.com/viem/98580.htm.

[3] 朱旭东,胡艳. 中国教育改革30年:教师教育卷[M]. 北京:北京师范大学出版社,2009:60,62.

[4] 教育部课题组. 改革开放30年中国教育重大理论成果[M]. 北京:教育科学出版社,2008:191.

[5] 王建磐. 教师专业化与教师教育政策的选择[J]. 高等师范教育研究,2001(5).

全球化视阈下我国教师教育改革动向

龙起香*
（钦州学院，广西 钦州 535000）

摘 要：全球化对教育的影响是广泛和深入的，教育进入了一个密集改革的时期。教师作为教育改革的中坚力量，如何适应全球化的国际环境，已成为世界各国普遍关注的热点。为了更好应对来自全球化教育的挑战，必须优先进行教师教育改革，以教师教育改革推动整个国家教育的发展。本文分析了全球化视阈下教师教育的发展特征（取向）并对我国教师教育改革动向进行了探讨。

关键词：教师教育；专业化；教育改革

The Trend of Teacher Education Reform in Our Country under Globalization

Long Qi-xiang
(Qinzhou University, Qinzhou 535000, China)

Abstract: Globalization has a extensive and deep-going influence, and ecducation has stepped into a intensive reform period. Teachers, as the core force in education reform, how they adapt to the international environment of globalization has became a focus in the world. For taking global education challenge well, we should give the priority to carry out teacher education reform to promote the whole national education development. The author analyses the development characters (trend) of teacher education in the view of globalization and studies teacher education reform in our country.

Key words: teacher education; specialization; education reform

* 龙起香，广西合浦县人，钦州学院讲师。

随着社会的发展及科技的进步，世界各国的经济、政治、文化、意识形态、生活方式等多层次多领域逐渐超越区域和民族国家界限，在世界范围内展现出全方位的沟通合作、相互依存的态势，即人类发展趋向于全球化。全球化的人类发展必然会改变人类的生活和思维方式，而担负着改变人们思想、观念、行为方式的教育也必然进行调整和改变。事实上，为了培养有国际意识、国际交往能力和竞争能力的人才，各国教育在制度及政策方面作了一系列的调整与变革，以适应国际交往和发展的需要，应对全球化的挑战。由于教师的教育是一个国家教育发展的内在生长机制，教师教育的发展直接关系到教师的质量，是提升教育核心竞争力的基础。为了更好地应对来自全球化教育的挑战，必须优先进行教师教育战略性改革与发展，以教师教育改革推动整个国家教育以适应全球化战略发展。

一、全球化视阈下教师教育的特征

在全球化视阈下，传统的教师教育正受到前所未有的挑战，教师教育呈现出新的特征，具体表现在：

1. 教师教育的专业化

在知识化时代的今天，教师的专业性越来越受到各国的强调。人们普遍认为，教师只有具备足够的专业能力和较强的自主性，才能更好满足社会日益发展和学生在认知、情意、学习等方面的要求。教师专业性不仅有利于肯定教师职业的特殊性和不可替代性，承认教师在教育中的重要地位和作用，而且有利于提高教师的专业素质，提高教师教育质量。实现教师的专业化必须实现教师教育的专业化，为此，必须为未来教师提供专业化的教育。近几十年来，各国对教师专业资格认定更为严格，对教师教育年限、专业知识、技能要求更具体，目的就是保证教师专业权威性和自主权。

2. 教师培养规格的高层次化

随着知识经济的重大转型及世界信息化浪潮的发展，各国对教师需求的重心从数量的增长走向素质的提升。许多发达国家不断提高教师资格证书的学历要求，如美国、加拿大、澳大利亚、新西兰、日本等国已经把小学教师职前培养纳入到高等教育体系。在此基础上，一些国家纷纷开设教育硕士、教育博士的学位以逐渐增加中小学教师中研究生和博士生的比例。如，美国近年来有些州已明文规定今后中小学教师必须具有教育硕士学位，其中华盛顿州于1992年开始实施中小学教师在申请更新教师证书时须同时具有双硕士学位。又如，英国为了不断增加教师研究生学历比例，目前已有30所大学的教育学院（系）参与设立了教育学士和研究生教育证书制度，这些制度使得英国具有研究生教育证书的中小学教师的比例不断增加。据统计，“美国1992年、英国1993年、日本1994年在职教师获得硕士、博士学位者分别占硕士、博士学位者总数的21.2%、7.1%、5.9%”。[1]可见，教师培养规格的高层次性已成为必然的趋势。

3. 教师教育机构的开放性

随着科技的进步和经济的发展，许多国家为了充分利用教育资源，纷纷要求培养教师的专业院校不仅仅只是培养教师，而且要拓展其培养目标，为社会输送更多人才；另一方面，人们认为师范院校培养出来的学生素质不高，偏重教学技能而忽视学术知识，知识领域狭窄，不能满足时代的要求，封闭式的教师教育体制遭到质疑。为此，二战后，一些发达国家通过将师范院校与其它院校合并或升格为综合性大学，或在综合性大学开设教师教育学院等形式以改变这一现状，致使教师教育逐渐从单一的、封闭的、定向的师范学校教育模式，走向由综合性大学或其它类型的学校为主，师范院校参与的多样化、开放、非定向的模式。开放的教师教育体系既可以充分发挥各院校学科专业的功能，加强教师教育专业化，又能满足学生个人的需要和社会对各种类型教师的需要。为教师教育的发展带来了生机与活力，也给原有的教师教育体系带来更多的机遇与更严峻的挑战。

4. 教师教育课程的整合性

随着信息社会的发展，对社会公民和劳动者的知识、能力和技术提出了新的要求，相应地对教师素质的要求也有了新的内涵，不仅要求教师具有深厚的学科专业知识，而且也要有指导学生学习和引导学生发展的技能素养。20 世纪 50 年代以来，大多数国家在改革师范教育时，一方面拓展普通文化知识教育，加强学科专业教育，注重了学术性；另一方面，教育理论学习与教育实践训练也越来越受到重视，师范性得到了强化。

合理制定教师教育课程结构，是实现教育师范性与学术性整合的重要手段。世界各国对教师教育课程的要求不尽相同，但大都形成一个共识，即把教师具有普通科学文化知识、学科专业知识、教育学科的基本知识，以及掌握教育教学的基本技能作为教师的基本要求或条件。因此，各国教师教育课程的基本结构大致上是由普通文化课程、学科专业课程、教育学科课程、教育技能课程和教育实践课程所构成。

5. 教师教育制度的一体化

20 世纪 70 年代以来，许多教育家从终身教育理念出发，指出了教师职后教育的必要性，认为教师在职前学习的知识会随着社会和教育的变革或者很快过时，或者存在局限性。基于此，各国教师教育制度逐渐趋向于一体化，由教师教育的一次性、终结性的培训变成连续性、终身性的教育，并且要求对教师的“训练模式”改变为“发展模式”。如美、德、法、日等国利用法律政策和强有力的教育行政措施来推进教师教育的一体化，在延长职前培养年限的同时，把教师职后教育提到前所未有的高度，保证职前教育和职后教育的关联性和连续性。法国在 1971 年就颁布了法令，规定初等教育教师在职期间享受 7 年在职进修权利。英国在 1992 年的教育《白皮书》中规定新任教师有 1/5 的时间进修，正式教师每七年轮流脱产进修一次。美国的许多州政府为了保证教师在职进修，立法规定了在职进修期限。

二、当前我国教师教育改革动向

1. 完善教师专业化的制度

教师专业化是现代社会发展对教师的基本要求，也是世界教师教育的重要特点和基本目标。这昭示着我们的教师教育工作必须进行以专业化为核心的改革。为此，必须要明确教师专业化的内涵和标准，确立教师专业标准和制定教师资格认证制度。教师专业标准的出台有助于明晰教师应具有的知识、理解力、技能、价值观等，教师培训必须达到这些标准才能授予教师资格证书，同时要加强教师资格证书的认定和管理工作，以保证教师专业化的实现。

我国于 1986 年 9 月 6 日由原国家教委颁布了《中小学教师考核合格证书试行办法》，根据教师的学历和工作经历的考核，颁发《专业合格证书》，这应该说是中国实行教师考核制度的萌芽。随后，1993 年颁布的《教师法》第 11 条规定中小学教师学历标准，继而在 1999 年、2000 年颁布并实施了《教师资格条例》,具体规定了中小学教师资格认定条件和方法。2001年教育部颁布的《关于首次认定教师资格工作若干问题的意见》明确规定,随着教师资格认定制度的实施,只有依法取得教师资格者方能被教育机构聘为教师。基于以上这些教育法规和政策,可以说我国教师专业标准制度已经基本完善。

2. 实行"开放型"教师培养制度

新中国建立以来,我国教师教育体制一直采取封闭定向型体制。这种体制能根据社会对不同层次的教师的数量或质量的需求进行有计划的统一培养,它有利于保证教师的数量供给和保证教师基本质量标准。这种模式对人口众多,义务教育普及率偏低的中国曾经起到积极的作用。但这种模式培养出来的学生和非师范专业的学生没有太多区别,非师范毕业生甚至不需任何教师专业培训也可以任教;另一方面认为教师培养"规格"的统一性致使教师缺乏开阔的视野,不能满足当前对复合型人才的需求;再者教师培养渠道的单一性致使教师有过强的职业安全感,不利于教师自身的发展。[2]因此,建立开放化教师教育体制已成顺应时势之举。

我国于1993年颁布的《中国教育改革和发展纲要》第41条明确提出:"进一步加强师资培养工作,其他高等院校也要积极承担起中小学和职业技术学校师资的任务"。此外,1993年颁布的《教师法》第18条强调了"非师范学校应承担培养和培训中小学教师的任务",教师教育的"开放型"模式初见端倪。随后,国家取消了大学毕业生的分配制度,就业的市场化已经在客观上打破了原有的封闭的师范教育体系,国家更顺应这种发展趋势,鼓励综合性大学和非师范类大学参与教师教育工作,使教师教育体系逐步走向开放。事实证明这种制度更能满足社会对于现代化、多元化、复合型教师的需求。

3. 实现职前培养和职后培训的统合

教师专业化是一个不断成熟、不断提升、不断创新的历程,教师的职前培养和在职继续教育作为教师专业发展的不同阶段,应有不同的目标、内容、方式,但应是连续的、相互衔接的,共同服务于教师专业能力的提高。因此,教师的教育从短期职前培训转向职前职后一体化专业学习,成为中国教育改革中的一个新动向。正如顾明远教授指出的"教师教育正从一次性终结式的教育向教师终身学习和专业发展转变;从职前职后培训相分离向培养培训一体化转变。"[3]

我国逐渐意识到教师教育发展是一个持续的过程,对于职后继续教育还通过相关法律法规来规范和完善,如2000年3月6日公布的《中小学教师继续教育工程方案》中规定的"中小学教师继续教育应异于教育培养,以提高教师实施素质教育的能力和水平为重点,以提高中小学教师整体素质为目的"。2001年国家颁布的《国务院关于基础教育改革与发展的决定》中论述完善教师教育体系时,再次强调要加强中小学教师的继续教育。然而我国教师教育主要是采取职前培养和职后培训的双轨制,而且着重的是教师职前培养和发展工作,教师的在职教育也只是补偿学历,是"教师学历教育",这明显有违于国家关于职后继续教育的宗旨。另外,虽然我国的教育政策、法规现已比较重视教师的在职培训问题,但在形成稳定的制度及出台具体的操作方案这些方面仍需要进一步完善。

4. 建立教师教育机构的申报、评估、监督体系

由于我国教师教育逐渐从封闭定向型师范教育向灵活开放的教师教育体系转变,许多重点综合大学正在加入教师教育行列,但教育课程上所投入的师资和经费设备等方面都有一个不断完善的过程,加上在经济利益的驱动下各种各样的教师继续教育培训机构泛滥,如果缺乏

有效的教育机构评估制度，办学水平良莠不齐的现象将难以避免。因此，为了保证教师教育的基本水准，规范教师教育机构的办学条件，确保教师教育机构的公信力，有必要建立教师教育机构资质认定标准，作为认定所有教师教育机构举办教师教育的基本资格要求。只有达到标准的办学机构，才允许进行教师教育工作。同时，在教师教育机构资质认定标准的基础上建立科学、完备的教师教育评价指标体系，定期对教师教育机构的教师教育质量实施评价，以确保教师培养目标的有效性和自律性。教师教育机构资质认定标准及评价内容应包括以下几方面的内容：

(1) 在教育课程设置方面，要强调教师的专业性、时代性与实践性；

(2) 教学方面，主要评价教学状况，教材、教具的使用情况以及实践活动；

(3) 教师方面，评价学科教育专业教师的确保率，教师教学成果、科研成果及指导能力；

(4) 学生方面，评价学生的学习安排、学习成绩、教育教学能力、奖学金制度及就业率等；

(5) 教育行政设施方面，评价教学软硬件的保障情况及教育教学实践基地建立及使用情况。

虽然我国已逐渐重视高等教育机构的教育、管理、科研等方面的质量问题，初步建立对高等院校的评价机制，但仍缺乏系统性、规范性，针对性。2003 年《教育部关于加强县级教师培训机构建设的指导意见》的出台也许将是国家开始关注教师教育机构评估制度的好征兆。

参考文献

[1] 黄赐英. 国际教师教育变革与发展基本趋势[J]. 衡阳师范学院学报，2005(10).

[2] 吕安琳. 建立健全教师教育机制，促进教师专业化发展[J]. 教育理论与实践，2006(8).

[3] 李琼，袁丽. 变革中的国际教师教育及其发展趋势[J]. 比较教育研究，2006(11).

社会转型期价值观嬗变与教师教育价值取向变化的思考

丁越华*

(钦州学院,广西 钦州 535000)

摘　要:本文对社会转型期教师教育价值观变化进行了研究,指出教师教育价值取向,教师专业价值判断标准和教师的思想品格、道德水准,都表现出开放多元化、复杂化、功利化和标准更高的变化特征,并充满了价值观念冲突。结合教师教育实践发展的现实问题,提出坚持教师教育核心价值观,思索在教师教育价值观念的矛盾中适时地进行正确价值观引领,实现整体价值的融合。提高教师专业化水平,树立教师基本的思想品格和道德水准。

关键词:社会转型价值观;教师教育价值观;变化;特征;思考

Thinking of Values Evolution in the Period of Social Transition and the Changes of Values Orientation in Teacher Education

Ding Yue-hua

(Qingzhou University, Qinzhou 535000, China)

Abstract: After studying the changes of value orientation in teacher education in the period of social transition, the paper points out that values orientation of teacher education, teachers' professional values criterion and teachers' character and moral standards become diverse, complicated, utilitarian and higher standard, being full of values conflicts. Combining the problems emerged from the practice and development of teacher education, it puts forward that we should stick to teacher education's core values, lead correct values timely among the confused

* 丁越华,女,安徽亳州人,钦州学院政经系副教授。

values to realize the integration of the overall values, improving teacher's professional level, building teacher's basic character and moral standard.

Key Words: values in the period of social transition; the values of teacher education; change; character; thinking

随着社会转型价值观的嬗变,教师教育价值观呈现出以"人"为魂、以"人"为本的核心精神,但教师教育价值观念取向多元化、复杂化,而且处于不断变化之中。教师教育现实存在的问题和实践发展,都要求我们深入研究和反思,找出答案。教师教育价值观应坚持什么?社会转型期的教师教育价值观与现行的教师教育观之间存在哪些问题?怎样科学合理地实现价值整合?

一、社会转型期价值观的主要特点

中国从计划经济体制向市场经济体制转变过程中,社会价值观念发生了全面而深刻的革命性变革。在新的历史条件下,价值取向带有明显的转型期特点:(一)价值取向呈现出多元化和分散化趋势,而且充满了价值观念上的矛盾和困惑,成为整个社会价值观裂变的典型反映。人的尊严与价值日益凸显,社会体现了对人的独立人格、尊严和价值的尊重,使个体需要与社会需要之间的矛盾更加尖锐,两种价值取向的冲突也日益明显。(二)竞争意识不断增强。不甘落后、敢于拼搏,把握今天,开拓创新,敢说敢干,体现强烈的参与意识。(三)思维开放,纳新意识增强。不轻信,不盲从,也不趋同,在判断、认识和分析问题方面有自己独立的看法。(四)道德价值观念复杂,并呈现出功利化趋势。竞争观念意识强,敢于竞争,但在竞争中掺杂极端个人主义。对传统道德基本肯定,但对多数人认同的道德准则产生怀疑并弱化。追求个人价值最大化,注重个人与社会并重,事业与利益兼得。对不良社会现象和风气,为顾及个人利益,普遍采取无所谓,消极观望态度。

二、社会转型期教师教育价值观的变化特征及思考

社会转型期价值观嬗变必然反映在教师教育价值观改革与发展上,正如马克思所说:"不是人们的意识决定人们的存在,相反,是人们的社会存在决定人们的意识。"(《马克思恩格斯选集》,2 版,第 2 卷,32 页。)社会转型期多元、开放、竞争及功利化特点的价值观必然对教师活动具有调节功能,决定教师活动的目的和方式,对整个教师教育价值观、教师教育体制、教师教学行为的改变与教师评价制度和标准的改革都产生了极其深刻的影响,使教师教育价值取向发生了一系列的变化,其主要表现为:

(一)教师教育的核心价值取向是回归到"人"的教育

在教师教育中,转型期价值取向是以权利、义务、平等的价值理念为核心,通过课程改革的理论研究和实践探索活动,培养和提高每个学生的全面健康发展的素质,并以构建起一个开放的、充满生机的、有中国特色的社会主义教育课程体系为最终目的。整个教师教育价值观念是以人为本,以尊重人的价值和人的主体性为主线,把学生放在学习主体地位上,教育是满足学

生的各种需要,实现个人的自我价值。这一新的教育价值观是我国教育的一大进步,对推进和不断深化教师教育改革与发展具有举足轻重的作用,也成为今后衡量教师教育质量的重要标准。

当前,教师教育存在对转型期的教师教育核心价值取向不明确,不理解的现象,缺乏对价值取向的认真思考与大力提倡。因此,办学定位不明确,基础教育和教师教育的改革与发展的方向、目标和人才培养模式上都存在问题。核心价值取向的迷茫和摇摆,导致了教师教育的弱化和边缘化,部分地方综合性院校的教师教育改革与发展不同程度出现停滞不前;也导致对基础教育新课改缺乏应有的重视,流于形式,培养目标不适应基础教育发展的时代需要;同样导致教师教育知识陈旧,综合素质跟不上变化,实践能力和创新能力有待提高。这说明,明确转型期的教师教育价值基本取向,明确核心价值是什么十分重要。在教师教育的改革与发展中,必须大力弘扬以人为本,突出个体价值及对人的尊重的社会与个体协调发展的教育价值观,起到价值导向作用,为教师教育改革确立主要价值目标。

(二)教师教育价值开放多元化,与现实的教师教育价值观存在冲突

教师教育存在核心价值取向不明确,是教师教育价值取向开放多元化的具体表现,其根本原因又是社会转型期价值观呈现出多元化和分散化趋势,充满了价值观念冲突造成的。长期以来,我国教师教育由各省市,各地方师范学校包办,教师培养和培训的方式、思想指导,课程设置都是整齐划一。指导教师行为的价值评价也是统一的。如今,教师教育冲破了独立封闭的旧体制,以开放的体制来发展,把教师教育纳入到整个高等教育体系中。教师培养由高等院校承担,师范院校也开办非师范类专业,在教师和学生来源上,课程设置和教材选择上,各类高校,发挥其所长,充分表现出开放多元化特点的价值观、人才观、施教观;在教师教育价值取向上,与国际接轨,又表现出区域性、民族性。有人认为,教育是实现人生理想和价值的途径;有人认为,教育是帮助学生成长的有效手段;有人认为,教育是提升人的生命质量的重要方式;有人认为,教育是帮助自身提高的重要因素。强调个体的自由、理性、自我意志以及个体之间的平等,是当代教师教育价值观变化最为显著的部分。

但现行教师教育价值取向与实际通行的教师教育价值观之间又存在着许多不一致。比如,教师教育价值取向追求个人全面发展的素质教育是其核心理念,但在高考制度下,学校要生存,就不得不追求升学率,搞应试教育,从而无暇顾及个体的全面发展、实践能力和创新思维的锻炼,与素质教育理念发生冲突。再比如,目前教育本体价值观大行其道,但教育社会价值观的呼声仍然存在,前者关注的是个体,以促进个人知识、能力的发展,达到个性完善为宗旨;后者把社会需要作为教育的出发点和落脚点,旨在促进国家政治经济文化的发展。这两种教育价值观的对立和区别在社会转型期,如何辨证统一起来?这个问题仍然没能解决。而且,社会发展有不同时期,人也有不同发展需求,什么时候以教育本体价值观为主?什么情况下抓教育社会价值观?这个问题不清晰。还有,理想的教师教育价值取向应该面向全体学生,给他们以均等的公平教育机会,促使每个人都获得成功,但为了更好地参与社会竞争,加快个人发展,在效率与教育公平问题上,实际通行的教师教育价值取向在很多时候把效率放在了首位。

总之,教师教育价值观取向表现为开放多元化,冲突明显,处于不断变化之中。如何处理好教师教育价值观的理想与现实矛盾?这就要求我们在教师教育价值观念的冲突中适时地进行正确价值观的引领,实现整体价值的融合。价值观冲突的融合,科学的态度应该是提倡多样

化，坚持主导性，在法制的基础上协调、解决各种价值观冲突，在实践探索中寻求交流、理解、沟通，逐步达成共识。任何一个社会的社会价值观都有一个以核心价值观为主导的并有多层面的价值观与之相结合的结构体系。在社会转型期间，第一，要以开放多元的心态吸取各种教师教育价值观的合理因素，承认其各自的合理性，避免用主导价值观去代替一切、将主导价值观与其他价值观对立起来的做法，使冲突各方融合或达成价值互补。第二，要确立教师教育主导价值观，并赋予其新的时代内涵。面对不同的价值取向，我们无法拒绝，但这与坚持主导价值取向不能混淆。道德价值导向机制主要通过良心自律、社会舆论监督和道德教育等途径得以实现，在教师教育价值观教育中既要坚持以核心价值观作为价值导向，又要与人的现实生活相联系，使个人利益得到应有的伸张和维护，在兼顾个人利益基础上维护集体主义，使教师教育主导价值观成为人民群众接受、认同和遵从的判断是非对错的标准。第三，健全各种价值观交流和对话的平台和机制，有效消除相互冲突价值观之间的隔膜和误解，实现多种价值观在新形势下协调发展。第四，为多元价值观念并存的社会提供有效的社会价值规范，健全法律法规，以引领社会转型期价值迷茫的人们走出价值冲突带来的阴影。

（三）教师专业化价值判断标准更高，教师专业化面临挑战

教师教育重点是教师专业化培养。教师专业化指教师素质、教师的专业能力，表现为：思想道德素质，渊博而扎实的专业知识素质，复合型的能力素质，健康的身心素质。今天教师专业化价值标准不再只是关注知识传授能力，还必须有培养能力，健全人格、品德形成能力。在教学行为上，与过去把立足点放在“教”而忽视“学”上，有很大的不同，教师专业化有新的更高的要求。教师专业水平高低、好坏的判断，不仅在于会传授知识，还在于会组织学生开展认知活动；不只是满足灌输现成知识，而是着力发展学生的智能，掌握学习本领，并注重培养学生的终生学习能力。可见，教师专业化标准是一个发展的概念，一个不断深化的过程。

教师专业化的价值判断标准变化，让教师教育专业化迫切需要改革。由于各地区经济发展不平衡，教师教育所需的条件各异，人力、物力和财力的投入也不同，使得各地教师教育专业化改革、发展水平不一，特别在经济基础较薄弱地区，教师教育观念的更新，知识结构的变化，教学技术的改进和新型教学手段的尝试，都不尽如人意。部分青年教师毕业于非师范专业的综合性大学，他们有学科专业知识，但教师教育学科基础知识不足，在教学方法和手段上基本素质缺乏，短期的岗前培训远远满足不了他们的需要。老教师们也认识到自身的观念、知识陈旧，教学方法落后，希望通过进修、回炉，更新知识，摆脱困境。然而繁重的教学与科研任务，很难让他们实现脱产培训的愿望。如何解决这些问题，提高教师专业化水平？首先，可以充分利用综合大学的学科资源，同时坚持师范性。结合现代教师专业化应具备的素质，构建一个由通识教育类课程系列、学科专业类课程系列和教师专业类课程系列的教育体系，向非师范专业的学生开放通识教育类课程和教师专业课程。其次，针对在职教师的进修和培训，政策上要有相应的措施，资金上有专项投入，按各地区，各学校实际，分批进行。第三，加强教师专业类课程比重，特别是配合新一轮课程改革，提高教师教育类课程内容的实用性，提升教师组织学生开展认知活动的能力和水平。被培训教师不只学习现成知识，还要掌握发展学生的智能，培养学生获得终生学习能力的方法和手段。最后，要使教师专业化的规模、结构、质量、效益上一台阶，必须有计划、有目的地与本校改革同时进行。教师培训中的“校本培训”、“教师发展学校”、“教师参与式培训”都是很好的形式。

（四）道德观复杂、功利化的特点，形成社会转型期教师的思想品格和道德水准

“德为师之本”，学生的未来与发展，需要从教师身上学习的不仅限于知识、能力，还包括优良的道德素质。市场经济条件下，个体作为经济主体的性质日益凸现，功利性与实用性成为衡量价值的重要尺度，适应这一转变而形成的价值观如奋斗、竞争、注重经济利益等，便与重义轻利、重“理”轻“欲”等传统价值观念相冲突，特别是当义与利相悖时，舍生取义、义利兼顾、取利忘义都可能成为个人行动的价值取向。这些也反映在教师道德取向和利益取向的价值冲突中，教师教育中职业道德要求教师认真学习，努力工作，以身作则教育人、培养人。但工作繁重，收入、待遇和权益维护等方面与社会其他成员之间的差距，尊师重教成为形式，教师由职业而带来的那种“文化威信”下降等，现实生活中累积起来的利益争端、利益需要，与教师的道德价值观的冲突在所难免。

如何引领迷茫的教师走出教师道德与利益取向的价值冲突？社会转型期教师思想品格和职业道德的基本要求是什么？什么是行之有效的教师教育中师德建设手段和方法？加强理论学习，是教师职业道德修养的必要方法；“内省”、“慎独”，也是教师职业道德修养的重要方法；与教育实践相结合，在教书育人中升化自己的道德水准，是教师职业道德提高的另一途径和方法。这些都可以帮助解决教师道德取向和利益取向的价值冲突，选择正确职业道德观。但道德调控最根本的是，道德教育必须实事求是才有效果，过低要求不对，过高要求不切实际，让教师科学地、全面地、深刻地认识社会转型期多元价值观，确立教育价值基本取向，把个人生命的意义、价值与自己从事的教育事业紧紧地联系在一起，转化为教师个人的内心信念。在平凡的岗位上肩负起教育的责任和使命，教书育人，这就是教师基本的思想品格和道德水准。我们要克服和防止对教师道德价值评价、判断、甄别上的单向性，片面地强调教师道德责任和义务，而忽略了对等的权利和义务，缺乏对教师道德体验的认同和尊重。社会转型期价值观的引领，平等意识、公民意识、关注自我利益等价值观，深刻而广泛地影响着教师的思想品格和职业道德，教师对自身的利益越来越重视，寻求奉献与索取相统一是现阶段教师向往的道德价值取向。

三、加强对社会转型期教师教育价值观变化发展研究

中国社会转型价值观念，带来了前所未有的教师教育价值观碰撞，历史与现实、传统与现代、本土文化与西方文明多重交织在一起，文中所述只是教师教育价值观变换的某些特征和对这些特征的思索，对现实问题及其矛盾的反思和现有解释范式的困惑，仍然没有结束，加强对社会转型期教师教育价值观的深入研究非常必要。马克思在《关于费尔巴哈的提纲》中指出：“哲学家只是用不同的方式解释世界，而问题在于改变世界。”（《马克思恩格斯选集》，2 版，第 2 卷，61 页。）要带着问题意识去发现研究问题，投入到教师教育改革实践的洪流中，做时代的弄潮儿，不断提出解决问题的路径和方法。

参考文献

[1] 教育部师范教育司. 教师专业化的理论与实践[M]. 北京：人民教育出版社，2003.
[2] 王瑛，胡恩华，梁芝兰，等. 现阶段高校教师价值观调查与分析[J]. 中国高教研究，2000(12)：36-37.
[3] 王腾. 浅谈如何提高教师职业道德素质[J]. 中国教师，2008(S1)：416.

教师教育:地方师范院校面临全新的挑战

郑国庆*
(阿坝师范高等专科学校,四川 郫县 611741)

摘 要:地方师范院校发展教师教育应当与时俱进,树立全新的教育观念;积极营造教师教育的氛围和环境;努力提高教师自身素质;并且在教育教学过程中全力培养师范生的教师职业技能。

关键词:地方师范院校;教师教育;创新教育

Teachers Education: Local Normal Colleges Facing New Challenges

Zheng Guo-qing
(Aba Teachers College, Pixian 611741, China)

Abstract: Local normal colleges developing teacher education should establish new educational concept to keep up with times, create positive atmosphere and environment, take effort to improve their own qualities and fully develop their vocational skills in the education process of teaching.

Key words: Local normal colleges; teachers' education; creative education

面对全人类教育事业的高速发展,人们对教育的关注达到了空前的程度,这就对从事教育工作的人——教师提出了更高的要求,当然也就是对培养教师的机构——师范院校提出了更大的挑战。师范院校原本是专门培养教师的高等教育机构,但是,今天它们必须面对非师范院校的竞争,必须面对受教育者对教育者的更高、更新的需求,必须符合教育事业高速发展的要求。师范院校正面临从师范教育向教师教育的根本转变和培养符合素质教育发展要求的研究型教师的全新挑战。

---

* 郑国庆,阿坝师范高等专科学校教师。

实施素质教育,要求具有开拓精神,善于与他人合作,具有全新教育理念的全面发展的人民教师。而师范教育无论在教育思想、教育理念或教育广度、深度,还是在方法等方面,都根本不能适应素质教育对教师发展的要求;必须全面开创全新的教师教育,培养研究型、创新型教师。江泽民同志指出:"创新是一个民族的灵魂,是一个国家兴旺发达的不竭动力。"[1]

现代教师教育发展的一个重要思想理念是"以人为本",使每一个未来的人民教师既得到全面而充分的自由发展,又能使其个性完全展示。教师教育的最高境界是使被教育者既成人又成才。从某种意义上讲,成人比成才更重要。成人的主要标志是:做人要有高尚的精神境界和健康的人格。成才的主要标志是:有科学的思维形式、方法、过程,有严谨的科学态度,有对事业的执著追求及在某一方面有所建树。这两者都需要创新才能达到相应的高度。因此,创新的教师教育是素质教育的基本要求,创新能力是个人素质的核心体现。根据我国国情,实施创新的教师教育已成为当今教师培养的重中之重。它的开展有助于教育观念的与时俱进,教育结构的改革,教育体系的完善和创新人才观的确立。地方师范院校实施创新的教师教育必须采取以下措施。

一、与时俱进,树立全新的创新教师教育观

什么是创新?创新是一种高级的思维活动。如何创新?创新要靠创新精神、创新能力。创新精神体现在:创新个性——好奇心、挑战性、冒险性;创新品质——理想信念、责任感、使命感、勤奋敬业;创新情感——意志、创新美感、计谋;创新思维——敏锐性、流畅性、变更性。创新能力是根据一定的目的,运用已知信息创造出某种新颖的、独特的、有社会或个人价值的产品的能力。创新精神、创新能力的培养关键在教师教育。

创新教师教育简而言之是培养有创新能力的教师的教育。它强调的是获取知识后创造性地转化,而不是单一地继承。教育的着眼点不是灌输了多少知识,而是着眼于开发学生的创新潜能。与传统师范教育相比,创新教师教育同样强调必要知识的积累,但更强调知识结构及获取知识的方式;同样强调培养教师的各种能力,但更强调教师创新能力的培养。在以"知识、能力、素质"构建新的教师培养模式的思想指导下,要求教师学会学习、学会思考、学会适应、学会教育、学会创造,具有不断追求知识、实事求是、独立思考、勇于创新的科学精神。

创新教师教育是一种全新的教育思想观念的革命,只有提高认识,更新观念,统一思想,形成共识,才能把创新教师教育真正落到实处。只有实施且强化创新教师教育,努力培养未来教师的创新能力,学校才能办出特色,地方师范院校才有存在的价值和意义,才能真正培养出适应国家经济和社会发展所需要的素质教育的合格人民教师。

二、积极营造创新教师教育的氛围和环境

师范院校要创建健康有序、宽松和谐、开放高效、激励上进的育人环境与氛围。每个师范专业学生都具有创新潜能。但是把他们潜在的创新力转化为现实的创新力,必须要有一个激发潜能、培养创新能力的环境和氛围。只有在浓厚的创新教师教育的校园氛围和环境中,才能实现对创新教师人才的培养。

1. 在管理中构建和谐氛围

现任英国诺丁汉大学校长(校监)的中科院院士杨福家先生在2000年中国科协学术年会上这样阐述他对世界一流大学的看法。他说,一流的大学不仅要有大楼、大师、更要有大爱。他认为这里的“大爱”来自于“仁、义、礼、智、信”的传统道德,来自于“捧着一颗心来,不带半根草去”[2]的无私奉献,来自于让校长、教师对“教育中享受生命”的深层次理解,来自于“蹲下身子看学生”的零距离尊重——尊重教师的个性,彰显他们的特长;尊重学生的差异,发挥他们的主体作用。这样才能使师生在愉悦、轻松的氛围中完成一定的教学任务,实现既定的培养目标。

2. 更新教师教育理念

我国传统的师范教育是以教师为中心的老师讲(只按教学大纲讲,教学内容陈旧落后),学生听;“课堂记笔记,考前背笔记,考试答笔记,考后忘笔记”的高分低能,明显不能适应现代社会素质教育对教师人才的需要。要扭转这种局面,就必须抛弃师范教育,发展教师教育,引导师范院校及教师经常开展三项调查:一是社会调查,看看自己的培养目标与社会发展对素质教育和人民教师的需求是否真正适应;二是课堂调查,看看在自己的教育教学活动中未来教师的主体地位是否真正落实;三是教育对象调查,看看自己的教育对象的个性是否真正得以张扬,特长是否真正得以彰显。使他们从中不断矫正认识,更新观念,尊重教育对象,尊重实践,成为未来教师学习活动的引导者(引导学习方向)、指导者(指导学习策略)和辅导者(辅导教育实践)。一句话,就是从人本思想的高度,把未来的教师看成学习的主人。

3. 尊重受教育者的主创精神

要满腔热情地尊重、鼓励和促进受教育者形成和表达自己的思想观点和认知,保护他们哪怕是萌芽状态的创造热情,善于发掘受教育者身上的闪光点,及时给予鼓励。教师教育是培养未来的教育工作者,他们既要学会学习,又要学会教育。教育人、培养人是目前人类社会面临的最复杂的工作任务,没有固定的模式,必须“有所探索,有所尝试,有所发现,有所发明,有所创造,有所前进”。彰显个性与特长是教师教育的重要特征,是培养研究型、创新型教师的保障。

4. 完善实验、实训、实习基地建设

现代化的实验、实训、实习基地极大地缩小了与教育教学一线的实际距离。实验、实训、实习基地应该做到设备设施先进,训练手段现代化,管理水平规范先进,环境氛围真实,实习过程正规、科学、严谨。因此,引进先进的教育教学技术设备,建立与现代教育理念相适应的、更贴近素质教育实际的实验、实训、实习场地,满足实践教学的要求,为未来教师提供良好的实践机会,对培养未来教师的创新精神和教育理念至关重要。

5. 建设精品专业,培养研究型、创新型教师

建设精品专业,就是打造学校的名牌产品,必须要不断地深化教育教学改革,要聘请知名学校和研究单位的专家、学者和基础教育一线教师与学校有关人员组成专家委员会,认真研究专业培养计划、课程设置、实践教学安排、要达到的目标。专业培养计划以培养未来教师的创新精神、满足素质教育发展要求为目标,按学分制把课程设置为几个模块,突出专业核心课程模块、专业拓展课程模块和学科教学与教育研究课程模块。每一模块必须按一定的比例安排理论课和实践课,把专业拓展课程模块瞄准当前学科研究发展方向,设计成几个方向的选修课,由学生根据自己的爱好兴趣选修课程,充分调动学生自主学习的积极性,自觉把自己培养成积极跟踪学科发展前沿的研究型、创新型教师。

6. 利用现代化教学手段，打造精品课程

课程是知识和技术的载体，把专业核心课打造成精品课程，用现代先进的教学技术教学，既能使未来的教师看到现代电子信息技术的创新应用，为他们利用先进的教育技术向基础教育融合渗透提供样板，又能尽早地使未来的教师介入当前的教育教学改革实践，缩短教师教育职前培养的适应期，彰显教师教育的现代特色、创新特色。

三、努力提高教师的素质

教师的素质是教师教育教学质量的重要决定因素。师范院校的教师必须具备准确的角色定位、良好的职业道德、广博的文化知识、宽厚的专业理论、扎实的研究型、创新型能力和健全的身心素质。而要培养创新人才，还必须提高师资队伍的创新意识和创造力。加强研究型、创新型教师培养，加强学科带头人的培养力度。举全校之力申请国家高水平研究课题项目；积极开展国际间、地区间、校际间的横向联合和科学研究；积极举办学术会议，开展学术信息交流；邀请名人、名家讲学或举办专题学术报告；鼓励教师攻读博士学位或访学开展专题研究；鼓励教师深入基础教育第一线开展教学实验研究。通过一系列的学术研究交流与教学改革活动与全方位工作，提升教师的综合素质，使师范院校拥有一支有着良好精神状态、丰厚的人文底蕴、孕育了忠信、勤朴、改革、争先的优秀精神和强烈责任感、高度事业心的教师队伍。这些对于师范院校面对师范教育向教师教育转轨，培养和激发未来教师勇于探索、敢于创新的精神是至关重要的，这是素质教育发展的必然要求。

四、在教学过程中注重创新教师教育

1. 注重教师基本技能训练

创新教师教育不是“空中楼阁”，它同样需要扎实的基础理论、广博的知识视野；不仅需要学科专业知识，还要具备教育专业知识与技能。这里的“基础”不仅是基本的知识体系，同样也包括实验知识和技术知识，也就是广义上的知识体系。因此要求和勉励未来教师学好基础知识也是创新教师教育的基本要求。另外还必须改进“填鸭式”的获取知识的教学方式，指导和帮助未来教师自主学习、自主探索，并在这种学习与探索中形成浓厚的兴趣。只有使未来的教师不仅会学，还要会教；不仅具有学科专业知识与技能，还要具有教育专业知识与技能，才能爆发研究与创新的火花。

2. 加强基础教育研究与实践教学

培养未来教师具有不断追求知识、实事求是、独立思考、勇于创新的科学精神是教师教育培养目标的重要内容。教学必须始终以培养未来教师的应用能力、研究能力和创新能力为核心，不断根据教育教学改革与发展的趋势和形势更新教育内容，狠抓基础教育研究与实践教学。知识来源于实践，能力来源于实践，素质更需要在实践中养成；基础教育研究与实践教学环节对于培养未来教师的实践能力、研究能力和创新能力尤其重要。因此，必须加强认识实习、课程实习、专业实习、毕业实习、实验教学、基础教育研究、社会实践和社会调查等各类研究性、实践性教学环节。通过实践、研究与探索培养未来教师的观察能力、认识能力、分析能力、概括能力、动手能力、协作能力、教学能力、研究能力等，为未来教师创新能力的培养奠定基础，同时使其在实践与研究中体验探索的艰辛和成功的喜悦。

参考文献

[1] 毛泽东、邓小平、江泽民论科学发展[M].北京:中央文献出版社,党建读物出版社,2009.

[2] 顾建军.小学综合实践活动设计[M].北京:高等教育出版社,2005.

第二部分
教师专业发展研究

中小学教师专业化发展影响因素的调查与分析
——以合肥地区中小学为例

陈 啸[1*] 赵 娟[2**]

(1. 合肥学院,安徽 合肥 230022;2. 淮北师范大学,安徽 淮北 235000)

摘 要:为了解教师参加专业化发展课题研究活动的基本情况,2007 年我们在合肥地区中小学中开展了一次问卷调查,调查重点为教师专业化发展的主要影响因素,并根据调查分析结果,对进一步深入开展"有效推进合肥地区教师专业化发展"课题研究提出了相关建议。

关键词:中小学;教师专业化发展;影响因素;课题研究

基金项目:全国教育科学"十一五"规划教育部重点课题的子课题《有效推进合肥地区教师专业化发展研究与实践》(项目编号:DMA060188);安徽省教育厅人文社科研究项目《有效推进合肥地区教师专业化发展的制度保障体系及运行机制研究》(项目编号:2009sk248)。

Abstract: Since 2007, the educational administrative department of Hefei have promoted professional development of teachers comprehensively in primary and secondary schools, the project research as the carrier. To understand the basic situation that teachers participate in the project research activities of professional development, we carried out a questionnaire survey in Hefei primary and secondary schools focusing on the main factors of professional development of teachers and, based on survey results of the analysis, we have made some suggestions to further carry out the project research.

Key words: primary and secondary schools; professional development of teachers; factors; project research

为全面提升教师素质,促进教师专业化发展,建立健全教师专业化发展的制度保障体系及运行机制,合肥市教育行政主管部门,于 2007 年 4 月向教育部中央教育科学研究所总课题组申报了教育部"十一五"教育科学规划重点课题"有效推进区域教师专业化发展研究"的子课题"有效推进合肥地区教师专业化发展研究与实践",获得批准立项。合肥地区的课题研究分四

---

* 陈啸,合肥学院副院长,教授,研究方向:高等教育学、教师教育。

** 赵娟,女,山东泰安人,淮北师范大学高等教育学硕士研究生。

个阶段进行，即课题研究筹备阶段、试点阶段、全面开展阶段和总结表彰阶段。目前已全面完成课题研究的筹备和试点阶段各项任务。在课题研究试点阶段，合肥市选择不同类型的136所学校，要求以学校为子课题组，具体围绕"有效学校研究与实践"、"有效教师研究与实践"、"有效教学研究与实践"、"有效技能研究与实践"、"有效研修研究与实践"(以下简称"五个有效")五个研究方向，结合学校实际，任意选择其中一个研究方向开展试点研究。两年多来，在合肥市、县(区)各级领导高度重视，首批136所实验学校的近五千名教师积极参与，努力探索实践下，课题研究取得了阶段性的丰硕成果，教师的专业化水平有了大幅度提高。但由于时间较短，缺少经验，不足之处也在所难免。为更加全面了解教师专业化发展情况，特别是以课题研究形式全面推进教师专业化发展的有效性和可行性，更好地促进整个课题研究有效进行，我们针对中小学教师专业化发展影响因素及广大教师对专业化发展活动的认识开展了一次调查研究。

一、研究对象与方法

本次调研结合教师的个人特征、任教学校类型、学校所在地等因素，面向上述136所试点学校教师，采用分层随机抽样的方法，抽取被试[1]，共随机发放调查问卷1000份，最终有效回收591份，其中针对中小学教师专业化发展影响因素调查的有效量表527份(有效教师被试的特征见表1)。调查问卷共有两大部分组成：第一部分为本次调查的重点，采用五等级量表法(从非常不符合、不符合、不确定、符合到非常符合)考察中小学教师通过参与专业化发展课题研究活动所表现出来的专业化发展状况，分析影响专业化发展的主要因素；第二部分为教师对专业化发展活动的认识。调查采取SPSS11.5进行统计分析。

表1　教师被试的基本特征(N=527)

类别		问卷	比例
性别	男	195	37%
	女	332	63%
教龄	5年以下	139	26.4%
	6～15年	234	44.4%
	16～25年	113	21.4%
	26年及以上	41	7.8%
任教学段	小学	237	45.0%
	初中	192	36.4%
	高中	98	18.6%
学校所在地	农村	49	9.3%
	城郊	173	32.8%
	市区	305	57.9%
学校层次	重点	177	33.6%
	普通	301	57.1%
	薄弱	49	9.3%

二、研究结果与分析

1. 中小学教师专业化发展的影响因素

通过分析调查问卷的具体量表,考察中小学教师专业化发展状况,分析得出了其影响因素结构。首先,对量表进行项目分析,证实了量表中所有题目都具有鉴别度。其次,经过 Bartlett 球形检验表明,KMO=0.893,$p<.000$,说明量表的相关矩阵差异显著,问卷适合进行因素分析。最后,采用主成分分析法抽取因子,分析转轴前后的因素矩阵可以发现,本问卷中所有题目都有一定的解释力度,均可予以保留。因素分析时特征值大于1的因素有三个,这一点从"因素分析陡坡图"(图1)的分布情形也可以看出来,第三个因素以后,坡度转为平坦。依 Kaiser 准则,共抽取三个共同因素进行分析。提取的三个因素分别为教师的专业理念与精神、专业交流与合作、专业自主发展能力,共解释了教师专业化发展总方差的54.168%(因素分析结果见表2)。

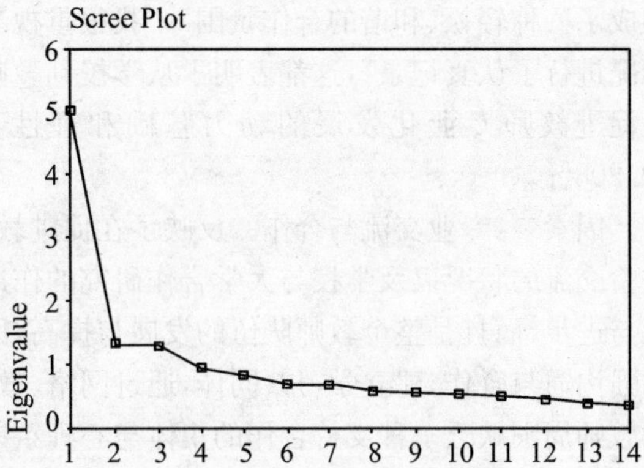

图1 因素分析陡坡图

表2 中小学教师专业化发展调查问卷的因素分析

抽取因素与相应题目	因子负荷量	解释率
因素1:专业理念与精神		20.208%
我愿意投入时间与精力,提升自己的专业素质	.760	
我支持学校开展的课题研究活动并愿意参与其中	.757	
在教育教学中,我除了教给学生如何学习之外,还注重教他们如何做人	.609	
参加课题研究并不是我自愿的,只是为了应付学校或上级教育部门的安排	.555	
我很重视教师专业成长档案袋的建立,对自身专业发展情况进行了认真记录	.521	
我们学校已经建立了教师学习发展共同体,形成了一种轻松、和谐的合作氛围	.520	
我们学校提供了宽松的支持环境有利于教师专业自主性的发挥	.481	
因素2:专业交流与合作		17.753%
我认为引进大学文化进入校园对教师的专业化发展很有帮助	.761	
我认为大学与中小学合作研究促进教师专业化发展成效显著	.737	
我建立了自己的教学博客,并经常在上面与其他教师分享教学心得与体会,交流教学经验	.675	
因素3:专业自主发展能力		16.207%
我能根据学生特点和教学内容合理进行教学设计	.751	
我具备教师所应具有的专业知识	.728	
我通常能够妥善处理课堂教学过程中遇到的突发事件	.700	
我对自己未来的专业发展规划有清晰的认识	.556	

因素一:专业理念与精神。主要反映了教师的专业发展积极性,教师及学校管理层主观上愿意投入时间与精力参与课题研究或其他教师专业化发展活动的程度,为提升教师专业素质、促进教师专业化发展作出努力。还反映了教师的教育观、学生观等。比如“在教育教学中,我除了交给学生如何学习之外,还注重教他们如何做人”,体现了教师真正尊重与关爱学生,对自己的职业充满热情,并有高度的认同感和责任感。“我们学校已建立了教师学习发展共同体,形成了一种轻松、和谐的合作氛围”,“我很重视教师专业成长档案袋的建立,对自身专业发展情况进行了认真记录”,这都表明了从学校到教师个体对教师专业化发展的重视程度。该因素是促进教师专业化发展的动力基础和理性支撑,对教师专业化发展的解释贡献率为20.208%。

因素二:专业交流与合作。反映了在促进教师专业化发展过程中,中小学教师与他人进行经验交流的状况以及学校与大学合作研究的作用。教师的专业化发展并不仅仅是单个人的发展与进步,而且是整个教师队伍的发展与提高,因而在专业化发展过程中教师与教师之间应该加强沟通与合作,建立学习共同体,通过网络、教研组讨论、评课议课等多种方式进行交流。如果教师周围缺乏一种支持合作的集体与心理氛围,将很难实现教学合作,从而不利于教师的专业化发展。在实施教师专业化发展活动过程中,学校需要积极争取与大学的合作,引进大学文化,大学可以为中小学带去新思想、新观念、新技术、新的发展方式,中小学教师可以在大学教师指导下自我引导、自我发展,并进一步成为教育改革的主导者。[2]从而有效实现以专业引领来促进教师的专业化发展。该因素有助于形成民主开放的交流气氛,拓展教师成长的空间,是促进教师专业化发展的有力保障,对教师专业化发展的解释贡献率为17.753%。

因素三:专业自主发展能力。反映了教师在教学情境中所具备的专业知识和能力,以及教师专业化发展的主体参与意识,教师在教育实践中的主体性参与,是教师发展的根本性动力。[3]比如,教师能否熟练掌握并运用专业知识;教师是否可以结合教学内容和学生的发展特点开发课程资源,进行合理的教学设计;教师的课题组织与管理能力如何,是否可以妥善处理突发事件;教师是否能够积极主动地学习,及时有效地进行教学反思;是否具备专业自主的规划能力等。该因素是教师专业化发展的核心内涵和坚实基础,对教师专业化发展的解释贡献率为16.207%。

对以上三个层面以及专业化发展成效进行描述性统计,由于各层面所涵盖的题项不同,因而不能直接从平均数的大小来比较,应将各层面平均数除以各层面题项数,得每题平均得分进行分析(教师专业化发展状况的描述统计见表3)。

表3 教师专业化发展状况的描述统计

层面	平均数	题项	每题平均得分
专业理念与精神	31.0019	7	4.4288
专业交流与合作	11.7666	3	3.9222
专业自主发展能力	17.0968	4	4.2742
专业发展成效	4.3472	1	4.3472
Valid N (listwise)	527		

从表3中可以知悉,专业理念与精神层面得分最高,表明教师的专业化发展积极性大幅提

高,对教育教学事业有较为坚定的信念。专业交流与合作层面得分最低,表明为促进教师专业化发展仍需加强校内与校际之间的交流与合作。从教师专业化发展成效方面看,平均数为4.3472,成效较为显著,标准差为0.52223,高低分差距不是很大,可见教师专业化发展个别差异情形并不明显,本次全员参与的研究试点对于整体推进教师专业化发展是可行的。

层面与层面之间积差相关分析结果显示,三个层面与专业发展成效均呈显著的正相关(积差相关分析结果见表4)。

表4 积差相关分析结果

		专业发展成效	专业理念与精神	专业交流与合作	专业自主发展能力
专业发展成效	Pearson Correlation	1	.454(**)	.364(**)	.526(**)
	Sig.(2-tailed)	.	.000	.000	.000
	N	527	527	527	527
专业理念与精神	Pearson Correlation	.454(**)	1	.488(**)	.514(**)
	Sig.(2-tailed)	.000	.	.000	.000
	N	527	527	527	527
专业交流与合作	Pearson Correlation	.364(**)	.488(**)	1	.429(**)
	Sig.(2-tailed)	.000	.000	.	.000
	N	527	527	527	527
专业自主发展能力	Pearson Correlation	.526(**)	.514(**)	.429(**)	1
	Sig.(2-tailed)	.000	.000	.000	.
	N	527	527	527	527

** Correlation is significant at the 0.01 level (2-tailed).

此外,用皮尔逊积差相关方法求两变量之间的相关程度发现,教师专业理念与精神、专业交流与合作、专业自主发展能力与专业发展成效之间两两显著相关。这表明,上述三个因素确实对教师专业化发展起显著的促进作用,并且三个因素之间相互促进、共同作用。

2. 不同特征的教师专业化发展特点

独立样本的 t-test 显示了不同性别教师在专业理念与精神层面有显著差异($p<.01$)。由 t 检验结果得出,女教师的专业理念与精神显著优于男教师(平均数 31.4578>30.2256)。这可能与教师这一职业特点以及女性心理发展特点有关。女教师往往更容易对教师职业产生认同感及依赖感,从而影响教师专业发展信念。

我们还采用单因子独立样本变异数分析法(One-Way ANOVA),对教龄、学校类型、学校所在地、学校发展层次与教师专业理念与精神、专业交流与合作、专业自主发展能力与专业发展成效是否有显著差异进行了分析。分析结果显示,学校类型、层次与以上各层面均无显著差异。而不同教龄的教师其专业自主发展能力有显著差异,6～15 年教龄的教师专业自主发展能力显著高于 1～5 年教龄教师的能力。学校所在地不同,教师的专业交流与合作有显著差异,市区学校教师专业交流与合作显著优于农村学校。另外,市区学校教师专业自主发展能力显著高于城郊地区教师的专业自主发展能力。分析其原因,这与教学条件及环境的限制等因素有关。市区学校由于它独特的地理优势以及人、财、物等多方面的优越性,其教师专业发展有更坚实的保障,教师获取资源及学习、交流的机会更为丰富,教师的专业自主发展能力也要高些。与之相比,城郊与农村学校明显处于劣势,尤其农村学校,其教学硬件及软件条件与市区学校都存在很大差距。

3. 教师对专业化发展活动的认识

为更加深入考察教师对专业化发展活动的认识,探索有效推进教师专业化发展的制度保障体系及运行机制,从而更好地规划及管理教师专业化发展活动,本研究还对以下三个方面进行了调查:

第一,促进教师专业化发展最重要的保障机制。表5显示,中小学教师认为促进教师专业化发展最重要的保障机制前三项分别为:与专家学者或优秀教师的互动机制、科学的用人机制、全面的评价机制。首先,合肥地区这次大规模的促进教师专业化发展研究活动是大学与中小学合作进行的,大学里专家学者的理论引领作用是有效促进教师专业化发展的最佳途径之一,而中小学一线教师有较为丰富的实践经验,因此专家学者与优秀一线教师的合理互动机制,是学校教育科研持续发展的重要条件和保障。其次,科学的用人机制是学校管理的重要方面,有利于组建一支具有专业合作精神的教师队伍,能较好地配合管理者实现管理目标及管理成果的最优化。再次,全面的评价机制强调不以考试结果作为唯一的评价手段,而是实行发展性评价,侧重考察教师的合作协调能力、教师工作态度及课堂教学效果等方面。也有教师对保障机制提出了自己的建议,比如课堂教学及论文评比、专业的培训等。

表5 教师专业化发展最重要的保障机制($N=533$)

保障机制	教师数(人)	百分比
科学的用人机制	259	48.6%
广泛的民主机制	217	40.7%
全面的评价机制	259	48.6%
合理的奖罚机制	152	28.6%
和谐的竞争机制	239	44.8%
与专家学者或优秀教师的互动机制	316	59.3%
与教育部门或各级教研机构的合作机制	157	29.4%

第二,教师参加专业化发展活动的最大动因。表6显示,提高教育教学水平是最主要原因,比例为93.5%,说明教师参加专业化发展活动主要是为了做好专业工作。其次是提高自身素质(89.3%),表明教师普遍具有专业发展需求,在终身学习的社会环境中,这种意识有利于教师的专业化成长。另有55.5%的教师认为新课改的要求是他们参加专业化发展活动的动因,说明大规模的新课程改革能够较大程度地调动教师专业化发展积极性。教师在问卷选项之外注明的其他动因有对自己教师理想的追求、把握本专业的发展前沿等。

第三,学校实施教师专业化发展最需要加强的环节。表7显示,占第一位的是教师专业化发展理念,教师专业发展理念是教师专业化发展的理性基础,只有观念上真正树立了专业发展的理念,在行动中才有可能实行。其次是满足教师发展需求的合理的进修机会,这说明目前的教师进修很大程度上仍存在问题,需要加以改善,保证提供给教师的进修机会真正满足教师的发展需求。排在第三位的是充裕的研究、讨论、交流与反思的时间。每个教师在教学过程中都会遇到一些困难和难以解决的问题,同行之间对教学问题的研究、讨论、交流、反思可以扩展教师的知识,促使教师更有效地进行思考,他们必须集中更多的时间和精力去从事那些有效果的和有创造性的活动:互相影响、讨论、激励、了解、鼓舞。[4]

表 6 教师参加专业化发展活动的最大动因($N=505$)

动因	教师数(人)	百分比
学历提升	58	11.5%
晋级、加薪、奖励	77	15.2%
提高教育教学水平	472	93.5%
新课改的要求	280	55.5%
听从上级主管部门和学校的安排	65	12.9%
提高自身素质	451	89.3%
个人的兴趣、爱好	112	22.2%

表 7 学校实施教师专业化发展最需要加强的环节($N=521$)

环节	教师数(人)	百分比
积极的文化	71	13.7%
教师专业化发展理念	284	54.6%
人员所尽职责的角色准备	67	12.9%
教师之间的专业沟通	231	44.4%
可靠的行政支持	122	23.4%
资源准备	81	15.5%
良好的研究环境	177	34.0%
充裕的研究、讨论、交流与反思的时间	262	50.3%
满足教师发展需求的合理的进修机会	268	51.4%

三、进一步深化课题研究的建议

调查分析结果表明,通过全员参与课题研究活动,中小学教师已形成了比较清晰的专业化发展理念;教师自主反思与发展意识由开始的较为迷惘转变为现在的比较明确;教师的专业发展能力有较为明显的提高;教师专业化发展活动的组织实施更为合理有效。实践证明,以课题研究为载体,推进区域教师专业化发展,是一种全新的教师专业化发展模式,是十分有效的,是完全可行的。

调查也反映出课题研究以及教师专业化发展活动实施中仍然存在的一些问题,比如:有些学校的课题研究缺乏深度,研究成果难以上升到理论高度;少数学校选题不当,致使未能深入开展课题研究;教师专业化发展的保障措施不够到位等。针对存在的问题以及影响教师专业化发展的几个主要因素,我们对今后在区域内全面开展教师专业化发展课题研究提出以下

建议:

1. 构建“1+3”组织架构,确保教师专业化发展课题研究的有效性

要想课题研究在更大范围推广,还应在市教育行政主管部门统一领导下,继续采取“专家分类指导,县区具体负责,学校互助合作,教师全员参与”的有效行动策略。一方面要充实专家指导力量,加大专家引领力度;另一方面要强化县区教育行政部门的主体作用,构建以市教育局总课题组为统领,县区教育行政部门、优秀实验学校、各参与学校为研究实施主体的“1+3”组织架构,并实行课题组长负责制,确保课题研究的有效性。

2. 明确“5+1”研究任务,增强教师专业化发展课题研究的针对性

参与学校和广大教师应当在“五个有效”子课题中,结合本校实际和自身情况选择某一个子课题开展研究,重点解决教师在教育教学中最迫切需要解决的问题。通过培育良好的研究环境,进一步全面强化教师对专业化发展的认知,培养教师研究主体意识,提高教师个人及集体反思能力。县区教育行政部门则应当围绕“建立促进区域教师专业化发展的长效机制”这一主题开展研究。通过研究,构建适合促进本区域教师专业化发展的评价指标体系与评估机制。

3. 按照“五阶段”实施步骤,保证教师专业化发展课题研究的有序性

教师专业化发展课题研究涉及面广,时间跨度较长,为使研究有序开展,建议具体划分为五个阶段进行:(1) 研究筹备阶段。成立相关研究组织机构,做好各项研究准备工作。(2) 理论学习阶段。通过学习、分析校情,选择适合本校实际的研究课题。(3) 研究实施阶段。制定研究计划,开展行动研究。(4) 自我评估阶段。各学校对阶段性研究成果进行及时的总结、提炼。(5) 结题总结阶段。在市教育行政主管部门统一领导下,由县区教育行政部门具体组织对区域内教师专业化发展课题研究进行结题。

4. 开展“1+ N”合作互助,充分发挥试点先行学校的示范带动作用

为发挥优秀实验学校的指导和示范作用,带动条件落后以及发展层次较为薄弱的学校,帮助他们更新专业发展理念,提高专业发展能力,各县区可根据实际,分类建立“1+ N”的课题研究“合作互助小组”。即在县区统一安排下,按课题研究“五个有效”研究方向进行划分,把选择相同子课题的学校进行组合,使先行试点为优秀的学校与两到三个相对薄弱学校结成合作互助小组,形成课题研究共同体,加强相互学习、交流与合作。另外,鼓励加强与大学的合作交流,引进大学文化,加强理论指导,营造良好的研究与学习氛围。

总之,以课题研究为载体开展教师专业化发展活动是一次全新的尝试,为确保课题研究的总体质量,要强调群策群力,除了市、县(区)、学校各级领导高度重视,负起责任,精心组织,周密安排之外,还要在经费、制度、资料、人员、设备、时间等多方面给予充分支持和保障,引领教师把课题研究做实、做深,确保教师专业化发展取得实效。

参考文献

[1] 李琼,曾晓东,杜亮.北京市中小学教师专业发展:结构与特点研究[J].教师教育研究,2008(11).

[2] 傅树京.PDS与TDS:教师专业发展的有效途径[J].教师教育研究,2004(11).

[3] 王长纯.教师专业化发展:对教师的重新发现[J].教育研究,2001(11).

[4] 联合国教科文组织国际教育发展委员会.学会生存[M].北京:教育科学出版社,1996.

Teaching Quality in Lower Secondary Mathematics Classes

Sarah Hopkins

Abstract: Based on a review of recent government reports released in Australia and the UK, the Teaching of Mathematics Observation Schedule (ToMOS) was developed to identify and help record the occurrence of specific teaching actions relating to teaching quality in the mathematics classroom. Findings from the pilot test indicated that the actions specified on the schedule can be reliably observed. The ToMOS is a useful reflective tool for mathematics teachers (inservice and preservice teachers) to help them examine and improve the quality of their teaching.

中学低年级数学课堂教学质量

莎拉·霍普金斯*

摘　要:数学教学监测表(简称 ToMOS)是在对英国和澳大利亚近年来发布的官方报告进行回顾总结的基础上形成的。该监测表明确了数学课堂上与教学质量密切相关的具体教学行为,并且帮助记录下这些教学行为出现的次数。试点测试的结果表明,监测表上所注明的具体教学行为均是可以观测得到的。这个数学教学监测表对所有数学教师(无论是在职的还是实习的教师)来说都是一个有用的工具。教师们可以借此监测表来反思教学,以检查和提高其教学质量。

Introduction

The Trends in International Mathematics and Science Study (TIMSS) data (NCES, 2003) and 1999 TIMSS Video Study (Hiebert et al., 2003) drew attention to a need to

* 莎拉·霍普金斯,澳大利亚西澳大学教育学院教师,博士。

improve the quality of teaching in lower secondary mathematics classrooms in Australia (Hollingsworth, Lokan, & McCrae, 2003) and in other participating countries (Desimone, Smith, Baker, & Ueno, 2005; MacNab, 2000). While investigative research has identified certain teaching practices thought to improve learning outcomes for students, some of which are espoused in standards documents representing excellence in mathematics teaching (AAMT, 2006; NCTM, 2000), very little research is available to empirically substantiate (or refute) findings and theories relating to effective teaching. Research that has tested whether or not measures of teaching quality account for student achievement gains is very sparse (Hill, Rowan, Lowenberg Ball, 2005; Schoen, Cebulla, Finn, & Fi, 2003). A limiting factor has been a lack of appropriate tools to measure teaching quality.

Traditionally in research, the quality of mathematics teaching has been considered in terms of easily quantifiable, proxy variables representing *teacher characteristics*, such as the teacher's qualifications in mathematics and mathematics education, number of years teaching, and verbal skills (e. g. , Akiba, LeTendre, & Scribner, 2007; Wayne & Youngs, 2003). Few measures to date have been developed to quantify *characteristics of teaching actions*. The aim of this research project was to build on existing research by developing an observation schedule that could be used to measure teaching quality in lower secondary mathematics classes.

Literature Review

The literature reviewed encompassed 10 recent large-scale, government funded studies in mathematics education (see Louden, Rohl and Hopkins, 2008, for details of the literature reviewed). The studies were chosen based on the criteria that they incorporated an investigation of where effective teaching was likely to be taking place (based on an analysis of achievement gains or the extent to which learning outcomes were enhanced) together with some examination of teacher characteristics and/or teaching practices.

To develop items for the Teaching of Mathematics Observation Schedule (ToMOS), the literature was reviewed to highlight teaching practices that have been associated with effective teaching and could potentially be observed during public time. Public time refers to segments in a lesson when the teacher and students are involved in public (rather than private) interaction. The findings were organised into eight themes (presented in no particular order): Choice of Task, Student Thinking, Consolidation, Feedback, Systematic Development of Content, Making Connections, Direct Teaching and Language.

Item Selection and Scoring the ToMOS

The aim of developing an observation schedule that could be completed in situ influenced the decision to restrict the ToMOS to ten teaching actions, however initially many items were considered. For each theme identified in the review findings, different items were written, describing associated teaching actions. Care was taken to describe actions that were equally likely to occur during a mathematics lesson, regardless of the content being taught. Preliminary testing of each item was then carried out. Preliminary testing involved the two developers observing four teachers teach one mathematics class each, at a school that was equipped with an observation room attached to a classroom. The observation room contained a one-way viewing window and was sound proofed. This set up allowed the developers to discuss any differences in the teaching actions each identified and to construct criteria for a coding manual to resolve these differences, without interrupting the class.

Certain items were eliminated because of difficulty achieving inter-rater agreement during preliminary testing and based on adhesion to the goal of keeping the teaching actions objectively observable (as far as possible) without assuming expertise on behalf of the observers. Eventually ten well functioning items were chosen to be represented in the ToMOS. These were categorized into two broad dimensions: Communicates Expectations and Focuses on Conceptual Understanding. A description of each action is presented in Table 1. A coding manual and recording sheet was developed to help observers identify each of the ten teaching actions (see Louden, Rohl and Hopkins, 2008 for details).

Table 1 Teaching actions in the ToMOS

Dimension 1: Communicates Expectations	
Intentions	The teacher makes verbal or written statements about the specific mathematics learning intended in the lesson
Quality	The teacher communicates in verbal or written form explicit criteria for quality responses to tasks assigned
Responsibility	The teacher makes statements that encourage students to take responsibility for their own mathematics learning
Respect	The teacher responds with respect to mathematical questions and comments initiated by students
Dimension 2: Focuses on Conceptual Understanding	
Emphasises Meaning	The teacher helps students interpret the meaning of solutions to worked examples by explicitly linking the solution to the question or interpreting the solution contextually
Multiple Solution Methods	The teacher draws focus to more than one solution method for a worked example
Summary	The teacher provides a summary statement that clearly links a problem to a more generalised case
Misconceptions	The teacher intentionally addresses common misconceptions by requiring students to analyse examples, solutions or ideas
Multiple Representations	The teacher uses two or more ways to represent a mathematical idea
Mathematical Language	The teacher clarifies key mathematical terms and/or symbols to promote student understanding of mathematical language

While the teacher actions identified in the ToMOS are thought to be indicative of effective teaching (an assumption requiring empirical support), the ToMOS is designed to measure teaching quality. It is not assumed that quality will be related to the number of times each action is observed in a lesson. Rather it is proposed that quality is related to a teacher's repertoire of these teaching actions. The scoring of the ToMOS is based on this proposition. The ToMOS is designed to be used in two, non consecutive classrooms and is scored out of ten: each action can be scored 1 if it is observed at least once during the two lessons or it is scored 0 if it is not observed.

Pilot testing the ToMOS

Method

Nine teachers agreed to participate in pilot testing the ToMOS. Teacher participation involved allowing the two developers to sit and observe them teaching two non consecutive Year 8 maths lessons, and agreeing to have these lessons videotaped. The instructions to the teacher were to choose two typical lessons. Written consent was required from all principals, teachers, students and parents involved.

The two coders sat together at the back or to the side of the classroom and the camera operator found a convenient position in the classroom to stand with a tripod. Individual students who did not have written consent to participate and be videotaped, were seated together behind the camera or to the side, and the camera operator was instructed to avoid recording these students. The teacher was fitted with a microphone.

During public time episodes, each coder recorded their observations separately. During larger episodes of private time, the two coders compared and discussed their records and resolved any differences to the satisfaction of both coders, if they were able to do so without disturbing students' work. Any differences that could not be quickly resolved were noted. Public time segments of each lesson observed were transcribed.

Results

Eighteen maths lessons were observed: two lessons taught by nine different teachers. In total, teacher actions specified on the ToMOS were observed 95 times and inter-rater agreement was reached during the lesson on 82 of these occasions (86%). The 13 differences were later resolved easily by viewing the video or reading the public time transcriptions and making minor changes to the wording of the coding manual.

Conclusion

There are few instruments that have been developed to measure teaching quality based on observed classroom practice. The ToMOS was developed in response to the need to measure teaching quality in lower secondary mathematics classes, enabling future research to validate findings and theories of effective mathematics teaching. While further testing of the ToMOS is required, pilot-testing of the ToMOS indicated it to be an instrument with good inter-rater reliability.

Robust instruments for examining teaching quality have many practical applications. For example, the ToMOS can be used as a reflective tool for preservice mathematics teachers, who can use it to critically analyse their use of public time based on a videotape of themselves in action. The consistency and type of feedback provided to preservice teachers during practicum can vary markedly and preservice teachers' own reflections may also very in terms of the depth and importance of the issues reflected upon. The actions identified in the ToMOS will help preservice to teachers focus on the quality of their teaching. Similarly the ToMOS can be used as a reflective tool for current mathematics teachers who are looking to improve their own teaching, or as a reporting tool for establishing teaching expertise.

References

[1] AAMT. Standards for excellence in teaching mathematics in Australian Schools [R]. Australian Association of Mathematics Teachers, 2006-1-17. http://www.aamt.edu.au.

[2] AKIBA M, LETENDRE G K, SCRIBNER J P. Teacher quality, opportunity gap, and national achievement in 46 countries[J]. Educational Researcher, 2007, 36(7): 369-387.

[3] DESIMONE L M, SMITH T, BAKER D, UENO K. Assessing barriers to the reform of U. S. mathematics instruction from an international perspective[J]. American Educational Research Journal, 2005, 42(3): 501-535.

[4] HIEBER J, GALLIMORE R, GARNIER H, GIVVIN K B, et al. Teaching mathematics in seven countries: Results from the TIMSS 1999 Video Study[R]. Washington, D. C.: National Center for Education Statistics.

[5] HILL H C, ROWAN B, LOEWENBERG BALL D. Effects of teachers' mathematical knowledge for teaching on student achievement[J]. American Education Research Journal, 2005, 42(2): 371-406.

[6] HOLLINGSWORTH H, LOKAN J, MCCRAE B. Teaching mathematics in Australia Camberwell [DB]. Victoria: Australian Association of Educational Research. Australian Council of Educational Research database, 2006-1-10. http://www.acer.edu.au.

[7] LOUDEN W, ROHL M, HOPKINS S. Teaching for growth: effective teaching of literacy and numeracy [J]. WA: University of Western Australia, 2008.

[8] MACNAB D. Raising standards in mathematics education: values, vision, and TIMSS[J]. Educational Studies in Mathematics, 2000, 42(1): 61-80.

[9] NCTM. Principles and Standards for School Mathematics [R]. National Council of Teachers of Mathematics, 2006-1-17. http://standards.nctm.org.

[10] SCHOEN H L, CEBULLA K J, FINN K F, FI C. Teacher variables that relate to student achievement when using a standards-based curriculum[J]. Journal for Research in Mathematics Education, 1999, 34 (3): 228.

[11] WAYNE A J, YOUNGS P. Teacher characteristics and student achievement gains: A review[J]. Review of Educational Research, 2003, 73(1): 89-122.

Research-based Programs Proven Effective with Minority Children

Carolyn B. H. Rogers*
(Capella University, Minneapolis, MN 55402 USA)

In an era of increased accountability, it is vital that teacher understand that effective instruction is vital to the success of *all* children. "The moral imperative of effective schools is the belief that *all* children can learn. That belief inspires the faculty and staff to be accountable for that learning" (Lunenburg & Irby, 2006, p. 102). Yet, in American schools there continues to be a growing disparity between White and Asian/Pacific Island students to that of Blacks, Hispanics and American Indians. According to National Center for Education Statistics (NCES), the average scale scores for reading, grades 4 and 8 in 2007 by race/ethnicity ranged from 232 to 203, an average of 28 point difference in the aforementioned groups. In light of the NCES results, teachers throughout America are turning to research based reading programs that have shown significant results for children in low performing minority groups in an effort to become more accountable in closing the achievement gap. According to the Comprehensive School Reform Quality (CSRQ) Center Report on Elementary School Comprehensive Reform Models, Success for All (SFA) and Direct Instruction (DI) were rated to show *moderately strong evidence* of positive effects in increasing student reading between the white and minority groups. The SFA reading program, founded by Robert Slavin and Nancy Madden, operates on the belief that every child can and will learn. SFA is a comprehensive reading approach designed to ensure that every child will read at grade level or above. As such, all team members are accountable for student success. The program, for grades Pre-K to 6, emphasizes prevention and early intervention to respond to and solve any child's learning problems. DI founded by Siegfried Engelmann and Wesley Becker, is a model for teaching that emphasizes well-developed and carefully planned lessons designed around small learning increments and clearly defined and prescribed teaching tasks. It is based on the theory that clear instruction can eliminate misinterpretations, thereby greatly improving and accelerating learning. SFA and DI are approved reading models in accordance with the *No Child Left Behind* legislation with

* Carolyn B. H. Rogers, PhD and Chair of Department of Educational Leadership, Capella University, Minneapolis, USA.

proven results in teaching minority children to read.

有效提高少数族群儿童学习成绩的教学模式

卡洛琳 B. H. 罗杰斯*

(开普拉大学,明尼阿波利斯 55402 美国)

当今时代,教师肩负的责任与日俱增。对教师而言,了解有效教学对所有孩子成功的重要性有着深远的意义。"高效的学校教育的道德准则是:所有的孩子都能学到知识。这一信念激励着所有教师肩负起教学的职责"(卢森博格 & 埃尔比, 2006, p. 102)。然而在美国,许多学校如今依然存在种群教育差异现象,白人学生与亚太裔、黑人、拉美裔及美国印第安人学生等在教育上都存在不同程度的差异,而且这种差异有继续扩大的态势。根据美国国家教育统计中心(NCES)2007 年的统计报告,四年级和八年级学生的阅读总体平均分在 232~203 之间,以上种群学生的成绩平均分差值为 28 分。根据 NCES 的统计,基于阅读研究的教学模式正受到全美国教师的青睐。这一模式旨在缩小学生学习之间的差距,研究表明,这一教学模式对提高少数种群中差生的学习成绩有显著的成效。根据学校整体改革质量中心(CSRQ)所做的《小学整体改革模式》报告,"让每个人都成功(SFA)"和"直接教学(DI)"被认为是在提高学生阅读能力方面有相当积极作用的教学模式。SFA 阅读模式,由罗伯特·斯莱文 (Robert Slavin) 和南茜夫人首创,其核心理念是每个孩子都能并且都愿意去学。SFA 是一种为每个孩子在标准水平或更高水平阅读而设计的综合的阅读方法。按照这一模式,小组的所有成员都要为团队的成功负责任,该课程模式分为学前班到六年级,强调预防和早期干预及解决学生的任何学习问题。教学模式由齐格弗里德·恩格尔曼(Siegfried Engelmann) 和韦斯利·贝克所创,是一种强调完善和精心设计的课程教学的教学模式,课程围绕小增量学习和完成规定的教学任务设计。这一教学模式的理论基础是:明确的指示能够消除误解,从而极大地改善和促进学习。通过少数种群孩子阅读教学的实据,表明 SFA 和 DI 是符合"不让一个孩子掉队"的规定和目标并得到广泛认可的教学模式。

References

[1] BORMAN G, SLAVIN R E, CHEUNG A, et al. Final reading outcomes of the national randomized field trial of Success for All[J]. American Educational Research Journal, 2007, 44 (3): 701-731.

[2] BORMAN G, SLAVIN R E, CHEUNG A, et al. The national randomized field trial of Success for All: Second-year outcomes[J]. American Educational Research Journal, 2005, 42 (4): 673-696.

* 卡洛琳 B. H. 罗杰斯,博士,开普拉大学高等教育管理系教授。

[3] BORMAN G D, HEWES G M, OVERMAN L T, et al. Comprehensive school reform and student achievement: A meta-analysis[R]. Johns Hopkins University, 2004. http://www. csos. jhu. edu.

[4] CARNINE D, SILBERT J, KAME'ENUI E, et al. Direct instruction reading [M]. 4th ed. Upper Saddle River, NJ: Pearson, 2004.

[5] COMPREHENSIVE SCHOOL REFORM QUALITY CENTER. CSRQ Center Report on Elementary School Comprehensive School Reform Models [R]. Washington, D. C.: American Institutes for Research, 2005.

[6] MARCHAND-MARTELLA N E, SLOCUM T A, MARTELLA R C. (2004). Introduction to Direct Instruction. Boston: MA, 2004.

小学教师校本成长的模式初探

——以安庆市健康路小学为例

曹长德*　黄义文**　孙朋***

(安庆师范学院,安徽　安庆　246011)

摘　要:教师专业发展的关键是校本成长。小学是我国义务教育阶段的起始阶段,是整个教师队伍中文化层次较低的一个阶层,小学教师的校本成长更具重要的意义。我们通过课题研究,探索出的小学教师校本成长的"三型六阶"模式,即指通过系统学习、岗位练兵、科研培训、专项研修、个性发展、风格生成等六个阶段造就、生成熟练型教师、研究型教师、特色型名师。

关键词:小学教师;校本;成长;模式

Preliminary Study on Model of Primary School Teachers Growth of School-based

——Take JianKang Road Primary School in Anqing City as an Example

Cao Chang-de　Huang Yi-wen　Sun Peng

Abstract: The key of teachers professional development is the growth of school-based. Primary school is on initial stage of compulsory education in our country and in a lower cultural class in all teachers, so primary school teachers school-based growth is more important significance. Through research by subject, we have explored and got a model of primary school teachers growth of school-based which is named three-type six-stage. It is generation of skilled teachers, research-

* 曹长德,安庆师范学院教育学院院长、教授。

** 黄义文,安庆市健康路小学校长。

*** 孙朋,安庆市健康路小学副校长。

oriented teachers, famous teacher with characteristics through a systematic study, job training, research training, special training, personal development, and style formation.

Key words: primary school teachers; School-based; growth; model

基础教育改革让教育管理部门和各个学校更加深刻地认识到教师队伍建设的重要性:优秀的教师队伍是提高教学质量和教学改革成功的根本保证,教师专业发展与学生的成长以及学校的发展密切相关;教师专业发展的关键是校本成长。小学是我国义务教育段的起始阶段,是整个教师队伍中文化层次较低的一个阶层,因此,如何有效促进小学教师在专业上可持续发展是一个非常具有现实意义的课题。我们通过课题研究,探索出的小学教师校本成长的模式,或许能够为同行们提供细微的参考。

一、研究的缘起

1. 基础教育课程改革的推动

2001年启动的基础教育课程改革是一项系统的改革工程,不仅对课程改革的目标、内容、结构等六个方面做了明确规定,而且对教师提出了相应的要求:即从知识的传授者变为"学生学习的促进者"、"教育教学的研究者"、"课程的建设者和开发者"、走出"象牙塔"与社区相联系的实践者。从以上所述的四个转变我们不难看出,教师首先必须研究学生,才能成为有效的学生学习的促进者;教师必须在深入研究课程的基础上,研究教育理论和教学实践,才能成为课程的建设和开发者;教师必须走出书斋、走出校园,研究社区,才能真正成为联系社区的实践者。一言以蔽之,教师必须提升自身素质、改变工作方式和范围,必须在教师专业上持续发展。

2. 国家对教师要求的推动

2002年12月27日教育部颁布了《关于积极推进中小学评价与考试制度改革的通知》(教基[2002]26号)明确提出建立有利于促进教师职业道德和专业水平提高的评价体系:"中小学教师评价制度的改革要有利于加强教师职业道德建设,促进教师业务水平的提高,建立有利于实施素质教育、发挥教师创造性的多元的、新型的中小学教师评价体系"。评价的内容主要包括职业道德、了解和尊重学生、教学方案的设计与实施、交流与反思。特别是新增加的"交流与反思",它要求教师能够主动与学生、家长、同事、学校领导进行交流和沟通,能对自己的教育观念、教学行为进行反思,并制定改进计划,能够不断创新,持续发展。

3. 学校自身发展的需要

教师的专业发展是学校发展的前提。就安庆市健康路小学而言,该校创办于1947年,是一所具有悠久历史和光荣传统的名校,学校秉承"全面发展,健康成长"的宗旨,引导教师和学生共同成长。学校自2002至2010年将有一大批老教师陆续退休,占学校教师总数的60%以上,刚刚走上小学教育岗位的师范毕业生占全校教师总数的34%。学生及学生家长对优质教育的需求与学校所能提供的教育服务存在着很大矛盾。这些新教师均具有大专学历,正值青春年华,精力充沛,时间充足。学校只有加强校本培训力度,采取科学有效的培训方式,让他们尽快实现教育理论学习与教学实践运用的统一,根据教育教学工作的需要不断学习新的知识与技能,研究和努力解决教学中的新问题,不断完善和发展自我,才能保证学校教育教学工作的可持续发展。因此,学校高度重视教师培训的研究与试验,努力探索适合于小学教师校本成长的模式。

二、小学教师校本成长的模式及形成过程

根据小学教师校本成长的特点,通过教育理论工作者与小学教师共同研究,经过六年多的实践探索,形成了小学教师校本成长模式,也叫"三型六阶"校本培训模式。

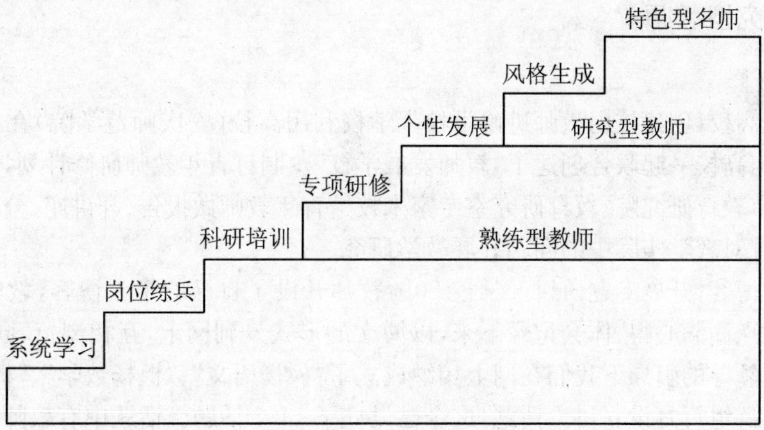

"三型六阶"校本培训模式

"三型六阶"校本培训模式是指通过系统学习、岗位练兵,科研培训、专项研修、个性发展、风格生成等六个阶段造就、生成熟练型教师、研究型教师、特色型名师。

(一) 熟练型教师

目前进入小学的教师基本上具有专科以上学历,并持有教师资格证书,基本上达到了合格要求,但是由于教育实习时间有限,他们对教育教学业务依然还很生疏,教师的角色意识、责任意识也需要进一步强化。因此,必须在教师岗位上进行系统学习和教学技能训练。

1. 系统学习

一是强化师德教育,激发教师的敬业情怀。二是强化教育专业知识,打好教书育人的基础,主要包括教育理论知识,学科专业理论与基本知识两个方面。三是强化教师专业技能,主要包括三个板块:

(1) 教师基础能力,如教师智慧、表达能力、审美能力、人际交往能力等;

(2) 教师职业能力,如教师的教育教学能力,班级管理能力,特定学科教师还应具备与学科相应的特殊能力;

(3) 教师自我完善能力,如教师自学能力、教学研究能力、网络信息处理能力等。

2. 岗位练兵

一是基本功训练。基本功是教师从事教学的基础。提高教师业务素质,应开展"一话"(普通话)、"二字"(钢笔字、粉笔字)、"三技能"(教具制作、课件制作、电化教学)的训练,并开展评比和奖励,激发教师学习、训练的积极性和主动性。

二是师徒结对。大胆启用校内实践经验丰富、理论水平较高的教师为校本培训的师资,实

行“一师多徒”和“一徒多师”，发挥好传、帮、带作用，促进教师快速成长。

三是岗位练兵课。“备课——上课——评课”是练兵的基本环节，在教师专业发展的不同阶段，提出不同的练兵课要求。第一阶段是辅导上课练兵。青年教师自选合适课题，在结对的指导教师帮助下备课，在一段时间准备后，分组展示评比。第二阶段是辅助上课练兵。学校确定教学主题与内容，青年教师集中抽选，在 24 小时内独立备课，结对教师参与辅导，集中展示评比。第三阶段是独立上课练兵。学校确定教学主题，青年教师集中抽选主题，结对教师不再参与辅导，青年教师在 3 小时内独立备课，自制课件，集中展示评比。

（二）研究型教师

1. 专项研修

一是依托高校，创建校内教师进修学校。学校利用高校（安庆师范学院）在学校设立的基础教育基地，与高校一起联合创建了“教师发展学校”。制订青年教师研修计划，邀请高校教育研究专家、省市教育研究院、教育研究室专家来校给青年教师做报告、开讲座，分析教育教学中存在的问题，针对教学实际中的问题开展教学研究。

二是借助博客，开展专题研讨。学校 80％教师开设了自己的个人博客，教师们将自己日常教学中的点点滴滴心得、体会记录下来，以博文的形式发到网上，互相浏览，同伴互助，资源共享。在学校领导的引导下我们在网上相继成立了“枫杨语文”、“枫杨数学”、“枫杨英语”等博客群组。博客群组每月设立讨论话题，迄今已设立了 14 个话题。话题中有教师们日常教学中碰到的问题（如期末测试情况分析、课堂评价语的运用），有对经典（如《论语》）教育论述的认识，有对名师教学观点的评析，有当前热门话题（如教师道德规范）的讨论等。在群组管理员的组织下，教师们在愉快和谐的氛围里畅谈教学的收获和困惑，思维不断碰撞，并享受着教研的快乐。在教师博客评比中，我校获得了“十佳博客团队”、“十佳博客教研团队”的光荣称号，青鸟的博客连续获得了区、市、省一等奖，更以 948 篇博文领全市教师博客之冠。学校为此专门编印了《教师精华博文》和《网络教研纪实》等资料。

三是开展专项活动，提高教师反思能力。主要从四方面促使教师反思：(1) 听课促反思。每学期开展教师间相互学习听课、师徒间指导听课、指导教师诊断听课等活动。(2) 评课促反思。开展教师示范课、公开课、研究课等评课活动。(3) 评教促反思。建立家长、学生评教制度，每学期开展一次家长学生评教活动。(4) 专题研讨促反思。以教研组为单位，每两周进行一次教学研讨；学校根据青年教师反映较为集中的问题，每月确定一个研讨专题召集青年教师、资深教师、相关专家一起进行集中研讨。

2. 课题研究

一是根据问题，确定课题。学校鼓励有研究能力的教师积极申请课题，要求青年教师必须参与课题研究，要求教师以解决教学中实际问题为导向，以提高教学质量为目标开展课题研究。例如语文组以“小学生课内外阅读有效融合的实践研究”为研究方向，数学组以“提高学生计算能力”为研究主题，积极申报省级、市级教研项目。

二是在行动中研究，在行动中成长。小学教师的研究始终与教学工作联系在一起，例如：语文组分为低、中、高三个年级段分别开展研究，低年级结合平时进行的识字活动，开展引导学生阅读《新三字经》、《古诗三百首》等课外文献的研究；中、高年级阅读教学开展读文、析文、赏文、评文学法指导研究。

(三)特色型名师

1. 个性发展

一是确定培养目标。小学教师成为研究型教师已经不容易,能够成为特色型名师的教师毕竟是少数,因此,学校需要对教师的师德、师风、师能等进行综合评价,确定师德高尚、业务能力优异、有强烈的钻研精神和进取精神的教师作为人选,为他们确立更高的专业发展方向和目标——成为在全市、全省乃至全国都有影响的名师。

二是促进个性成长。哈佛大学心理学家加纳德认为人的智力是多元的,每个人身上都不同程度地具有九种智力的潜能,因而每个人的智能结构都是独特的,就像光通过棱镜透射出五颜六色的光谱一样,如果再加上每个人的气质、性格的差异,生活背景、知识背景的不同,学习的方式方法、成长路径自然也就各具特色,具有个性化的特征。因此,每个教师都应该对自己的成长进行反思,对未来的学习进行系统地设计,并探索出一条适合于自己的成长之路;学校帮助能够成长为名师的教师发现特色,支持教师强化自己的特色。

2. 风格生成

个性发展与风格生成是相辅相成的,个性发展是一个长期的过程,是风格生成的前提条件;而风格生成是个性发展的高级阶段和最终目标。对于一个研究型教师而言,研究是一种态度,一种职业生活方式,他(她)不再简单重复别人的劳动,而是在自己的专业世界中创造性地发挥自己的特长和优势,并在此基础上形成自己的教学风格,在此过程中他(她)是将自己的生命融进职业生活来强化自己的教学特色,从而使自己的特色日益鲜明。

三、小学教师校本成长的保障机制

安庆市健康路小学的成功经验和形成了相对稳定的小学教师校本成长模式,说明虽然小学教师文化水平在教师中属于低层次,但是校本研修同样是有效的。当然小学教师校本成长同样需要相应的保障机制。

1. 领导重视是小学教师校本成长的政治保障

对于一所学校来说教师的成长与学生的成长同样重要,建立一支高素质的教师队伍是学校领导的重要任务。领导重视是教师队伍成长的第一要素。一个好校长可以带出一支优秀的教师队伍,一支优秀的教师队伍可以造就一个优秀的学校。

2. 经费投入是小学教师校本成长的经济保障

校本成长虽然投入较低,但是,仍然需要经济保障。教师的外出学习、研究资料的添置、研究场地的提供、网络资源的开发都需要经费的投入,因此,经费的投入是不可或缺的。

3. 校本成长模式的形成是小学教师校本成长的方法保证

教师的校本成长是有规律可循的,它必须遵照一定的环节和程式,按照一定的方法来进行,因此,小学教师的校本成长需要有先进的理论指导,需要切实可行的方法和途径,需要促进教师发展的评价机制等,也就是说小学教师的校本成长必须遵循一定的模式。

4. 教师发展学校、教研组、课题组的建立是小学教师校本成长的组织保证

校本培训活动、校本教研等活动的开展主要依靠学校领导发动,但是必须要有一定的抓手,必须建立相关的组织机构来执行和监督。

5. 文化氛围的形成是小学教师校本成长的环境保证

学校良好的文化氛围是学生也是教师成长的环境，是教师校本成长的外因，是教师成长的条件。

6. 专家引领是小学教师校本成长的方向保证

教师校本成长并非闭门造车，需要高层次的理论指导，需要借助高校教育理论专家和教育研究机构专家的指引，以避免教师成长中的方向误差和低效重复。

7. 鼓励成长晋升机制的形成是小学教师校本成长的制度保证

建立支持教师自主发展的激励制度，形成与教师专业发展热情、态度、成效挂钩的精神与物质鼓励的机制，包括经费支持、评比考核、职务晋升、进修机会的获取等；建立教师发展学校运行制度，教研组、课题组的工作制度，确保教师校本成长常态化。

"三型六阶"校本培训模式注重了教师专业发展的阶段性，采取阶梯式培训步骤，分类开展教师培养，具有很强的实践性和可操作性。但是，学校管理者在进行校本培训时应注重以下三个问题：(1) 要看到教师专业发展的长期性，不能急功近利。教师的专业发展是一个长期的过程，要成为名师还需要更多更长的时间。(2) 要看到教师专业发展的差异性，不能搞一刀切。虽然教师专业发展需要经历"三型六阶"，但是因个人能力、经历的差异，表现出在专业发展上会有不同的需求，每个阶段所需要的时间也不尽相同。(3) 要看到教师专业发展的无限性，不能只培养技能。教学技能培训是有限的、低级的，而教师的专业发展是无限的。教师自主成长意识的形成、可持续发展能力的获得、教学特色和教学风格的形成才是最高的境界和最终的目标。

参考文献

[1] 教育部基础教育司组织. 走进新课程[M]. 北京：北京师范大学出版社，2002.

[2] 叶澜，等. 教师角色与教师发展新探[M]. 北京：教育科学出版社，2001.

[3] 于漪. "师徒帮带"的教师培训模式[J]. 外国教育资料，1993(3).

[4] 林崇德. 教育的智慧[M]. 北京：开明出版社，2000.

合肥地区中小学教师专业化发展情况实证调查

赵 娟[1*] 陈 啸[2**]

(1. 淮北师范大学,安徽 淮北 235000;2. 合肥学院,安徽 合肥 230022)

摘 要:通过对合肥市中小学教师的专业化发展情况的问卷调查,文章指出合肥地区中小学教师专业化发展存在的一些不容忽视的问题,并提出了有效推进区域教师专业化发展的对策建议。

关键词:中小学;教师;专业化发展;调查

基金项目:全国教育科学"十一五"规划教育部重点课题的子课题《有效推进合肥地区教师专业化发展研究与实践》(项目编号:DMA060188)、安徽省教育厅人文社科研究项目《有效推进合肥地区教师专业化发展的制度保障体系及运行机制研究》(项目编号:2009sk248)。

Abstract: In order to through understand the present situation of Hefei area primary and secondary school teachers professional development, then base on that, research and establish a more perfect safeguard system and operational mechanism of teacher professional development, speed up the integration process of teacher education, we had carried on a questionnaire survey to Hefei primary and secondary school teachers which is about the situation of their career specialization. Through the investigation and analysis, we had pointed out that there were some problems that could not be neglected in Hefei primary and secondary school teacher professional development, and proposed the effective countermeasure and the suggestion of improving region teacher professional development.

Key words: Primary and secondary school; Teachers; Professional Development; Survey

为全面了解合肥地区中小学教师专业化发展的现状,研究建立教师专业化发展的制度保障体系及运行机制,加快教师教育一体化进程,我们对合肥市中小学教师的专业化发展情况展开了一次问卷调查。调查采取分层随机抽样,分别在合肥市区、乡镇、农村三个不同区域,选择重点、一般、薄弱三类不同学校,覆盖小学、初中、高中三个学段,共发放教师调查问卷 1540 份,

* 赵娟,淮北师范大学高等教育学硕士研究生。

** 陈啸,合肥学院副院长、教授。

回收问卷1508份，其中进行统计的有效问卷1434份，问卷回收有效率为95.1%。另外，我们还通过对学生的调查，间接反映教师的专业化发展情况。学生问卷调查内容主要包括教师的课堂教学情况、上课方式、教学效果的反馈、师生关系以及学生心目中的好教师。学生问卷调查同样采取上述分层随机抽样，共发放学生调查问卷1236份，有效回收1189份，问卷回收有效率为96.2%。

一、调查结果与分析

1. 教师对"专业化发展"的认识普遍提高

调查显示，58.99%的中小学教师认为"专业化发展是自身不断完善的需要"，37.42%的教师认为"专业化发展是基本教学规律对教师提出的必然要求"。对于"教师专业成长最关键的因素"，79.81%的教师认为要"通过自己的刻苦努力、掌握教科研方法"。调查表明绝大多数教师已经认识到专业化发展的重要意义以及积极掌握教科研方法开展行动研究的重要性。调查还显示，学校领导对教师专业化发展重要性的认识也有很大提高，比如，认为学校领导"普遍比较重视"的比例为53%，"非常重视"的为26.50%，两项合计为79.5%。对于教师所处的专业化发展阶段，20.33%教师认为"处于适应期"，49.73%的教师认为"处于发展前期"，两项合计为70.06%。说明有七成教师开始或已经步入专业化发展时期。但能够依此制定相应专业发展计划的只有56.18%。在回答教师"最希望自己哪方面从师素质提高"的多项选择时，56.57%的教师选择"教学能力"，14.34%是"新课程理念"，但选择"师德教育"的仅为1.07%，选择"班级管理"与"反思能力"的所占比例更是微乎其微，仅分别为0.40%、0.67%。这表明多数教师已经认识到提高综合素质的重要性，但对综合素质的理解不够全面。在工作中遇到困难时，50.27%的教师采用的处理方法是"请业务领导帮助或与同事交流解决"。对于"探究式教学的态度"，43.43%的教师"非常赞同"，49.06%的教师"基本同意"，认为"不可行"的只有1.47%，另有6.03%仍处于迷惘状态。

综合分析以上调查数据可以发现，大多数教师和学校领导已经认识到专业化发展的重要性并能够积极投入到专业化发展活动中，但是对教师专业化发展的认识仍不够全面，理念并不非常清晰，很多教师虽然认识到专业化发展的重要性，但却并没有制定明确的专业发展规划投入实际的行动。特别是还没有充分认识到，教师除了要不断提高自身素质和教学能力之外，还要注重提高专业自主发展能力，完善专业发展理念，培养积极的专业发展精神以及加强专业交流与合作。

2. 教师专业化发展的方法与途径正在发生一些积极的变化

对"教师参加教育科研情况"的调查显示，50.54%的教师"参加过学校确立的教科研项目"，25.61%的教师"参加过省、市、县及以上教科研项目"，9.95%教师虽然"没有参加科研项目，但自行选题、自行研究"，三项合计为86.1%。调查显示，当前教师专业化发展主要采用的形式：52.09%为听课评课，12.55%为优秀教师经验交流会，11.47%为校际课题教研活动，10.53%为教师基本技能大赛，7.56%为教材教法研讨会，5.94%为校际人员交流。另外，教师对学校开展的教研课、观摩课、自学笔记、集体备课等教研活动的参与率分别为36.96%、32.88%、8.97%、21.20%。对上述师训方法，48.53%的教师表示"基本满意"，22.40%的教师表示"满意"，两项合计为70.93%。针对"学校对教师专业化发展情况应采取的考核评价方式”选择，其比例从大到小排序为：教学评比（61.43%）、笔试、按成绩评价（12.45%）、评聘职称时综合评价（10.83%）、论文及答辩（8.93%）。针对教师在专业化发展过程中现代教育技术应用情况的调查显示，74.05%的教师“经常使用计算机”。其中，83.14%的教师“使用计算机来上网查资料，做课件或备课”。对学生的调查也显示，教师上课方式正逐渐由传统教学模式向现代教学模式转换，教学手段也正呈现多样化趋势，并且注重在课堂上引导学生进行自主探究式学习。但是目前这些做法的力度还不够，覆盖面还不是很广，尤其在高中阶段，即使在教学条件及教学水平很高的合肥市属中学，教师的上课方式也仍以传统方式为主，这可能跟高中仍面临高考的压力有关，要完全转变教师上课方式任重道远。

上述调查表明，教师专业化发展活动中采取的方式、方法及途径正在发生一些转变，但传统方法仍占主流。这里并不是否定传统做法的作用及优点，只是在现代教育技术手段广泛应用于教育教学的今天，要加快提高教育教学质量，促进教师专业化发展，教师就应该努力掌握现代教育教学方法，并能合理运用。其次，教师培训的方法与途径也要加快改革的步伐，学校应加强校本培训的规划和管理，将教师培训与教师参加教科研活动有效结合起来，并能采取合理的考核评价方法调动教师积极性，探索更加有效的方式加强校内教师之间以及校际间的交流与合作，真正有效促进教师专业化发展。

3. 教师专业化发展取得初步成果，教学质量有所提升

调查显示，63.05%的教师表示“通过培训，自身的专业素质有所提高”；21.69%的教师表示“有较大提高”；也有15.26%的教师表示“收获不大”。教师“对目前自己讲授的课程能熟练掌握并轻松驾驭”的有57.53%；而“感到有难度，经过努力才能完成”的占39.76%；“感到吃力，经常完不成进度”的有2.71%。所授课程在市、学校等历次考核中“平均为上等水平”的有33.10%，“平均处于中等水平”的有60.16%，“平均水平为及格”的有6.59%，0.14%的“处于不及格水平”。另有数据显示，60.95%的教师“对自己所教专业和从事的工作非常喜欢，信心十足”；21.09%的教师“将从事的工作视为谋生手段，谈不上喜不喜欢”；“对自己工作表示不满意，认为工作压力大”的有17.01%；还有0.95%的教师表示“非常厌倦从事的工作，有机会就跳槽”。这表明，多数教师的专业精神状态较好，少数教师的专业精神状态比较消极。对中小学教师如何选择学科教学内容的调查表明，66.22%的教师会“结合教材、学生、社会对学科课程的要求”，还有33.78%的教师是“根据教材，面向考试，传授系统的学科知识”。调查显示，教师课堂教学效果总体不错，受到学生欢迎。但不难发现初中与小学相比有较为明显的差距。例如，教师布置的作业对学生是否更有吸引力的调查中，回答“是”的比例，小学生为82.89%，初中生为54.16%。这跟初中教学内容更复杂、教学任务更重有一定关系。除此之外，初中教师应该进行自我反思，对课堂教学进行全面、深入分析，找到差距产生的根源，以便及时补救。师生关系方面的调查表明，中小学师生关系正得到一定的改善，教师的课堂教学已经摆脱了完全“一言堂”的传统模式，不过教师的成长空间仍然很大，师生关系的不民主、不平等还是存在的，师生双方还没有达成全方位的有效互动。比如，只有38.07%的高中理科生回答上化学课时，自己有了更多参与课堂演示实验的机会；“教师是否向你们征求过对课堂教学的意见”的肯定回答比例，小学生为69.33%，初中生为71.75%，高中生为78.97%。通过调查反馈，学生心目中好老师的样子大体可以描述为：仪表良好，和蔼可亲；知识渊博，兴趣广泛；公正，民主，宽容；有幽默感；有耐心，认真负责；教学能力高，教学质量好。

综合分析以上调查结果表明，当前合肥地区中小学教师课堂教学情况总体不错，较之以前

有一定进步,也在一定程度上反映了教师自身素质和能力有所提升。但是教师的专业化发展仍然存在一些问题,教师进一步提升的空间还很大。

二、教师专业化发展存在的主要问题

1. 专业化发展的认识还不够深入、理念模糊

调查显示,学校领导对教师专业化发展"不太重视"及"很不重视"的比例分别为 17.7%、2.8%。说明仍然有少数学校领导对教师专业化发展的认识还不到位,行动迟缓,以学校工作繁忙、任务繁重、教师工作量较大等为理由,使学校促进教师专业化发展的工作处于停滞状态;调查还显示,部分教师对专业化发展进程中需要学校的支持和保障并与同伴合作的认识还不足。比如,只有 12.47%的教师认为"(教师的专业化成长)需要学校领导重视和关心",而选择"(需要)同行帮助"的只有 5.83%;甚至有 3.59%的教师认为是"评职称的需要"或表示"没想过这个问题"。有 18.82%的教师认为自己已经"处于发展后期",甚至有 11.13%的教师认为"处于创造期",这表明部分教师对"教师的专业化是不断发展的过程"这个概念认识不清,并不真正了解自身所处的专业化发展阶段,因此,有 45%左右的教师"没有制定相应的专业发展计划",等等。

2. 专业化发展的路径还不够合理、方法欠佳

调查显示,对教师传统的以课堂授课为主的三项培训形式的满意度普遍不高:专家讲座(报告)型(31.25%)、名师课堂(实录)型(18.07%)、同行介绍经验、共同研讨型(16.30%)。对学校目前开展校本培训所采取的三项保障条件认同度也不高:培训规划和管理(25.73%)、培训经费(22.41%)、培训课程和教材(15.35%)。对上述师训方法表示"不太满意"的有 24.27%,"很不满意"的有 4.80%,两项合计为 29.07%。另外,有些教师不善于运用现代教育技术进行教育教学及科研,专业化发展步伐缓慢。对"现代教学媒体"的应用调查显示,只有 12.52%的教师"很熟练地掌握,并且上课经常使用",26.78%的教师"能熟练掌握,但不常用",44.41%的教师"掌握程度一般,有时用",还有 16.29%的教师"掌握程度不熟练,且几乎不用"。有 21.48%的教师上课经常使用的教学手段还是"挂图"。在回答"教师日常获取教学资源的途径是什么?"选题时,只有 37.97%的教师选择"计算机网络",而 45.81%的教师选择"传统方式——教学参考书",另有 7.30%教师选择"图书馆(资料室)",8.92%的教师选择"报刊等新闻媒体",可见绝大多数教师都不习惯或甚至不会利用现代技术获取教学资源。更有 10.73%的教师使用计算机"主要上网看新闻",6.14% 的教师"聊天、玩游戏或随便浏览网站"。两项合计比例高达 16.87%。

3. 教师之间的交流还不够广泛、合作较少

调查显示,教师采取的课题教研还不能做到全员覆盖,校际之间的交流也很不够。比如,有 13.90%的教师表示"既没有参加过任何教科研项目,也没有自行开展过研究"。只有 11.47%的学校开展过"校际课题教研活动";参加过"校际人员交流"的教师更少,比例仅为 5.94%,等等。以上调查结果表明,由于缺少组织等多种原因,在教师专业化发展进程中,多是学校的个体行动,未能很好地建立起研究共同体,缺少相互之间的学习、借鉴和交流,"成果共享"机制尚未形成。另外,学校内部教师与领导、同事之间的交流与合作仍然不足。实践证明,没有充分有效的教学合作,将不利于教师的专业化发展。少数科研能力不强的学校缺乏专家

的指导，也走了不少弯路。调查中，一线教师们普遍反映应加强对教师专业化发展的理论指导，不能简单用新课改的培训代替教育科研的培训，等等。

三、有效推进区域教师专业化发展的行动策略建议

教师的职业专门化已经成为当今国际教师教育的一个重要发展方向。其核心价值导向就是使教师从过去满足于从前辈经验或自己的积累中吸取灵感的“教书匠”，转变成为现代具有反思能力的专家型的“教学大师”。这实际上就是要求教师走上一条理论—实践—反思—再实践—再反思的专业化发展之路。而实践证明，以课题研究为载体，采用行动研究的基本方法，在专家引领、行政推动下，循序渐进，不断发展，是教师专业化发展的最佳路径之一。按照这一思路，我们提出有效推进区域教师专业化发展的行动策略。

1. 依靠专家引领，讲究策略，保障教师专业化发展的科学性

有效推进教师专业化发展，专家引领至关重要。为确保专家指导的实效性，一要逐步建立专家指导和引领的网络体系，即建立以专家指导组为核心、课题研究组（学校）为纽带的教师专业发展共同体。二要讲究指导的策略。专家在教师专业化发展中的作用，主要体现在理念、思路与方法三个层面。因此，首先要讲究指导的“三层次”：一是教育思想、教育观念的指导；二是教育实践与反思方法与策略的指导；三是针对教育教学中实际问题进行的指导。其次要讲究过好“三关”即发展初期的“开题关”、发展中期的“瓶颈关”和发展后期的“结题关”。以保证教师专业化发展沿着科学的轨道前行。

2. 加强行政推进，分层管理，增强教师专业化发展的有效性

由于教师专业化发展涉及面广，时间跨度较长，因此只有依靠“行政推动”，使教师的专业化发展和日常的教育教学紧密结合起来，才能做到健康、可持续。所谓“行政推动”就是要探索建立教师专业化发展的制度保障体系及运行机制。对于一个区域来说，其关键要素是以“宏观统领”为着力点，以“分层管理”为落脚点，即按照市、县、学校三级，以市教育行政管理部门为宏观统领，其总揽全局，抓宏观组织、指导、督查和验收；以各县区教育行政部门为承上启下，其分工负责，抓具体的落实、协调、督促和指导；以各学校为基本单元，负责具体开展教育教学研究，确保教师专业化发展所需的一切保障条件，使区域的教师专业化发展整体有效推进。

3. 深入研究校情，明确方向，确保教师专业化发展的针对性

教师的专业化发展，不仅是教师群体的发展，更是教师个体的发展，归根结底是教师在解决教学实践问题的过程中不断得到发展。因此，一要深入分析学校现状及所面临的问题，明确学校层面教师专业化发展的方向；二要引导教师，深入分析并提出自身所面临并迫切需要解决的问题；三要考虑学校的层次、规模、教师的科研能力等客观条件，等等。对于规模较大的学校，还可再细分校内的若干课题研究小组，或根据学科、年级等不同纬度来设计和精选校内子课题，并将课题研究与常规的校本培训、教研活动有机整合，做到全员参与，人人受益。

4. 开展校际合作，联手高校，促进教师专业化发展效益最大化

进入21世纪以来，教师专业化发展日益具有开放性特征。因此，建立校际研究共同体，开展广泛的学校间交流与合作，是教师互助学习、分享经验、共同发展的成功模式。尤其对于城市薄弱学校、农村偏远学校而言，与城市重点学校结成对子，开展“捆绑”帮扶，更是快速提升教学水平，促进教育均衡，实现教育公平的行之有效的好办法。另外，中小学与地方高校“联手”，

加强深度合作,也是教师专业化发展的有效途径。因为这种合作不仅是“人力”的合作,更是“理论与实践”的结合。高校的专家学者指导广大中小学教师,将教学实践与各种专业知识联系起来,在解决教学的实际问题中,通过实践总结和提炼,最终上升到理论。这种理论来自于鲜活的教学一线,不仅使教师更易接受,而且增强了教师的自信心,提高了教师自我更新意识,更好推进自身专业化发展。高校学者在双向互动中,不仅把理论应用于实践,而且在实践中又不断丰富理论,其收获自不待言。

5. 采取强力措施,强行入轨,强力推动教师的专业化成长

教师的专业化发展总体呈现良性态势。但调查显示,始终存在“二八”现象,即总有 20% 的教师行动迟缓甚至原地不动。为有效解决这个问题,可采取一些“强力”措施,仍然原地不动的教师“强行入轨”。比如,成立研究小组,建立“教师专业成长档案袋”,建设教师专业化发展研究网站和个人网页,定期开展研究成果的提炼和交流,制定教师专业化发展的考核评价体系,把教师专业化发展纳入绩效考核,等等。

总之,通过有效的行动策略,在学校层面,更好地营造浓厚的学习氛围,丰富校园文化,优化学校资源,提高学校整体的办学水平;对教师个人而言,使教师逐步树立清晰的专业化发展理念,激发专业化发展内需,制定明确合理的专业化发展规划,提高专业技能,优化专业品质,促进有效教学。教师专业化发展的根本目的是实现学校的有效发展,从而带动和引领学生实现全面发展。

参考文献

[1] 叶澜,等. 教师角色与教师发展新探[M]. 北京:教育科学出版社,2001.
[2] 吴卫东. 教师专业发展与培训[M]. 杭州:浙江大学出版社,2005.
[3] 王长纯. 教师专业化发展:教师的重新发现[J]. 教育研究,2001(11).
[4] 傅树京. PDS 与 TDS:教师专业发展的有效途径[J]. 教师教育研究,2004(11).

关于综合型教师及其培养机制的研究

苏春景*

（鲁东大学，山东　烟台　264025）

与教育部2001年6月颁布的《基础教育课程改革纲要（试行）》相配套的新课程与新教材，已于2005年在全国范围内推广应用。这是建国以来中国教育史上里程碑式的改革，虽然在具体的实施过程中引起了不同的看法，但它在教育理念上确实引发了一系列的重大变化。注重课程的综合性与设置综合实践是新课程改革的一大亮点。基于综合性的课程标准与教材版本，眼下已基本构建起来。但新课程的实施，迫切需要一大批适应新课程标准的"综合型"教师。调查表明，尽管新课改已进行了多年，但在教学实践与课堂教学中，占据统治地位的仍然是"学科型"教师。学生接受的是分科的机械灌输或强化训练模式，学生很少接触国家规定学科以外的东西，造成知识面狭窄，学生既缺乏浓厚的人文素养，又欠缺必备的科学精神；学生获得的是一大堆供考试用的死记硬背的知识，而缺乏渗透智慧的灵性与悟性。当代中国教学实践的残酷现实，呼唤以综合性课程为核心的育人环境，而当务之急是进行"学科型"教师向"综合型"教师转变的机制研究，为课程改革提供强有力的人力资源支持。

"学科型"教师指只能教授某一门学科或只关注本学科自身知识体系的教师，属传统课程的产物；"综合型"教师指不仅可以教授多门学科而且可以胜任综合学科（如品德与社会、历史与社会、科学等），或在各科教学中有机渗透研究性学习、社会实践活动的教师，属新课程改革的产物。作者认为，"学科型"教师转型为"综合型"教师是当前课程改革顺利实施的重要前提。这就要强化"学科型"教师转型为"综合型"教师的机制的研究。

一、综合课程的设置呼唤"综合型"教师

新课程标准明确要求把"综合性"作为课程设置的基本原则之一。它体现为三个方面：

1. 突出学科的综合性

作为一门学科，应联系儿童经验和生活实际；针对不同学科，应提倡彼此关联，相互补充。这就要重视社会生活和学生经验的整合，加强各学科之间的相互渗透。对高中生而言，要有宽厚的综合知识，应有一定的选修课学分。当前的高中新课程具有极强的综合性，它把课程分为基础课程和拓展课程，基础课程分语言与文学、人文与社会、体育与健康等8个学习领域，分60个大模块若干小模块，学生可以自己选择学习内容、难度，每个学习领域都必须获得一定学分。学生高中阶段共88个学分，约有20个学分必修，其余选修。这就为学生的进一步发展打

* 苏春景，鲁东大学教育科学学院院长，教授。

下了良好的基础。对大学生而言,要硬性要求文科专业必须选学理科课程,理科专业必须选学文科课程。早在20世纪40年代,美国麻省理工大学,就设立了文化科学艺术学院。新世纪的大学更是呈现出学科综合化的趋势。目前我国的清华大学也在加强建设人文社会科学,因为一流人才不仅包括各类专门人才,也包括各类综合性人才,而文科对培养人才具有重要的作用。当代高校的课程改革都重视"通才教育",如淡化专业的主辅修制、双学位制、学分制等,旨在改变学科型、专业型人才。大学之大,就在于大学能为学生提供包罗万象的文化,使大学生了解古今中外的历史、文学、艺术、哲学和科学,欣赏人类丰富多彩的文化的结晶,开阔大学生的视野。

2. 设置综合课程

在新的基础教育课程结构中,综合课程已经成为学校课程体系中的重要组成部分。新课程标准明确规定,小学阶段以综合课程为主,初中阶段设置分科与综合相结合的课程,高中以分科课程为主(但强化了基础课程,并要求有60多个学分的选修课程)。在"综合型"的课程计划中,原有的物理、化学和生物被整合为科学,历史、地理被整合为历史与社会,美术、音乐被整合为艺术,还有品德与生活、品德与社会。这是符合科学发展规律的。爱迪生没有自己的学科专业,却有世界上最多的发明;爱因斯坦既是一个杰出的物理家,又是一个优秀的小提琴演奏家;十九世纪末二十世纪初的大物理学家都具有很高的音乐素养;大数学家华罗庚、苏步青都是热情洋溢的诗人。通才教育背景下的综合课程观应成为教育工作者的永恒追求。

3. 增设综合实践活动

综合实践活动属非学科领域,是一门密切联系社会实际与学生生活实践的课程。它是基于学习者的直接经验,密切联系学生自身生活和社会生活,体现对知识的综合运用的实践性课程。其内容包括:信息技术教育、研究性学习、社区服务与社会实践、劳动与技术教育等。与《纲要(试行)》配套出台的《义务教育课程设计及比例》明确规定,综合实践活动课程的实质是综合性学习,综合性学习强调不同学科和内容的联系与综合,强调学科知识与学生自身学习经验的整合,它的主要目标是培养学生的综合性能力。

要想完成以上三方面的任务,必须尽快造就一大批"综合型"教师。

二、当代所谓优秀的特级教师大多为"学科型"教师

长期以来,我们培养了一大批优秀的语文、数学、外语、物理、化学、历史等学科型的特级教师,他们在学科教学方面经验丰富,又有高超的教学艺术与风格,但让他们承担综合课程或以"整合性"观点突出学科的综合性,真正培养学生的综合性能力,还是一个难度较大的问题。他们中的相当一部分人会感到力不从心。学生需要的,教师不讲,或者无能为力去讲;学生不需要的,讲得太多。著名优秀教师李镇西曾对学生进行这样一个调查:"除了学习之外,目前你还有哪些最关心的问题得不到解答?"结果47名学生共提了106个问题,内容涉及人际关系、心理保健、性知识教育、宗教信仰、职业选择、国际政治、自我评价、社会风气、男女感情、人格塑造、哲学流派、环境保护、生与死等方面,而这些几乎全是学校教育内容的空白。(李镇西:《爱心与教育》,四川少年儿童出版社,1998年7月第1版,第218页。)

现实呼唤综合课程教师的到来。正如有学者提出,中国课程的最大问题不是"难"、"繁"、"旧"等,而是缺乏内在的关联和结构,由于现在的教材编写少有一流科学家的参与,导致教材

内容缺乏对学科发展的整体性把握和理解，更谈不上相关学科的协调。（吴刚:《迈向新千年的课程改革》,《全球教育展望》,2002 年第 10 期。）因此，集中优势兵力，精选知名的一专多能的科学家参与教材编写，将加速综合性教学的到来。如何培养胜任综合课程的教师更是我们从未遇到的工作。可以说，尽快造就一大批合格的综合课程教师与“综合型”教师，是新课程改革的重大课题。

三、“综合型”教师的培养是一个长期的系统工程

建国以来，我国一直沿用学科课程的模式，没有“综合型”教师产生的土壤。造就一大批综合型教师必须从根本上抓起，在一个相当长的时间内逐渐培植综合型教师产生的土壤。

（一）将通才教育观落到实处

我国古代思想家主张培养“博学鸿儒”，古希腊、罗马思想家提倡“博雅教育”，曾创造古代教育的辉煌。夸美纽斯的“泛智教育”、纽曼的“自由教育”、洪堡的“全面教育”、蔡元培的“文理兼习”、美国的“哈佛报告”等，都曾在教育史上产生广泛的影响。日本教育界从“博中取胜”的实践中，积极呼吁“通识教育”，强调“没有综合化，就不会产生伟大的文化和伟大的人物”，教育就是要培养“理想的在世界上通用的日本人”。当前相当一部分大学教师把功夫放在培养学生的实用技能上，有的大学生则把精力全部放在各种证书的获得上，以迎合社会的需求，谋取好的职业。这是一种十分短浅的行为，因为“学生在大学期间的学习，更多的是学习理论，打好知识基础，学会学习的方法和科学的思维方式，培养自己不断吸纳新知识的能力；要求他们什么都会干，要求他们走出校门就能挑大梁，这不但是不切实际的，也是不可能的”。（中国人民大学校长纪宝成:大学应教给学生什么，《中国青年报》2002 年 4 月 6 日。）为此，要采取多种形式营造阅读经典名著、学习元典文化的氛围，扩大知识面。元典文化尤其是中国古代的六艺、四书、五经等，古希腊、罗马思想家的著作等，大都是百科全书式的知识，囊括了多种多样的学科。经常接触元典文化，会自然而然地形成自身的综合知识。

（二）改革传统模式，开辟新的课程资源

从宏观上讲，改变由国家单一办学的模式，采用多种形式办学，如国家多部门的联合办学、高校间的联合办学、跨越国界的联合办学、教育部门和工矿企业的联合办学等，可为复合型、综合型人才的培养提供许多实质性的内容。从微观上讲，可推广查有梁同志提出的“整体—融合”教育模式。（查有梁,《“整体—融合”教育模式建构》,《课程教材教法》,2000 年第 7 期。）

（三）建构一体化的综合性教学体制

改变学科教学的传统模式，建议尽快落实“小学以综合课程为主，高中取消文理分科，大学低年级不分专业”的构想。

采取各种措施，鼓励高层次、高素质教师到中小学任教。解放前，许多国外留学的学有所成者以及作家、科学家都在中小学校当过教师。

适当推广北大等高校的“培养大师计划”、华东师范大学教科院的“本、硕、博连读试点”。淡化师范教育与综合大学的界限，逐步建立“综合大学＋师范教育”的教师培养机制；师范大学

可尝试进行“4＋2”模式，让一部分大学筛选部分学生在完成第四年专业学习后，免试进入教育学院进行专业化学习后获得硕士学位。通过“4＋2”模式毕业的学生，将会成为专业知识与教育技能都非常到位的复合型、研究型和有后劲的教师。

四、关于“综合型”教师培养的建议

（一）教师要集师范性与学术性于一身

中国现代史上，有许多文化名人如老舍、胡适、闻一多、蔡元培等，既在自己的研究领域有很高的成就，又都在学校里担任过教师，以自己的学识、风范与人格赢得学生的爱戴。作为一名综合型教师，固然要掌握一定的教育理论，热爱教师这一职业，创造性地把教育理论知识运用到教学实践中去。但更要强调，要有较强的学科拓展能力，在现有的基础上，以研究的方式去探究本学科领域中的未知，进而起到推动学科知识发展的作用。当代社会是一个飞速发展的社会，新成果、新发明层出不穷，利用多种渠道丰富教师的科学素养和人文精神，是一个非常重要的任务。

（二）构建学科互补机制，从单独性教学转轨为协作性教学

“学科性”教师终身教授某一门学科，经过潜心钻研，也可以取得明显的教学效果。综合课程或综合实践活动所设计的主体内容具有跨学科性、复杂性，有时学生选择的研究课题往往是教师从未接触到的。在这种情况下，教师之间的协作、研究与交流、就显得十分必要。为解决难度较大的课题，我们认为风马牛不相及的两个学科的教师，可以同堂上课。如讲一首诗，语文教师从文字的阅读上引导，美术教师则从图画欣赏的角度展示。如讲“声音”，物理教师从科学的角度探讨，音乐教师从艺术的角度讲解。这是对传统教学模式的一场革命。

（三）充分发挥教师集体的教育作用

组织不同学科的教师经常开展集体备课，深入了解横向学科、相关学科的基本结构，学习其他学科教师的思维方式。为不同学科的教师创造交流的机会。不仅包括学科内容的交流，更重要的是思维模式和研究方法与手段的交流。如，原有的文科教师应着重学习统计、测量和实验的方法；原有的理科教师要掌握文献分析方法、质的研究方法。

（四）提高教师的教学设计的综合能力

“学科型”教师一般是借助教学大纲的要求、教科书的具体内容以及教学参考书的建议提示等，设计板书，写出教案，追求有逻辑、有步骤地实施教学。综合课程尤其是综合实践活动的课题，多为学生自由选择，具有差异性、多样性和复杂性，没有固定的学习内容；综合实践活动的目标具有生成性的特点。教学过程的自由度较大。这就要求教师具有高超的教学设计能力。一般来讲，教师应考虑以下几个方面：

(1) 确定学生感兴趣的主题，尽可能多地掌握该主题的知识与背景材料。

(2) 通过不同途径，拓宽课程资源，如其他学科的教师与家长、自然景观与公共设施、文献资料与网络媒体等。

(3) 组织学生开展有教育性质的各种活动，让学生分析问题、提出假设、解决问题。

(4) 考虑协作学习的具体措施。

(5) 制作能够探索学生长期学习轨迹的评价工具。

(五) 改革与完善当前的“中小学骨干教师培训工程”

为使新课程标准顺利施行，每位教师应根据自身的条件，制定切实可行的进修与学习计划。我国已花费大量的人力、物力、财力开展国家级、省级教师培训。但绝大部分仍然是采取单科课程的思维模式，很少有进行综合课程的培训，这没有抓住新课程改革的真谛，培训的结果还是脱离不了原有的“学科模式”。这就要加快对“品德与生活”、“品德与社会”、“科学”、“艺术”等国家规定的综合学科课程教师的培养与培训，加强对教授单一学科教师的拓展性训练。范围应包括本学科的现代教育理念、现代教育教学内容、现代教学方法与手段。

(六) 构建开放性教师生长机制

综合课程具有开放性的特点，要给教师一定的“观光旅游”时间，使他们不仅读万卷书，而且行万里路，从寂静的书斋走向沸腾的社会。真正了解由个人、社会与自然组成的多样化的世界，不断洞察由科学、道德与艺术构成的多元化的文化。这样的教师，才能培养一流的人才。首先，可以利用寒暑假参观我国的一流大学，感受名校的文化特色。如北京大学的爱国传统，清华大学的求实精神，天津大学对实践能力的重视，南开大学对人文精神的关注等。其次，可分期分批组织教师访问我国有特色的中小学。如辽宁盘锦中学的自学文化氛围，江苏洋思中学的课堂教学模式，山东杜朗口中学的课堂教学改革，民办学校的别具一格的创意等。还可以利用节假日到祖国的名山大川远足旅行。领略泰山之雄伟、华山之险峻、雁荡之巧石、峨眉之清凉、衡岳之云烟……体验曲径通幽处的岳麓书院、白鹿洞书院、嵩阳书院之旧址的学术气息……

(七) 弘扬“探究性”教学

综合课程具有探究性。组织学生“研究性学习”，教师自身首先应成为一个合格的研究者。这就要求教师根据教育改革的发展趋势和所在学校的具体情况，选择适合自身特点的课题研究。可以对所教学科的某一问题进行纵深研究，可以进行教育教学改革尤其是课堂教学模式的研究。因此，一方面教师要根据教育发展的需要，积极申报各级部门的课题立项。另一方面，教师要根据自己的研究兴趣确定自己的研究意向。承担或参与一定的课题研究，对加快“学科型”教师向“综合型”教师的转变具有“催化剂”的作用。因为每一个课题的研究，都需要教师综合运用各门学科的知识与技能，更需要深厚的教育素养。

(八) 构建全方位、立体化的交流机制

积极创造条件，开展“走出去，请进来”活动。给教师一定的“学术休假”时间(多读书、多思考问题)，一定的参加学术会议时间(了解同行的研究成果、了解学科的前沿动态)；利用各种渠道，邀请国内外的专家学者到学校为师生作学术报告。利用网络与全世界的同行专家建立合作联系。

(九)开设特色课程

加快培养指导“辩论课”等包含各学科知识课程的教师。指导此类课程,客观上要求教师具备宽广的知识面,刺激他们精通自然科学、社会科学以及思维科学等跨界学科,还要求掌握该学科的研究方法。经常与思维敏捷、表达流利的学生打交道的同时,也有助于自身综合知识水平的提高。

(十)尽快提高小学教师的素质要求

我国的《基础教育课程改革纲要(试行)》明确规定,小学以综合课程为主,因此培养综合教师应从小学教师入手。解放前,许多小学教师多才多艺,具有精深渊博的知识,培养出了许多高质量的小学生。美国对小学教师提出了很高的要求,小学教师必须拥有学士学位,现在很多州明文规定,新的小学教师必须是硕士研究生。除学历达标外,还要具有学识丰富、诚实正直、身体健康等过硬的素质,才有资格应聘教师。如教师在课堂上能够轻松地利用各种现代化的软件进行辅助教学,让学生通过计算机、电视机、监听录音获得书本以外的大量的信息。(李芒,《论综合实践活动课程与教师的教学能力》,《教育研究》,2002 年第 3 期。)

我国著名的小学教学教学法专家,尝试教学理论创立者邱学华先生一生致力于教学实验,尤其把培养高素质的教师作为重任。他曾提出中国学校的办学宗旨应体现民族化、国际化、人文化的特色,要求教师实施“六个一工程”,即写一手漂亮的中国字,练一套中国功夫,熟悉一种中国乐曲,演奏一种民族乐器,学会一种民间工艺,有一颗诚挚的中国心。这对综合型教师的培养具有重要的启示。

"3+2+3"本科学历小学教师培养模式研究

葛明荣*

(鲁东大学,山东 烟台 264025)

摘 要:培养本科学历的小学教师是社会经济和教育发展的必然要求。"3+2+3"本科学历小学教师培养模式把中师丰富的小学教师培养经验和高师的优秀师资、先进设备以及浓厚的学术气氛有机结合起来,培养出来的小学教师职业角色明确、职业技能扎实、科研能力较强、综合素质较高,是适应基础教育改革发展需要的新一代小学教师培养模式。

关键词:"3+2+3"模式;本科学历;小学教师;培养模式

Study of "3 + 2 + 3" Model of Training Primary School Teachers with College-level Education

Ge Ming-rong

(Ludong university, Yantai 264025, China)

Abstract: The training of primary school teachers with College-level education is a logical requirement of social economy and educational development. "3+2+3" model is to expose experienced primary school teachers of normal school education to normal outstanding teachers of higher education, advanced equipment and strong academic atmosphere, so that primary school teachers trained in specific job roles will have professional skills, good research capacity, and integrated high-qualities, which is a new generation of primary school teacher training model adapt to fundamental education reform and development.

Key words: "3+2+3"model; College-level education; primary school teachers; training model

* 葛明荣,山东青岛人,鲁东大学教育科学学院副教授。

中等师范学校改制以后，在中国山东省出现了“3＋2＋3”本科学历小学教师培养模式，即通过三年中专教育、两年大专教育、三年专升本教育培养小学教师的模式。中国山东省鲁东大学一直负责该模式专升本阶段的教育任务，学生毕业后直接输送到全省各地区小学教师队伍中，到目前为止已经有四届毕业生。根据初步调查，这部分经过八年小学教师教育的本科学生在教学、管理等岗位上大部分成绩突出，能够出色承担起小学教育中各种岗位的工作，受到用人单位的好评。对该模式的优缺点进行研究探讨，对于培养优秀的本科学历小学教师无疑具有重要的现实意义。

一、问题的提出

（一）基本概念的界定

1. 小学教师

小学教师是一种专门的职业，即专门从事小学教育工作的专业人员（professional）。有专门的专业范围——小学教育；有特定的服务对象——处于儿童期的小学生；必须掌握专门的知识技能——从事小学教育必备的教育学、心理学知识，学科基础知识以及较高的教育教学技巧，一定的音体美技能等；有公认的伦理规范——强烈的事业心、责任心，善待孩子，以及活泼开朗、机智耐心等专业个性品质。[1]小学教师的培养有其特定的模式。

2. 培养模式

所谓培养模式，一般认为是为实现培养目标而采取的培养过程的构造样式和运行方式，它主要包括培养目标、课程设置、教学设计和教育方法等构成要素。[2]本科学历层次小学教师的培养模式不是唯一的，而是可变和多样的，有风格或特征较为稳定的基本范型。

（二）当前中国小学教师的培养模式

中国小学教师的培养正逐步由高等专科师范院校培养向大学本科层次的培养过渡，本科层次的小学教育专业在中国已有近10年的历史，纵观目前对于本科学历小学教师培养模式的探索和研究，主要有以下几种模式：“3＋4”模式、“5＋2”模式、“3＋3＋2”模式、“3＋2＋3”模式等。

1. “3＋4”培养模式主要有两种：一种是学生在中等师范学校学习三年后参加选拔考试，在高等师范院校进一步接受四年本科教育的培养模式，这种模式已经逐渐被取消。另一种是招收高中毕业生，通过高考选拔学生，由普通高等师范院校专门的教育学院培养小学师资的小学教育本科专业的培养模式，目前对于后一种模式的研究居多。

2. “5＋2”培养模式即学生在初中毕业后连续攻读五年的小学教育专科，成绩合格，颁发大专学历，学生可直接参加工作，也可参加教育部门统一组织的本科入学考试，进入高等师范本科院校进一步深造两年，获得本科学历。[3]有人认为“5＋2”培养模式是培养本科学历小学教师的有效模式：选择初中毕业生的“5＋2”培养模式与高中起点四年制培养模式相比具有明显的优势，它把中等师范院校和高等师范院校的各种优势资源有机结合，培养出的小学教师综合素质较高。[4]

3. “3+3+2”培养模式是高中毕业后，接受3年高等师范专科学院的教育，再参加考试进入高等师范本科学校进行2年的学习，获得本科学历。

4. “3+2+3”培养模式是学生先接受三年的中师教育，再进入高等师范专科学校进行两年深造，然后通过考试进入高等师范本科院校学习三年。这种培养模式有学者称之为“5+3”培养模式，这也是本文所研究的内容。

（三）小学教师培养模式研究的意义

第一，理论的意义，加强小学教师培养模式的研究可以进一步改革和完善小学教师专业化培养机制，使中国的师范教育在改革小学教师培养课程结构上更趋于合理化，有利于建立小学教师终身学习的机制。

第二，实践的意义，小学教师担负着培养祖国未来的重担，责任重大。加强小学教师培养模式的研究可以使大学层次的小学教师的培养在培养目标、课程设置上更能理性化、合理化，培养的小学教师更能符合时代的要求，在道德素养、专业素养和人格魅力方面更能体现一名现代教师的要求。

（四）小学教师培养模式研究的现状

目前在中国有不少学者对本科层次小学教师培养进行了研究。黄正平同志在2008年第1期《教师教育研究》发表论文“‘5+2’：培养本科学历小学教师的有效模式”，阐述了江苏省“5+2”培养本科学历小学教师模式的形成，分析了该模式的比较优势，提出了该模式的策略建议。王智秋教授在2007年第5期《教育研究》发表论文“小学教育专业人才培养模式的研究与探索”，提出了“综合培养、发展专长、注重研究、全程实践”的小学教师培养模式。牛晓东同志在2007年第1期《濮阳职业技术学院学报》发表论文“本科小学教育专业培养模式探析”，张巧文同志在2006年第9期《教育探索》发表论文“对小学教育本科专业教师培养理念的思考”，黄伟娣同志在2005年第2期《课程·教材·教法》发表论文“小学教育本科专业课程方案比较研究”，惠中同志主编的2003年上海科技教育出版社出版的《教师教育新视野——本科学历小学教师培养模式初探》等，从本科学历小学教师的培养理念、培养目标、课程设置、培养模式等方面进行了研究与探讨。以上文献大多阐述的是四年本科学制小学教师的培养，针对专科升本科小学教师培养的研究相对不多，黄正平同志阐述的“5+2”模式，实际上是“3+2+2”模式，即：3年中专教育、2年大专教育、2年专升本教育，本课题所研究的是3年专升本教育，就笔者所收集到的资料来看，目前国内还没有关于“3+2+3”本科学历小学教师培养模式的研究和调查。

二、“3+2+3”本科学历小学教师培养模式的形成

“3+2+3”本科学历小学教师培养模式，是指学生在初中毕业后接受三年的中师教育，再进入高等师范院校进行两年专科深造，然后通过考试进入高等师范本科院校学习三年。这一模式的开始是培养五年一贯制(3+2)专科学历小学教师。

五年一贯制专科是指在初中教育的基础上施行的将中等师范的综合性教育与专科阶段的分科教育融为一体的专科教育。在中国，招收初中毕业生、培养五年一贯制专科学历小学教

师，是1984年从江苏省南通师范学校开始的。在教师专业化发展和基础教育课程改革的背景下，1995年2月，国家教委师范司在总结10年探索的基础上，制定了《大学专科程度小学教师培养课程方案》，并颁布全国试行。教育模式是"学制五年，在全面发展的基础上分科"。要求培养"具有从事小学多学科教学的知识、技能和基本能力"的教师。课程设置实行全面发展的综合性教育与一门学科基本达到大专程度的专业定向教育相结合。山东省是较早开设小学教师专科培养试验的省份之一，1999年全省统一将原先的中等师范学校通过与其它院校合并(与高等师范院校合并培养专科学段的学生或与其它职业学校合并建立职业技术学院等)、升级成师范专科学校等途径完成了"五年一贯制专科"改革。2002年9月，教育部在《关于加强专科以上学历小学教师培养工作的几点意见》中指出："招收初中毕业生，实行'五年一贯制'专科教育，有利于小学教师职业道德、知识、能力和素质的综合培养，有利于提高教师专业化水平，是当前我国培养专科学历小学教师的重要补充。"

在培养五年一贯制(3+2)专科学历层次的小学教师的基础上，通过专升本考试进一步深造三年的"3+2+3"培养模式是高等教育大众化的必然要求，是小学教育专业与新课程改革相结合的必然产物，同时能较好地满足五年一贯制师范毕业生继续深造、全面提高自身素质的需要。1997年，根据国家教育部提出的在师范教育体系格局调整中，将小学教育专业纳入普通高等教育的范畴，成立"培养本专科学历小学教师专业建设研究"课题组，经过两年多的努力，完成了"面向21世纪本、专科学历小学教师专业建设研究"等课题。1999年，中国国家教育部正式批准南京师范大学等4所本科师范院校作为首批正式设置"小学教育"本科专业的高校。从此，中国小学教师的培养不仅在培养层次上，而且在培养机构上都真正纳入了高等教育体系与本科教育专业范畴，中国大陆地区的教师培养体制也由三级师范培养体制逐步走向二级师范培养体制乃至一级培养体制。山东省在2003年允许应届的小学教育专科毕业生参加专升本考试，升入高等师范本科院校接受三年本科教育。2004年山东省淄博师范学校升格为淄博师范专科学校，成为山东省内唯一一所专门以培养专科层次小学教师为主的高等师范专科学校，其五年一贯制专科学生的两年专科阶段依然在原来学校完成。2007年山东省莱阳师范学校、蓬莱师范学校、文登师范学校在当年招收的五年一贯制专科学生，2007年9月～2010年7月三年中专阶段在原来学校完成学习任务；2010年9月～2012年7月两年专科阶段将到鲁东大学教师教育学院完成学习任务；参加专升本的学生2012年9月～2015年7月也将在鲁东大学教师教育学院完成本科阶段的学习。至此，"3+2+3"本科学历小学教师培养模式正式形成。

三、"3+2+3"本科学历小学教师培养模式的比较优势

"3+2+3"小学教师培养模式兼具五年制专科教育和三年本科教育的优点，使学生具有扎实的教师专业理论素养和教育教学能力，具备了教师发展性的能力——科学研究能力和创新能力。与其它各种培养本科层次小学教师的模式比较来看，"3+2+3"本科学历小学教师培养模式具有明显的优势：

(一)"3+2+3"本科学历小学教师培养模式有利于学生牢固树立明确的职业角色

1. "3+2+3"本科学历小学教师培养模式有利于培养学生深厚的职业道德修养

"3+2+3"小学教师培养模式在历时八年的教育过程中,通过开设师德修养课程,对学生进行了严格的职业道德教育,不但使学生养成爱岗敬业、为人师表的教师基本道德素质,更具备了对待小学生所特有的强烈的爱心、充分的耐心、细致的关心、可爱的童心和无私的奉献精神,这样一来才能在以后的教育教学中以身示范,言传身教。

2. "3+2+3"本科学历小学教师培养模式有利于培养坚定的职业信念

在正确的专业思想的指导下,学生能广泛地参与小学教育实践,全身心地投入到小学教育实践中去,最终形成对小学教育事业的执著追求,并将这一追求内化为持久的职业信念。

3. "3+2+3"本科学历小学教师培养模式有利于培养学生深厚的职业情谊

通过教育见习、实习和教育调查等实践活动,让学生直接接触到小学教育教学实际情景,深入地了解教育对象——小学生的活泼可爱、充满发展的可能性的特点,深切地体会小学教师肩上神圣的责任,认识到小学教师这一职业的价值,渐渐从认可到接纳到喜欢直至热爱小学教师这一职业,并立志献身于小学教育事业,建立深厚的职业情感。

4. "3+2+3"本科学历小学教师培养模式有利于培养学生深厚的职业知识能力素养

小学教育的对象和任务的特殊性决定了小学教师这一职业需要一套特殊的知识能力系统,从初中毕业进入中师开始,学生便意识到自己将来要从事小学教育教学工作,较早地对自己的职业角色进行了明确的定位,树立了职业意识,学生在以后8年的学习生活中围绕小学教师这一职业目标不断地塑造和提高自己,培养小学教师这一职业所需要的职业知识和职业能力,形成了小学教师职业角色心理,由此在参加工作后能较快地融入小学教师职业角色中去。

(二)"3+2+3"本科学历小学教师培养模式有利于培养学生扎实的小学教师职业技能

小学教师主要的职业技能表现为八个方面:即知识的处理能力、教学组织能力、言语表达能力、书面表述能力、研究能力、书写能力、计算机操作能力、制作能力。[5]

1. 宽厚的小学教师职业技能

学生生源是年龄较小的初中毕业生,可塑性较强,更容易接受新事物,学习新技能。在中师浓厚的重视教师基本功训练的气氛中,在专业的书法、美术、普通话、音乐、计算机教师的指导下,通过开设相应的课程和采取多种形式的实践活动,如:教师基本功比赛、基本功十佳标兵评选、演讲比赛、参加省内乃至全国的书法绘画大型比赛等,营造一种扎实练习基本功的氛围,经过学生自身的刻苦练习,学生在"三字一画一话"(钢笔字、粉笔字、毛笔字、简笔画、普通话)技能、语言表达能力、制作能力、计算机操作技能等方面达到较高的水平。

2. 较强的小学教师实践能力

在五年一贯制和本科阶段都开设了实习见习课程,让学生在教育教学实践中感受到教育对象的真实性,了解小学生的身心状态,深入理解教育理论,体验到教师的责任,帮助学生超前获得了教育教学实际经验,在实践运用中提高职业技能和本领。这些都使学生未毕业就具有扎实的职业技能,毕业后能够在较短的时间内适应岗位的要求,担当重任。

(三)“3+2+3”本科学历小学教师培养模式能培养学生的教育科研能力

三年本科阶段开设教育科学研究方法、教育统计与教育测量、小学语文教学法研究、小学数学教学法研究、小学英语教学法研究、小学音乐教学法研究、基础教育改革研究等科研类课程，使学生结合当前基础教育课程改革的实际情况，发现问题，运用所学的知识探讨解决问题的方法，使学生具有了初步的小学教育教学反思和科学研究能力，最终成长为综合素质较高的科研型小学教师。

总之，“3+2+3”小学教师培养模式有明确的办学方向和稳定的职业趋向，使小学教师的培养免受高考指挥棒的影响，有条件按照素质教育的要求，实施全面的教育，促进学生健康、个性地发展，在知识结构上，学生能将一般科学文化知识、学科专业知识和教育专业知识加以综合，在能力结构上，学生具备了一定的教育能力、教学能力和科研能力，由此，培养出的学生能写会画、能说会弹、能唱会跳，具有综合型的素质结构，因此，“3+2+3”小学教师培养模式能培养适应21世纪教育教学改革需要的、具有实施素质教育能力的、能胜任小学教育教学和科研工作的综合型高素质小学教师。

四、“3+2+3”本科学历小学教师培养模式优化策略

(一) 实行8年一贯制

招生的时候就让学生知道自己考的是8年一贯的本科学历小学教师教育，中间没有再升学选拔环节。“初中毕业就决定了自己将来是大学本科毕业生”，有利于吸引优秀初中生报考小学教育专业；中间没有再升学环节，更容易保障培养目标的实现。

实行8年一贯制有利于吸引优秀初中生报考。目前国内高中阶段的学习又苦又累，即使经过高中3年学习也不一定考上大学本科，而初中毕业就可以圆自己上大学本科的梦想。经过8年的小学教师专业培养，每位学生在本科毕业时很容易成长为合格的小学教师，更容易找到工作，并且近年来，国家越来越重视教师待遇的提高。从上大学和就业角度来看，8年一贯制小学教育专业对初中毕业生很有吸引力。

实行8年一贯制更容易保障培养目标的实现。学生的培养计划按照8年来安排，可以避免课程的重复设置，更加有效地利用资源，科学地进行教育资源分配，更加有利于培养出优秀的小学教育师资。

(二) 3年中专教育策略

选拔优秀的初中毕业生到中等师范学校接受3年中专教育，充分发挥中等师范学校丰富的小学教师培养经验，强化小学教师基本技能培养。

该阶段的教育工作由中等师范学校承担，突出学生小学教师基本技能的培养。在这个阶段不分专业，注重培养学生的动手能力，发挥刚毕业初中生年龄小、可塑性强的优点，对学生进行书法、普通话、计算机、体育、美术、音乐等方面的教师基本功培养，这是目前我国中等师范学校的优势。

(三)2 年大专教育策略

进入高等院校接受 2 年大专教育,本阶段主要强化小学教师专业技能培养,按照小学语文、小学数学、小学英语、小学音乐、小学美术、小学体育等专业到高校相对应的院系选修到规定学分,同时接受相关教育教学基本理论教育。

该阶段教育由高等师范本、专科院校承担。3 年中专教育结束时,按学生志愿分配专业:首先由学生按照自己的爱好、特长等选专业,然后由高等师范本、专科院校根据学生志愿和成绩进行专业调配,保证小学语文、小学数学、小学外语、小学音乐、小学美术、小学体育等各专业的相对均衡。学生到中文、数学、英语、音乐、美术、体育等院系选修专业规定学分,提高专业知识,同时接受教育教学基本理论教育,提高教育、教学技能。

(四)3 年本科教育策略

本阶段主要是强化小学教师科研创新技能培养。

该阶段教育由高等师范本科院校承担,注重培养学生的教育科研能力、教材分析能力、教学改革能力、课程设置能力等。首先学生带着问题到小学进行一年的顶岗实习,讲授自己所学专业课程,在自己大学老师指导下进行相关的实践调查。完成后面两年的本科学习,开设课程重点在教育科学研究方法、课程、教材、教法的研究,克服学生在实习中的不足,完成老师布置的科研课题、做好本科毕业论文等。

(五)“理论-实践-理论”的培养理念

在 8 年培养过程中始终坚持“理论-实践-理论”的培养理念,注重学生实践能力的培养,紧密与小学教育教学实践相结合。除了顶岗实习以外的各个学期都要有 4~6 周到小学进行教育实习或教育见习的时间,把课堂中学到的理论、方法、技能应用到教育实习中,在教育实习中不断观察、实践,发现问题回校研究解决。

参考文献

[1] 李建辉. 高师小学教育专业定位与课程建设问题探讨[J]. 漳州师范学院学报,2004(2).

[2] 李跃文. 小学教师“三二分段”培养模式研究[J]. 重庆教育学院院报,2005(11).

[3] 黄幼岩,吴言明. 新时期我国小学教师培养模式探讨[J]. 现代教育科学,2006(2).

[4] 黄正平. “5+2”:培养本科学历小学教师的有效模式[J]. 教师教育研究,2008(1).

[5] 蒋亦华. 我国小学教师培养路径的现代特征与实践结构[J]. 教育理论与实践,2007(5).

Transforming Education: Hardware, Software, Wetware

—The Need to Reinvent Teaching Practice

Song Hong-zhuan* Tom P. Abeles**

Introduction

Education is a lagging indicator. Its function has been to transmit knowledge about the "world" and societal values. Thus, what it delivers has been historic by nature. Additionally, it is the well understood cliché that the "classroom" has been essentially the same since the first "schools" were established. The technologies for delivery have changed, but the core holds.

The entrance to the digital age via global connectivity with the internet, cell phones and computers represents, as suggested by Clayton Christensen and others, a disruptive innovation, one that has yet to be fully addressed by society at large and the educational community in particular. The education system appears to see these technologies as the equivalent of new sources of information, delivery and production in an effort to avoid fully confronting the disruption and the opportunities.

Rather than change, like the oyster which coats a grain of sand to make a pearl, they map bricks or the traditional classroom, into "clicks" or virtual space rather than embracing the transformative. Failure to address the shift is leading to the rise of competitive alternatives which will eventually lead, as with the US automotive industry, to the system's collapse up the chain from preK to the undergraduate institutions with a wholesale disruption of both the institutions and the workforce.

The Destruction of the Knowledge Guilds

At one time the libraries of Alexandria housed a large portion of what was "known". Scholars used the libraries and created knowledge objects. They earned a living by serving

---

* Song Hong-zhuan, Dr. President and CEO, International Council for Education Development PO Box 14068 Minneapolis, MN USA 55414.(宋红专,博士,国际教育发展委员会总裁。)

** Tom P. Abeles, Dr. President Sagacity, Inc 3704 11th Ave South Minneapolis, MN 55407.

others who sought this knowledge. This guild of scholars sallied forth like knights from castles to disseminate the knowledge or held forth in these hallowed institutions, schools and universities. The printing press made knowledge more readily available and there was a slight shift in mission as the role of the scholar/teacher expanded to interpret that knowledge. And these functions have remained largely unchanged up to the present day. The arrival of the Internet freed knowledge from the confines of the Ivory Tower. Today, knowledge wants to be free. The pressure from the rapid expansion of knowledge, where it cannot be contained within the walls of the Ivory Tower or controlled by the "keepers" has radically changed the business proposition of the systems of education. Like Teilhard de Chardin's Noosphere, the growing computational "cloud" not only yields to knowledge's desire to be free, but it also creates a plethora of social networks connecting people across space and time which means that the interpretation of the "meaning" of that knowledge is no longer just the domain of those who reside in the Ivory Towers. In this environment, corporations and even the military have understood the multidimensional challenges of creating, disseminating and interpreting; and they have adapted. Education, because it has traditionally thrived on transmitting the "historic" has not acknowledged this pressure with regards to content. In particular, the entire process of education itself has changed little, except to replace the pen with the word processor. What, indeed, happens when the classroom is a cloud, freed from time and space?

What happens when "digital natives" who are "multi-taskers" can access information faster and more completely with the click of a mouse (or the blink of an eye) and create links to larger resources than can ever by accomplished by being confined to a linear pedagogical, lock-step, age- defined, learning cohort? What is the function of a brick-spaced facility? And, more importantly, what is the function of an "educator" and the academic "guild" infrastructure?

Deconstructing the Infrastructure

The education "system" is basically understood to be the preK-12 system which has been supported by public fiscal resources. The public post secondary institutions, grade 13～16 have, up to the present been held out as separate. But with increasing demands for further education, the system is, by default gradually expanding from K-12 to the community colleges, grades 13～14 and to the four year institutions, grades 13～16. The pieces that has stood outside, which one can label the "departments of education" and which executes the will of the public through legislative mandates now needs to be added to the mix.

Introducing these two pieces, particularly schools or colleges of education, changes how we view the picture. While corporations and, even, the military have a degree of autonomy in restructuring to meet change, the core, preK-12 systems have a variety of external, vested, interests in any changes. Colleges of Education which train personnel for the system, while seeking to respond to changes, have to address the regulatory requirements. Additionally, faculty in universities have multiple responsibilities where the success of introducing innovations into the current system often is not rewarded adequately. In other words the ability of faculty to advance their careers are predicated, not on the success of the students who graduate and go into teaching but on other criteria where even their own performance in the classroom are not the dominant factor.

Similarly, executive agencies, which serve the needs of legislatures, provide oversight and thus transfer the responsibility of performance of the public education onto the schools themselves. The success or failure of the school systems within a political domain is duly reported. A variety of sticks and carrots to encourage change are provided, but the responsibility is removed from the agency. They have successfully positioned themselves to be able to measure success by their increase in budgets providing ever greater oversight or encouragement but not by a measure in their performance with respect to the schools under their oversight.

Post Secondary Institutions

Society's demands for knowledge workers has required increased schooling, advancing from grade 6 to grade 12 and today, minimally through grade 14 via community colleges, vocational and technical schools. But the understanding is that knowledge acquisition is a life-long process. Furthermore, there is an increasing recognition that institutions can no longer be segmented into neat, age-defined, experiences such as primary, secondary and post secondary or that individuals will so progress. Community colleges that offer bachelor degrees overlap between post secondary and secondary programs and home schooling and similar optionsblur the lines. Thus the post secondary, 13～16 programs become integrated and the ultimate competency of an individual, a measure of the effectiveness of public investments at all levels, requires an involvement of all institutions from preK to post secondary. With more faculty in the primary and secondary schools obtaining advanced degrees, including doctorates, the distinction between faculty is also becoming a blur.

With the addition of the internet, location of students and faculty starts to become moot. It points out that the need for a physical presence of either students or faculty is not an absolute requirement. The ability of software to track and evaluate students, faculty, administration, programs and other critical values across space and time ties the systems together, even with mobility. International reciprocity, which is increasing, allows programs to go across geo-political boundaries.

Institutional responsibility should not cease upon a student passing a course or walking out with their tassel tossed to the other side. This should hold, not just for preparation of faculty in the primary/secondary schools but in any position obtained by virtue of a certification of proficiency. In this case, the analysis is confined to the education system.

Departments of Education

The true cost of oversight of the preK-12 education system as it is currently constructed has not been measured, both the direct and indirect (administrative) costs as well as the cost of the inability to restructure the system from the Department to the personnel in the schools. The military has seen the need to flatten the organization and get more control and decision making at the local level in spite of similar demands. This has included changes in lines of authority on activities as well as control of funding. The education system as a lagging indicator has assiduously resisted such structural adjustments. Rather it has chosen to add layers of bureaucracy as a response to defined problems, adding cost to its infrastructure while shifting responsibilities downward, increasing requirements without increasing authority or control. This has often resulted in increased burdens and conflicting missions and opportunities.

As with other government agencies, the legislature creates the laws and the department writes the rules for execution and oversight. There is little flexibility in working with the schools to reach accommodations which might not fit within an adamantine structure. Thus, the flexibility to meet local situations, except through a set of bureaucratic rules does not exist. The system "appeal" process becomes long, laborious and expensive in time and fiscal resources. As with the post secondary institutions, there needs to be a re-alignment of the relationship between the administrative agencies and the institutions, faculty, staff and students. Administrative cylinders must be bridged or eliminated.

While it is recognized that it is the student experience that is critical, one needs to realize that the success of the child depends in a large part on the support infrastructure which makes the entire system responsible to that student. It is also important to understand that the student's experience and success also depends on the larger context in which the student exists. The education system cannot expect to shoulder the shortcomings of the larger infrastructure. This defines new relationships, not just between the education system and the students but between the system and the larger community. The burden for this outreach cannot fall entirely on the schools but becomes the responsibility of the larger system, including the Departments of Education and the post secondary institutions working in and with the society at-large, not as supplicants, rule seeking bureaucrats or experts acting at a distance.

Disruptive Technologies

Social Networks

The world outside of the classroom is built on networks. This includes teams located in a physical space, or, today, individuals and organizations linked by communications technologies, including the Internet. Education focuses on the individual where collaboration,except in select incidents, is considered unacceptable or even "cheating". The arrival of the internet with on-line games/simulations, virtual worlds, and social networking tools pushes ever harder. The individual is forced to test against a system which increasingly resists as it has with each new technology from calculators to smart phones.

The current system, with its legal and administrative infrastructure, resists change and offers little flexibility, thus, increasing the opportunity that public education will lose those who are able to find alternative paths both within and outside. The relationships at all points will become contentious and increasingly costly to support.

The post secondary system, while being more flexible in bringing these options into use, still, for its own students, maps bricks into clicks. In other words, in a world where knowledge is becoming unbound, the system still maintains the roll of faculty as the keeper of knowledge. For the most part, within colleges of education, little is being done to engage the system into which their students will enter as faculty. The post secondary institutions are separate from the industry unlike other post secondary programs which prepare professionals.

Digital Natives/Digital Immigrants

While the terms, digital natives/digital immigrants originally was used to separate youth from the older generation not "growing up digital", the term now has a broader connotation which differentiates those who are at home with the emerging information/communication technologies and those who still miss the rotary dial phone. The key issue at hand is the ability of the "natives" to multi-task. Marketing companies have a clear picture that this is occurring for example, while many watch television and simultaneously use their computer and even maintain smart phone connections. They find that to effectively reach this increasingly important audience that they have to simultaneous engage this audience at all levels.

Education is still linear, age or grade defined and cohort bound even knowing that individuals learn at different rates for different areas of knowledge. The system is defined, not for the students, but for a system which did not have the tools, insights, or skills to be responsive to these needs in the past and even less so today though digital tools do exist. Lessons from the "one room" school house have been discarded rather than adapted to modern opportunities and needs.

Knowledge Wants to be Free

Hardware and software for ICT's are becoming cheaper, more powerful and ubiquitous. Thus access is becoming almost universal. This changes the entire nature of the educational experience. Dedicated brick-spaced venues do not have to be the only learning venue and knowledge acquisition does not have to be meted out in standard time-bound units on a standard basis. The "little red schoolhouse" exists as a memory and a habit driven delivery model. The vested interests from school bus sales and drivers to architects, energy companies and administrators as well as teachers maintain a capital intensive system tied to the past.

Knowledge has leaked out of the Ivory Tower faster than water leaking through a broken levee. This changes the nature of education which now must be driven by other objectives than constantly repackaging that which is available from many sources. In many ways this presents the needed catalyst to bring all players together around problem-based learning which can be unique to an individual or what might be defined as a class, program, school or system which can transcend geopolitical boundaries.

Throwing Down the Gauntlet

In today's world, life-long learning is becoming an imperative. It is doubtful that the requirements will formally increase as it has in the past going formally from grade 6 to grade 12 to two years of a post secondary education. In fact the distinction, created by separate institutions is becoming moot as individuals at all levels are crossing these historically defined but some what arbitrary boundaries.

As with the change in medical records, it will become standard for a person's educational path will be able to be traced, not only by levels of accomplishment but performance evaluations. For education, this becomes increasingly important, not just for students as they advance, but for all elements including faculty, institutions, administrators and, even programs. Thus, for public institutions there needs to be continuous opportunities for improvements for all areas. Because of the increased reliance on social networks and open access to knowledge, there needs to be a collaborative relationship between both individuals and institutions. This requires a changing role for all parties, particularly the post secondary institutions and the regulatory arms of government responsible to the legislature, the public and the educational institutions.

Post Secondary Institutions

In the past, undergraduate institutions have seen themselves to be autonomous, or semi-autonomous entities. While private universities can maintain this position, public universities, particularly at the undergraduate level, must see themselves as an extension of the traditional primary/secondary system. The issue of graduate programs and graduate faculty, particularly in colleges of education, must also re-assess their roles. Right now the separation is eroding faster than a stream bank at flood stage, never to be restored.

A new role needs to be carved with the graduate programs and the current primary, secondary system. With the ability of individuals and institutions to undergo continual improvement, learning, the systems, working with graduate schools need to be able to define unique relationships which utilize the unique capabilities of both types of programs. This will and must vary depending on the institutions. Thus the team will provide skills development and certification, new programs for faculty and institutions and paths for student advancements through the system in all disciplines.

Departments of Education

Departments of education have a multiple personality syndrome. On one hand their function is to develop plans to implement the will of the people as manifest in the legislation passed at the level of the state. On the other hand, the federal mandates, often tied to funding, force the departments to steer between Scylla and Charybdis while providing guidance to the school systems. What makes this more complex is that those schools and their faculty on the front line know the situation that they are facing and which may not be the same for all situations.

Unlike the military that has ceded local control, the education departments, see themselves as walking the tight rope of their funders and legislators and see their ability to allow such increase in dimensions of freedom at the local levels extremely limited. This, in turn requires them to return to both the state and federal trough to study ways in which these mandates and conflicts might be resolved, leading to further, but different constraints and increases in regulatory mandates. Departments of education must re-constitute themselves to be "school friendly" which may require how they align themselves in relation to regulators/funders and the schools themselves.

Education reform cannot occur unless there is a re-alignment of the three key participants in shaping the educational system, the regulators, the post secondary institutions and the schools themselves. There are a number of other pressures operating. For example, teachers' unions which have used "student rights to an education" as a vehicle for promoting the economic agendas of the membership under the guise of school improvement. These too must be brought to the table in a constructive manner recognizing that their purpose and function may also have shifted. That requires significant re-assessment on their parts, also. If such accommodation can not be addressed satisfactorily, as Clayton Christensen has pointed out for other sectors, alternative competitors will rise where the carrot of increased funding will fall under the weight of past sins. The cost will become too great to be off-set by additional funds.

教师教育一体化的教师继续教育刍议

黄家庆*
（钦州学院，广西 钦州 535000）

摘 要：教师继续教育是教师职业生存与职业发展的内在诉求；是保障教师持续正确代表政府意愿的需要；是保障教师获得社会职业认可的需要；是教师专业发展的推进器；是教师教育一体化的应有之义。教师教育一体化教师继续教育的实施，需要转变教师继续教育的旧观念；制定与教师职业岗位相对应和促进其专业发展的培训规划；建构与教师职前培养相互衔接，重在促进专业发展的专业课程体系；建立教师教育一体化下的继续教育机构；创新教师继续教育的模式；各要素形成分工明确、协调配合的责任运行机制。

关键词：教师教育；一体化；继续教育

基金项目：新世纪广西高等教育教学改革工程项目："教师职业适应性提高的研究"。

Discussion on Teacher Continuing Education in the Integration of Teacher Education

Huang Jia-qing
（Qinzhou University，Qinzhou 535000，China ）

Abstract：Teacher continuing education is the inner demands of teachers' professional survive and career development；is the demand of ensuring teacher to continue to correctly represent the government's will；is the demand of ensuring teacher to acquire social and professional recognition；is a propeller of teacher professional development；is a must of integration of teacher education. In order to implement it，change the old concept of teacher continuing education，develop

* 黄家庆，男，广西合浦人，钦州学院副研究员。

training plans that fit the posts for teachers and promote their professional development, build a professional course system that converges with Pre-service Training and emphasizes to promote professional development; set up continuing education agencies based on the integration of teacher education; reform teaching patterns and form an operating mechanism of clear division of labor and coordination are needed.

Key words: teacher education; integration; continuing education

当前,教师教育一体化已成为各国加强和改革教师教育的共同目标以及教师教育发展的一种趋势。但在实践中,教师教育的职前培养与职后培训相脱离的现状还没有从根本上得到改变,还没有形成有机的整体。如何发挥教师教育一体化的作用做好教师继续教育,并贯穿于教师的整个职业生涯,促进教师成长与专业发展,是教师教育的一个课题。

一、继续教育在教师职业生涯中的专业发展意蕴

教师继续教育发展到今天,已经不是一般意义上的教师在职培训,它不是仅仅满足于教师知识与技能补差补缺的教育,而是在终身学习理念指导下,以促使教师专业发展为目标,实施的有目的、有计划、有组织的促使教师专业化发展的教育。它在教师职业生涯中,是教师专业发展的根基。

1. 教师继续教育是教师职业生存与专业发展的内在诉求

随着社会的发展,教师职业的性质与功能发生了变化,经历了长者即教师,学者即教师,到教师即文化知识的传播者,以至于教师即促进者、引导者的多重角色转换。由原来的单纯传授知识,发展演化为通过激发和调动学生的主观能动性,引导学生全面发展。教师的教学不再只是对知识的传授,更重要的是引导学生对知识的主动建构。[1]高质量的教师不仅是有知识、有学问的人,而且是有道德、有理想、有专业追求的人,不仅是高起点的人,而且是终身学习的人。[2]然而,高质量教师的职业素养和对职业不断发展的适应能力,不是职前教育所能独自培养的,它还需要职后连续的学习经历和活动来不断建构。两者是联为一体的阶段性与连续性相统一的不断成长与成熟的持续过程。这一发展过程的实现,不仅需要教师主动地努力学习和实践,以提高自己的专业能力,而且需要创设良好的教师继续教育条件。经常不断地在职进修,是专业性职业的标准特征之一。教师作为一个专业性职业,从业者要实现在专业知识和技能方面不断丰富和发展,除有赖于在从教过程中,通过对自己教学实践和经验的不断反思和探索外,同时还需要接受继续教育,通过在职进修、学历提升等各种方式来不断提升专业知识和能力,否则就会落伍,被淘汰。继续教育既是教师职业的社会期待,也是教师个人职业生存与专业发展的内在诉求。

2. 教师继续教育是保障教师持续正确代表政府意愿的需要

随着社会的发展,教育巨大的社会功能不断显现,教育的功用不断纳入国家与民族发展的轨道,由此强化了教育的受控地位,利用教育手段对人施加影响在不断深化,使教师与教材作为代表政府意愿的中介显得更为重要。教师作为教育的主导要素,由于其在社会与学生发展之间起着重要的中介作用,为了保障其持续正确地代表政府的意愿,教师也就必须进行继续教

育,以把握当时的社会政治、经济与文化背景,不断地获取国家与民族发展的各种信息,学习掌握反映政府意愿的新知识及其技能。教师作为人才的培育者,不仅需要不断地更新教育理念和教学内容,不断学习和掌握新的教学方法和教学媒体,而且也需要响应和反映政府建设终身学习社会的目标,积极参与继续教育,为各行各业做出典范,在社会上率先建构行业终身教育体系。

3. 教师继续教育是保障教师获得社会职业认可的需要

教师要适应职业的发展,树立教师职业的社会威信,必须走专业化发展的道路。实现专业化的发展,从客观条件要求上来讲,它要以带有强制性的制约机制来促进教师职业的专业性提高。如制定严格的教师职业规范,订立执行较高的教师资格认定和入职标准,以及实行职业规范与专业制裁等。这些制度像一张筛子,把不符合要求的教师滤掉,为教师职业专业化获得社会认可提供依据。但是,这些制度只能提高教师行业内的群体素质,自身却不能促使经筛选的教师更好地提高其自身素质。因此,还必须提供良好的继续教育条件,并充分激发教师的主观能动性,使参加继续教育成为教师的自觉行动,通过实施继续教育,发展教师的职业工作能力,提高其职业适应性,让教师主动在继续教育中获得专业自由和专业发展,从而以更强的职业适应性赢得教师职业专业化的社会认可。

4. 教师继续教育是教师专业发展的推进器

社会职业发展的现实告诉我们,确立教师职业专业地位和加速教师专业发展,必须加大教师继续教育。教师继续教育是专业发展的推进器,它帮助教师克服其职业发展中的"高原现象"。实施强有力的继续教育,通过采取多种教育模式,启发和帮助教师进行职业体验,增强职业自我解读能力,深化对教师职业以及职业发展与个人发展关系的理解;通过回归进修的形式,使教师摆脱原有文化环境、现实利害关系的负影响,同时,增加专业知识、专业理论、专业技能、教育科学知识,增强教育教学能力,而能更好地随着社会环境、教学环境、自己身份以及所面临的关系的变化,不断提高适应能力,适应教师的社会期待、他人期待以及自身期待发生的变化,促进教师的专业发展。

二、我国教师教育一体化的形成及其本质

1. 传统师范教育向一体化现代教师教育的转型

教师教育在教育部《关于"十五"期间教师教育改革与发展的意见》中明确为:"在终身教育思想指导下,按照教师专业发展的不同阶段,对教师的职前培养、入职教育和在职培训的统称。"教师教育一体化,就是在不断提高教师专业水平这一总体目标的前提下,实现教师教育的纵向各阶段和横向各方面辩证统一的一种教师教育的理念和实践。但相当长的一个时期,我国培养师资的专业学校只负责新教师的"生产"——教师职前培养,各类教育培训机构只管老教师的"保养"——教师职后培训。在教师职业发展中,两个原本相互联系的教育阶段却处于分离、脱节的状态。

20世纪80年代开始,随着我国各行各业改革开放的深入,教师教育也进入了从职前培养职后培训分开向一体化转型发展的过程:1986年3月,原国家教委《关于加强和发展师范教育的意见》提出,师范院校也要承担一部分在职教师的培训;1998年12月,教育部颁布《面向21世纪教育振兴行动计划》,要求继续推进师资培养的开放化进程,把中小学教师的继续教育纳

入教师教育的一体化建设;1999 年 6 月,中共中央、国务院《关于深化教育改革全面推进素质教育的决定》提出,将师范教育的内涵扩展到教师职前培养和教师的在职培训,积极推进教师教育的一体化建设;2001 年 5 月,国务院《关于基础教育改革与发展的决定》首次使用“教师教育”的概念,并决定:完善以现有师范院校为主体、其他高等院校共同参与、培养培训相衔接的开放的教师教育体系;2007 年 5 月,《国家教育事业发展“十一五”规划纲要》再次提出,要构建“开放灵活、规范有序的教师教育体系,提高教师教育的层次和水平”,进一步从制度上促进了传统师范教育向一体化现代教师教育的转型以及与国际教师教育接轨。

2. 教师教育一体化继续教育的本质

继续教育不同于在职培训,它是在成人在职培训实践基础上发展而来的,是根据社会与人发展的需要,对具有高中阶段教育及以上学历的人员,实行的一种帮助其实现专业发展的有目的、有计划以及有组织的教育活动。教师继续教育是指根据社会以及教育的发展和在职教师的需要,对从事教师职业的人员所实施促使其专业发展的一种有目的、有组织以及有计划的教育活动。它既包括在职教师的学历提高教育,也包括教育教学研究和职业工作与专业发展交流的学习活动,还包括促进教师自我教育与自我成长的活动。

教师继续教育是教师教育一体化的应有之意。现代教师继续教育以追求学习者专业发展与全面提高教师素质为目标。教师教育一体化的教师继续教育,是以教师专业化为价值取向,促进教师职业发展的职能教育。一体化的教师教育包括三层含义:一是职前培养、入职教育、职后提高的一体化,即建设教师终身教育的协调体系;二是中小幼教师教育一体化;三是教学研究与教学实践的一体化,即建立师范大学与中小学的伙伴关系。[3] 从这三层含义来看,教师继续教育是终身教育理念下根据教师职业发展需要进行的再教育活动;它是一个体系内的组成部分;它的开展,应该与教师职前培养相协调,与中小学校互为合作伙伴;它的实施,应是教学研究与教学实践相结合,职前职后课程优化整合,不断促进教师教育整个课程体系既有阶段性、针对性,又有连续性,实现与职前培养统一起来的过程。一方面,它要不断拓展教师在职教育,强化职前与职后教育活动之间的有机联系;另一方面,它要通过继续教育中的相关科研活动,促进继续教育各模式的构建与优化,探讨教师教育改革的理论,提供实施改革的策略建议,提升教师教育质量。

三、教师教育一体化教师继续教育的实施

教师教育一体化继续教育的实施,就是要做到教师职后提高与职前培养的有机链接与沟通,各种教师培训符合各成长阶段教师的特点和要求,保障教师专业的持续发展。

1. 要转变教师继续教育旧的观念

当前,在一些基层学校和教师中,继续教育的意识不强,把继续教育看成是上面安排的任务,没有认识到继续教育既是自己应该履行的义务,同时又是自己应该享有的权益;不认同继续教育是教师职业生涯中专业发展的必要,是国家和终身学习社会对教师的要求,有的甚至错误地认为参加继续教育会影响教学。在现实中,不少教师是为了获取一纸证书来履职晋级参加继续教育的。而另一方面,现有的教师继续教育制度从上到下往往只强调:参加教师继续教育,是教师职务评聘、晋级的必备条件之一;规定拒不参加继续教育或擅自中断培训、进修的教师,不得参加职称评聘和晋级。这样一来,继续教育就变成了强制性活动,成为教师职务评聘

的限制条件,导致课程目标错位;教师接受继续教育只是履行义务,而不是享受权利,缺失了促进教师专业发展的应有之意。[4]

因此,在教师教育一体化下实施教师继续教育,一是要改变长期以来形成的重职前培养轻职后培训的现象,将教师继续教育的实施贯穿于教师的整个职业生涯中,依靠一体化的"终身性"教育来促进教师成长与专业发展。二是要转变基层教育单位和教师中普遍存在的教师继续教育是一种知识技能型的"补短教育"的观念,实现教师继续教育的观念转型。三是要以调动教师的学习积极性为基点,"培养自主成长型教师",摒弃"灌、喂、抱"的被动强迫式的继续教育活动,让教师感到接受继续教育既是履行义务又是享受权利,参加继续教育是自我专业发展的需要。

2. 要制定与教师职业岗位相对应和促进其专业发展的培训规划

我国《教师法》第十九条规定,"各级人民政府教育行政部门、学校主管部门和学校应当制定教师培训规划,对教师进行多种形式的思想政治、业务培训。"教育部颁发的《中小学教师继续教育规定》,规定中小学教师继续教育原则上每5年一个培训周期。这都要求做好教师继续教育的规划。目前,我国教师学历层次总体偏低,同时,我国小学、初中教师取得的学历专业与所教课程不对口问题突出,如初始学历合格的初中语文、数学、外语、美术、音乐、艺术和体育教师,约有1/3是学非所教,而初始学历不合格的教师,取得合格学历的专业与所教课程对口率更低,据国家教育督导组织的抽样调查表明,初始学历不合格的初中教师,取得合格学历的专业与所教课程对口率为58.2%,问题突出。[5]

作为一门专业,教师的发展空间是无限的。教师作为发展中的专业人员,要经历内涵多层面、多领域的不同的专业发展阶段,需要不断接受在职进修和培训,从各个方面不断汲取知识,自我完善,自我提高。同时,一方面,因工作环境与个性的差异,教师对各个目标层次的学历与非学历教育有着不同的需求;另一方面,教师也会由于不同的工作阶段产生不同的学习需求。因此,教育行政部门、教师所在学校,要根据不同的需求,制定与教师职业岗位相对应和促进其专业发展的教师继续教育规划,合理安排、统筹管理,防止为了取得合格学历而学非所教。在做好总体提升教师学历规划的同时,又要按层次、学科专业分类,制订中长期促进教师专业发展的各级各类非学历进修计划。如制定国家级、省级、地市级三级层次、任务不同的每5年一个培训周期的在职教师培训计划。

3. 要建构与教师职前培养相互衔接,重在促进专业发展的专业课程体系

继续教育是使教师通过培训在原有的基础上不断得到提高的活动,不是某一层次或某一项学习任务。它的每次学习培训活动,从教师专业发展来讲,应是相互衔接的再上升。然而,长期以来,我国教师继续教育培训的课程体系比较单一,或是重复在师范院校时已经学过的内容,或是对教师所担任的课程进行教材疏通,或是带有某些行政主观性的从上到下的集训。教师继续教育阶段与教师培养阶段的课程设置缺乏专业发展上的衔接,如师范院校忽视培养学生教师专业思想和专业能力的课程开设,教师培训阶段课程开设只重解决眼前的实际问题,为用而开设课程,又忽视了教师的持续发展。[6]

因此,教师继续教育要注意把当前需要与长远需要结合起来,进行宏观整体设计,建构一体化的教师教育课程体系。在培训课程设置上,教师职前培养阶段与职后培训阶段的课程既要避免重复,又要相互衔接;既满足教师职业的一般需要,又满足单个教师的个别需要;在教师发展各个阶段的衔接上,实现不同阶段,不同目标,不同层次,不同类型的沟通和连贯,实现学

历教育与非学历教育的有效衔接，实现教师实践成长和理论学习的吻合。通过课程设置的一体化，使课程设置前后兼顾，适应现代教育与科技的发展，符合各成长阶段教师的特点和要求。如，教育手段现代化的步伐日益加快，中小学校的电教设备陆续配置起来，有的已达到相当高的水平，教育信息技术对教师的要求越来越高，但中年以上教师往往由于职前培养时缺乏相应的课程学习，或理论知识不足，或技能不够娴熟。对这些教师应考虑开设现代教育技术的培训课程。另外，应针对教师职前培养课程设置有限，继续教育的培训课程还应考虑分学科设置选修课，使教师学习相近相关的课程，以利于开阔视野，改善知识结构，学以致用，提高深层素质。教师继续教育的课程设置应重在帮助教师更新教育观念、优化知识结构、促进专业反省能力的培养和提高，帮助他们形成自己的教学风格和教学特色，成为专家型或学者型教师。[7]

4. 要建立教师教育一体化的继续教育机构

实施教师教育一体化下的教师继续教育，促进教师专业不断发展，必须整合教师职前培养和职后培训机构，对现行的教师教育机制进行改革与创新，改变教师职前培养和职后培训相脱离的现状，把教师职前培养与职后培训有机结合起来，并贯穿于教师职业发展中。

其一，整合教师职前培养和职后培训机构，把地方教育学院、教师进修学院等教育培训机构与地方师范院校或综合性高校合二为一，建立隶属于地方高等院校的教师教育培训机构——教师教育学院或教师发展学院。通过资源优化重组，增强教师教育实力，并为实现教师教育一体化的职前培养与职后培训的有机结合，提供机构的组织保障。

其二，借鉴天津市和广州市教师继续教育体系构建方面的经验，在师范院校或综合性高校设立教师教育学院，使之成为一个地市的教师教育主体，在区(县)的教师教育机构设立教师教育分院，形成市、区(县)和中小学的三级教师教育网络，统筹、规划、实施教师教育。[8]方便地方高等院校的教师教育与基础教育联动，促进教师职前培养和职后培训能够更好地衔接。

5. 要创新教师继续教育的模式

实施教师继续教育是为了保障教师能够适应社会的不断变化，帮助教师形成终身学习和研究的意愿和能力，基于终身教育的理念，为教师建立终身学习体系。教师继续教育是一个系统工程，需要以教师专业化为取向，根据教师的不同需求，通过对系统要素的科学配置，创新教师继续教育的模式，开展多层次、多形式、多规格、多样化，能满足不同层次教师学习需求和选择的培训。如为了满足社会现实和教育事业发展要求，对教师进行的必修课和选修课相结合的全员培训；为了促进教师专业发展，组织开展的专家报告、名校研修、挂职锻炼、访问学习、教研培训等个性化强、联系教学实践紧的针对性、应用性培训；为了提高教师学科专业知识或教育理论知识，由教师选择的专项系统培训或学历提高学习培训。

在新的历史时期，教师教育一体化的教师继续教育，必须改变传统的职前教师教育模式和教与学分离的状况，解决中小学教育教学问题和受教者自主性被淡化的问题，采取由高等院校、地方教育行政部门和中小学三方密切合作的模式，如建立"教师教育合作共同体"，共同体在地方教育行政部门指导参与下，由地方高校与作为师范生实习基地的和作为教师培训研修基地的中小学组成。即在地方教育行政部门、地方高校与中小学校通过制订相应的合作计划和相关的实施办法，形成相互促进的机制、互利共赢的稳定的共同体，在平等合作的基础上，开展教师职前培养和教师职后培训活动，走高校与基础教育共同培养师资之路。

四、教师教育一体化教师继续教育的运行机制

2004 年国家教育部制定的《2003～2007 年教育振兴行动计划》强调，要构建以师范大学和其他高水平大学为先导，专科、本科、研究生三个层次协调发展，职前职后教育相互沟通，学历与非学历教育并举，促进教育专业发展和终身学习的现代教师教育体系。然而，由于以高校为主导的一体化的教师继续教育其各要素的责任不明确，与职前培养相衔接的职后培训活动难以取得突破性进展。究其原因之一，就是缺乏相应的措施机制。

教师继续教育机制的形成要素主要有教育行政部门、承担继续教育院校、教师所在学校和教师个人。一体化下的教师继续教育要有效地促进教师专业发展，就要使这四个要素呈现出良好的相互作用的状态。在教师教育已纳入高等教育体系的现阶段，应积极构建教育行政部门、承担继续教育院校、教师所在学校分工明确、协调配合的责任运行机制。

1. 教育行政部门，负责教师继续教育的宏观调控、统筹规划、政策保障和资源整合，制定培训规划和要求；组织开展继续教育的督导与质量评估；对基层学校的教师继续教育工作进行检查与指导，提供教师继续教育政策咨询服务。

2. 承担教师继续教育院校，负责根据教育行政部门制定的培训规划和要求，开发建设教师继续教育课程，具体实施继续教育各阶段的培训计划和活动的组织、管理；对经培训考核合格的教师，发给相应层次的继续教育证书或认定学分；开展教师教育和中小学教育研究，并为基层学校的教育科学研究等活动提供服务。

3. 基层学校，建设学习型组织；组织开展校本培训；配合承担教师继续教育院校开展的各项培训活动；做好外出培训教师的管理，协助承担教师继续教育院校开展培训质量管理及学员档案的收集整理等工作；承担必要的教师研修课程任务，参与教师继续教育院校进行的教育教学研究活动。

上述责任，通过教育行政部门、承担教师继续教育院校和基层学校签署的共建“教师教育创新实验区”或“教师教育一体化合作共同体”协议书确定下来，并设立专门机构或专人负责，形成工作机制。以保障“教师教育创新实验区”或“合作共同体”的健康发展，使其成为培养新教师的摇篮、教师继续教育的园地、基础教育的科研基地，成为大学教师和中小学教师实现教师专业发展的平台和沃土。

另一方面，建立以学习型组织为载体的学校内部教师继续教育机制。教师继续教育由强制行为转变为自主行为，核心要素是动力系统的建构以及个体动力的形成。教师继续教育目的的实现，需要教师以专业发展为取向，把继续教育作为自身工作与生活的诉求。为此，应建立以学习型组织为载体的学校内部教师继续教育机制。创建学习型组织不但可以为教师继续教育工作的改革注入新的活力，同时对教师继续教育机构的自身建设也有一定的促进作用。[9]把学校创建成学习型组织，在学校内部建立完善的学习制度，用科学的、人本化的评价和公开、公平、公正的奖惩分明的组织管理，把参加继续教育与教师的切身利益紧密结合在一起，组织教师在工作中学习，在学习中工作，让学习成为工作新的形式，形成有助于教师自我发展、实现自我价值的民主、和谐、上进的学习组织氛围，从而激发教师参加进修、不断学习的积极性，促进教师专业化发展，内化教师的“知识经济建立在知识和信息的生产分配和使用基础之上，以创造性的人力资源为依托”的知识价值观和人力资本价值观。[10]并以此推动教师继续教育工作。

参考文献

[1] 耿文侠,冯春明.教师职业的专业特性分析[J].教育研究,2007(2).

[2] 司孟月,薄红英.谈谈教师专业化问题[J].河南商业高等专科学报,2002(3).

[3] 袁振国.中国教育政策评论[M].北京:教育科学出版社,2002:25.

[4] 刘志文.广东教师教育人才培养模式一体化改革的思考[J].高教探索,2009(4):91.

[5] 国家教育督导报告2008(摘要):关注义务教育[N].中国教育报,2008-12-05.

[6][7] 赵慧君,李春超.实现教师教育一体化所引发的问题与启示[J].长春师范学院学报:人文社会科学版,2006(5).

[8] 童宏保.教师继续教育问题与对策[J].集美大学学报,2009(1).

[9] 吴樟兴.学习型组织与师资培训[J].教育发展研究,2001(8).

要从观念和体制上解决问题
——谈中小学教师学历培训的若干问题

颜　燕*
(钦州学院,广西　钦州　535000)

摘　要:随着社会的发展和教育的发展,对我们教师提出了更高的学历要求,学历培训也随之如火如荼地展开,经过几年的努力,我国教师的学历大幅提高,但同时我们也发现了不少问题,如教师学历培训过程出现了"四重四轻"的现象,即重数量轻质量,重结果轻过程,重职前轻职后,重功利轻实绩,使得学历含金量大幅下降。笔者认为要解决这些问题,必须从观念和体制上入手。

关键词:教师;学历培训;观念;体制

Solving the Problems from the Concepts and Systems
—On the Issues of Primary and Secondary School Teacher Education Training

Yan Yan
(Qinzhou University, Qinzhou 535000, China)

Abstract: Teachers need higher educational background with the social and education development. Educational training develops rapidly after several years of efforts, but some problems appear at the same time. The "four emphasis and four ignores" phenomenon, namely, emphasis on quantity rather than quality, emphasis on the results rather than the process, etc, declines the qualities of educational training. The key points to solve these problems are concepts and systems.

Key words: teachers; education training; concept; system

* 颜燕,女,广西钦州人,钦州学院政治与经济系教师。

社会发展对国民的素质提出了更高的要求，提高国民的素质主要靠教育，教育的质量要靠教师，而教师素质的提高靠教师培训。通过教师培训可以不断完善教师的知识、能力结构。教师的知识结构、能力结构处于一个不断充实和不断改进之中，换句话讲就是教学相长的过程。近年来，教师学历培训如火如荼地开展，教师在一定程度上拓宽了知识面，提高了教师技能。但是也存在不少的问题，针对教师的学历培训所存在的问题，笔者想谈谈一些浅薄的看法。

一、当前中小学教师学历培训状况

近年来，社会越来越多地关注教师教育的问题。2004 年教育部颁发了《关于加快推进全国教师教育网络联盟计划，组织实施新一轮中小学教师全员培训的意见》实施 200 万中小学教师学历学位提高培训，促进全国教师学历学位水平整体提升。到 2007 年底，使全国小学教师具有专科以上学历者提高到 60%左右；初中教师具有本科以上学历者提高到 50%左右；高中教师在学历达标基础上，具有研究生学历者达到一定比例。很多地方教育机构就此提出了“高中研究生化，初中本科化，小学大专化” 的口号，中小学校也制定了相应的政策。从此我国的教师学历培训呈现出一片“繁荣”景象。

2007 年，小学、初中、高中专任教师的学历合格率分别达到了 99.1%，97.2%，89.3%。分别比 2006 年提高 2.7，0.9，2.8 个百分点。高学历教师比例逐年提高。2007 年，专科以上小学教师达 66.9%，比上年提高 4.8 个百分点；本科以上初中教师占 47.3%，比上年提高 6.2 个百分点；研究生学历高中教师达到 1.8%，比上年提高 0.4 个百分点。在新增教师中，具有大学专科、本科学历的教师成为主体。[1]

随着教师学历培训的开展，教师队伍学历合格率显著提高。然而在这些所谓的高合格率背后中，存在着“四重四轻”现象。即重数量轻质量，高校为了追求利益最大化，盲目扩大招生，降低门槛，缩短培训时间，降低教学成本，疏于管理，教学质量下降，学员素质降低；重结果轻过程，中小学教师为名（文凭）而学，对学历培训的认识不足，忽视学习过程对自身素质提高的作用；重职前轻职后，中小学校重视教师任职前的学历，忽视教师任职后的教育培训。重功利轻实绩，政府主管的数字政绩意识，导致其重视学历达标的结果，忽视学历培训的效果。这些现象的存在使得教师培训应有的要求及实际学习情况相差甚远，导致了学历含金量大幅下降，高学历的背后是与其不相符的知识、能力结构，教师素质的下降，教学质量的下降，进而导致学生质量下降。

二、问题在于观念和体制

鉴于中小学教师学历培训存在的问题，我认为问题主要出在观念和体制上。

第一，教师为名（文凭）而学，缺乏素质意识。部分教师不重视学历培训，对提高自身专业知识意识淡薄，重结果轻过程，认为学历培训只是为了一纸文书，只是作为晋级或评职称的一个阶梯。往往是要晋级或评职称时，才会考虑参加培训。再者学历与工资不挂钩，评聘不同步，教师进修后的学历对其意义不大，因而教师积极性普遍不高。加之中小学教师受到教学任务繁重，升学率压力和经济条件等因素的影响，大都只好选择函授的培训模式进行学习。而函授学习的特点是时间短,课程多,一门课程两三天就结束,不到一个月的培训时间安排了十几门课程。为了能按时完成教学任务,高校教师挑选一些重点或考试内容讲解,其它内容只能靠函授学员自学,而中小学教师由于日常教学任务繁重,很难安排自学的时间。

第二,中小学校重职前轻职后,缺乏长远意识。中小学校往往存在重职前学历忽略职后培训的观念。中小学大都没有制定教师培训的计划,或者为了应付上级检查而制定相关教师培训计划,现实中却没有真正贯彻落实。再者学校教育经费紧张,在教师培训问题上,多采取消极的政策。如有些学校不允许教师脱产进修,采取离岗脱产进修政策;认为教师的培训是个人行为,对教师培训的费用不予报销,甚至实行扣发部分工资、相应津贴;进修期间不得参加职称评定等消极的政策。这些消极的政策严重地打击了教师参加培训的积极性。

第三,学校为钱而办学,缺乏质量意识。在经济利益驱使下,教师培训普遍存在的自欺欺人现象,把学历培训当成一种赚钱的手段。各高校一方面为了抢夺生源,采用五花八门的招生手段和"优惠政策",如降低门槛,易进易出等。另一方面疏于教学管理,甚至有些高校可以说是放任管理,采取睁一只眼闭一只眼的方法,忽略了对函授学员应有的要求。不管是否到校学习,学习情况如何,是否有代考行为,只要交钱,一律及格毕业。在这种"管理"理念的影响下,函授学员消极学习,对自身要求不严,想方设法通过各种途径和关系与授课教师联系,以求教师透露考试重点,或采取考试作弊等手段达到成绩合格。这样一来学历培训就完全变味,成为了一种纯商业行为的举动。难怪有人说,学历培训与满大街的办假证的毫无分别,只是一个名正言顺,一个涉嫌违法。

第四,政府主管为功而管,缺乏实绩意识。胡鞍钢博士曾提到:"建国以来,我国一直实行注重物质资本,轻视人力资本的发展战略。"由于物质资本投入周期短、见效快,能短时间出政绩,给政府官员带来实际的效益。而教育投入周期长,见效慢,短时间看不到实绩,且我国对政府官员晋升的考核往往只注重经济效益。教师培训是一项长期的投资项目,需要政府大量经费的投入,短时间看不到其实效,出不了政绩,不能给政府主管带来实际的政绩效果。究其两者利害关系,政府主管忽视教师培训的观念就不难理解了。

第五,国家对教师教育经费投入严重不足,是导致教师培训问题的关键因素。从中央到地方出台与教师培训的相关法律条文都比较少,条文也比较笼统,且没有明确而具体的规定。自1993年我国中央政府在制定90年代教育改革与发展规划时,明确提出到2000年国家财政性教育经费占GDP的4%。1995年颁布实施的教育法也对此作了相应的规定。然而教育投入占GDP的4%提出16年,仍未达标。目前我国教育的公共投入占GDP的比重只有3%,经过调整后,我国实际的公共教育投入占GDP的比例仅为2.4%,和发达国家的差距也就进一步扩大。[2]远远低于世界平均水平,甚至低于发展中国家的平均水平。由于受国家教育经费投入严重不足的影响,使得学校基础教学资源也相对落后,教师参加培训的经费更得不到相应的保障。

三、从端正人才观念和深化体制改革入手

如何解决上述问题,我认为应从端正人才观念和深化体制改革入手。

第一,继承传统思想,树立素质观。我国自古以来有尊师重道的传统美德,有"一日为师,终身为父"、"名师出高徒"、"三教圣人,莫不有师;千古帝王,莫不有师"之美说。作为教师要转

变重结果轻过程的观念，把“要我学”转变到“我要学”，端正求学动机。“学历培训”更注重学的经历，学的过程，学的内涵，加强责任意识，树立名符其实观、实事求是观、为人师表观、学高为师观。在知识爆炸的经济时代，教师要不断更新知识、更新观念，坚持理论与实践相结合，在教学中不断发现自身的不足，做到缺什么补什么，补什么专什么。

第二，转变狭隘观念，树立长远观。中小学校要转变重职前轻职后的观念，根据学校发展需要，制定积极有效的培训计划和相关优惠政策、奖励措施，妥善地解决教与学的矛盾，减轻教师个人教学压力和培训经费的压力，有效保障培训工作的顺利进行。中小学校应加强与高等院校的联系，构建一个教与学的互助机制，以降低经费的投入。教师的素质提高，最终的受益者是学生，是学校，是国家。没有过硬的教师便没有优质教育，没有优质教育便没有优秀人才，没有优秀人才便没有强盛国家。

第三，端正办学方向，树立质量观。学校要把“为钱而办学”转变为“质量办学”的观念。坚持为国家的未来培养合格师资的办学方向。近年来，由于高校的扩招带来的教学质量下降，学生质量下降等问题已引起了多方的关注。兵家有言：“兵不在多而贵精”。人才素质的缺陷很难以数量进行弥补。我们不能只片面地追求量的增长而忽视质的提升。学校应根据不同的生源，合理地安排培训时间，采取多种形式的培训方式，走培训模式多样化的道路，提高培训的效果。再者，学校应建立质量评价机制，制定相应可行的标准，严格考核，端正教风学风考风，对教师的教学质量和学生的学习质量进行有效地评估。

第四，端正“投资观”，树立实绩观。我国的教育经费投入主要靠中央政府和地方政府财政拨款，而实行地方财政包干后，由于我国缺少财政资金使用的绩效考核制度，有的地方政府把经费投入到见效快、出政绩的物质资本投入中，使本来不多的教育经费难以足额及时到位。制度、体制上存在形而上学主义、十分松懈。教师素质的提高不是一蹴而就的，需要加强政府指导，端正“投资观”，构建健全教育投资和培训的长效机制。

加大监督力度，确保教育经费的投入落实到位。人们往往关注教育经费的投入多少，却很少关注到教育经费的投入是否落实到位。有的学校追求规模扩张，追求校舍和基础设施建设方面的高标准、高档次，却忽视教学和科研的投入。如何使得有限的钱，切实地落实到位，这需要我们构建一个有效监督机制，使得教育经费投入公开化、规范化。

第五，建立以政府投入为主，社会投入为辅的机制，拓宽教育经费的筹集途径。对于教育经费的筹集途经，我们不妨来学学美国的做法。美国教师教育经费来源途径多样且具有自己的特色，教师教育资助方式多样，社会捐资用以培养教师的风气浓厚，为教师参加各种培训提供经费以及通过强制手段如立法等以提高教师教育经费投入的执行率。[3]政府要加大教育经费的投入力度，完善师资培训网络体系。但是仅靠中央政府和地方政府的投入是远远不够的，还应广泛发动社会的力量，多渠道筹集经费，构建一个政府和民间共助的机制。同时，还要营造尊师重道的良好氛围，提高教师的社会地位，提升学校的社会影响力，以拓宽教育经费的投资途径。

总而言之，要解决教师学历培训中出现的各种问题，我们要端正办学思想、端正求学动机，端正人才观和用人观。克服为钱、为名、为功（政绩）观念，批判唯文凭的用人观。树立名符其实观、实事求是观、为人师表观、学高为师观。办学单位应从严要求，制定严格的学籍管理、听课、考试、毕业等制度和纪律。学员单位应采取灵活措施，适当照顾。学员要端正求学思想，任课教师应加强责任意识，最终具有决定意义的是政府、社会及用人单位应端正人才观、用人观，

"投资观"，克服片面的"年轻化"、僵硬的"行政化"和"唯学历主义"。

参考文献

[1] 我国中小学专任教师达1052万人趋向高学历化.教育部网站.

[2] 专家称我国实际公共教育投入占GDP比例仅为2.4%. http://money.163.com/09/0908/09/5IM9F5LV00253CAA.html.

[3] 曹惠容.试论美国教师教育经费来源的特点及其对我国的启示[J].中国高教研究，2009，01. http://www.gxqingyuan.com/Forum/showtopic.aspx? topicid=12959&page=end.

第三部分

师范院校教师培养的探索与研究

Development of the Quality Management System for Teacher Training at Nakhon Pathom Rajabhat University, Thailand

Somchit Janjai Benjawan Sahavacharin Jesada Boonmahome
Wirat Nadsawang Suwanna Chaiyathon
(Faculty of Education, Nakorn Pathom Rajabhat University
NakhonPathom 73000, Thailand)

Abstract: After the education reform in Thailand in 1999, school teachers must obtain new bachelor degree in education. Instead of the 4-year education program used before the reform, this new bachelor program needs 5 years to obtain the degree. During the study, the students of this program have to do practical teaching training in schools. Since this program is relatively new, lacking efficient management system, we have developed the quality management system and proposed criteria and indicators of factors for this system. Afterward, the system developed in this work was used to evaluate the current teacher training practice at Nakhon Pathom Rajabhat University, Thailand. It was found that the practice meet the proposed criteria at the average level. Therefore, six strategic plans were proposed to improve this situation. One of this plan was implemented and teacher training handbooks and teaching guidelines were developed for the practical uses.

泰国佛统皇家大学教师教育质量管理体系的发展

摘 要:泰国在1999年教育改革以后,从事教育的学校教师必须获得新的学士学位。改革前获得学生学位需要四年时间,改革后需要五年。改革后学生在攻读过程中必须在学校里进行实践教学培训。这一制度相对比较新,管理体系亟待完善,所以我们已致力完善这一管理体系并提出相关的标准和指标。并已把它用来评价在泰国佛统皇家大学目前的实践教学培训。研究表明所提出的标准总体上切实可行。我们已制定出了6条战略性计划以完善这一体系,其中之一已实施。相应的实践教学培训手册和教学指导用书已相继出笼。

1. Introduction

Thailand proclaimed its first National Education Act in 1999[1], as a consequence of the educational reform movement . According to this Act, the government has to provide the education which responds to global, social and economic changes and corresponds to technological innovation. The National Education Act cover three main topics. These are the reform of education administration and management, the learning reform and the reform of teacher education and development. For the teacher reform and development, the government has issued the working policies to change teacher education from 4 years to 5 years and to grant scholarships to teachers whose major subjects are in urgent demand of the country. The target number of teachers to be graduated is also specified. In addition, more educational technologies and active learning are encouraged to use.

Nakhon Pathom Rajabhat University, situated about 60 kilometers west of Bangkok, was first founded as the Women's Teacher School in 1936. Then it was promoted to be Nakhon Pathom Teacher College in 1975. At that time, it was among 36 teacher colleges existing in the country. Each college provided teacher education as well as other programs at diploma and degree level according to the need of the community. Because of this expanded function, all teacher colleges were upgraded to the level of institutes of higher education and were bestowed the name "Rajabhat" which means "the King's academician". In 2004, the government passed the law that transformed all Rajabhat Institutes into Rajabhat Universities. These universities provide the community with higher education and vocational training. With this reform, Nakhon Pathom Rajabhat University was reorganized. As a result, the University is divided into four faculties: Faculty of Education, Faculty of Science and Technology, Faculty of Humanities and Social Science and Faculty of Management Science. Each faculty is sub-divided into programs. In total, there are 46 programs for under graduate and 12 programs for graduate levels. Within the Faculty of Education, there are the program of early childhood education and the program of physical education. In addition, it also provide fundamental education courses for other 7 joint-programs with the other faculties. These are science education, mathematic education, Thai education, English education, social education, music education and arts education. This year, there are 1500 students attending these programs. Officially, it is required 5 years to complete the study. During the study, the students have to practice teaching in schools. Especially, the fifth year students have to spend one year for the teaching practice in schools. In order to provide their teaching experience, the Faculty of Education set up the Teacher Training Center, coordinating with various partnerships involving with teacher training. The Faculty use the demonstration school, the kindergarten school of the University as well as the partnership schools for the training of these students. The partnership schools are good schools in the community, which can host these students. The staffs of the Faculty as well as teachers in the partnership schools were nominated by their own organization to supervise the students. Both supervisors work together for this training process. The problem challenging teacher training now is how to provide teaching experience which is both of high quality and high standard in order to enhance students to be knowledgeable, competent, professionally skillful, holding high moral standards and becoming good social models. This research aims to develop a quality management system for teacher training. The objectives of this research are as follows:

(1) To develop criteria and indicators of various factors within the quality management system of teacher training.

(2) To evaluate the current situations of the teacher training of Nakhon Pathom Rajabhat University.

(3) To propose strategic plans to improve the management system of the teacher training.

(4) To develop the teacher handbooks and teaching guidelines for using in the teacher training.

2. Research method

There were 3 groups of participants in this research. The first group was the teacher training team from the University consisting of 5 researchers, 7 heads of the education programs, 10 teacher training supervisors and 2 former directors of the Teacher Training Center. The second group was the partnership school team consisting of 12 school administers and school supervisors . The third group was 14 students selected from all education programs.

The research procedure can be summarized as follows :

Step 1 Studying the current situations and the problems of teacher training management at Nakhon Pathom Rajabhat University. To get this information, we interviewed the directors of the Teacher Training Center and carried out brainstorm among the students. Then the content analysis was made to get the conclusion.

Step 2 Doing the SWOT analysis of the current situations in providing teacher training experience. This analysis was involved by the first group of research participants.

Step 3 Setting the philosophy, vision, mission and strategies in teacher training management of the Teacher Training Center. The conclusion of this setting was made from the SWOT analysis and the result from step 1.

Step 4 Setting criteria and indicators involving all the input and process factors in the teacher training management system. The principles of the quality management system [2] were synthesized and used to obtain the criteria and indicators.

Step 5 Evaluating the current status of teacher training management system according to the criteria and indicators as set up in step 4. A rating scale questionnaire was made and used for this evaluation. The answers of the questionnaire were from all the heads of the teacher education programs.

Step 6 Forming strategic plans in order to improve the teacher training management. A workshop whose participants were the teacher training supervisors and heads of the education programs, was organized to get the strategic plan.

Step 7 Developing the teacher handbooks and teaching guidelines for teacher training.

3. Results and discussion

The results of this research can be summarized into 2 sections. Section 1 include the results obtained from step 1 to step 3, enabling the research team to collect necessary data to be analyzed and synthesized in order to lay down the quality management system. Section 2 is the research results responding to the objectives of the research. The results of each section are described as follows:

Section 1 Basic data used for laying down the quality management system of teacher training

1.1 The results of the study of the current situations and the problems in teacher training management are as follows:

- Lacking of supporting factors such as transportation needed by the supervisors from the University to the partnership schools where students are practicing.
- Accreditation of work loads for the supervision was lower than the normal teaching loads, this does not correspond to the actual work done and the time spent.
- Lacking of monitoring system, following up, and evaluating the work of the supervisors.
- Lacking of coordination and cooperation among the university supervisors and the supervisors in schools.
- Insufficient numbers of supervisors from the University.

1.2 As the result of the SWOT analysis of the current situations of teacher training, it was found that there were both internal and external factors which were either positive or negative as shown in Table 1.

Table 1 The result of the SWOT analysis of the teacher training situations

INTERNAl	Positive factors	Negative factors
factors	Strengths	Weaknesses
	1. There is a Teacher Training Center, which co-ordinate the various groups of participants in teacher training. 2. In the University, there are Science center, the demonstration school at secondary level and kindergarten which can be used as laboratories for science, mathematic and kindergarten teachers. 3. There are many school teachers who graduated from the University; these alumni are very helpful for the teacher training process. 4. The University has 70-years experience in teacher training. The community has confidence in education programs of the University.	1. Most experienced supervisors of the university have retired. 2. New supervisors have not enough experience. 3. The information about the partnership schools and the school teachers is not sufficient. 4. There are insufficient evaluation and following up processes for teacher training.
factors	1. The government has announced the 15 year free education for children. 2. Teaching is a career still needed by the country; therefore, there are many students interested in education program. So the faculty can recruit more suitable students to enroll in the education program. 3. The government grants scholarship to the good students to study in the education program. 4. There are more competent and skillful school supervisors; therefore, the Center can assign competent school supervisors to supervise the students.	1. There is still an imbalance between the quota of new supervisors and those who are retiring. 2. There are other government niversities that also provide education program. So there is high competition in this field. 3. The government has policy to control the number of teachers so they will not be excessive. 4. The University receives less budget than other big universities.

As the result of the SWOT analysis, the Faculty of Education should make use of the strengths to increase the opportunities and to decrease the threats by the following measures: First, the University should develop the curriculum of science education, mathematic education and early childhood education programs. Second, good quality students from high schools in the community should be recruited with a provision of the scholarship to study in the programs. Finally, job positions as teachers should be provided by related organizations in the community after the completion of their studies. To overcome the weaknesses and threats, the following measures should be implemented: First, on-line database of information on teacher training such as names of partnership schools and supervisors, academic record of the students and activities of students and supervisors in the schools should be established. Second, criteria and indicators for the quality management system of the teacher training should be set up and implemented. Third, a strategic plan to promote the supervisors of the university and to recruit young supervisors should be made. Finally, sufficient financial support and facilities for teacher training activities such as transportation and communication should be provided.

1.3 Setting the philosophy, vision, mission and strategies for the Teacher Training Center. The outcomes from the meeting of the teacher training team from the University are as follows:

Philosophy Outstanding coordination, excellent service, high-quality teacher training management were set up as the philosophy of the Teacher Training Center.

Vision In the next five year, it is expected the students who have been trained with this quality management system will become qualified teachers. They will be competent in teaching and capable of using information technology for teaching activities. In addition, they will be hard-working, life-long learning and public devoting people.

Mission The mission of the Teacher Training Center was proposed as follows:

(1) Establish a quality management system and network for teacher training.

(2) Provide training activities for the development of students.

(3) Help improving the schools and the teachers that join with the Faculty of Education in Teacher training.

(4) Develop the curriculum for teaching training.

Strategies The followings strategies are suggested.

(1) Create school network to host students.

(2) Develop supervision process which involve the participation from partnership schools.

(3) Develop the potentials and personality of students so that they can become skillful professional teachers.

(4) Improve database of information on the teacher training.

(5) Coordinate and cooperate with partnership schools and the community in fulfilling the potentials of students.

Section 2 Results responding to the research objectives

2.1 Based on the total quality management control[3], we have proposed criteria and indicators of input factors and process factors as shown in Table 2.

Table 2 The criteria and indicators of factors involved in the management system of the teacher training

Factors	Criteria	Indicator
Input factors 1. Curriculum for teacher training	Criteria 1 There is a curriculum that aims to develop high quality teacher.	1. There are handbooks for students to use during their pre-service teacher training. 2. The outcome of learning must reflect the consequence of the high quality teachers. 3. The content of the teacher training curriculum must give knowledge, skills and experience for teaching profession. 4. There are processes for training teachers in partnership schools under the supervision of supervisors from the Faculty and the partnership schools. 5. There are evaluation processes and the results are used for the improvement of the curriculum and students.
2. Supporting factors for teacher training	Criteria 1 There is an adequate provision of transportation for the University supervisors	1. There are available vehicles for the supervisors. 2. University provides accidental insurances for the supervisors. 3. There is financial support for transportation in case that the supervisors have to travel to schools in remote areas.
	Criteria 2 There are enough equipment and materials for teacher training.	1. There are student handbooks on teacher training, supervision record forms and supervision evaluation forms. 2. There are enough audio visual materials for using in teacher training.
	Criteria 3 There is adequate allocation of budget to support the teacher training.	1. There is sufficient budget for the education programs and the Teacher Training Center. 2. There is accountability system in which all expenses can be inspected whether the money has been spent efficiently.
3. Information system for teacher training	Criteria 1 There is database of information for planning the teacher training.	1. There is complete and up-to-date information about students, teacher, partnership schools, supervisors from schools and from the University, with reflect the current status and the tendency within the next 5 years. 2. There is information service that can provide counseling in both academic and self development in order to coach students in their effort to improve themselves. 3. There is information technology which can be effectively used.

续表

Factors	Criteria	Indicator
4. The students	Criteria 1 The students have basic qualifications ready to enter teacher training in schools.	1. The students have to pass all of the required education courses before starting to practice teaching in schools. 2. They obtain not less than grade "C" in all education courses. 3. They have to participate in all compulsory activities that are intended to mould high quality teachers. 4. They behave properly and comply to the rules and regulations of the University.
	Criteria 2 The students have adequate knowledge and ability and they are proud of their profession.	1. They admire and have faith in their teacher profession. 2. They show their effort in trying to help develop their pupils. 3. They improve their lesson plans that can be actualized and truly achieved. 4. They always develop their teaching aids that can be used effectively. 5. They prepare learning activities by keeping in mind the good effect that will happen to their pupils. 6. They can systematically report the effectiveness of the learning process of their pupils. 7. They behave themselves and serve as good social models for their students.
5. The supervisor	Criteria 1 The supervisors are well qualified to supervise students.	1. The supervisors are proficient in the subject area they supervised and understand the process of teacher training. 2. The supervisors are knowledgeable in the preparation of learning activities and classroom action research so that they can coach their students in improving the learning and teaching process in the subject area. 3. The teacher training supervisors are knowledgeable in the schools' management system and the school-based curriculum of the schools where the students are to put theory into practice. 4. Both the content supervisors and the teacher training supervisors join in the teacher training seminars with the students and the school supervisors, which is held before and after teacher training. 5. The supervisors have at least 2 years experience in teaching courses that related to teacher training.
	Criteria 2 The supervisors have incentives and morale to do their jobs.	1. Make an official annual announcement of outstanding supervisors. 2. Give appropriate weight for supervision working load so that it corresponds to the time spent and the number of students under supervision.

续表

Factors	Criteria	Indicator
1. The process of teaching training	Criteria 1 There are processes of effective teacher training practice.	1. There is data collection and research necessary for using in planning teacher training. 2. There is a working plan for teacher training practice. 3. There is work performance completion according to the plan. 4. There is continuous monitoring and evaluation of the teacher training practice. 5. There are records and evaluation reports. 6. There is an application of the data and evaluation reports in the decision making stage and in improving teacher training.
	Criteria 2 There is a management system that supports effective teachetraining practice.	1. There is a Teaching Training Center whose functions are to plan teacher training experiences, to coordinate with all concerned partners, to supervise and monitor as well as to evaluate teacher training practice. 2. There is an officially appointed working committee in which the roles, responsibilities and tasks are clearly specified. 3. There is a permanent officers at the Teacher Training Center who take care of the office duties, coordinate with and provide convenience for supervisors in doing their jobs. 4. The Teacher Training Center has the philosophy, vision, mission and strategic plans to launch the management of teacher training. 5. There is an establishment of cooperative network with the partnership schools and the communities.
	Criteria 3 There is tracking and follow up system as well as the evaluation the teacher training practice.	1. There is an obvious plan for supervision, monitoring and follow up with teacher training. 2. There is research tool for collecting data in the supervision process and the use of the data to improve the process. 3. There is an annual report on the teacher training practice which is sent to all partners.
2. The personnel development process.	Criteria 1 There is personnel development for those concerned with teacher training so that they become life-long learners.	1. There is a plan for personnel development to improve work efficiency. 2. There are activities for supervisor development. 3. There is a supportive atmosphere that induces self development and exchanges of knowledge among working personnel. 4. There is a system and network for mutual learning with partnership schools. 5. There is evidence showing the curriculum development.

2.2 We have evaluated the current teacher training performance of Nakhon Pathom Rajabhat University by using the proposed criteria and indicators of the quality management. It was found that the evaluation of almost all the criteria was at average level, except for the criteria for the curriculum for teacher training which was at low level.

2.3 Six strategic plans were created for using to improve the teacher training. These are:

-The plan for the development of the teacher training curriculum which aims to develop the curriculum and handbooks for teacher training experience.

-The plan for setting up the information system for teacher training.

-The plan for the development of the University supervisors and the school supervisors.

-The plan to provide supporting facilities for teacher training activities.

-The plan for supervising student teachers which aim to recruit partnership schools for teacher training practice.

-The plan for the development of the Teacher Training Center.

2.4 We have developed the guidelines for students on how to prepare lessons and 5 handbooks for the training, as listed:

(1) Guidelines for supervisors on how to set up activities where they can observe students while practice teaching in schools.

(2) Guidelines for supervisors on how to prepare activities for students to practice in the role of teacher assistants in schools.

(3) Guidelines for supervisors to prepare activities in practice teaching for students in schools.

(4) Guidelines for supervisors to design activities for students who will spend one year with teacher training in schools.

4. Conclusion

In this work, we have developed the quality management system for teacher training at Nakhon Pathom Rajabhat University. In the development, we have set up the criteria and indicators for the teacher training. The criteria and indicators were used to evaluate the current situation of the teacher training of the University. From the evaluation, we proposed the strategic plans to improve the performance of the teacher training. One of the strategic plan was implemented. Finally, we produced the handbooks and guidelines for the supervisors and students in teacher training programs in schools.

5. Acknowledgement

We thank Office of Higher Education Commission for the financial support of this research.

Reference

[1] National Education Commission. National Education Act (1999). Bangkok: Prikwhan Graphics, 2002.

[2] EVANS J R, LINDSAY W M. The Management and Control of Quality. Singapore: Thompson, 2005.

[3] RICHARDSON T L. Total Quality Management. New York: Delmar Publishers, 1997.

地方综合性院校教师教育一体化体系的构建

莫华善* 徐书业** 张传月***

(钦州学院,广西 钦州 535000)

摘　要:构建一体化的教师教育体系以教师专业化和终身教育思想为理论基础。相对地方综合性院校而言,当下教师教育存在机构设置不合理、职前职后教育失范、师范专业去师范化、课程有效性不高等问题。地方综合性院校教师教育体系一体化构建应体现连续性和整体性,在培养培训机构与教学管理机制、培养与培训目标以及实施教育教学过程等方面体现一体化要求。

关键词:地方综合性院校;教师教育;培养模式;一体化

基金项目:新世纪广西高等教育教学改革工程"十一五"第五批立项项目"教师教育一体化与新建地方综合性院校教师教育师资队伍建设的研究与实践"(项目编号:2009B084)。

Construction of Integrated System of Teachers' Educational Local Comprehensive Colleges

Mo Hua-shan, Xu Shu-ye, Zhang Chuan-yue

(Qinzhou University, Qinzhou 535000, China)

Abstract: Construction of integrated system of teachers' education shall be based on the theories of specialzation of teaching profession and lifelong educations. Compared to local comprehensive institutes, currently teachers' education facilities are still having problems such as improper teachers' education setting, unregualted pre-and-post educations, normality loss in normal specialty and ineffectiveness of

* 莫华善,钦州学院教育系副研究员。

** 徐书业,钦州学院副院长,教授,博士。

*** 张传月,钦州学院教育系副教授。

various courses. Consistency and integration shall be fully demonstrated throughout the process of construction of intergrated system of teachers' education at local comprehensive institutes, that is, from the cultivation of teaching facilities and teaching management systems, the goal of education and training to appliance of education and teaching.

Key words: local comprehensive colleges; teachers' education; cultivation mode; integration

本文所指的地方综合性院校主要是指由原来独立设置的高等师范专科学校(或中等师范学校)与其他大中专院校合并升格而成立的高校。在我国教师教育机构开放化和多元化格局逐渐形成的背景下,地方综合性院校如何发挥已有教师教育资源的优势和特色,完善教师教育体系,推进教师教育教学改革,这是本文思考和探讨的问题。

一、教师教育一体化体系构建的外部环境和理论基础

詹姆斯·波特从终身教育的理论出发,提出现代师范教育应分为三个阶段,即个人教育阶段(职前教育阶段)、准备教育阶段(试用阶段)、在职教育阶段(继续教育阶段),率先阐发了职前培养与职后培训一体化的思想。[1]从 20 世纪 80 年代以来,教师教育一体化开始成为世界范围内教师教育变革的主要趋势之一。

1. 终身教育思想

1965 年联合国教科文组织促进成人教育国际委员会主席保罗·郎格朗首先提出"终身教育"的称法,这一概念在 20 世纪 70 年代兴起。[2]联合国教科文组织的报告《从现在到 2000 年教育内容发展的全球展望》对终身教育的内涵作了进一步的揭示。终身教育作为一种教育思想,它具有整体性特点,面向全体人民,并把一切具有教育功能的机构(子系统)联系或连接起来,使各种教育机构一体化;教育是连续性的,它贯穿于人生发展的始终,把人生成长的各个阶段连接起来,使人生各个发展阶段一体化。[3]自 20 世纪 60 年代以来,终身教育作为一种最有影响的教育思潮和教育策略引起世界各国的关注,从西方到东方,从发达国家到发展中国家,它已被不同社会制度的国家普遍接受,并对世界教育的理论和实践产生了深远的影响。

2. 教师专业发展理论

教师专业发展问题也是国际组织一贯强调和重视的问题,早在 1963 年和 1980 年世界教育年鉴的主题分别就是"教育与教师培养"和"教师专业发展"。教师专业发展理论认为,教师作为一个教学人员,要经历一个由不成熟到相对成熟的发展历程。已经取得合格学历和相应的教师资格证书并踏上教学工作岗位的教师,虽然经过了职前教育,但这并不意味着就是一个成熟的教学人员,教师的专业发展空间是无限的,成熟是相对的,而发展是绝对的。首先,教师的专业发展是一个连续的、动态的、终身的过程。教师教育并不仅限于职前的师资培育,其外延应一直延伸到教师专业生涯的最后阶段,教师教育机构要为教师专业成长提供全程支持,这种教育的支持应包括职前的培养、新教师的入职教育与辅导、教师在职培训;其次,教师专业发展具有一体化的内涵。它包括:专业理想的建立、专业知识的拓展、专业能力的发展、专业自我的形成,这几方面只有相互配合、相互关联,构成一个完整的整体,才能造就出一个成熟、优秀、和谐的教学专业人员。特别是 20 世纪 80 年代以来,教师专业发展日益成为人们关注的焦点,

许多发达国家中小学教师的培养目标呈现高层次化趋势，师范教育全部纳入高等教育序列。教师专业化形成了一股强劲的世界性潮流，推动了许多国家教师教育新理念和新制度的建立。

二、地方综合性院校现行教师教育管理体系运行中存在的问题

以广西为例，目前广西有河池学院、钦州学院、贺州学院、百色学院、梧州学院、北海职业学院等多所地方综合性院校，这些院校尽管已经不属于师范类高等学校，但仍然承担本地区中小学教师的培养培训任务，因此这些院校仍具有教师教育机构的特性和功能。但在综合性院校的教师教育实践中，人们发现原有的教师教育优势在逐渐失去，教师专业培养目标的师范性在一定程度上被弱化，师范专业毕业生质量也受到了中小学校的质疑。从教师教育一体化理论的视角，我们认为制约当前地方综合性院校实现教师教育一体化进程以及教师教育人才培养质量的因素主要体现在以下几个方面：

1. 学校内部教师教育管理机构设置的合理化问题

当前，虽然地方综合性院校主要由原来的师专与教育学院、中师或其他大中专院校等教育机构合并升格而成，本区域的教师教育资源已经由多校共享整合到一校独有的格局，实现中小学教师培养培训一体化具备了基本的前提和基础，但是落实到学校实践上仍然存在不少障碍，教师教育的效果并不显著。学校合并升格转轨的过程中因人设事、机构重复设置的问题仍然存在，教师教育职能未能做到条块管理，校内教师教育资源分属不同管理机构，并列的教师教育教学单位缺乏协调沟通，给管理上带来一定的难度和障碍，造成有限的教学经费重复投资。如目前一些院校内部职能机构中由教务处管理职前教师培养，成人教育处既管理在职教师学历提高也负责在职教师培训，在院系教学系列设教育系或初等教育系负责教育学类专业教学，学科类师范专业则由其他院系负责，从事教师教育的师资分属不同的教学单位。这种教师职前培养和在职培训分别由不同职能机构承担的分离的教育教学模式与一体化的教师教育理念是对立的，在实践中对提高教师教育人才培养培训质量造成了极大的阻力。

2. 职前培养和职后培训的失范问题

新升格的综合性院校试图构建一种综合性大学的框架，往往把更多精力和财力集中在新设置的非师范专业的建设上，将工作重心放到如何提高学校的办学层次和整体实力上，忽略了对教师教育专业的内涵建设和经费的投入，甚至导致多年积累的高师教育特色与优势逐渐淡化和边缘化。而在开放的教师教育体系下(包括教师教育机构多元性、取消师范院校毕业生国家分配制度、允许非师范专业人员认证教师资格等)，综合性院校对职前教师培养目标的认识容易倾向专业的学术性、应用性而忽视了师范性，体现在学科课程比例增加，教师教育课程比例被挤压，计算机、外语等工具性课程受到重视而教育基本原理、教师口语、演讲、书写、教学技能、教学实践等教师职业课程逐步被弱化；职前实践训练时间不足，目前，许多院校安排师范专业学生的教育见习和教育实习时间一般在 4～6 周左右，远低于国外一些发达国家的水平。如美国教师教育专业的学生有大约一个学期的时间集中用于教学实践，英国则达到 24 周。[4] 教育实习时间过少，师范生很难将专业知识综合用于具体教学环境，也延长了毕业生走上工作岗位之后由新手教师向成熟教师的过渡时间，这对教师成长是不利的。教师职后培训的观念落后，不注重职前培养和在职培训目标设计之间的连贯性。培训方式比较单一，仍然是知识传授式、单向式的，缺少教育现场与实践情景。教学管理的规范程度不高，片面追求培训规模和经

济效益。教师学历补偿教育与提高培训之间的衔接机制不健全，如一些中小学教师在学历提高培训中，避开自己多年从事的学科教学现实而选择就读所谓容易拿到学分的学科课程，这是不正常的，反映了管理环节上的疏忽，教学管理者没有根据继续教育学分登记、学科素质提高的连贯性、人才使用以及职称评定等来综合考察并实施教学管理。

3. 师范专业设置与教师教育师资的去师范化问题

由于综合性院校的人才培养定位主要以应用型为主，为满足迅速增长的新专业教学需要，不少师范专业教师通过转轨培训而成为担任非师范新专业课程的教学人员并从师范专业院系分流出来，导致师范专业的师资紧张，教师教育课程建设力度减弱，尤其是教育学科课程与教师职业技能课程师资不足，专业实践技能训练不够充分，师范生技能培养质量下降。教师教育师资的转轨导致学校课程文化建设的去师范化现象，这种现象与我国新一轮基础教育课程变革的形势是不相适应的。新课程改革对目前高校的教师教育课程设置必将产生更加深刻的影响，需要教师教育院校进行对应的课程革新。而课程变革的资源是无限的、多种多样的、强有力的，所有学科不断增长的知识冲击着课程内容。这些都是进行教师教育课程改革与教师教育师资队伍建设必须予以重视的外部背景和条件。综合性院校的去师范化现象实质是一个学科本位思想的取向问题，目前一些院校仍然以实施“公共类课程＋学科专业类课程＋教育类课程”的传统培养模式为主，这种培养模式的最大特点是将学科专业类课程和教育类课程在培养计划中混合编排，尽管学生毕业后自然获取教师资格，但实践证明，这种培养模式培养的学生在学科专业性上先天不足，在师范性上优势不强，就像“两个半桶水相加”。[5]这是重“学术性”轻“师范性”观念的外在表现，在这种观念的支配下，教师教育实践活动结果的最大缺陷就是不能突出教师职业的特殊性，而在校园文化建设上，片面重学术取向、轻师范氛围的营造，极不利于学生教育情感的养成。值得注意的是，由于我国大批地方区域性综合性学院均为办学在5年内的新办院校，这些院校的办学兴奋点还在如何改善办学条件、如何扩大非师范专业规模、如何设置适应地方经济建设的专业等方面上，教师教育课程设置与人才培养模式创新改革工作有所淡化，教师教育工作出现边缘化趋势已是在所难免。

4. 课程设置的实效性问题

中小学校对师范生实习后反馈回来的信息表明，目前综合性院校教师教育院系关注和研究我国基础教育新课程改革不够，训练师范生的教学技能没有很好把握新一轮基础教育课程改革的实质，教师教育内容还停留于教育学、心理学基本原理的灌输，理论与具体教育实践相脱节，教学方式和技术手段落后，脱离中小学现实教育生活，专业训练缺乏务实性，师范生的课程开发和教育技术等能力缺乏，人才培养活动脱离了教师对自身教学实践情景问题的关注，培养规格与中小学师资的实际要求尚有一定差距，这些都是教师教育课程设置针对性缺乏、实效性不高以及教师职业教育特征被弱化的体现。比如目前最能体现教师教学技巧能力并区别于其他职业技能的课程包括：普通话、钢笔字、粉笔字、毛笔字、演讲、演唱、体育裁判、教学设计技能、班主任工作技能、摄影、板报设计、双语教学、教育技术辅助教学技能等还未能引起承担教师教育任务的综合性院校足够的重视。

三、地方综合性院校构建一体化教师教育体系的对策思考

要解决当前地方综合性院校教师教育一体化进程中出现的问题，提高区域性教师教育人

才培养质量，需要构建与选择适合地方综合性院校特征的一体化教师教育体系，这一体系的核心构想应包括：

1. 教师教育培养培训机构和教学管理机制一体化

在我国教师教育体系改革实践中，一批高校已探索总结了一些切实可行的教育教育一体化培养和管理模式。如将教师培养转移到高校教育学院的“4＋2”模式，这种模式最早在北京师范大学等教师教育机构实施，强调教育研究和教师教育资源的有机整合，突出教育研究与教师教育的优势与特色，使教育学院在教育科学研究和培养教育类专业本科生、硕士生及博士生基础上，强化了教师培养的功能。但是这种模式目前还不具备在全国教师教育院校推广的基础，尤其是大量地方高校并没有相应的政策；有的院校实施职前培养和职后培训集中整合的教学管理模式，将教师教育资源统合到学校的教师教育学院（或教育系）归口管理，行政管理职能则分属不同的职能机构，教师教育学院（或教育系）需要与学校其他职能部门如教务处、成人教育处等协调下工作，教育管理权限分散，协调与管理环节比较多。针对地方综合性院校多个层次不同类型学校合并、教师教育资源分散、师范功能有所弱化的特征，我们认为，需要寻求和建立有别于上述运行模式的实现培养培训机构和教育教学管理机制一体化的新机制，确保教师教育质量。要进一步理顺校内教师教育机构管理职能，对管理、教学科研资源进行调整，成立新的教师教育教学管理机构（如教师教育处），进行全校教师教育工作的协调和管理，这一机构与教师教育学院（或教育系）可以分设也可以合署，所有教师教育事务从教务处、成人教育学院或其他培训机构中剥离并归口教师教育机构管理。强化教师教育机构教学管理自主权，对校内教师教育资源进行充分整合，实施学科专业教育与教师专业教育、师范专业与非师范专业分离的人才培养模式，师范专业学生、学科教学论教师和师范教育实践环节的组织实施从原来的各专业学院（系）分流出来，这样处理更利于组织教育专业教学和研究活动，既可能避免学科教学论教师被专业学院（系）边缘化的倾向，又可以解决教师教育课程与师资的去师范化问题；既可保持教师教育在综合性院校中的传统优势和地位，又突出教师教育和教育科学研究的特色。新的教师教育教学管理体系同时包括中小学师资培训中心、中小学校长培训中心、教育行政管理干部培训中心等机构。这样的体系将能最大限度地全面负责和开展教育类本专科专业学生的职前培养、教育科学研究和咨询、教师的岗前培训和职后培训、高校教师岗前培训、教育管理干部培训、师范生支教顶岗实习、非师范生教师资格培训认定等工作。

2. 教师教育人才培养目标和培训要求一体化

社会经济以及教育的改革发展需要高素质的师资。“从世界范围看，教育的未来在很大程度上依赖于未来教师的数量和质量。……未来的教师要具有很好的学术素养，有良好的个性品质，并具有专业化的资格”。[6]培养能适应新课程改革需要的，开展素质教育的德才兼备的专业化教师依然是综合性院校教育人才培养的基本目标和要求。实现这个目标，必须处理好师范性和学术性关系，设计连贯性的一体化的培养培训目标：一是在职前培养阶段强化接触基础教育实践，加强与中小学校教育的合作与衔接，避免综合性院校的教师、师范专业学生普遍关注基础教育不够、研究基础教育不够、服务基础教育不够的现象，扭转基础教育课程改革搞得轰轰烈烈而教师教育院校的教师对此缺乏关注与理解，职前培养滞后于基础教育改革的尴尬局面；二是在职后培训阶段强化接触新的教育思想观念的熏陶，树立促进教师发展为本的职后培训观念，改变职后培训仍停留在学历补偿教育和知识传递阶段的做法，促使教师在定期的回流教育培训中能够对自身的教育实践进行反思，获得教学艺术提升的机会。在此方面，美国教师专业化运动中曾实施推广的教师专业发展学校至今仍然是我们实现教师培养与培训一体化的一种有效方式，其基本做法是大学教育学院与中小学合作培养教师，由大学教师与实践经验丰富的中小学教师共同合作完成对实习生的培养，中小学教师定期走进大学校园，承担教师培训的课程，使得中小学教学实践中的具体问题得以回归大学课堂，大学教育情景才变得鲜活真实，有效解决职前培养和职后培训教学中的冲突问题。大学教师教育理论工作者通过与中小学实践的结合、中小学在职教师通过对实习生的指导，共同实现对教师自身教育历程的反思、自我提高和专业发展。

3. 教师教育教学过程一体化

依据终身教育思想和教师专业发展理论，教师的个体成长是终身职业社会化的过程，在不同阶段有不同的职业发展需求。教师教育应该遵循这一规律构建贯通教师教育职前与职后的课程体系和教学内容，既满足教师发展的阶段性需求，又能体现终身教育的整体性，强化教师职业教育特征。设计一体化的教师教育内容和要求，关键是加强对教师教育课程体系的整体设计，注重职前培养课程与职后培训课程的衔接，改变职前培养、职后培训在课程教学上相互割裂和低水平重复的状况。[7]我们认为，培养培训同时也是一个共生互动的过程，作为师范类专业，不论是职前培养计划还是职后培训计划，必须从一体化的角度进行设计，需要考虑并认识到教师的成长是一个生成的、长期的过程，理应靠职前培养和职后培训共同承担完成，最终确保在职前培养与职后培训的课堂教学以及教学质量评价等方面的教学管理设计要求上体现一贯性。在理论教学与实践教学环节的关系上，无论是职前培养与职后培训，实践环节是不可或缺的，毕竟教育始终是一门实践的艺术，实践的智慧和实践的能力是教师应具有的重要素质。因为，教师教育的理论教学主要是以讲授教师所需理论性知识的课程，而单纯依靠理论教学不可能培养出具有实践能力的合格的师资。[8]目前，职前培养的课程应注重基础性、综合性以及通识教育，而在职后培训环节上，更要注重对教师已有教育观念和教育行为的反思。

参考文献

[1] 吴文侃，杨汉清. 比较教育学[M]. 北京：人民教育出版社，1999：531.

[2] 胡森. 教育大百科全书[M]. 重庆：西南师范大学出版社；海口：海南出版社，2006：67.

[3] 拉塞克，维迪努. 从现在到 2000 年教育内容的全球展望[M]. 马胜利，等，译. 北京：教育科学出版社，1990：142-143.

[4] 教育部师范教育司. 教师专业化的理论与实践[M]. 北京：人民教育出版社，2003：155.

[5] 钟秉林. 师范大学转型与高师教育走向[M]. 北京：教育科学出版社，2002：87.

[6] 胡森. 教育大百科全书[M]. 重庆：西南师范大学出版社；海口：海南出版社，2006：498-499.

[7] 荀渊. 教师教育一体化改革的回顾与反思[J]. 教师教育研究，2004(4).

[8] 曲铁华，马艳芬. 论教师专业化与职前教师教育课程改革[J]. 教育科学，2004(4).

发达地区农村顶岗实习支教的探讨

李 彬* 黄翠红**
(湖州师范学院,浙江 湖州 313000)

摘 要:本文以浙江省顶岗实习支教为例,通过顶岗实习支教实践过程中出现的问题,按教育实习的规律,从操作层面提出了改革措施,为推进教师教育实习改革和促进顶岗实习支教发展提供依据。

关键词:顶岗实习;支教;实习;农村

基金项目:省教育规划课题"面向农村基础教育——师范生教师能力培养体系的研究与实践"(SCG369);校级课题"我校师范生顶岗实习工作中存在的问题与对策研究"(GJC09008)。

Study on Student Teaching Exchange in Well-developed Rural Areas

Li Bin, Huang Cui-hong
(Huzhou University, Huzhou 313000, China)

Abstract: The thesis takes the student teaching exchange in Zhejiang as an example, through the problems caused in the exchange and due to the rules of educational practice, proposed reform measures from the operational level, and provide a basis to promote the teacher education reform and the development of teaching exchange.

Key words: teaching exchange; teaching; teaching practice; rural areas

---

* 李彬,湖州师范学院教务处。

** 黄翠红,湖州师范学院教务处。

一、引言

目前,发达地区的农村学校师资数量基本达到要求,但还存在着农村教师老龄化和优秀教师匮乏等现象。为提高农村教育质量、促进义务教育均衡发展、加快社会主义新农村建设,浙江省启动了"农村素质教育提升工程"和"农村中小学教师领雁工程",考虑到在实施过程中出现的严重"供学矛盾",提出了"师范生顶岗实习支教"。顶岗实习支教是一个涉及高师院校、地方教育行政部门、实习基地中小学及带队教师、实习指导教师、实习生、中小学生等多层次、多元素、多方位、多领导的系统工程[1],这对教育实习的模式带来新的挑战。高校教育实习是教师教育教学中的重要环节,改革教育实习环节,提高教师培养质量,同时兼顾农村教师短缺的矛盾,提高农村教育水平,是非常目前重要的问题。下面以浙江省为例探讨顶岗实习支教与教育实习的改变。

二、顶岗实习支教过程中存在的问题

1. 政策执行

浙江省开展顶岗实习支教工作是新形势下加强师范教育实习的一种重要形式,将师范生实习与农村中小学教师"领雁工程"有机结合,选派优秀师范生到农村中小学顶岗实习,不仅为农村骨干教师参加"领雁工程"培训提供时间,还能引导学生深入基层,了解农村中小学教学现状,增强社会责任感和使命感,更有利于教师教育与基础教育建立密切联系,帮助高师院校更深入地参与基础教育尤其是农村基础教育的改革发展和实践研究,对推进地方基础教育均衡发展具有十分重大的意义。但是,还有些地方教育行政部门和高校部分老师不能准确理解顶岗实习这项工程的内涵和真正意义,因此,在执行过程中会遇到来自校内外的各种阻力和压力,比如:学校对教学计划和正常教学秩序的调整不及时;任课教师对顶岗学生单独进行理论课程考试和学分认定不理解;学生家长对顶岗子女的不理解;教育行政部门和中小学校政策不完善等等,严重影响了高校顶岗实习工作的开展。

2. 思想认识

顶岗实习是一个制度化、长期、有效的模式与机制,在一定程度上可以实现教育系统内部教师资源的合理配置,是一个将学生培养与农村教师队伍建设联系起来的现实思路[2]。要真正实现顶岗实习这个工程,需要教育行政部门、实习学校和高师院校共同来完成,缺一不可。特别是地方教育行政部门是高校和实习学校之间的纽带,起桥梁作用,所以,教育行政部门的认识到位和重视更为重要。然而,从目前情况来看,有些地方教育行政部门对农村中小学教师的"领雁工程"培训很重视,对顶岗实习支教工作不够积极,常常持被动和观望态度。部分高校老师对顶岗实习工作也不支持,认为顶岗实习只是教育行政部门让学生去填补领雁工程培训教师的缺岗,打乱高校正常教学计划,不符合人才培养目标,而且教学成本增加,高校可以拒绝安排,从而出现了双方沟通难、落实任务难、实习管理难和思想不统一、步调不一致、信息不通畅的"三难三不"倾向。

3. 工作落实

顶岗实习是融教师教育培养模式改革与农村师资更新于一体的一种新型的教师实践培养

模式。在我国最早起源于1975年四平师范学院(现在吉林师大)数学系对顶岗实习的探索,作为师范院校教育实习破旧立新的典范。2000年以西南大学张诗亚教授向教育部师范司提交"关于贫困地区基础教育师资'更新工程'建构的报告"并得到师范司的支持和采纳为标志,顶岗实习在西部贫困地区得到大力支持和推广,在西南地区确实解决了农村义务教育教师数量不足和质量不高这一现实而紧迫的问题,促进区域间、城乡间教育的均衡发展[3]。然而,在地处经济较为发达的地区和城市,顶岗实习的实践与探索才刚刚开始,还属于尝试探索阶段。教育行政部门、高校、实习学校以及实习生对顶岗实习支教的真正目的还不够明确,工作上不够主动,沟通上不够及时,从而会出现学生到岗率低、顶岗学生专业与被顶岗教师学科不相符、到岗不能顶岗、顶岗实习时间不统一、管理不规范等现象。特别是上半年的顶岗实习与学生就业、考研的冲突,导致学生不能够安心顶岗,实习学校意见大,高师院校管理难。因此,如何做到将学生顶岗学科和实习学校缺岗学科统一,学生顶岗实习时间与农村教师培训时间统一,有效地利用实习生资源,真正达到"雪中送炭"的目的,成为高校和地方教育行政部门必须考虑与协调的问题。

4. 运行质量

在顶岗实习实际过程中,一是由于"领雁工程"有省、市、县三级,培训教师岗位空缺数多,学生参加顶岗的报名数少,为了满足数量要求,学校没有办法进行删选,只是要求学院对报名学生进行强化培训,但有的学院报名学生只有2～3个,无法按照学校的要求进行培训,导致培训流于形式。二是"领雁工程"每年四期培训,上半年顶岗实习支教学生如选择大四学生,与就业冲突,学生无法安心顶岗支教;如选择大三学生,学科教学论、教育教学实践技能等课程开设通常在三年级下学期。也就是说,参与顶岗实习支教的学生可能还没有接受过教育教学理论与实践技能的培训,当他们进入到实际教学中时会面临着一个较长的适应期。三是无论是教育行政部门还是高校,对顶岗实习的检查,都只重顶岗实习学生的数量,忽视顶岗实习的质量。

三、顶岗实习支教的实践

1. 做好实习前的工作

顶岗实习支教是以强化学生从教技能为主题,以促进学生成长成才为核心,以服务农村基础教育、促进教育均衡发展为责任的一种新型教师教育模式。

高校组织学生开展顶岗实习支教的首要任务是改革教师教育实习模式,提高实习质量,而"领雁工程"的实施为高校加强教育实习,开展顶岗实习支教工作提供了难得的机遇。同样是两个月的实习,在传统教育实习中平均每个实习生正式上课8～10节,而顶岗实习支教生平均上200节课(来自2008～2009学年顶岗实习带队教师的统计),是前者的20倍。拥有更多的实践机会,实习生能更好地在实践中变压力为动力,寻找差距,掌握具有实践价值的教学技能,提高其教育教学的"临床经验"。另一方面,在经济、文化、教育水平相对落后的农村地区支教,既是对师范生师德的考验,也是对师德的磨砺。增加了他们对中国农村现状特别是教育现状的了解并进而更加明确了服务于教育的决心,改变了就业观念,热心投入农村基础教育事业,达到解决大学生就业与农村教师老龄化的"双赢"效果。

另一方面,以提高农村教师执教能力为重点,浙江省启动了农村中小学教师"领雁工程"和学生顶岗实习工作,做到教师培训与顶岗实习相结合,着力改善农村师资,提高农村基础教育质量，适应国家重视农村教育、建设社会主义新农村的政策。高校选派优秀学生参加顶岗实习支教，不仅为农村中小学教师参加“领雁工程”培训提供时间，而且为农村基础教育输送新鲜师资力量，引进先进的教育思想、教育理念和教育技术，对推进全省基础教育均衡发展具有重大意义。

因此，地方行政部门和高校要充分认识到顶岗实习这项工作的重要性，本着对农村基础教育和广大学生负责的态度去重视并做好选派、管理等工作。顶岗实习既是学校行为，更是政府行为。教育行政部门的到位、补位是学校顶岗实习工作顺利开展的坚实保障。要强化政策和经费保障，制定相关政策，加大专项经费投入，确保顶岗实习能长期有效开展。

2. 处理好教学与实习的关系

知识经济社会，大学的人才培养应该以培养学生综合素质和能力为导向，适时地在培养方案、方式和途径上寻求突破，改变学生在传统教育实习中被动的角色定位，从上岗起就被推上前台。同时，考虑到专业特点和学生考研、就业的实际情况，以及农村学校岗位的实际需求，顶岗实习支教作为一项新的改革，它的开端不能“全面开花”，应该从点上突破。做法是将教育实习与顶岗实习支教有机结合，选拔优秀学生参加顶岗实习支教或模拟顶岗实习，其他同学参加常规教育实习，为下半年第一批“领雁工程”教师提供培训时间；两个月的教育实习结束后，选拔优秀实习生参加下半年第二批“领雁工程”教师培训的顶岗支教。这样既不会打乱教学计划，又可以让优秀学生真枪真刀在农村中小学得到强化训练，更重要的是保证了“领雁工程”教师培训的顺利开展。

同时，针对实习期间暴露出来的问题，高校应及时做出相应的调整。一方面临时调整教学计划，可以将一些教育基础理论课程以选修课的方式提前，保证师范生在实习支教前完成相关课程与培训，缩短适应期。另一方面，重新修订教学计划，适当调整教育教学理论与技能课程安排，在三年级有计划地开设相关课程，采取 3.5＋0.5 模式[4]，即：3.5 校内教育，0.5 顶岗实习。延长实习时间，改革教育教学课程内容，增加所学专业中小学教学大纲、中小学教材课等内容，克服教育教学理论教学与中小学实际脱节的矛盾。

3. 理顺顶岗实习系统关系

顶岗实习支教是一项涉及面广，组织实施极为复杂的系统工程。要深入持久地开展下去，既需要高校持之以恒的努力，也需要地方教育行政部门和农村中小学校的大力支持，要理顺各级关系，明确工作职责。在制度建设上，要尽快出台相关文件，明确工作职责；在实习管理上，要组建顶岗实习管理领导小组，充分发挥团队精神，通过教育行政部门、实习学校和高校三方在观念、人才、资源的互动和互助，稳步推进顶岗实习支教工作。

教育实习的制度化除了它以必修课的形式进入教学计划外，还表现在一系列实习制度的配套实施。顶岗实习应在继承传统教育实习管理方法的基础上，建立新的规章制度，如：顶岗实习管理办法、学生顶岗实习成绩考核与评定办法等，同时要明确高师院校、县区教育局、实习基地学校、实习生四方在顶岗实习中的权利和义务。[5]

由教育行政部门、实习学校和高校共同建立顶岗实习教学团队，充分发挥团队精神，研究探索以基础教育，特别是农村基础教育对教师教育毕业生人才需求为前提，以学生综合能力和就业为培养目标的顶岗实习支教管理模式，采取“双重管理”和“双导师制”，确保顶岗实习保质保量完成。

4. 配备建设基地

以农村中小学教师“领雁工程”培训为契机,拓展学生顶岗实习支教内涵,在农村建立稳定的顶岗实习基地,高校、地方教育行政部门和基地学校共同制定长远规划,每年选派优秀学生到基地参加顶岗实习支教,将顶岗实习支教拓展到为农村基础教育事业发展服务,源源不断地为农村中小学校输送新鲜的师资力量,架起大学生和农村教师“双向培训”的桥梁和纽带,不仅实地锻炼了师范生的教学技能,而且提高了农村中小学的教育教学水平。湖州师范学院已率先在吴兴区、南浔区5个师资相对紧缺的农村学校建立了顶岗实习基地。目前,这几个学校既作为申请参加顶岗实习学生的培训基地,又是学生参加顶岗实习锻炼的实地战场。一方面,高校可以派新教师或教学法教师或大学生去农村顶岗基地学校顶岗支教;另一方面,要充分发挥高校教师教育基地,为顶岗实习基地学校教师提供免费培训机会,高校师生下农村基地学校顶岗实习支教和农村基地学校教师上高校免费培训,真正建立“顶岗实习、置换培训”的“合作、互利、双赢”的长效机制。[7]

四、结语

发达地区农村顶岗实习支教有其特殊性,教育实习改革要因地制宜。另外,顶岗实习支教是教育实习的新模式,它比传统教育实习时间长、工作独立性强,内容也相对丰富,是一种义务性的“全职”教师岗位锻炼,体验从学生到教师再到学生的角色转换,经历理论到实践再到理论的循环,对教师职业、理论学习的认识及评价达到一个新的高度。发达地区农村顶岗实习支教的实践需要高师院校、地方教育行政部门、实习基地和中小学等部门根据当地的特点,多方协调,同步改革,同时在教学方法、课程设置和教学内容等方面也要进行系列改革,把教育实习的方式、方法和内容不断拓宽,为培养出高素质的教师人才奠定良好基础。

参考文献

[1] 左静妮.对顶岗实习支教的几点思考[J].中国教师,2009, S1:90.
[2] 易连云,等.探索与实施“顶岗实习支教”模式 促进农村中小学师资更新[J].西南大学学报,2008(2).
[3] 荀渊.华东师范大学:不断探索师范生实践教学新模式[N].中国教育报,2009,16(5).
[4] 杨玉梅.我国高师师范专业顶岗实习实施效果现状调查研究[D].重庆:西南大学,2008.
[5] 高月春,等.高师教育实习改革实践探索:以河北师范大学“顶岗实习”为例[J]. 河北师范大学学报,2007(6).
[6] 赵夫辰,等.深化顶岗实习支教工程 提高师范大学生能力素质[J].河北师范大学学报,2008(9).
[7] 张璇.高师教育改革与农村基础教育发展的新尝试:对顶岗实习、置换培训实践的思考[J].继续教育研究,2009(1).

论师范生教育智慧的培养

许占权*

(湛江师范学院,广东 湛江 524048)

摘　要:在当前的教师教育中,教育智慧的培养比较欠缺。教师教育要站在教师专业化的高度培养富有教育智慧的教师。提高师范生教育理论智慧的方法主要有:引导师范生形成教师专业化意识,提升教育理论课程的实效,指导学生阅读教育名著,加强师范生教育科研能力的培养。培养师范生教育实践智慧之路是改革理论课程教学模式,加强教育实践课程。

关键词:师范生;教师专业化;教育理论智慧;教育实践智慧

基金项目:广东省教育科研"十一五"规划重点课题(06TJZ002)。

Study on Training of Normal Students' Educational Wisdom

Abstract: The training of educational wisdom during teachers' education has been ignored for a long time. We should train teachers at the height of teacher's specialization. There are so many approaches for upgrading normal students' wisdom of educational theory, such as guiding normal students to form consciousness of teacher's specialization, advancing efficiency of curriculum of educational theories, supervising students reading classics within education domain and intensifying the training of normal students' ability of educational scientific research. It is a practice approach for us to train normal students' wisdom of educational practice by means of reforming the instruction styles of theoretical curriculum and putting more emphasis on educational practice curriculum.

Key words: Normal students; Teacher's specialization; Wisdom of educational theory; Wisdom of educational practice

* 许占权,湛江师范学院教育科学学院副院长,教授,研究方向:教育学原理。

相对一般智慧而言,教育智慧是一种特殊智慧,即合理认识与解决教育理论与实践问题的才智[1]。有学者指出:“教育智慧在教育教学实践中主要表现为教师对于教育教学工作的规律性把握、创造性驾驭和深刻性洞悉、敏锐反应及灵活机智应对的综合能力。”[2]教育智慧可以分为教育理论智慧和教育实践智慧。

师范教育已走向教师教育,教师的培养已不局限在师范院校,本文中的“师范生”是指就读于各类院校的教师教育专业的学生。

教育智慧是教师专业化素质的重要组成部分,然而以往职前教师教育重视的是对师范生进行专业知识传授和教师技能的训练,忽视教育智慧的培养。在师范教育阶段,学科知识、教育知识的传授以及教师技能的训练固然重要,但教育智慧的启迪与培养也不可忽视。智慧虽然不能像知识一样直接传授,“但它需要在获取知识、经验的过程中经由教育的悉心呵护而不断得到开启、丰富和发展”[2]。

一、教育智慧:教师教育的缺失

举一个教育学案例。一个师范生,学教育学的时候,听老师讲了这样一个故事:有一次,一个教育家发现一个孩子在摇晃一株小树苗,便走上前去说:“小朋友,小树苗可不能摇呀,你一摇,它头就晕了,要叫痛的,就要流泪了。”孩子于是很懂事地不摇了。这个师范生很佩服这位教育家,于是一直记着。毕业后,该师范生竟也遇到了这样的事情。有一个小朋友在路边摇晃着小树苗。他把那位教育家说过的话说了一遍。而小朋友却说:“老师,你骗人,小树怎么会头晕,怎么会想事情,怎么会说话呢?”[3]

这个案例给我们带来了什么思考呢?为什么教育家用过的方法到了师范生手中就不灵了呢?道理很简单,教育方法是不能简单照搬的。没有放之四海而皆准的教育方法,教育需要针对不同情境及不同教育对象而采用不同的教育方法,教育需要创造性,教育需要智慧。接受了几年的师范教育,师范生获得了什么?恐怕更多的是教条的学科知识以及初步的教师技能,而缺乏应对具体教育情境的教育智慧。上述案例中的师范生恐怕是很多师范毕业生的典型代表,正如一些用人单位的抱怨:“受过师范教育的人不会和学生打交道。”教育智慧是教师专业素质中最重要的素质,“学会了教学的所有技术,但仍然不适合做教师,这是有可能的。显然,教师的培训内涵要比传授知识和技巧深得多,甚至也比教授职业道德规范深得多。成为一名教师还包括那些不能被正式传授的东西:教育智慧的最具个性色彩的体现”[4]。

二、培养师范生教育理论智慧

教育理论智慧不仅仅可以为教育家或教育理论研究者所拥有,而且可以为每位普通教师所拥有,从而形成教师个人的教育哲学。同时,教师专业化发展也需要教师提升教育理论智慧。专门化职业与普通职业的区别之一是:专门化职业有一套有学术地位的理论系统,从事专门化职业的专业人员要把服务和研究融为一体。在教师专业化进程中,“教师作为研究者”的理念逐渐深入人心。但是,在我国,“教师作为研究者”的理想与现实还有很大距离。在教师职前教育中加强对师范生教育理论智慧的培养是促进教师成为研究者不可缺少的重要举措。

(一) 师范生教育理论智慧缺失的原因

教师拥有教育理论智慧的表现是:对教育理论及教育研究充满兴趣;能够把教育理论转化为自己的教育理念;能够将教育理论运用于教育实践;在教育理论研究或实践研究上有所创新。然而作为准教师的师范生,大部分学生对教育理论兴趣不高,具有研究教育兴趣和意识的学生更是不多。师范生普遍缺乏提升自己教育理论智慧的意识。造成这种局面的原因是多方面的,其中主要原因有:

第一,师范生对新时代教师所应具备的素质缺乏全面认识,对教师专业发展缺少真正的了解。很多师范生认为只要具有一定的学科知识和教师基本技能,就能成为好教师。大部分师范生没有树立"教师作为研究者"的理念,对教育理论及教育研究的重要性缺少应有的重视。突出的表现是:师范生重视学科课程、教育实践课程以及教师技能类课程的学习,而对教育学、心理学、教育研究方法等教育理论课程及学术论文的撰写不重视。一些师范生仅仅把教育学、心理学等教育理论课程看成是普通的公共课,而没有把教育理论课程当成专业课,学习态度很不认真,应付考试的现象比较普遍。

第二,教育学、心理学等教育理论课程缺乏实效。近年来,一些师范院校不断对教育学、心理学等教育理论课进行改革,取得了一些成效,但仍然存在很多问题,教育理论课的效果不佳仍然是比较突出的问题。主要问题有:大部分教师教育专业的教育专业类课程还停留在教育学、心理学和教材教法老三门上,远远不能适应培养专业化教师的需要;公共教育理论课程的研究与建设被边缘化;一些教育理论教材粗糙、空洞、脱离实践,引不起师范生的兴趣;一些院校教育理论课教学过程还停留在单纯的知识灌输水平上,缺少对学生思维的启迪以及教育理念的引领。

第三,一线中小学教师轻视教育理论的现象波及师范生。由于很多中小学教师对教育理论不感兴趣,再加上个别从事理论工作的学者急功近利,发表出版了一些缺少真正智慧的理论文章和著作,损害了教育理论工作者的形象,影响了教育理论的声誉,导致一线中小学教师轻视教育理论。而一线中小学教师对师范生影响很大,他们的言行也影响到了师范生对教育理论的不重视。

第四,教师教育专业的学生对教育理论的期望和认识存在偏差。教育理论不是技术手段,学了就可以在实践中直接使用。但很多师范专业的学生却期望教育理论像技术手段一样,学习了就可以直接应用。也就是说,他们对教育理论的价值缺乏合理的认识。

(二) 如何培养师范生的教育理论智慧

1. 引导师范生形成教师专业化意识

师范教育中,我们首先要让师范生树立明确的职业意识,对教师这一职业的特点及发展有正确认识。师范生要正确认识教师这一职业的专业化特性及发展趋势。师范生只有对教师的专业化内涵有清晰的认识,才能按教师专业化的素质要求来打造自己;师范生只有对教育事业的智慧品性有充分的认识,才能重视对自身教育智慧的锻造。

2. 提升教育理论课程的实效

教育学、心理学等教育理论课程的价值不在于教给学生多少概念性的知识和条条框框的原理,而在于使学生形成富有智慧的教育理念和教育价值观。教育理念和教育价值观是教育智慧的灵魂。教育学等教育理论对于师范生教育智慧的形成具有特殊的作用,教育理论有助于师范生形成教育的理解力、反思力、想象力、转化力和创造力等。以教育学特有的立场、视角和思维方式,对人的生命成长与发展进行理解与阐释,是教育学智慧的特殊功能,它使教育学拥有了强大的解释力、理解力和反思力[6]。在此基础上,教育理论可以转化为师范生的教育智慧。

教师教育要不断改革教育理论课程,使教育理论课程在提高师范生教育智慧中发挥应有的作用:首先,要让学生明确教育理论课程在教师教育专业中的地位和作用,正确认识教育理论课程在师范生专业成长中的作用;其次,应该增加教育理论课程的比重,可以通过开设教育科研方法、教育思想史、教师专业发展等选修课程,丰富师范生的教育理论;第三,改革灌输式的教学方法,开展研究性学习;第四,改革教育理论课程考试方式,改变只能反映学生记忆情况的考试内容和方式,以能反映学生理解、应用及创新的考试方式为主。

3. 指导学生阅读教育名著

指导师范生阅读教育名著是汲取教育理论智慧一个很好的途径。教育名著是经过历史检验,得到公认的人类教育财富,它积淀着前人深邃的思想精华,蕴含着丰富的教育理论智慧。教育现实的改进与提升需要我们不断地返回经典,去吸收与借鉴前人的思想与智慧。"当较深入地研读教育思想家的作品之后,发现几乎所有现在我们深觉困惑的问题,都早已为以前的教育思想家讨论过。为了解决这些问题,在发表意见之前,如能知悉先人的主张,则有事半功倍的作用;尤其在与杰出教育思想家神交之时,可能冒出智慧的火花,对于敏锐思考,效用甚大。"[7]

4. 加强师范生教育科研能力的培养

在教师专业发展中,教育科研能力是教师专业能力不可缺少的组成部分。师范生教育科研能力的养成不仅有助于未来教师素质的提高,从而提高其在早期求职阶段的能力,而且有助于提高其在专业成长的后续阶段的发展潜力。中小学教师教育科研能力发展与其在大学期间形成的教育科研能力基础有关。培养师范生教育科研能力是提高师范生教育理论智慧的重要途径之一。

师范生教育科研能力的培养要从教育科研意识、教育理论兴趣和教育科研方法等方面着手。教育科研能力培养的途径有很多,常见的有课程论文、学年论文、毕业论文、大学生科技创新活动和参与教师课题研究等。有效培养师范生教育科研能力的方法在于理论学习与科研实践训练相结合,不能只满足于教育科研方面的陈述性知识的传递。

三、培养师范生教育实践智慧

(一) 培养师范生实践智慧的必要性

美国教育社会学家洛蒂(D. C. Lortie)在《中小学教师》(1975)中提出"不确定性"是教师的显著特征。正如洛蒂所巧妙指出的,教师的工作几乎是由"不确定性"所支配的。在某课堂中有效的计划,在别的课堂里未必有效。"不确定性"提出了教育实践的创造性与探究性,也就是要求教师要具备实践智慧。

教育实践智慧是教师在教育活动中所形成和表现出来的有效解决具体教育问题的聪明才

智,是教师对教育情境和问题的深刻洞察和敏锐把握。教育实践智慧是教师的人格、学识、能力、经验、教育机智等综合素质的体现。教育实践智慧表现在教师面对复杂的、充满变化的教育教学活动,与问题情境对话,与学生对话,敏锐把握教育教学活动发展的脉搏和契机,既继承前人又突破陈规,既借鉴理论又不照搬别人,创造新办法,高效地开展教育教学活动[8]。

有学者把实践智慧与实践知识视为同一个概念,笔者认为二者是不同的。实践知识所表现的是在实践中知道怎样做和会做,而实践智慧所表现的是创造性地做。创造性地解决具体实践问题是实践智慧的本质特征,而实践知识不一定要有创造性。实践知识是实践智慧的基础,实践智慧是实践知识的创造性发展。教师的实践智慧不是仅仅表现在能够按部就班地管理好班级或上好课,而是表现为在具体班级管理、课堂教学等教育教学活动中,面对变化不定的具体教育情境或者不同的学生,独到地解决问题。

实践智慧主要从实践中来,那么,还没有完全进入教育实践领域,作为准教师的师范生是否需要培养实践智慧?实践智慧能否培养呢?回答是肯定的。实践智慧是作为准教师的师范生人才素质结构中不可缺少的重要组成部分,承担培养教师任务的院校不能向社会输送仅仅具有理论知识和初步教师技能的"半成品"。师范院校不能培养只会纸上谈兵的书生,而是要培养具有一定实战能力的教师。师范院校不能培养只会照本宣科和模仿的低层次教师,而应该培养具有创新意识和创新才能的教师。

(二)培养师范生教育实践智慧的途径

1. 加强教育实践课程

教育见习、教育实习等教育实践课程是培养师范生教育实践智慧的主渠道。教育实践课程不能仅仅停留在教师技能的提高,还要重视培养师范生教育实践智慧。但就我国教师教育的现状分析,教育实践观还比较陈旧,教育实践的课程还存在不尽合理的方面。长期以来,我国的教师教育过分偏重学科专业教育的学术性,忽视教师教育的实践性,教育实习等实践活动被边缘化。存在的问题主要有:教育实践投入不足,教育实践课时比例太小,教育实习时间短,教育实践形式单一,教师实习指导不到位等。因此,我们要重建教师教育实践课程体系,使教师教育实践课程的附属地位得到改观,为师范生的教育实践智慧的提升提供必要的条件。

我们应该对教育实践课程做出如下改革:

第一,提高教育实践课程比例,延长教育实习时间。我国是世界上教育实习时间比较短的国家,多少年来,我们的教育实习时间一直是8周左右,占全部课时的6%左右。我国也是世界上教育见习时间比较短的国家。例如在美国宾夕法尼亚大学的本科初等教育专业教学计划中,要求学生每周花三天半在小学担任教师助理,另外还要完成12周的全日制教学实习[9]。教育实践课程的薄弱导致师范毕业生缺乏实践智慧,改革教师教育职前培养阶段的课程结构,大幅度提高实践课程比例势在必行。

第二,学习美国"教师专业发展学校"经验,改变大学和中小学的关系。专业发展学校是1986年霍姆斯小组在《明日的教师》报告中提出的,是指大学教育学院与附近中小学合作培养师资的一种"新型学校"。专业发展学校为准教师提供一个理论和实践结合的场景,也为职前和在职教师的各种学习提供制度支持。专业发展学校建设的理想是,通过大学与中小学的共同努力,使各自的教学质量和教学效果都能得到明显的提高。美国教师专业发展学校的经验很值得我们借鉴。

2. 改革理论课程的教学模式

培养师范生的教育实践智慧，不仅要强化教育实践课程，而且要改革理论课程的教学模式与教学方法。案例分析、"虚拟现场"等教学模式有助于师范生教育实践智慧的培养。

学生根据案例所提供的情境，不仅能学会如何教学，而且能学会如何提出教学问题、分析问题、着手解决问题，依据案例展示的线索，检验假设和评价，通过这样的过程学生获得专业自主和发展。但是，要防止学生仅仅停留在对案例中的教师的简单模仿。案例的作用在于使学习者间接感受、领悟教育智慧，而不是照搬某种具体的教育方法。

所谓虚拟现场，是指创设一种较为真实的课堂教学的问题情境，师范生或是扮演教师，或是扮演学生，或是作为观看教学活动并要发表观点与见解的观众，共同建构模拟课堂教学的实践活动[10]。虚拟现场模式通过师范生亲身去做、去体验、去揣摩"当"教师的过程，进而体会到教育现场的丰富性、多变性和生成性，关注教育现场中随时发生的种种问题，从而促进教育实践智慧的形成。

3. 教育实践智慧的培养与教育理论智慧的培养互为依托

虽然教育实践智慧主要发生和体现在具体的教育实践活动中，也不同于教育理论智慧，但是汲取教育理论智慧非常有助于提升教育实践智慧。理论虽然不是解决问题的具体方法，但能为处理问题提供某种理念和思路，因此对实践问题具有重要的指导意义。一个富有思想和教育理论的教师比一个相对缺乏思想和理论的教师更能显示出教育智慧。实际上，教育理论智慧与实践智慧是互相影响互相促进的。纵观古今中外教育历史和现实，我们会发现，凡是有大智慧的专家学者，他们的理论智慧一定离不开实践智慧；凡是有大智慧的教师，他们的实践智慧无一不受到教育理论智慧的影响。所以，我们在培养师范生教育智慧过程中，不要割裂教育理论与教育实践的关系，教育实践智慧的培养与教育理论智慧的培养要互为依托。

四、结论

教育是智慧的事业，教育智慧是教师素质的综合体现。智慧无止境，教师教育智慧的提升，贯穿教师整个职业生涯。职前教育阶段是奠定教师教育智慧的重要阶段，师范生教育智慧的培养不可忽视。教师教育，在向师范生传授专业知识，训练专业技能的基础上，还要注重师范生教育智慧的提升。如何在职前培养师范生的教育理论智慧和教育实践智慧，需要在实践中进一步探索。

参考文献

[1] 熊川武，江铃. 理解教育论[M]. 北京：教育科学出版社，2005：246.
[2] 田慧生. 时代呼唤教育智慧及智慧型教师[J]. 教育研究，2005(2).
[3] 王晓春. 教育智慧从哪里来：点评 100 个教育案例[M]. 上海：华东师范大学出版社，2005：11.
[4] 加马克斯·范梅南. 教学机智：教育智慧的意蕴[M]. 李树英，译. 北京：教育科学出版社，2001：14.
[5] 王帮左. 中学优秀教师的成长与高师教改之探索[M]. 北京：人民教育出版社，1994：46.
[6] 李政涛. 论教育学的智慧[J]. 教育理论与实践，2006(3).
[7] 林玉体. 西方教育思想史[M]. 北京：九州出版社，2006：3.

[8] 许占权. 提升教育实践智慧，促进教师专业发展[J]. 教育导刊，2007(8).
[9] UNIVERSITY OF PENNSYLVANIA. Graduate School of Education Catalogue：1995-1996 [M]. Philadelphia：University of Pennsylvania Press，1995：2.
[10] 姜勇，高维华，朱文佳. 教师教育转型研究："虚拟现场"与教师成长[C];周南照，赵丽，任友群. 教师教育改革与教师专业发展：国际视野与本土实践. 上海：华东师范大学出版社，2007：88-94.

学前教育专业的目标定位与课程体系的建构

蔡勇强[*]　魏　蕾[**]
（漳州师范学院，福建　漳州　363000）

摘　要：高师下嫁、幼师升格把学前教育师资的培养推进了高等教育的范畴，使学前教育本科专业面临专业重构。该专业能否健康发展，涉及到培养目标、课程设计、教材建设诸方面的因素，其中最核心的是课程体系的构建。

关键词：学前教育；本科；培养目标；课程体系

Cultivation Goals and Curriculum Plan for the Majors of Preschool Teachers Education

Cai Yong-qiang　Wei Lei
(Zhangzhou Teachers' College，Zhangzhou 363000，China)

Abstract：With the extension of higher education and normal school for preparation of preschool teachers attaining higher educational institution status，preschool teachers' preparation is incorporated into higher education，which makes it necessary to redesign the preparation program. The proper development of the program is influenced by many factors，i. e. the cultivation goals，curriculum plan，and instruction resources. Among the factors，the designing of curriculum system is crucial to development of the program.

Key words：preschool teachers education；undergraduate program；cultivation goals；curriculum plan

高等教育由精英化走向大众化，既给我国高等教育带来了发展的机遇，也给高等教育提出

---

* 蔡勇强，漳州师范学院教育系副主任、教授。

** 魏蕾，漳州师范学院教育系讲师。

了全新的挑战,如何生存和发展,成为高校不可回避的问题;如何进行专业调整与专业定位又成为高校面临的首要任务。专业的目标定位关系到专业发展的方向性选择,而课程体系的构建是否合理则关系到专业培养目标能否实现。本文试图从高师院校学前教育专业定位分析入手,重新设计当前高师学前教育本科专业的课程体系。

一、高师院校学前教育专业的目标定位

高师作为为国家经济和文化发展服务的高等院校之一,其人才培养目标和规格定位应该凸显出层次性、应用性等特点,充分考虑社会需求和个体发展要求。学前教育专业的定位势必也应以此为导向。

(一)以社会对学前教育人才的素质要求为导向

设计培养目标,首先应适应我国学前教育的实际需要,充分体现社会对学前教育人才的素质要求。

随着社会的发展,学前教育形成了正式教育与非正式教育的教育体系,它包括家庭教育、托幼教育机构教育和学前社会教育,这些教育机构的形成和发展,均需要既具有宽厚的学前教育理论,又具有学前教育职业技能的专门人才。与此同时,随着各类幼儿园的办园水平的不断提高,需要高素质、高层次、高学历的幼儿园教师。因此,关于学前教育专业的定位,我们应明确以高标准、高素质为基准,它隶属于高等师范教育范畴。它不同于以往的中等幼儿师范教育,生源定位于普通高中毕业生,无论是学历层次、课程要求较前者都有极大的提升;它也不同于以往高师学前教育专业,培养目标不再是幼师的师资,而是直接培养幼儿教师,幼教行政管理人员和幼教社会工作者。这些学前教育的一线工作者,是研究型的教育工作者,他们既有扎实的理论功底和宽广的知识基础,又有出色的教育技能,能将教育实践和理论结合起来,通过个体的终身的研究性学习,聚沙成塔,给学前教育领域注入自下而上的自我更新的原动力。

(二)适应个体发展的需要

培养目标还应该体现培养人才的个性特点,即鼓励学生形成个性,培养个人能力特长。现代幼教发展需要有不同专长的幼教专业人才,如语言教育类、艺术教育类、体育类等,要使学生在全面发展的基础上,能够学有所长,充分发展个性,以适应我国幼教事业发展的需要。

对学生来说,在高师学习只是他们人生发展历程的一个阶段。因此在设定培养目标时应关注三个层次的发展需要,即作为人的发展需要、作为教育者发展的需要、作为本科学历教育者发展的需要,促进学生健全人格、文化修养、人生发展与教师专业的成长。

高师学前教育专业的培养目标的确定,应当从过去狭隘的,需求量较少的幼师教师转移到为幼儿教育机构和教育行政部门培养高层次的应用型人才上来,因此可将高师学前教育专业的培养目标定位为:培养掌握宽厚的学前教育科学理论知识,熟练掌握从事学前儿童保育与教育教学技能,能够胜任托幼机构保教工作和研究工作的幼儿教师、幼教行政管理人员及其他儿童工作机构的专门人才。

二、构建学前教育专业课程体系的依据

构建学前教育专业课程体系是以上述对学前教育专业的培养目标和专业定位的认识为基础的。

(一) 课程体系必须反映高等本科教育这一层次上的要求

纵观世界各国,幼儿教师的学历标准都在提高,越来越多的国家要求幼儿教师必须具备大学本科及以上的学历。为保证基础教育的发展,提高师资素质,国家教委从 1985 年起进行了中师毕业生再读两年大专的试点,并在师范院校开设了学前专科,逐步使幼儿教师的学历提高到大学专科以上的层次。近年,一些幼师幼专相继并入师范院校,设立学前教育本科专业,又把学前教育师资培养推进了高等教育本科的范畴。这种学历接轨,不仅是教育全球化的要求,更是我国学前教育发展的自身要求。

学前教育本科专业培养的是学前教育工作者。在学前教育的领域中,其"工作者"可以是搞教育教学的,也可以是搞管理和科研的,也可以是社区、少年宫的儿童教育工作者,当然也可以是与学前教育有关的文化产业如影视、报刊、网络、出版、图书馆等的从业者,但最主要的是培养托幼教育机构的一线教师。"立足幼教师资、兼顾相近相关"的培养目标使专业口径相对较宽,有利于吸引考生,也有利于适应就业市场。在本科生的培养层次性上不仅要凸显掌握知识的广博性,更要显示出扎实的专业知识功底,以及灵活的社会适应性。

既然学前教育专业属于高等本科教育体系,这一定位在课程体系构建中应有两方面的体现:

第一,就通识课程和人文素质而言,应与其他大学本科专业有同样的要求。

第二,就专业课程的深度和广度而言,应与过去中师培养中专学历幼儿教师或高专培养专科学历幼儿教师的课程体系不一样。因为本科专业培养的不仅仅是一般的幼儿园教师,而且是既有扎实的理论功底和宽广的基础知识,又有出色的教育技能,能将教育实践和理论结合起来的研究型的幼教工作者。

(二) 课程体系必须反映学前教育这一专业特色上的要求

学前教育专业以培养幼教领域的高级人才为己任,因此在课程体系上决不能套用传统高师其他专业的模式。高师原有的各个专业,主要是针对中等教育师资需求而设,历经发展完善,各自拥有一套较完整的学科课程体系。而学前教育专业则应以自己的专业定位作为出发点来设计课程体系。

学前教育专业定位应是为社会经济和基础教育改革与发展服务的,因此课程体系的设计必须体现应用性,要强调专业能力、实践能力的培养,以及基本操作技能的训练,避免培养出"眼高手低"的传统人才。"实践型"的人才,不是单一的,而是多元的,在学前教育领域有相对较强的适应性。这样的定位体现了高等教育大众化的背景下学前教育专业与时俱进,主动与社会的变迁和进步接轨,根据幼教人才市场的需要办学,同时为自身的专业建设和学科发展拓展广阔空间的理念。笔者认为学前专业本科人才的应用性体现在四个方面,即教、保、研、管。

1. 教,即教育教学能力。应培养热爱教育事业、热爱儿童,具有开发学前儿童潜力,对学

前儿童能实施正确教育，具备一定教学能力的教师。目前，我国幼儿园教育质量的水平相对不高，其中关键的原因是幼儿园教师的综合素质水平低，学历水平低。在教育工作中，甚至有一些教师不会设计幼儿的活动，缺乏开展幼儿各方面艺术活动的技能技巧，这必然影响到幼儿各方面潜能的开发。因此，应重视学生教育能力和所需的各项教学技能的培养。主要有：其一，了解幼儿：幼儿教师必须了解幼儿身心发展特点与教育规律，并具有以此为依据开展教育活动的能力；幼儿教师必须具有观察了解和评价幼儿的能力。其二，创设环境：教师应具有创设安全、尊重、支持和挑战的物质环境的能力；教师必须具有促进师幼互动和同伴互动，形成良好的班级心理环境的能力。其三，设计与组织活动：幼儿教师必须具有组织和指导幼儿一日活动的能力；幼儿教师必须具有创造性地制定教育计划，灵活选择教育内容和教育组织形式，生成课程的能力；幼儿教师必须具有创编所需教育内容的能力。其四，使用教学策略：幼儿教师必须具有个别教育和因材施教的能力；幼儿教师必须具有综合素养和综合教育的能力。其五，利用资源：幼儿教师必须具有利用生活中的教育资源，在生活中寻找教育契机的能力；必须具有与家长、社区及同伴合作，利用家庭、社区和同伴教育资源的能力。

2. 保，即保育能力。现代幼儿园的保育工作已不仅是对幼儿日常生活的安排和护理，身体的保健和养育，生长发育指标的达成，而更重视如何提高幼儿的生活质量，包括提供增进幼儿健康的物质生活环境条件和创设宽松、和谐的人际心理环境，更关注幼儿的情绪和需要，养成幼儿健康的行为习惯，帮助其形成积极、合理的生活态度和生活方式从而促进幼儿身心和谐发展。因此，未来的幼教工作者除了具备一定的保育知识技能，还必须掌握对幼儿进行身心保育的策略与方法。

3. 研，即研究能力。应具有从事学前教育理论与实践研究的能力。我国学前教育事业及其学科的发展，主要依赖于它的科学研究，依赖于掌握了本学科理论知识与科研方法的人才。高师学前教育专业原有的人才培养目标，不重视学生科研能力的培养，即使是从事幼儿园的教育工作，也很难将实践中获得的经验上升到理论高度。不会独立地进行教育科学研究，这是当前学前教育质量难以提高的关键所在。因此，我国所有幼儿园所急需的是能进行科学研究的幼教工作者。

4. 管，即管理能力。应具有管理各级各类学前教育机构的能力。随着社会的变化，管理在各领域的发展壮大中起着越来越大的作用，哪个领域能做到科学管理，能将人力、物力和财力等各项因素合理地组织起来，并能调动其积极性，这个领域就能兴旺发达。因此，要使我国学前教育领域能获得大的发展，取得最大效益，就必须具有一批既掌握了学前教育理论与实践知识，又能将各种兴办学前教育的条件和因素合理组织与利用的管理人才，这是促进学前教育事业快速发展的一个重要方面。

（三）课程体系必须符合幼儿教师的成材规律

一专多能的复合型师资是相当长一段时期内我国幼教对师资的要求。对幼教领域的教师而言，执教的“广度”甚至比中小学教师更大，这就要求学前教育专业的课程设计中，更应重视综合性教育，先求博再求专。客观地说，任何一个新的毕业生也不可能在幼教的各个领域都达到专家的水准。因此，在课程方案中，可考虑“分流培养”，在前五个学期设置基础课和专业课，使学生达到本专业的基本要求；第六学期开始设置系列选修课，让学生自主选择。这样能使课程体系具有一定的开放度和弹性，改变过去千人一面的做法，达到培养学生某方面特长的目的。先博后专，形成特色，符合教师的成材规律。

三、学前教育专业的课程设计

靳玉乐认为："课程设计是一个有目的、有计划、有结构地产生课程计划、分科课程标准以及教材教科书等的系统化活动"[1]。黄甫全认为："课程研制是将预期教育结果结构化、序列化和现实化的过程"[2]。课程设计过程中最核心的是课程结构的编制，既包括课程体系结构的整体编制，也包括具体课程的编制。

以下着重谈谈课程体系结构的整体编制问题。课程体系结构的整体编制涉及课程分类问题。基于上述的思考，学前专业课程体系应包括以下几类课程：

（一）必修课

1. 公共必修课即通识类课程。开设科目和要求与其他本科专业相同。

2. 专业必修课即学前教育专业课程。此部分课程最能体现本专业的特色，旨在培养学生达到本专业本科层次所需的质量要求。包括：① 专业基础课：教育基本理论、普通心理学等。② 专业主干课：学前卫生学、学前心理学、学前教育学、幼儿语言教育、幼儿艺术教育、幼儿社会教育、幼儿科学教育、幼儿健康教育、幼儿园课程、幼儿园管理、学前教育科研法等。③ 专业技能课：声乐、琴法、舞蹈、美术等。

（二）选修课

1. 模块选修课（限定性选修课）

根据"分流培养"的思路，可围绕幼教领域"教学"、"科研"、"管理"三个专业方向构建若干组课程模块，或设置语言类、艺术类、社会类、科学类、健康类等方向或选修课程组，供学生选择，每个学生均应至少选择一个模块课程组。以选修课程组的形式供学生选择，既满足学生多元发展需要，也使课程方案具有一定的灵活性和弹性。

2. 任意选修课（非限定性选修课）

任意选修课的开设旨在扩大学生知识面，完善知识结构，实施因材施教，实现文理渗透，培养学生综合素质。此类选修课程应由学校统筹，实行跨专业任意选修。

（三）实践环节

实践环节旨在理论联系实际，促进师范生知识向能力的转化，培养锻炼各种技能技巧，包括教育实习、见习、教育调查、科研实践等。

具体课程的编制涉及课程设置及课时（学分）分配问题。至于各类课程的设置可由各院校自行编制。

构建学前教育专业的课程体系，关系到该专业的培养目标能否实现，进而影响到未来幼教师资的专业化水平，应视为专业建设中的重中之重。需要从理论上不断探索，在实践中不断完善，以期建立起较为科学合理的课程体系。

参考文献

[1]　靳玉乐.现代课程论［M］.重庆:西南师范大学出版社,1995:217.

[2]　黄甫全.阶梯型课程引论［M］.贵阳:贵州人民出版社,1996:227.

教育学课程群建设初探

杨超有* 陈庆文**

(玉林师范学院,广西 玉林 537000)

摘 要:教育学课程群的提出旨在探寻教育学课程之间的内在联系,为高师教育学课程改革提供理论依据。教育学课程群是以《教育概论》课程为基础,围绕高师培养目标,根据教师教育理论和教育学学科发展状况和基础教育发展需要而开设,结构合理、内容科学、关系密切的课程体系。教育学课程群建设的基础有三:教育学科的发展是其学科基础;教师教育改革趋势是其实践基础;基础教育改革的迫切需要是其外部动力。我们认为教育学课程群建设首先要明确课程群选择的依据,其次是推行学分制管理体制,最后是打造优秀教学团队。

关键词:教育学;课程;课程群;建设

The Initial Research on the Construction of the Pedagogy Course Group

Yang Chao-you Chen Qing-wen

Abstract: The research on Pedagogy Course Group seeks the inter connection among the pedagogy course. It provides theoretic basis. Pedagogy Course Group is a course system which tades the course Introduction to Education as its core, and includes other pedagogy course according to the development of pedagogy and the need of the basis education development. The system is reasonable in its structure, scientific in its contents and close in interrelation among each course. The construction of Pedagogy Course Group is based on three principles. First, the

* 杨超有,玉林师范学院教育科学系主任,教授,玉林师范学院教育科学研究所所长。

** 陈庆文,玉林师范学院教育科学系副主任。

development of pedagogy is the basis of pedagogy. Second, the trend of teachers education reform is its pratical basis. Finally, the urgent demand for basis education reform is its momentum. The construction of the Pedagogy Course Group should first of all make clear the priciple of the selection of pedagogy course, then carry out the credit system, and finally establish a team of excellent teaching faculties.

Key words: pedagogy; course; course group; construction

教育学是我国教师教育课程体系中的核心课程和标志性课程,教育学课程改革一直以来是我国高等师范教育课程改革关注的焦点和热点,但不可否认教育学课程改革在一些学校仍然没有达到预期效果,尚存在种种问题:如课程体系结构不合理,课时比例失调,教学内容跟不上教育改革的步伐等等。随着基础教育改革的深入,教育学课程的作用日益彰显,同时也对高等师范教育学课程体系不断提出新挑战。因此,进一步调整高师教育学课程结构,更新教育学内容,是当前高师教育学课程改革一个紧迫的任务。

一、教育学课程群的界定

1990 年,北京理工大学基于"在课程建设中应当以教学计划的整体优化为目标",提出要注重课群的研究与建设。之后,一些高校陆续开展了"课程群"的理论研究与实践探索。目前我国学者普遍认为所谓课程群是为实现某一培养目标而以某门课程为基础,由 3 至 6 门性质相关或相近的子课程整合而成的课程体系。课程群应具有以下几个方面特征:第一,课程群中必须以某门课程为基础,在这个基础上开设出若干门子课程;第二,课程群中的所有课程是彼此独立而又相互密切联系的课程;第三,课程群应是指从属于某个学科,相互之间有着合理分工的系统化的有机整体。

早在 1896 年梁启超《论师范》即提出师范教育中应设"教育"课程,包括"教育学"、"教育史"、"教学法"、"教育管理"、"教育实习"等;建国后,教育学课程的地位得到提升,逐渐形成所谓"老三门"的格局,即:教育学、心理学、学科教材教法;当前,许多师范院校提出教师教育课程板块,包括教育概论、心理发展与教育、教学设计、班主任工作、青少年心理健康等。不管是梁启超的"教育"课程还是当前的"教师教育课程板块",它们的出发点都是为了培养合格的师资队伍,它们之间都具有密切的联系,且它们都由几门课程组成。教育学课程是一个不可分割的有机整体。从"课程群"的视角去探索教育学课程体系的内部关系,从而优化教育学课程体系,是当前高师教育学课程改革较好的一个突破点。我们认为所谓教育学课程群就是以《教育概论》(或称《教育学原理》等,下同)课程为基础,围绕高师培养目标,根据教师教育理论和教育学学科发展状况和基础教育发展需要而开设,结构合理、内容科学、关系密切的课程体系。

二、教育学课程群建设的基础

教育学科在中国已有百余年历史。改革开放之后,教育学科的研究与应用更是日趋深入和广泛,教育学科自身的发展,教师教育课程改革的趋势与基础教育改革的迫切需要,为教育学课程群的构建提供了深厚的基础。

1. 教育学科的发展

教育科学在英文中有“Educational Science”和“Educational Sciences”两种译法，前者被称为“单数教育科学”，后者被称为“复数教育科学”。瞿葆奎先生认为：复数的教育科学所蕴含的观念是教育科学是大量社会学科、还包括某些自然学科应用于教育领域而形成的，它们绝大多数以教育现象为对象；在方法上博采众家，其发展以这些学科的发展为前提。

以教育活动为研究对象，采用不同的学科方法就产生了教育学的分支学科。如分析教育中形而上问题的学科：教育哲学、教育美学、教育伦理学等；分析教育中社会现象的学科：教育社会学、教育经济学、教育法学、教育生态学、教育文化学等；分析教育中个体的“人”的学科：教育心理学、教育生理学等；运用方法直接分析教育活动的学科：比较教育学等；研究如何运用方法来分析教育活动的学科：教育统计学、教育测量学、教育评价学、教育实验学等；分析与其他领域共有的实际问题：教育卫生学、教育行政学、教育技术学等；分析教育领域独有的实际问题：课程论、教学论等。教育学分支学科的发展成熟形成了教育学科系统群，为高师教育学课程群建设提供了深厚的学科基础。

2. 教师教育课程改革趋势

早在1904年《奏定学堂章程》中规定初级师范学堂设教育学，包括教育史、教育原理、教授法大要、教育法令、学校教育管理法以及“实事授业”（实习）；优级师范学堂所设教育学包括：教育理论、教育史、教授法、学校卫生、教育法令以及“授实事练习”（实习）。建国后，我国教师教育课程体系受苏联教育模式的影响，逐渐形成“教育学”、“心理学”、“学科教学法”老三门的格局课程，而且都是必修课程，可供学生自由选择的课程比较少，目前许多师范院校还沿用这种模式。在教学实践中，教育理论课程比较注重传授基本理论，与学生面临的实践联系甚少。同时，教育学类课程学时在总学时中所占比例偏低，如教育学、心理学、学科教学法约有54学时，有些学校甚至压缩为36学时，教育学科包括教育实习占总课时的10%左右。

建国以来，教育学课程的改革一直是人们关注的话题，不管是课程结构、课时比例还是课程内容，但相对于基础教育改革等其他领域，教师教育课程体系相对封闭，与基础教育课程体系相比具有较强的稳定性。在社会发展迅速，基础教育改革日新月异的今天，教师教育课程体系必须做出回应，高师教育学课程体系的稳定性必将打破。教师教育课程改革的趋势为教育学课程群建立提供了实践基础。

3. 基础教育改革的迫切需要

近年来，以课程改革为中心的基础教育改革在我国全面展开，教育观念、课程内容、教学方法、评价手段等都发生了很大的变化，高师院校对此必须作出回应。余文森教授曾对国家课改实验区作调研，发现在教学改革中仍然存在很多问题，如：把课堂中的“对话”变成“问答”，为夸奖而夸奖，把自主变成自流，有活动无体验，合作有形式无实质，探究的“泛化”和“神化”等，这些问题说明我们的改革仍然没有完全深入实质。作为教师教育培养“母机”的高等师范院校，我们不得不反思我们的课程体系，特别是教育学课程是否发挥了应有的作用。2005年对广西普通高中教师抽样调查发现教师的课程观、课程知识、课程开发能力以及课程行动研究能力等方面素质还比较低，部分教师弄不清课程的基本概念，无法正确解读课程纲要、课程标准、课程目标、校本课程、研究性学习等现象。当然基础教育改革从教师观念、教育教学技能、教师专业素养等方面都提出了新的要求，这为高师教育学改革提供了外部动力。

三、教育学课程群的建设思路

正如前文所述，随着基础教育改革深入和教师教育的不断发展，我国高师院校在教育学课程改革方面也进行了不同程度的研究和探索。作者查阅多所重点师范大学和一些地方性师范院校，他们的教育学课程都不再局限于“老三门”，或是在课程结构，或是在课时设置，或是在课程内容上都有所创新。在此，我们提出教育学课程群的概念，旨在探索这些课程之间的内部关系，从而更好地发挥它的效用。

(一) 明确课程群构建的依据

明确课程群构建的依据具有重要意义，假如依据不明确可能会导致课程体系的混乱，甚至有些学校根据教师开课。在课程理论研究领域，课程选择无非考虑两个方面：一是个体发展，二是社会发展。对于基础教育而言，课程选择应更多考虑个体发展需要，而在高等教育实践领域，课程选择则应更多从社会发展需要出发。教育学课程设置的目标直接指向培养合格教师，无疑教育学课程设置的最重要依据是教师素质；其次是教育学课程之间的关系。

1. 教师素质结构

早在1961年，美国“全国师范教育与专业标准委员会”和“美国教育协会”组成的研究小组在研究报告中就提出将师范教育的课程分为“普通课程”、“专业课程”和“教育课程”。教育课程指有关教育专业本身的课程，旨在使学生了解教育的意义、目标及方法，通常包括两类：一是“教育学基础课程”，如教育史、学校与社区关系、教育哲学思想、人类行为发展、心理学等；二是“教学方法课程”，指与教学设计与方法有关的课程。人们普遍认为，教师素质包含三个方面：学科专业知识、教育专业素质和一般文化素质。我国有些学者认为新课程改革给教师素质提出了新要求，体现在教育理念、教育技能和专业素养三个方面。也有人对教师教育素质进行划分，认为教师必须具备的教育素质包括五个方面：教育理论素养，教育实践技能，教育临床经验，教育研究能力，教育学理念。

综合以上观点，并考察我国中小学教育实践，我们认为中小学教师至少应具备从事教育教学、学生管理工作、科研发展这三个方面能力。因此，教育学课程群应由三个方面课程组成：一是教育基础理论课程，包括“教育概论”、“发展与教育心理学”；二是教育技能课程：“学科课程与教学论”、“课堂教学策略”、“班主任工作”、“青少年心理健康”、“教育科学研究方法”；三是教育实践课程：“教育见习”以及“教育实习”。除此之外，还应开设一些选修课程，如“课程理论与课程改革”、“中外教育名著选读”、“学校管理”、“教学技能训练”等。至于课时安排及课程顺序，考察我国多所师范大学教育学课程设计及西方发达国家教育学课程，按170学分计算，教育学课程应占20%左右，即34学分。据此，我们对教育学课程所包含的课程、学分和学年安排作出构想(见下表)。

教育学课程群构想

类别	所含课程	学分	学年
教育理论课	“教育概论”、“发展与教育心理学”	4	二年级
教育技能课	“学科课程与教学论”、“课堂教学策略”、“班主任工作”、“青少年心理健康”、“教育科学研究方法”	11	三年级
教育实践课	“教育见习”以及“教育实习”	13	四年级
其他选修课	“课程理论与课程改革”、“中外教育名著选读”、“学校管理”、“教学技能训练”	6	三、四年级

2. 课程间的关系

课程群中的单门课程具有关联性、整体性和独立性特征，教育学课程群亦具有以下特征。

第一，教育学课程群中的核心课程是《教育概论》。课程群理论最重要的一个特点就是必须有主干课程，其他子课程围绕核心课程开设。在教育学课程群中无疑《教育概论》就是核心课程。《教育概论》是关于教育学一般原理的概要论述，是学习教育学的入门课和基础课，是教育学课程群中其他课程的出发点，它的地位是毋庸置疑的。

第二，教育学课程群中的课程具有整体性。课程群中的单门课程都具有它的地位和作用，我们不能仅限于具体的各门课程自身的调节，而没有考虑课程在课程群中的位置和相互关系，没有从整体上使整个课程系统得到改善。教育学课程群中的各门课程是处于整个课程体系及整个教学体系之中，每一步骤，每一环节，都是从整体的需要出发，不应片面追求某一门课程的完备性，扩大或改变其在课程体系结构中的位置。课程群建设是整体的、联系的，而不是孤立的、割裂的。

第三，教育学课程群中的课程具有独立性。这里的独立性已不是先行的单门课程建设所具有独立性意义，而是指根据培养目标和培养规格，从专业课程体系、课程结构上进行总体上的设计和探讨，从系统结构优化着眼，从课程结构和教学体系的优化上着手诸课程的建设，注重课程设置的科学性，力求减少诸课程内容的重复，压缩不必要的课时，使其建设的目标，既达到课程结构和教学体系的优化又使诸课程具有相对独立性。

（二）推行学分制管理体制

学分制作为一种课程管理体制，在教育学课程群建设中具有重要作用。学分制的核心是实行选课制，选课制的前提是提供给学生若干具有导引性的课程。学分制是以人才培养的多样化为主旨，以发展学生兴趣与特长为中心，课程体系也相应具有多种模式，两者之间形成了相辅相成的关系。

学分制促使教育学课程群建设处于一个不断变化的动态过程中，根据基础教育改革以及高师教育发展的需要，不断改革课程结构，教学内容、方法等，假如课程群始终不变，那么最终会变成“老四门”、“老五门”；学分制同时又能满足学生个体选择的多样性。

（三）打造优秀教学团队

教师是高等学校实现其教育观和教育理念的最关键因素。高校的教学水平主要取决于教师水平，而教师水平除了自身努力和功底外，还取决于教师之间的有效沟通和交流。教育学课程群是一个复杂的课程体系,绝不是一人可以胜任的,因此,我们认为教学团队是教育学课程群得以有效实施的重要保证。教学团队是以课程群为核心组成的教师群体,该教师群体通过成员之间的协作与交流,开展教学研究和教学改革,从而提高教学水平和教师整体素质。

一个优秀的教学团队应具备以下几个特点:第一,团队成员必须具有积极创新精神。通过团队的努力,在课程群教学中开展创新性教学,通过团队成员在教学方法上的创新来培养具有创新精神的学生。第二,教学团队具有可持续发展潜力。教学团队的成员既要开展教学研究,同时必须开展科学研究,科学研究是提高教学水平的深层次动因。一个有持续发展和竞争力的高水平教学团队,必须有高水平的科研作支撑。第三,团队规模适度,结构合理性。团队组成人员在职称、年龄、教学经历等方面自然形成梯队形式,既保证了成员在教学交流中的各层次的全面性,又保证了团队发展人才的不断层。同时团队规模适度,保证成员之间能保持充分的沟通与交流。

参考文献

[1] 约翰·R·霍尔,玛丽·乔·尼兹.文化:社会学的视野[M].周晓虹,徐彬,译.北京:商务印书馆,2002:320.
[2] 戴维·伯姆,李·尼科.论对话[M].王松涛,译.北京:教育科学出版社,2004.
[3] R·本尼迪克特.文化模式[M].王炜,等,译.北京:三联书店,1988:39.
[4] 贺来.宽容意识[M].长春:吉林教育出版社,2001:7.
[5] 埃德加·莫兰.复杂性理论与教育问题[M].陈一壮,译.北京:北京大学出版社,1999.
[6] 韦政通.中国文化与现代生活[M].北京:中国人民大学出版社,2005.
[7] 联合国教科文组织.教育:财富蕴藏其中[M].北京:教育科学出版社,1996:46.
[8] 高亚萍."亚文化"视野中的青年流行文化[J].中国青年研究,2003(5).

教师教育模式创新的构想
——“顶岗实习置换培训”的启示

黄家庆[*]　徐书业[**]
(钦州学院,广西　钦州　535000)

摘　要:适应新时期教育发展对教师的要求,教师教育应构建“教师教育合作共同体”,以培养高质量的师范生,造就未来优秀的教师;促进教师的专业发展,不断提高教师职业适应性。教师教育一体化的研究、教育部相关的文件和“顶岗实习,置换培训”的实施,为“教师教育合作共同体”的构建提供了基础。“教师教育合作共同体”要以“顶岗实习,置换培训”为载体,以经常性合作交流活动为纽带,以制度和机制为保障,来运作和巩固发展。

关键词:教师教育;合作共同体;大学;中小学

基金项目:新世纪广西高等教育教学改革工程项目:“教师职业适应性提高的研究”(2008B022)。

Innovation of Teachers Training-Implication of Teachers Training
—by Exchanging Roles

Huang Jia-qing　Xu Shu-ye
(Qinzhou University, Qinzhou 535000, China)

Abstract: Aiming to meet the needs of education development, educate high-level normal students, train excellent teachers and promote the development of career of teachers, an integration of teacher-training and cooperation should be constructed. Based on the relevant research and documents, the integration realizes

* 黄家庆,钦州学院副厅级调研员,副研究员。
** 徐书业,钦州学院副院长,教授,博士。

the exchange of roles between the teachers and would-be teachers in middle schools and primary schools, with the guaranttee of relavant system and cooperation.

Key words: teachers training; integration of cooperation; university; primary and middle schools

实现我国教育强国的战略目标,需要培养高素质的教师,建设一支高水平的教师队伍。而要适应新时期教育发展对教师的要求,必须深化高校教师教育改革、创新模式。教师教育模式的创新,是一项实践性很强的改革课题。近年来各地开展的高校选派高年级优秀师范生到农村中小学实习支教,让置换出来的教师离岗培训的“顶岗实习,置换培训”活动,不失为教师教育改革的一个尝试。这一活动,既是高校提高教师教育质量,培养未来中小学教师教育实习的制度改革;又是高校与地方共同开展中小学教师培训,促进教师专业化发展的有益探索。教师教育应以这一活动为契机和切入口,创新模式——构建“教师教育合作共同体”。

一、“教师教育合作共同体”的模式构想

“教师教育合作共同体”的模式,就是在地方教育行政部门的协调下,大学与中小学校通过制订相应的合作计划和相关的实施办法,形成相互促进的机制、互利共赢的稳定的共同体,在平等合作的基础上,开展师范生培养和在职教师培训的活动。共同体由作为教师培训研修基地的大学与作为师范生实习基地的中小学组成。

具体形式是:一方面,由大学有计划地组织师范教育专业的高年级学生到实习基地学校,在一定时间内,进行“一对一”或“二对一”的顶岗实习支教,以强化师范生实践教学,加强教师养成教育,培养师范生教师职业的基本知识和基本技能,增强其为农村基础教育服务的意识和能力。另一方面,通过顶岗实习支教置换出来的实习基地学校的教师,到派出顶岗实习支教师范生的大学,按照大学与地方教育行政部门拟定的培训研修计划,接受培训和到研修基地学校进行观摩、研修。同时,大学教师就中小学教育实践中的问题进行探索,与研修基地、实习基地学校的教师共同开展教育教学研究活动,促进各方的发展,并成为学习与发展的共同体。它是一种把教师职前培养与职后培训有机紧密结合起来的教师教育新模式。

“教师教育合作共同体”与教师专业发展学校(PDS)和教师发展学校(TDS)有所不同。教师专业发展学校是以中小学为基地,由大学或教育科研机构和中小学合作建立的旨在促进教师专业发展的教学研究共同体。[1]教师发展学校是大学、教育科研机构、教育学术团体、教研培训部门和中小学合作建立的以人为本、以教学教育实践为基础、以教学相长为意义取向的、旨在促进教师专业发展的学习与发展的共同体。但是它们都是以中小学为基地,都是平等的合作“伙伴”关系,都旨在通过大学与中小学合作实现教师专业发展,并促进大学与中小学的共同发展。

二、“教师教育合作共同体”的意义作用

“教师教育合作共同体”的模式,是学习与发展的共同体,各方都是学习者,在教学教育实践的合作中相互学习,理论文化和实践文化相互沟通,大学和中小学都获得生存和发展的可能

性,都有未来发展的希望,而不是大学搞实验,中小学做被试者。因为中小学校若要变革进步,成为模范学校,就必须不断提高教师的水平,不断地从大学接受新的思想和新知识;大学若想培养出未来更好的教师,就必须将中小学校作为师范教育实践的场所。[2]而当大学与中小学双方处于分离状态时,双方的缺点呈现显性状态,双方的优点没有充分体现出来。只有双方合作才能为对方提供其所需、但又不具备的要素,才能有利于双方共同促进教师专业发展,共同从事教师教育。[3]“教师教育合作共同体”的构建就是旨在从根本上提高教师的专业发展水平——培养高质量的师范生,造就未来优秀的教师;促进教师发展的主体性、主动性和创造性,不断提高教师职业适应性。

从大学的层面上看,师范生需要具备一定的教师职业知识、技能和意向,要形成的专业判断能力,可以在实习基地学校的“临床”教育教学实践中取得或实现。大学不能完全提供教师教育需要的真实的教育教学情景,可以在“教师教育合作共同体”完全获得。同时,中小学真实的教育教学情景和教师丰富、鲜活的教学实践经验,会给大学的研究和教师教育注入新鲜血液。大学教师把中小学的鲜活、生动的教育教学案例带进课堂,可使其教学内容更富有吸引力和说服力,而成为师范教育专业的课程资源;大学教师就中小学教育实践中的问题进行探索,其研究成果会更富有针对性和适切性。大学的教育理论只有扎根于中小学丰富的教育实践,从鲜活的中小学教育生活中源源不断地汲取营养、提取经验,才能促进自身的发展,才能在教育实践中检验自己。

从中小学的层面上看,相当多的教师在参加工作以后很少有机会系统学习理论知识,亟须得到理论知识的补充和将感性认识上升为理论。“教师教育合作共同体”的模式将为他们提供很好的条件和机会。大学教师具备丰厚的教育理论基础和及时获取新知识的优越条件,具有敏锐发现问题的洞察力和运用相应理论研究问题的能力,能给中小学带来一些新思想、新知识、新技能、新技术、新的发展思路和研究问题的策略及方法。[4]大学根据需要,针对中小学教师实践问题开办教育理论讲座,为中小学教师进行专业知识和现代教育技术的培训,唤醒他们积极、主动追求专业发展的愿望,使教育教学工作的实践在中小学教师眼里变成研究的对象,从而逐渐开始以研究的态度和方式对待教育教学的日常工作,不断适应教师职业的发展。

从大学与中小学的相互关系来看,高质量的大中小学教育来自优异的教师教育,提高教师教育质量是大学与中小学共同发展的基础,大学与中小学在教师教育合作中取长补短,可“形成一种互补关系”,结成一种平等、共生、有机合作的伙伴关系。即实习基地学校给大学师范生提供实习情境和场所,研修基地学校给大学组织培训中小学教师提供研修条件,促进教师教育质量的提高;在与大学的合作中,中小学可有效地利用大学的教育资源,更好地促进学校和教师专业的发展。大学则充分运用中小学的教育情境和场所,更好地释放自身应有的功能,实施教师教育职前培养职后培训的一体化;并通过与中小学校合作开展教育科学项目研究和教学改革实验,探讨教育实践问题等各种途径,为中小学教师提供培训服务和教师专业发展提供广泛的支持。“教师教育合作共同体”可为教师教育理论与实践的融合、大学与中小学的共同发展,提供一个崭新的平台,实现教育理论与实践、高等教育与基础教育的双向沟通。

三、“教师教育合作共同体”的构建依据与基础

“教师教育合作共同体”作为一种教育思想,落实为具体行动进而成为现实,良好的基础是

十分重要的成功条件。

1. “教师教育合作共同体”构建的理论依据

教师教育一体化的研究认为，在当今世界教师教育改革中，教师教育一体化已逐步成为各国教师教育发展中的一种新模式。要提高教师培养培训质量，促进教师持续的专业发展，师范生的培养和中小学教师的在职培训必须利用中小学的资源，加强与大学的合作。目前，我国教师培养系统和培训系统水平倒挂的现象存在，显然不利于教师的继续教育，不能达到促进教师专业发展的目的。教师教育要提高办学层次和质量，必须改变培养、培训分离的状态，对教师职前培养和职后培训进行全程的规划设计，实现一体化，并纳入高等教育体系。

研究还认为，教师教育一体化包括三层含义：一是职前培养、入职教育、职后提高的一体化，建设教师终身教育的协调体系；二是中小幼教师教育一体化；三是教学研究与教学实践的一体化，即建立师范大学与中小学的伙伴关系。[5]而要实现教师教育一体化首先是在教育组织上的一体化。“教师教育合作共同体”无疑是实现教师教育一体化的一种教育组织。

2. “教师教育合作共同体”构建的政策依据

2007 年 7 月国家教育部下发的《关于大力推进师范生实习支教工作的意见》(教师[2007] 4 号)，为“教师教育合作共同体”的构建提供了工作依据。《教育部关于大力推进师范生实习支教工作的意见》要求：高师院校要因地制宜地组织高年级师范生，到中小学进行不少于一学期的教育实习；各地要将师范生实习支教与加强农村教师队伍建设紧密结合，根据实际需要，创造有利条件，积极安排和接收高师院校师范生到农村学校进行实习支教；地方各级教育行政部门、高师院校和中小学要不断创新师范生实习支教的途径和方法，积极探索三方合作、协同开展师范生教育实习工作的有效机制。教育部还要求高师院校会同教育行政部门，因地制宜地选择确定一批条件适宜的中小学作为实习基地，建立相对稳定的师范生实习基地。这就有意无意地为“教师教育合作共同体”的建立起到了引导的作用，从而成为相应的依据。

3. “教师教育合作共同体”构建的实践基础

各地教育部门和大学贯彻落实教育部的意见，实施“顶岗支教，置换培训”工程，为“教师教育合作共同体”的建立提供了良好的现实基础。在实施“顶岗支教，置换培训”工程中，各地教育部门和高校通过顶岗实习支教和对置换出来的教师进行培训，把大学与实习基地的中小学校联系结合起来，开展合作。即高校选派优秀师范生到实习基地学校顶岗实习支教，顶岗实习支教结束，由实习基地学校对顶岗实习支教学生在实习支教期间的思想表现及业务水平做出鉴定；实习基地学校把被顶岗的教师送到派遣师范生的高校参加培训，培训结束，经考核合格，由高校颁发相关的培训证书。这一“顶岗支教，置换培训”项目工程的实施，不论是组织形式，还是实施内容，客观上都为“教师教育合作共同体”的建立打下了基础，而可称之为其雏形。如钦州市教育局和钦州学院在实施“顶岗支教，置换培训”项目工程中，制定了“钦州学院师范生顶岗实习与师资培训实施方案”，教育局下文明确了 13 所中学为钦州学院师范生的实习基地学校，确立了 2 所先进中学为师资培训的示范性研修基地学校。钦州学院为做好师范生顶岗实习与师资培训工作，还制定了《钦州学院师范生顶岗实习支教工作管理办法》、《钦州学院师范生顶岗实习与师资培训试点工作教师基地研修计划》以及《被顶岗教师培训方案》，并与师资培训示范性研修基地学校的领导及有关人员成立了培训机构。不仅形成了一套顶岗实习支教的管理办法和一套完整的师资培训模式，还形成了在教育行政部门协调下建立起来的大学与中小学合作的框架。

四、“教师教育合作共同体”的形成与运作

“教师教育合作共同体”的建立,目的是使合作学校成为教师职前培养与教师职后培训的场所,并在教师教育中实现共同发展。在具体的实施过程中,目的的实现是需要形成稳定的工作统一体和相应的运作载体与运作策略作为依托的。

(一)“教师教育合作共同体”的形成

“教师教育合作共同体”是大学与地方“校地合作”的一种形式。它由地方高校与接受师范生实习的中小学和接受教师研修的示范性中小学组成。地方教育行政部门是“教师教育合作共同体”的组建者,各相关中小学由教育行政部门协调组织参加。它应有一个从教育行政部门组织安排到自愿加入的过程。目前,即以实施《教育部关于大力推进师范生实习支教工作的意见》,开展“顶岗实习,置换培训”为切入口,由地方教育行政部门有选择地确定接受师范生实习和接受教师研修的中小学校,明确为师范生实习基地和教师培训研修基地,把这些相关的学校与大学组成“教师教育合作共同体”。将来,经过实践成熟和认识的提高,并随着教师教育的发展,各方均有强烈的合作意愿,寻求合作发展时,进入“教师教育合作共同体”的中小学校,则由教育行政部门安排转为自愿要求参加。然而,它的运转和发展能否顺利进行,则取决于各方权利与义务的确定、是否达成共识、形成的制度和管理的规则等因素。

(二)“教师教育合作共同体”运作的载体与策略

1. 以“顶岗实习,置换培训”为载体,开展合作,促进教师教育发展

在过去的教师教育中,大学是教师学习理论的场所,中小学是教师实践的基地,二者没有必然的联系,相互隔阂,各行其是,没有得到很好的结合。现在开展“顶岗实习,置换培训”活动,让师范生到农村中小学教育实习基地实习支教,同时置换出实习基地学校的教师离岗到高校接受培训,高校又把培训的教师带到研修基地学校去观摩、研讨。这样把“教师教育合作共同体”的成员紧密地结合起来,实现大学与中小学双方真正意义上的合作,提供对方所需,相互弥补,实施教师的职前培养和职后培训,促进教师的专业化和合作双方的发展,实现双赢。“教师教育合作共同体”也就能在工作中得到巩固和发展,并较好地促进教师教育发展。只有建立起了这种紧密的工作合作关系,大学与中小学之间的合作才可能是稳定和长久的。

2. 以经常性合作交流活动为纽带,巩固合作成果,发挥合作共同体的效能

一是开展合作研究项目,发挥双方的专长,共同探讨教育实践与理论问题,通过科研活动中的文化磨合,增强合作意识。

二是利用网络平台,与大学教育科研人员和中小学教师开展交流。学校利用自己的网站,开通与本校教科研相关的 BBS ,邀请教育科研人员在线主持,与中小学教师进行教育教学研究过程中有关问题的探讨。

三是针对中小学教师教育教学实践中出现的问题,大学不定期地举办教育理论讲座等,定期进行交流,以座谈会的形式就出现的新问题进行探讨。

四是合作成员中的中小学开展重大的教育教学活动邀请大学师范教育专业的师生参加,大学积极响应,并予以支持和帮助。

在双方平等的合作过程中，大学帮助中小学获取了更多促进教师专业发展的思想、技术和方法，使中小学有意识地去展示促进教师专业发展的功能，使其处于隐性状态下的促进教师发展功能得以充分释放；在双方相互交流中，大学了解了中小学对教师教育的需求，得以及时对教师教育计划、内容、方式方法作出反应；在与中小学的实际接触过程中，大学了解中小学的实际情况，便于更有针对性地进行教育科学研究，这有利于充分释放教育科研为中小学服务的功能。[6]这些建立在平等互动基础上的经常性合作交流活动，既巩固了"顶岗实习，置换培训"的合作成果，又发挥了"教师教育合作共同体"的效能。

3. 以制度和机制为保障，推动合作顺利进行，提高教师教育合作效益

在合作共同体的层面上，应在教育行政部门的参与指导下，制定"教师教育合作共同体"章程，明确其宗旨、目的和各成员单位的权利与义务等有关事项；建立"教师教育合作共同体"成员单位的校长联席会议制度。校长联席会主要研究决定合作的重大问题和合作项目，沟通信息，交流情况，每年召开1～2次。"教师教育合作共同体"应设立工作协调机构，由教育行政部门、大学和实习基地、研修基地的学校代表有关人员组成，主要负责制定教师教育的合作规划、完善合作活动制度、编制活动计划等，如拟订"顶岗实习置换培训实施方案"、"教师培训研修合作计划"、"合作备忘录"、"项目合作管理办法"等。每学期召开一次工作会议或根据需要由教育行政部门组织召开。

此外，大学应建立健全师范生实习支教工作规章制度，制定为中小学教师提供多样化教育服务的计划、方案，形成与教育行政部门、中小学互动的有效机制。如"选派骨干教师担任实习支教的指导教师，在教师考核、职务聘任和表彰奖励等方面体现积极的政策导向，鼓励和支持教师参加师范生实习支教工作，并深入中小学第一线开展教育教学研究"（教育部教师[2007]4号文件）。同时"吸收一部分中小学优秀教师担任教育类课程的教学和教育实践的指导工作"[7]，让中小学优秀教师将生动的教学实践经验带入大学讲坛，以便在课堂教学以及科学研究中注入实践的元素。各相关中小学校和教育行政部门应主动拟订教师培训计划和需要大学提供帮助支持的项目，以能较好地与大学对接。

总之，在"教师教育合作共同体"这一模式下，形成地方教育部门关心师范教育、重视教师培训，大学积极融入地方教育教师的态势，教师职前培养和职后培训成为一个连续的、有机的、相互联系的一体化过程，将有力、有效地促进教师专业发展。

参考文献

[1] 钟智.教师专业发展学校的构建[J].教师教育研究，2005(4).

[2] 苏智欣.美国教师教育改革中的思想争论.国际教育纵横：中国比较教育文选[D].北京：人民教育出版社，1994：342.

[3][4][6] 傅树京.大学与中小学合作发展：理念及实践[J].辽宁教育研究，2003(5).

[5] 袁振国.中国教育政策评论[M].北京：教育科学出版社，2002：25.

[7] 教育部关于"十五"期间教师教育改革与发展的意见.http://www.moe.edu.cn/jsduiw.

师专升格为综合本科院校后的教师教育资源整合探讨

梁 庆*

（钦州学院，广西 钦州 535000）

摘 要：师专升格为综合本科学院以后，教育资源向非师范专业转移削弱了教师教育力量，教师职前教育环境的弱化、学术本位的思想、教师职前教育实践的缺失导致了教师教育质量的下降。新升格的综合本科学院，要承担起为当地教育事业发展培养、培训教师的重任，整合师范教育资源是势在必行。整合的内容是：整合管理力量，加强教师教育管理；整合师资力量，把师资力量做强；整合生源，吸引优秀学生来接受教师教育；整合课程结构，突出师范性课程；整合校内、校外资源，提高师范生的教育实践能力。

关键词：综合本科学院；教师教育；资源整合

基金项目：广西教育科学“十一五”科研项目“师专升格为综合本科学院后的教师教育资源整合研究”（2008A29）。

On the Integration of Teacher Education Resources at Newly Upgraded Normal Colleges

Liang Qing

（Qinzhou University，Qinzhou 535000，China）

Abstract：The power of teacher education is weaken after the upgrading from a Teacher's College to a comprehensive undergraduate university. The main reasons to reduce the teaching qulity are the change from education major to non-education major，the weaking of teachers' pre-vocational education，academic-based thinking，and the lack of pre-vocational education practice. The newly upgraded university is

* 梁庆，男，广西浦北人，钦州学院教育科学部副教授。

to undertake the development of local education and training, so it's imperative to integrate the teacher education resources. The integrations in clude management strengthen, teaching staff, source of students, curriculum structure, internal and external resources.

Key words: comprehensive undergraduate university; teacher education; resource integration

师专升格为综合本科学院后，学院的办学性质发生了从师范教育向综合教育的转变。由于这些新升格的综合本科学院大多分布在各地、市，故升格以后，这些学院就要承担起为社会经济培养人才和为当地培养教师的双重任务，学院变成了师范教育与非师范教育并存的格局。随着九年义务教育的普及和计划生育政策的贯彻落实等原因，中小学教师的需求逐渐趋于“饱和”。但另一方面，随着“教师工资待遇不低于当地公务员工资”政策的落实，教师将逐渐成为一种令人羡慕的职业，将会吸引越来越多的学子来从事教师职业。因此，师专升格为综合本科学院之后，在教师教育方面的工作重心是要把教师教育“做精做强”。“做精”就是要把教师职前教育(师范教育)从原来的数量扩充转向精英的培养上来，走内涵发展的道路；“做强”就是努力突出教师的双专业性，即要根据现代教师发展的要求在突出教师的学科学术的同时也要突出师范性。师范教育的特色是师范[1]，不能把师范这个特色凸显出来，师范教育就失去了它的本质。此外，这些新升格的综合本科学院，除了承担教师职前教育这一任务之外，还承担着当地中小学在职教师入职教育和在职培训的重任，不把自身做强，就难有承担教师培训重任之力。

教师教育是师专升格为综合本科学院以前的强项，做精做强教师教育是时代对师专升格为综合本科学院的要求。但不少师专升格为综合本科学院以后，教师教育被挤到了边缘，教师教育质量下降也初见端倪，如果不及时对教师教育资源进行整合，这些升格的本科学院原有的教师教育的优势将不复存在，师范教育与非师范教育并存将是徒有虚名。

一、师专升格为综合本科学院后的教师教育质量下降的原因分析

(一) 教育资源向非师范专业转移削弱了教师教育的力量

升格以后，学院的性质发生的重大的变化，从体制上看是师范教育与非师范教育并存。非师范教育对新升格的本科学院而言是一个全新的领域，学院在专业开设、资源配备上向非师范专业倾斜是无可厚非的。但随着非师范专业的扩张，师范专业的萎缩，原来从事教师教育专业的教师也纷纷转投它向，造成了教师教育资源的流失。另外，由于非师范专业的人才紧缺，地方和学院的财力有限，学院新引进的教师都是为非师范专业服务的教师。如此下来，一方面原来从事教师教育工作的教师在流失，另一方面新的教师教育方面的教师又得不到补充，势必造成从事教师教育工作的教师越来越弱。教师是教育的根本，教师教育的师资力量得不到加强，教师教育质量的下降也就在所难免。

(二)师范教育环境的弱化将引发教师教育质量下降

师范教育的特色是师范，师专升格为综合本科学院后，原有的师范教育的环境不复存在，没有了师范特色的环境，可能会导致师范生的方向迷失。从管理环境看，由于非师范专业对这些新升格的综合本科学院来说是一个全新的领域，学院的各管理层次必然要把管理的中心转向非师范专业的管理上来。由于人力有限，对师范专业的管理只能靠“吃老本”，对其管理只能“暂时搁置”。没有了研究，更谈不上创新，久而久之，必然会引发教师教育质量的下降。从师范生的学习环境上看，由于没能对师范教育资源进行整合，师范教育仍分布在各系里，随着非师范专业的扩张，师范专业逐渐萎缩，师范教育在这些学院里从原来的中心走向了边缘。这些夹在非师范教育缝隙或被挤到边缘地带的师范生失去了良好的教师专业成长的环境，也导致了教师教育质量的下降。

师范生的专业成长需要良好的环境，这里所说的环境包括培养目标、课程设置、师范性专业的教师资源、师范性教育活动的安排、日常性的教师教育技能的训练和科学的教育实习安排等。师范生在由这些因素构成的教育环境中接受教师教育，对其专业素质提高会起到非常重要的潜移默化的作用，对教育质量的提高会起到重要的促进作用。这种师范生成长的育人环境在这些学院升格以前是我们所熟悉的。但升格以后，师范专业与非师范专业并存的各专业系成了一个“大杂烩”，传统师范生的这种专业成长环境不复存在。没有了这种文化环境，师范生得不到良好教师教育文化环境的熏陶，这将影响到师范生的专业人格的养成。可以说，师范教育环境的弱化，对教师教育质量会产生不可估量的负面影响。

(三)学术本位的思想降低了教师教育质量

学术性还是师范性的问题一直是师范教育争议热烈的问题。在教育理论界折中了这两性的争议:师范教育既要强调学术性，也要突出师范性。但在具体实践过程中，学术本位仍然是主流。原因多样，但最根本的原因是体制问题。传统的师范院校，师范专业是按学科专业来分块管理的，中文、数学、地理、政治、英语等，除了一些公共课(含教育科学课程)，专业与专业之间几乎是井水不犯河水。在课程的开设上，各专业以我为主，对最能体现师范性的教育科学课程只开了老三门(教育学、心理学、学科教育学或学科教学法)。从课时安排上看，教育科学课程只占总课时的7%左右，师范教育的师范性没能从根本上得到体现。各专业的学科课程的安排，绝大多数是按照学科的逻辑顺序来进行安排，根本没考虑中小学教育的实际需要，这样的课程体系培养出来的学生的结果是处在学术上不去，师范体现不出来的尴尬境地。升格以后，这矛盾非但没有解决，反而有日趋彰显之势，在这学术本位思想的指导之下，师范也就无所谓师范了。

(四)教师职前教育实践环节的淡化导致了教师教育质量的下降

教师职业是一种实践性很强的职业，它需要具有较强的教学实践能力。师范生要成为一名合格的教师，在校学习期间必须掌握从教的基本技能，否则，这些师范生就算能成为“学者”，也难成为“良师”。要使师范生掌握从教的基本技能，师范院校必须加强师范生实践环节的教学。

要把师范生的教育实践工作做好，教师职前教育必须具备两个条件:一是具有熟悉基础教育前沿动态、教育基本理论扎实、教学水平较高并能引领教师教育发展的教育理论和科学教育学教师。二是具有相对稳定的教育实习基地。这两条件,新升格的本科院校在没升格前是比较注重建设的,但在升格之后,由于重心转移,建设被严重淡化。

1. 师范专业严重萎缩,各系每个年级只保留一个师范班,甚至隔年才招一个师范班,导致原来从事教育理论教学和学科教育学教学的教师没课可上。为了生存,这些教师纷纷"改行",原来以教育理论或学科教育学为主业,现在把学科教育学变为副业。既然是副业,有时间时就多做一些,实在忙不过来,只能吃老本了事。没有了专业研究,一年两年也许还能应付,时间长了,剩下的只是混了。其结果是培养出来"21世纪的学生,20世纪的教学方法"就不足为怪了。

2. 要提高师范教育的质量,必须做好师范生的教育实习工作。一般地,师范院校在其所服务的区域都有一些定点实习学校(或称实习基地)。每年,师范院校都组织学生到定点实习学校进行教育实习工作,这是师范生的专业成长所必需的。但是由于各种原因,一些新升格的本科学院的师范专业的教育实习变成了"走过场",根本达不到锻炼的目的。表现有三:其一,由于师资有限,学校无法派出更多的实习指导教师指导学生的实习,通常是一个班的学生由一、二个带队老师带队到一个实习学校进行教育实习,学生得到的指导相当有限。其二,一个班的学生同时挤到一所中、小学进行实习,而实习学校的容纳有限,每个实习生得到上讲台的实习机会实际很少。据本课题组对广西新升格的地方本科学院的调查,有些新升格的本科学院的师范生在教育实习时只能上2节课。上2节课就结束了教育实习,根本达不到锻炼的目的。其三,更有甚者,个别新升格的本科学院的一些专业系还鼓励学生"自主实习",由学生自己联系实习单位,自发去实习。实习时间结束,学生能把学院需要的实习材料上交即可。不排除这种实习模式可能给了实习生更多的实习机会。运用这种实习模式,如果学院对学生的实习过程有跟踪、指导,这不失为一种值得称道的实习模式。但据我们课题组调查,采取这种实习模式的学院,是在实习经费有限、指导教师不足,找不到合适的实习学校的情况下做出的无奈的选择,这种实习的质量如何也就难以预料了。

师范生的教育实习是最能体现教师职前教育质量的一个环节,一些新升格的本科学院的学科教育学教师学无专攻、学生实习缺乏专业指导、实习时间没有保障、实习学校不稳定等,在这种情形下,还谈什么教育质量?

鉴于此,师专升格为综合本科学院之后,要承担起为当地教育事业的发展培养、培训教师的重任,对教师教育资源进行整合势在必行。

二、师专升格为综合本科学院后的教师教育资源整合内容探析

教师教育从封闭走向开放是教师教育发展的历史必然。但开放不是放开,开放的最根本目的是为了提高教师教育的质量。师专升格以前进行的师范教育是一种封闭的教师教育。升格以后,师范教育与非师范教育并存其实就是教师教育开放的表现形式。但万变不离其宗,只要教师教育存在,提高教师教育质量的根本目的就不会变。但话也说回来,在师专时,师专培养的师范生离社会的要求还有差距;升格以后,如前所述的原因,要提高师范教育的质量,使教师教育能满足社会的需要谈何容易?所以,师专升格为综合本科学院之后,要提高教师教育质量,对他们来说是一个严峻的大挑战。根据世界各国教师教育改革发展的经验,结合各升格本科学院的实际情况,进行教师教育资源整合将是提高教师教育质量的一条根本的出路。

(一) 整合管理力量,加强教师教育管理

管理是教育质量提高的保障,有什么样的管理,教育就有什么样的质量。在教师教育的发展史上,教师教育经历了从封闭性的师范教育到开放性的教师教育发展过程,我国目前的教师教育正进入开放性的教师教育阶段。但教师教育开放以后,如何培养适合基础教育发展甚至引领基础教育发展的高质量的教师,成为从事教师教育的高校必须思考和解决的问题。师专升格为综合本科学院之后,教师教育的模式实现了从封闭到开放的转变,但这转变不等于教师教育质量就提高了。要提高教师教育质量,必须寻找一种行之有效的管理模式。在这方面,西方一些国家的做法值得我们借鉴。如美国伊利诺大学,是全美最优秀的理工大学之一,其师范教育也在一流之列[2]。伊利诺大学在师范教育中,为了有效地配置和整合学校资源,充分发挥综合大学的优势,它建立了一个跨越多个学院,甚至跨越校内外的完善的组织系统。包括教师教育理事会、执行委员会、专业委员会、相关各系及教职工、实习学校的合作教师共五个子系统[2]。各个子系统分工明确,职责分明,正是因为有了这样严密的组织管理机制,才确保了该校的教师教育的质量。新升格的综合本科学院,其办学性质与综合大学办教师教育的性质有许多相同之处,但与原来就是非师范性质的综合本科大学相比,这些学院办起教师教育来更有优势。但这优势不可能是从天而降,需要我们对这些传统的优势进行整合,尤其是在管理方面。为加强教师教育的管理,须成立一个专门的管理机构,就目前从师专升格而来的综合本科学院而言,成立教师教育学院是一个比较理想的选择:成立教师教育学院之后,教师教育的事务由教师教育学院来统管。这样一来,一方面教师教育的管理得到加强,教师教育质量的提高就有了保障。另一方面,教师教育从其它各系分离出来以后,各系可以更加集中力量去进行其专业建设,这是两全其美的事,何乐而不为?因此,整合管理力量,加强教师教育的管理,无论从教师教育的角度还是从各系专业发展的角度乃至学校发展的角度看都是十分有利的。

(二) 整合师资力量,把师资力量做强

教师是教育的根本,高质量的教师教育需要高素质的教师教育团队的支撑。师专升格为综合本科学院之后,学院的办学性质发生了改变,但以专业为主的管理格局并没有发生改变,在这样的管理格局下,师范教育散落在各系里,这不仅使师范专业学生失去了原有的专业成长环境,更重要的是导致了教师教育师资力量的分散。在这种状态下,要把教师教育的师资力量做强谈何容易?当今的教师教育已不像传统的师范教育,传统的师范教育是封闭的、终结性的教育,而当今的教师教育是教师职前教育(师范教育)、入职教育、在职教育一体化的教育,这种教育是开放的、专业性、终身性的。所以这些新升格的综合本科学院除了承担教师职前教育外,还在肩负着教师入职培训和教师在职培训的历史使命。一直以来,师范教育就有滞后于基础教育的通病,自从我国的基础教育进行改革之后,我国的基础教育已发生了翻天覆地的变化,而不少师范院校的师范教育还是五十年不变,这种"以不变应万变"的教师教育模式,其教育结果怎样是可想而知的。因此,新升格的综合本科学院要把教师教育的职前培养、入职培训、在职培训承担起来,必须建立一支学术有专攻、技能有特长、教育理念超前的教师教育团队。由于师专升格为综合本科学院以前就是师范院校,其原有的教师教育力量尚存,稍加整合便可建立起一支教师教育的团队。如前所述,为加强教师教育的管理,成立教师教育学院,教师教育学院成立以后,把原有的教育科学教师、各系的学科教育学教师整合起来便可组成一支

教师教育团队。以后，教师教育学院根据每位教师的专业特长确定其专业研究方向，根据教师教育发展的需要，选送相关教师到教育科研水平较高的大学进修提升，分期分批派遣教师教育教师到中小学去蹲点研究。这样，一方面确保了教师教育师资有先进的教育理念，也确保了教师教育教师对基础教育的前沿动态有充分的了解，有了这双管齐下团队建设模式，一支精干的教师教育团队才能建成，把教师教育师资做强的这一目标才有可能实现。

（三）整合生源，吸引更多优秀学生来接受教师教育

有学生才有教育。多年来，国家为了确保师范院校的生源，出台了许多优惠的政策，如在招生上优先录取，实行低学费、甚至免费教育等，这些政策对促进我国师范教育的发展乃至我国教育事业的发展起到了巨大的作用。但是，随着义务教育的普及，中小学教师需求的“饱和”，再加上从事教育职业的门槛提高、就业途径的不畅、教师待遇迟迟不能得到提高等方面的原因，造成了报读师范专业的学生迅速下降。像我区一些新升格的本科学院的一些专业，近几年的师范招生计划都不能完成。了解基础教育情况的人都知道，并不是中小学不需要教师，现在我区义务教育初中阶段的教学班，无论是城里还是乡下，几乎班班爆满，少则五六十人一班，多则上百人一个班，按照标准班进行编班，义务教育初中阶段的教师至少要增加一倍以上。而乡村小学，由于条件艰苦，工资待遇又低，许多师范生毕业后又不愿意到艰苦的地方从教。这样一来，一方面基础教育的教师需求短缺，另一方面又有大量的师范毕业生无业可就或改投他行，学生不愿报读师范专业也就不足为怪了。但从今以后，这一现象将会发生根本的改变。按照《教师法》、《义务教育法》的规定，教师的待遇不低于当地公务员的水平，但因各地的经济发展水平跟不上，这一政策在一些经济欠发达地区迟迟未得实施。2008 年 12 月，国务院总理温家宝主持召开了国务院常务会议，审议并原则通过《关于义务教育学校实施绩效工资的指导意见》。意见指出，为贯彻落实《义务教育法》，深化教育改革，吸引和鼓励各类优秀人才长期从教、终身从教，促进教育事业发展，义务教育学校实施绩效工资。《意见》决定从 2009 年 1 月 1 日起，在全国义务教育学校实施绩效工资，确保义务教育教师平均工资水平不低于当地公务员平均工资水平，同时对义务教育学校离退休人员发放生活补贴[3]。现在，各地正在贯彻落实这一政策。这一政策的实施，将会吸引大批学子来报读师范教育，教师教育将迎来一个新的春天。但这一政策的实施，也将意味着对教师教育提出了更高的要求，无论是教师职前教育、入职培训还是在职培训都会有更高的标准和要求。对于新升格的综合本科学院来说，做精做强教师教育是一个前所未有的机遇，但也是一个前所未有的挑战。把握这一时机，多渠道组织生源，教师教育将焕发出春天的气息，以下几点值得参考：

1. 在中学对国家的教师政策进行广泛宣传，使更多的优秀毕业生来报读师范专业。

2. 改革师范生的招生制度，在农村初中毕业生中招收五年一贯制的师范专科学生就读师范专业，专门培养农村小学教师。

众所周知，我国师范教育从旧三级（中师、师专、本科）向新三级（专科、本科、研究生）转变之后，本科层次的师范生毕业后不愿到小学，尤其是农村小学任教，专科学生愿到小学任教，但由于专科学生入学的分数相当低，而且由于年龄偏大，可塑性小，再加上就业的压力，许多学生实际到了第三年就去找工作了，这样培养的教师的质量很难满足小学教育的要求。对师范专科教育的招生进行改革，在农村初中招收一批优秀的学生来就读师范专业，把“中师阶段的重教育学、心理学的教学，重视书法、音乐、美术、舞蹈方面的训练”[4]的传统继承下来，加上初中

生的年龄小，可塑性大，更利于培养素质全面的小学教师。况且，这些学生从农村来，经过五年的教师专业训练，无论从思想上还是专业素养上都能适合农村小学教育的要求，这一举措，对农村小学教育师资的培养来说无疑是一种比较理想的选择。

3. 在校内对国家的教师教育政策进行宣传，吸引更多的非师范专业学生来参加教师教育培训，采用“3+1”、“4+1”或“渗透式”等培训模式对欲从事教育工作的非师范专业学生进行系统的教育专业培训，考取教师资格，使一些优秀的非师范专业的学生也有机会竞争教师职业，这些非师范专业学生有扎实的专业知识，经过系统的教师专业训练后能通过竞争当上教师，对教育事业来说也将会起到促进作用。

4. 拓展教师教育渠道，使教师教育向中小学延伸，真正承担起中小学教师入职培训和在职培训的重任。

（四）整合课程结构，突出师范性课程

“课程设置是师范教育改革的核心”。[5]长期以来，学术性之争和师范性之争一直困扰着师范教育，争论的结果是两者都重要，但在实践中学术中心丝毫没有动摇，各师范院校的课程设置便体现了这一点。有调查表明，“目前我国高师课程设置主要包括三个板块：公共基础课程、学科专业课程和教育专业课程。这三块课程占总学时比例大致是，公共基础课程约占20%，学科专业课程多于70%，教育专业课占7%”。[6]这样的课程结构，师范教育根本不能体现其师范性。从本质而言，学术性问题解决的是教师教什么的问题，而师范性问题解决的是教师怎么教的问题。本课题组通过调查表明，师范院校毕业的学生从教以后，在大学期间所学习的大量的学科专业知识在实际工作中很难用上，而他们最需要的怎么教的知识、技能却又远远不够，其原因也就不言而喻了。为充分体现教师职前教育的师范性，也为教师的终身教育做准备，改革教师职前教育的课程体系势在必行。至于如何改，国外的一些经验可以值得我们借鉴。事实证明，教育理论的缺失是阻碍基础教育质量提升的重要根源，增加教育类课程也就成为教师教育课程改革的切入点。我们不妨借鉴一些西方国家的经验。如美国教师教育中教育类课程占全部课程的20%，英国占25%，德国占25%，法国占20%。[7]有了这突出师范性的教师职前教育的课程体系，师范院校培养出来的教师才不至于出现有米不会炊的尴尬现象。

对于公共课程和学科专业课程的改革，我们不能因为增加了教育类课程而盲目地削减这两类课程，而是应深入中小学实际，进行深入地调研，根据中小学的实际需要来开设课程。总而言之，满足中小学教育的实际需要是我们进行教师教育课程改革的根本原则，而不是想当然或照抄照搬，从而避免出现师范院校的教师教育与基础教育“两张皮”的现象。

（五）整合校内、校外资源，提高师范生的教育实践能力

教育是一种培养人的艺术，教师职前教育培养的是应用型的教育人才，教育实习是师范生专业成长不可或缺的重要课程。长期以来，教育教学实习是我国教师职前教育阶段的一个薄弱环节，绝大多数师范院校的师范生在校学习期间仅经历教育实习这一种教育教学实习形式，教育见习、教育调查等机会少之又少，甚至没有。即使有，也由于时间太短而流于形式。[8]师范生的教育实习时间短而集中，一般是6周左右，在校内进行试教训练2周，到实习单位进行见习、实习4周，占总课时的3%左右。由于师范院校的人力紧缺，一个教学班的实习通常只有一、两个教师带队，实习学校通常也只是一个。这样，一个教学班四、五十人同时拥到一所学校

实习，而且实习生通常只能在实习学校的非毕业班进行学习，这样一来，学生能真正上讲台的机会则少得可怜。如前所述，我区的一些师范院校的学生到实习学校实习时只能上2节课，仅上2节课就完成了实习任务，师范生的教学技能怎样形成？师范院校怎能培养应用型人才？名誉上，师范院校都有固定的实习学校，但在实际操作过程中，由于实习学校只是单方向师范院校提供服务，再加上由于实习学校校舍紧缺等方面的原因，师范院校的师范生很难固定到一所学校进行教育实习，实习学校少而多变，学习指导教师相对匮乏，师范生的实习质量就很难保证了。

应用型大学的特点就是培养应用型人才，师范院校要培养应用型人才就必须给学生充足的教育教学实习时间和实习学校，同时必须具有充足的校内、校外（实习学校）的实习指导教师。这三点，对于刚从师专升格的综合本科学院来说，如果仍然按照原来以学科专业为主的教师教育管理模式进行动作，做好任何一点都不容易。为加强师范生的教育教学实践，提高师范生的教育教学技术水平，缩短师范生从教后的适应时间，提高师范生的竞争力，师范院校对教师职前教育的教育实习工作必须进行改革。

1. 适当增加见习、实习时间，变集中实习为分散见习、实习。

2. 增加实习内容，在传统的教育教学实习的基础上增加教育教学见习、教育调查、教育行政实习等内容。

3. 与实习学校建立合作伙伴关系，实习学校给师范院校的师范生提供实习场所和技术指导，师范院校给实习学校提供专业引领，通过师范院校与实习学校的共赢来建立起良好的合作伙伴关系，师范院校的稳定的实习基地才能建立起来。

4. 与中小学联系，建立更多的教育实习基地，对传统的专业系的各自为政的教育教学实习进行改革。成立教师教育学院后，各专业的教育教学实习实行由教师教育学院统一安排，统一调度，把传统的同一专业的学生的同时拥进一所实习学校进行实习的状况改为各专业分组交叉的方式进行教育教学实习。这样，到一所实习学校进行实习的学生人数与一班学生同时到一所实习学校实习的人数相当，但由于专业分散，实习生上讲台进行教学实习的机会则更多。这种实习模式，更有利于师范生的教育教学技能的形成。

5. 与实习学校建立合作伙伴关系后，在实习学校选聘合作教师，以解决师范院校实习指导教师不足的问题。对实习学校的实习合作教师的选聘要有严格的标准，伊利诺大学的合作教师的选聘值得我们借鉴：(1)有资格教相应的课程；(2)直接教与学生实习领域相关的课程或指导实习领域相关的学习活动；(3)有三年以上的教学经验；(4)愿意与大学方的相关人员合作；(5)愿意帮助实习生完成实习项目。[2]

以上这五点的贯彻落实，必须要有相应的统一机构来组织实施，否则，再良好的愿望也只是空中楼阁、海市蜃楼！

教师专业化是时代的呼唤，要实现教师专业化，教师职前、入职、在职教育必须一体化。师专升格为综合本科学院之后，顺应了教师教育从封闭走向开放的发展潮流，但师专升格为综合本科学院以后，要把为当地培养、培训教师的重任承担起来，必须把现有的教师教育资源整合起来，用科学发展观的思想来指导自身的教育工作，这是师专升格为综合本科学院以后办好教师教育的根本出路。

参考文献

[1] 陶立志.师范教育的特色是师范[J].甘肃教育,1998(6).
[2] 宫振但胜.综合性大学中师范教育资源的配置与整合[J].教育研究,2006(2).
[3] 新华社.国务院会议审议并原则通过《关于义务教育学校实施绩效工资的指导意见》.2008-12-21. http://politics.people.com.cn/GB/1024/8553342.html.
[4] 顾明远.谈谈我国教师教育的改革走向[J].求是杂志,2008(7).
[5] 李春超,曹华.论教师教育一体化中的职前课程改革[J].长春师范学院学报,2006(3).
[6] 刘秀平,张传学.综合性大学教师教育的综合优势及发展策略探讨[J].湖北函授大学学报,2007(6).
[7] 刘景颖.教师专业化与教师教育改革[J].闽江学院学报,2002(10).

关于整合新建本科院校教师教育资源的思考

何雪玲*
（钦州学院，广西 钦州 535000）

摘 要：新建本科院校教师教育资源的管理存在不足。探讨新建本科院校教师教育资源的整合途径：即提高教师队伍素质、优化学科课程设置、加强教育实习管理等。从而使有限的资源发挥其最大的效率，全方位提升教师教育水平，为地方教育事业发展发挥应有作用。

关键词：新建本科院校；教师教育资源；资源整合；管理

基金项目：广西教育科学“十一五”规划 2008 年度立项课题（2008A29）“师专升格为综合本科学院后的师范教育资源整合研究”。

Thoughts on Integration of Teacher Educational Resources in New Undergraduate Colleges

He Xue-ling
(Qinzhou University, Qinzhou 535000, China)

Abstract: In new undergraduate colleges and universities, there are some insufficiencies in the management of teacher educational resources. The article discusses the ways to integrate the management of teacher educational resources in new undergraduate colleges and universities: to improve the teachers' inner quality, to optimize curriculum provision, to strengthen the educational practice base construction, and so on. Thus it enables the limited resources to display its maximum efficiency, promote the teachers' educational level in many ways, and play a role for the development of the local education.

key words: new undergraduate universities; teacher educational resources;

* 何雪玲，钦州学院教育科学部副教授，研究方向为学校管理、教师教育。

resources integration; management

为顺应教师教育的发展趋势，广西的河池、百色、贺州、钦州等多所师范高等专科学校通过重组、合并而升格为普通本科院校。这些学校自从升格成功后，各校重新对学校的发展进行定位，由原来以教师教育为主的办学思路改变为综合发展为主，学校把更多的办学资源投向了非师范专业的办学，这使得本应随着学校升格而得到更好发展的师范专业逐步丧失发展的优势。本文拟就笔者所在的学校为研究对象，对新建本科院校的教育资源整合问题进行相关探讨，以期为新建的本科院校的教师教育资源管理提供依据。

一、新建本科院校教师教育资源管理的现状

教师教育资源，主要是指教师职前培养过程中各种资源要素的整体组合。在本研究中，这些基本要素是指教师队伍资源、学科课程资源、教育实习资源等。

（一）新建本科院校教师教育师资队伍资源管理的现状

1. 教师队伍数量相对不足

从统计资料看，目前我校的学生规模 7568 人（含全日制本、专科），663 名在岗教职员工中，有专任教师 416 人，占 62.7%，生师比为 18：1，基本达到《本科办学人才培养工作水平评估》中 16～18：1 的要求，但这是整个学校的平均数，具体到各专业系，生师比就有很大差异。以我校专门培养小学教师的初教系为例：目前，初教系共有学生 354 人，而本系任课教师 17 人，生师比达到 20.8：1。由于专职教师人数少，专业教师的工作负荷非常重，只有用外聘教师来完成教学任务。可见，教师队伍数量相对不足已经成为制约学校教育发展的突出问题。

2. 教师队伍学历偏低，结构不尽合理

首先，师资队伍中硕士学位以上教师（不包括外聘教师）仅有 112 人，占教师总数的 26.9%，但博士仅有 8 人，约占教师总数的 2%。除此以外的教师学历为本科及以下，这与本科院校教师的任职条件尚存距离。其次，职称结构有待改善，具有正高级职称的教师为 9 人，占教师比例约为 2%，副高级职称的教师为 65 人，仅占教师比例为 15.6%，在一定程度上反映了教师队伍的学术水平，教学科研工作的能力层次有待提升。

3. 教师教学与科研水平较低

由于新建本科院校前身是专科学校，教师的主要任务是从事教学工作，许多教师很少进行科学研究，即使有小部分教师从事科研工作，但其科研级别不高。目前，学校在研项目中，国家级课题 1 项、省级的课题共 71 项（含 2006～2008 年度）；发表的论文数量比较多，但所发表的刊物级别较低。其中，从 2006 学校升格以来，共在中文核心刊物发表论文 140 篇，在 SCI、EI、SSCI 等三大文献检索系统发表论文仅 8 篇。可见，与本科教育对教师的要求相比，教师的专业素养、科研能力等水平整体较低。

4. 教师教育理论素质欠缺

据调查，当前我校的教师来源主要有：大部分是原来师专任教的老师，这部分教师因为多年以来从事的是教师教育与培养的工作，因此教师教育理论与实践水平相对较高；另外，随着学校办学规模的扩大，从综合性大学毕业后直接进入新建本科院校的教师越来越多；还有一些

是原中等(含中学、中专、中师)学校调入的教师,这部分的教师,他们虽然在入职时大部分接受过自治区高师培训中心组织的高校教师资格培训,取得高校教师资格。但是,这短短几周的培训,很难让这些教师真正掌握现代教育的理论与从事教师教育的实践经验,对教师教育的性质、特征、规律和发展趋势普遍存在模糊认识,不能将现代教育理论的精髓融入到教学当中,形成符合教师教育规律的课程与教学体系。教师教育理论的欠缺使得教师在教学过程中不能恰当地针对教师教育的特殊性进行教学,容易忽略教师教育的规律,这就影响了教师教育培养目标的实现。

(二) 新建本科院校教育实习资源管理的现状

1. 教育实习基地建设滞后

随着我国高等师范教育的快速发展,教师教育发生了很大的变化,新建本科院校的教育实习基地建设虽然逐渐受到了重视并进行了一些改革,取得了一些进展。但从我校的现状来看,目前尚缺乏数量充足的较稳定或固定的教育实习基地。

2. 教育实习的组织管理机构与组织管理工作不够健全

据了解,当前我校的教育实习管理体制不健全。根本没有组成由地方教育行政部门、地方院校、实践学校参加的“三位一体”的教育实习领导联合体,来共同负责教育实习的计划、组织、督导、考核与评估。学校制定的实习管理制度尚不健全,对教育实习的组织、要求、内容、过程等的规定也不详细具体,缺乏全面管理和检查、监控教育实习过程的机制。

3. 教育实习经费短缺

教育实习经费仍沿袭多年前的标准,没有根据社会发展情况进行相应的调整,且多年来增长幅度甚微,不能满足实习需求。据了解,目前我校教育实习经费一般专科生、本科生为80元左右,但开支项目含实习费、补贴费、管理费等等,不含交通费、指导教师补贴费用等。这不仅对实习时间、实习学校的选择有明显制约,而且也限制了不少学校的实习方式。

(三) 新建本科院校教师教育课程资源现状

1. 当前教师教育课程设置理念落后,课程内容陈旧

一直以来,课程重视传统经典理论的知识讲授,而对于现代的新信息新理论的介绍却不够重视。学校教师教育的基础学科课程至今仍然是老三门体系:普通教育学、普通心理学、学科教育论(教学法)。这些学科教育理论很经典,确实值得我们继承,但学科缺少活力和前沿的信息,与现在社会的需要尚有一定距离,实用性比较差,这样就会导致教师在职前学习中教育理论掌握不足,教育观念还有待更新。

2. 学科专业课程与教育类课程比例失衡

在我国教师教育的传统课程里,通识课程、学科专业课程和教育科学课程,在结构比例上一直是重学科专业课程,轻教育科学课程。如我校的音乐教育2008级本科专业只开设心理学与教育学,其课时为140课时,仅占总课时3329节的4.2%,其学分总共为8学分,占总170个学分的4.2%;而教育实习也只有4个学分,仅占总学分的4.7%。据统计,教育理论课占总学时的比例,“前苏联为25%,英国为25%,法国为20%,德国为30%,美国为20%”[1]。

二、整合新建本科院校教师教育资源的思考

学校升格后，办学规模扩大了，但能否产生预期的效果，关键在于管理，而管理的关键在于教育资源的重组整合。教育资源整合的优劣，直接关系到办学效益和质量。下面，拟从教师队伍建设、学科建设、教育实习基地建设等方面入手，探讨我校教师教育资源整合管理的途径。

（一）新建本科院校教师教育教师资源的整合

教育组织的效益在很大程度上取决于其人力资源的质量情况[2]，特别是教师的质量状况，是新建本科院校资源中最重要的资源。

1. 加强对现有教师的培养，全面提升教师的素质

教师作为高校教育教学和科研实践的主体，是影响新建本科院校发展的关键所在。新建本科院校应采取学历教育与非学历教育相结合，加强教师的培养。一是对原来长期从事专科教学的教师，要分层分类制定培养提高计划。可以派送他们到国内重点高校和科研院所进行学习、培训和进修。以此更新其教育教学思想，形成与时俱进的现代教育观、教师观和学生观；掌握现代教育技术，更新教学方法和手段，提高本科教学水平；同时，鼓励教师发挥团队精神，积极开展科学研究，强化科研意识，以科研促教学，并且形成学科优势，以提高科研的档次和水平。二是对教学经历不长或刚走上工作岗位的青年教师，可以采取校内培养的方式。如以老带新，帮助他们真正掌握现代教育的理论与从事教师教育的实践经验，对教师教育的性质、特征、规律和发展趋势有清醒的认识，能将现代教育理论的精髓融入到教学当中；同时加强青年教师的人文素养、心理品质等方面的培训，让他们尽快成长为合格的教师。

2. 教师的合理引进

教师人才的引进是新建本科院校教师队伍建设中最快捷的方式，通过人才的引进，可以在较短的时间内弥补学校教学、科研中的薄弱环节，改善教师的知识结构、学历结构以及带动校内人才的培养和成长，使教师队伍结构更趋向于合理化和科学化，促使教师的数量和质量适应新建本科院校发展的需求。

（二）新建本科院校教育实习资源管理的思考

1. 完善管理制度，科学合理地制定实习规划

学校应该建立和健全教育实习的管理规定，使之科学化、制度化、规范化，确保教育实习的顺利开展。各专业要根据专业发展规划和专业特点及本专业的优势，制定本专业教育实习规划，明确实习的目标、内容、进程，组织力量，有计划地开展工作。

2. 健全管理机构，促进教育实习的有效实施

组成由地方教育行政部门、地方院校、实习学校参加的“三位一体”的教育实习领导联合体，来共同负责教育实习的计划、组织、督导、考核与评估。高师院校和基地学校还应分别设有相应的部门和专兼职负责人，特别是要争取教育行政部门的支持，签订三方协议，分别制定教育实习年度计划和具体工作计划，进一步明确三方的责任，争取长期合作，建立起稳定性好的基地，保证教育实习工作的顺利实施。

3. 不断加大投入，保证教育实习工作的运转

设立教育实习专项资金，加大对教育实习基地建设的投入。该专项资金主要用于共建项目的资助（包括共建实践实验室等实践保障设施、与中小学实践单位共设教育科学研究项目）；研究成果的奖励；年度实习基地建设工作表彰；共建研讨、检查、总结等会议支出。

（三）新建本科院校专业课程资源整合构想

事实证明，学科建设是本科院校建设的基础与龙头[3]，是高校办学水平高低的重要标志。“高师课程体系改革应大力加强教育类课程，积极拓宽基础课程，努力精简学科专业课程。”[4]

1. 强化教育专业课程

教育专业课程是指为各专业学生开设的有关教育教学理论方法、技巧等培养教师专业内涵的课程，这类课程体现了教师的专业特点，是教师教育区别于其他教育的重要标志，是提高教师教育专业化水平和教师职业专门化程度的重要保证。我国教师教育专业课程设置过于薄弱，这一现状值得我们反思和改进。设置大比重的教育专业课程是使师范生走向专业化的重要途径。因此，基于师范生的特点，参照世界先进国家的成功经验，应该学习的教育专业课程包括教育学、心理学、教育心理学、中外教育史、师德教育、教育社会学、教育经济学、教育人类学、教育行政管理学、学习与发展心理学等。

当然，强调增加教育专业课程的课时量不能忽视教育专业课程、公共课及学科专业课程的平衡关系。教育专业课程的教学可以采取必修和选修两种形式：必修课程要精选基础性的核心课程，保证足够的课时；选修课要体现广度和深度，授课形式可多样化。即便如此，课时的有限性和内容的丰富性之间依然存在矛盾，解决这个矛盾一方面要靠内部调节，另一方面有学者也提出了新的学制模式，即“4＋1”模式，将本科修业年限延长至五年。将一年的时间用于教育理论课、教育技能课和教育实践课的学习，以增强教育专业性，缓解矛盾。

2. 拓宽基础类课程

基础课旨在拓宽学生的知识面，优化学生的知识结构，提高学生的综合素质，为将来教育教学工作打下坚实的基础。目前我国教师教育中，基础课程不仅种类少，而且结构不合理。就种类而言，除政治类课程、教育类课程、外语、体育和计算机外，别的课程几乎没有；就结构而言，政治类课程又占时较多。有鉴于此，新建本科院校的公共基础课程应该调整、拓宽。首先，要适应当代通识教育、素质教育的潮流，开设哲学、历史、艺术、文化、伦理道德等通识课程，开启学生智慧，提高文明修养，激发青春意气，造福人类社会。其次，要按照宽基础的要求，开设交叉性学科课程，促进文理渗透。再次，要根据加强能力的原则，大力加强工具性课程的开设。在普遍开设外语、计算机、普通逻辑等课程的基础上，文科要开设古代汉语、中外文化史、高等数学等课程，理科要开设大学语文、美学等课程，以增强学生的思维能力和表达能力。

3. 优化专业类课程

学科专业课程是教师教育课程的核心和基础，教师必须掌握一定的学科专业知识。因此，要整合学科专业课程，把学科专业课程压缩在 35％～40％。同时，调整学科专业课程内部的比例，必须按照少而精、博而通的原则对学科专业课程进行整合：一是整合必修课程，对内容相近的课程进行有机整合，开设综合课程；二是确立核心课程，每个专业都要确立 2～3 门核心课程，核心课程必须达到同类专业的学术水平，从而确保学科专业课程的整体水平；三是减少必修课程门类，更新课程内容，压缩授课时数；四是增加选修课程的比重。

参考文献

[1] 文胜利.高师院校的课程体系要作根本性变革[J].高等师范教育研究;1998(1).

[2] [美]欧文斯.组织行为学[M].孙绵涛,等,译.武汉:华中师范大学出版社,1987.

[3] 刘献君.关于师资建设和管理的几个问题[J].高等教育研究,2003(4).

[4] 文胜利.高师院校的课程体系要作根本性变革[J].高等师范教育研究,1998(1).

试论地方学院教师教育资源的整合

冼秀丽*
（钦州学院，广西 钦州 535000）

摘　要：在地方升本高校中，有一批以师范教育为主的高校随着高等教育大众化发展进入综合化过程中。如何在这一过程中改革传统的师范教育模式，适应现代教师教育体制改革要求，不断提高教师教育水平，是地方升本高校综合化面临的紧迫任务。本文分析了此类高校在这一过程教师教育资源利用存在的问题及进行教师教育资源整合的必要性，提出了教师教育资源整合的模式，为解决综合化趋势中的教师教育问题提供了可资借鉴的启示。

关键词：地方学院；教师教育；整合；模式

On the Integration of Teacher Education at Local Colleges

Xian Xiu-li
(Qinzhou University, Qinzhou 535000, China)

Abstract: Among the local newly-promoted universities, some teacher education-oriented ones will go into the integration process with the development of the popularization of higher education. It's an urgent task for these universities to reform the traditional teacher education modes to adapt to the modern teacher education system, and continually improve the teachers' education level. The paper analyzes the problems of using the teacher education resource in this process, and the needs and modes of the integration of teachers educational resources. It also provides the ways to solve these problems .

Key words: local colleges; teacher education; integration; mode

---

* 冼秀丽，钦州学院副教授，主要从事教育基本理论、教师教育研究。

近几年来,随着我国高等教育迅速发展,一批新升格本科综合性学院(以下简称地方学院)在精英教育向大众教育过渡的背景下应运而生。这一批新建地方学院不少是处在过去的师范教育为主过渡到综合性院校的办学发展过程之中。这些地方学院为满足经济社会对人才的多元需求,同时也是为了自身的生存和发展,都纷纷提出了"师范向综合转变、专科向本科转变"的办学思路,于是重点拓展了许多新的专业(其中主要是非师范专业),学院的办学变成了师范专业与非师范专业并存的名副其实的综合性本科院校。但是,在这些地方学院的办学过程中用综合性办学去遮蔽师范教育的倾向十分明显,教师教育处在师范性和综合性的夹缝之中,既否定了过去的传统,又没有新的路径,应该说是处境尴尬,前途迷失。教育部师范教育司管培俊司长曾指出,"在师范院校基础上合并改制的地方综合性本科院校,要明确学校定位和办学方向,发挥优势,更好地承担为当地培养培训中小学教师的责任和义务。"[1]为此,探讨在办学转变中既具师范特性,又具综合性的教师教育模式,对走出目前综合趋势化中的教师教育的尴尬,并为综合趋势化中的教师教育寻求新的发展出路具有十分重要的意义。笔者认为,教师教育资源的整合正是解决这一难题的有效途径。

一、教师教育资源整合的内涵

"整合"一词出自英文"Integration",最早是由英国哲学家赫伯特·斯宾赛(Herbert Spencer)1862年在《第一原理》中提出来的。他认为:从哲学的意义上说,整合是由系统的整体性及系统核心的统摄、凝聚作用而导致的使若干相关部分或因素合成一个新的统一整体的建构、序化过程。1969年劳仁斯(Lawrence)和罗斯(Lorah J. W.)在《组织与环境》中,从组织行为角度对整合加以阐述,认为整合是一个组织内部不同部门之间用来协调其活动所采取的行为和所使用的结构。整合不是简单的结合,更不是"拼合",整合是对现有资源进行合理地调整、有机地结合,追求资源整体结构的最佳化和整体效益的最大化。

教师教育资源整合是教育科学研究中的一个崭新领域,是指通过调整、协调、重组现有教师教育资源实现配置优化,提高整体效益的一个系统工程,从而把系统内部彼此相关但却彼此分离的职能以及系统外部既参与共同的使命又拥有独立经济效益的主体整合成一个系统,使之形成相互联系、相互渗透,实现规模、结构、质量、效益的协调发展,提高教育的运行质量和整体水平,在资源共享、学科交叉融合的平台上增强学校的综合实力和竞争优势。这一发展平台的建立,需要对学校教育资源如办学思想、学校文化、课程专业、组织机构、人力资源、硬件设施等进行全方位的整合与重构,以期形成可持续发展的教育资源,产生 $1+1\gg2$ 的整体效益。[2]

二、地方学院教师教育资源整合的现状分析

地方学院近期因忙于从专科向本科、从单科向综合型的双重转型与实质性合并,可能疏于考虑或无暇顾及,师专升格为综合性学院后,随着非师范专业的增加,师范专业逐渐从原来办学的中心走向学校办学的边缘,教师教育的优质资源流失严重,有被削弱、淡化甚至边缘化的倾向。由于有限的力量没有得到整合,各种教师教育资源得不到充分利用,教师教育质量下降已初见端倪,教师教育的各种问题日显突出。

(一) 学校缺乏对教师教育的投入与关注

由于升格为综合性学院后，学院战略发展的主攻方向是“综合化”，呈现较为明显的“去师范化”现象。[3]学校发展重心放在非师范专业上，将大部分资源和精力投放在其相关专业的发展。究其原因，一是当前市场上技术型、应用型人才奇缺，在其相关专业进行投资，不仅见效快、效果好、效益高、影响大，还能给学校办学带来一定经济上的实惠。由于学校加强对非师范院系、专业的建设，大力发展非师范专业，严格控制师范类学生的招生数量，使师范生人数在各系里迅速减少，师范生成长的文化氛围被削弱，这就势必导致削弱对原师范类专业的投入与关注。师范类专业陷入了“吃老本”的境地，只能凭借以前师范院校保留下来的师范性来支撑教师教育，长期以来形成的师范教育办学优势未能有效发挥，这无疑影响了学院师范类专业的长远发展。

(二) 教师教育的专业性得不到充分发挥

由于综合大学建设要求，地方学院往往把学术发展水平视为学院“强”“大”的体征，而过分追求，极易诱发“重研究，轻教学”的倾向和对原有师范特色的掩埋，再现了学术性与师范性的纷争与失衡，不利于教师专业化发展。同时，由于片面追求“综合化”和办学重点的迁移，也进一步削弱了对教育理论的研究和对现实教育问题的关注，忽视了对教育学科人才队伍的培养和对教育学科的投入。在学科专业建设上，往往只注重学科专业的本身建设，在教师教育中不顾及学科间的交叉与融合，使教师教育学科和专业结构的单一性仍未能改变，难于培养出合格的复合型师资，出现了师范毕业生教师专业化程度不高的现象，师范生素质不尽如人意，教师教育的专业性得不到充分发挥。[4]

(三) 师范教育的管理水平有待提高

为实现学校战略发展，目前教学管理和学生管理未能很好体现教师教育的特殊规律。从学校与外部的关系看，不能与教育部有效衔接；从学校内部关系看，也表现出诸多不协调现象。随着非师范专业的增加，各专业系必须把力量集中在自己并不擅长的非师范专业的管理上，而对师范专业则无暇顾及，教师教育的管理被削弱。同时，各系为了确保所属师范专业的质量，必须做好相应的教育、教学、实习等方面的工作，本来是同一性质的工作变成了各系的重复劳动和重复的投入，造成了有限的人力、物力资源的极大浪费。教师教育的师资力量散落在各系里，没有形成团队，造成师资的效能未能充分发挥，也不利于教师的专业成长。由于有限的力量没有得到整合，各种教师教育资源得不到充分利用，教师教育质量下降已初见端倪。

总而言之，地方学院从师专升格为综合性本科院校的综合化过程中，师范专业散落在各系里，导致各种教育资源的分散，造成了极大的浪费，教师教育从传统的“集约化”教育变成了“小农”教育模式，教育质量的下降也就在所难免。

教学质量是一个专业乃至一所学校的生命线，教师教育要生存，必须要确保自身的教育质量，要提高教育质量，就必须改革现行的运行模式。从形式上说，就是对现有的教师教育资源进行整合。通过教师教育资源整合，师范生由相应的部门进行管理，一方面有利于这些新升格的院校发挥传统的专业优势，另一方面也利于各专业系集中力量去发展非师范专业。同时也有利于减少重复劳动，共享各种师范教育资源，客观上促进了学校的开源节流。

三、地方学院教师教育资源整合的模式选择

（一）目前国内教师教育的几种模式[5]

1. 学科教育与教师教育混合的模式

这是沿用了40多年的培养模式，目前仍为多数高师学校所采用，但作了调整改进。该模式基本保持传统的师范院校的教师培养模式，学科教育与教师教育不相分离，学科系同时设有师范类专业和非师范类专业，各专业科系在承担专业学科教育任务的同时，还须独立承担部分教师教育的任务。我校目前正采用这种模式。

这种模式的优点是，真正承担起了基础教育一线教师的在职培训职能，对基础教育的需求逐渐清晰起来，使学校教师教育体系更加完整。学校内部机构勿需调整，教师教育专业课程教学、组织教师教育科学研究和职后培训任务也由这一机构完成。但这一模式的不足是，不能有效整合校内资源，学生、学科教学论教师和教育实习的组织实施仍分散在各专业学院，无法实现学科专业教育与教师专业教育的分离，学科教学论教师无法有效组织教研活动，被专业学院边缘化，教师教育被普遍弱化。

2. 虚拟联盟形态的模式

在该模式中，学校将职前培养有关的行政职能，从学校教务处分离出来，加上职后培训任务，成立专门的教师教育管理机构，如教师教育处或教师教育部，整合校内教师教育资源，进行专业化培养，加强对教师教育的管理和协调。统一协调和管理学校的教师教育活动，而学校教师教育资源并没有进行实质性整合，教师教育资源仍然保持原有的相对分离状态，包括学校师范类学生的培养活动、教师继续教育活动等，具体的教师教育教学活动由学校中的多个教学组织机构来实施。

该模式的主要优点在于学校有专门的教师教育机构，可以有效协调全校的教师教育资源，将教师教育活动从学校其他教学活动中分离出来，自成系统，使教师继续教育和职前教师教育纳入统一的管理轨道。该模式面临的主要问题是，如何清晰地划定教师教育管理机构的权利和职责范围，如何协调教师教育管理机构与教务处、继续教育管理部门以及教师教育教学实体之间的关系。同时，这种模式在教学上与传统师范教育体系没有大的区别，也不能将教师专业化教育与学科专业教育相分离，无法建立满足教师发展的平台。

3. "大教育学院"模式

这种模式是将分散在学科专业教学院系的学科教学论课教师集中起来，共同研究如何将完成了学科专业学习的学生培养成为符合当今基础教育需要的教师的问题。在该模式下，学校整合全校教师教育资源，归并相关机构、人员以及权利和责任，成立实体性的大教育学院。大教育学院负责学校全部教师教育教学活动，包括职前教师教育和教师继续教育。

该模式的优势首先是将学校分散的教师教育资源和教师教育职能进行有效整合，提升学校整体的教师教育能力。学科教学教师与教育理论学科教师归并于统一组织，可以形成优势互补，彼此间可以生成更加有效的互相学习、彼此合作和共同进步的效应。其次，大教育学院对全校教师教育职能的整合，有利于提升学校教师教育工作的效率和效益。但实行该种模式至少面临三个问题：一是会深刻地触及到各院系部门之间的利益，协调各方面的关系阻力不

小;二是教师的职后培训质量难以保证。由于不是对等整合,教师的职后培训工作就很难保证不被削弱;三是隐含着教师教育队伍流失的危险,部分教师教育的教师会转向学科专业教育;四是失去了学科专业根基的支撑,也没有建立起以教育学理论为背景的学科体系,因而难以提升教师教育学院的办学层次。

(二)目前地方学院教师教育资源整合模式的选择

从目前地方学院教师教育的现状看,虽然学校类型发生了改变——由单一的师范院校转变为多科性或综合性地方院校,但教师教育模式并没有改变——仍然是传统的、封闭的、定向型教师教育模式,一般采取“公共基础课+学科专业课+教育学科课”的模式。这种教师教育模式,由于历史的原因,在一定时期内发挥了重要的作用,完成了中小学教师培养培训任务。同时也造成了办学模式封闭和教师来源单一、培养任务专一和培养口径过窄、职后教育水平偏低、教育经费重复投入、教育资源难于优化等弊端,直接影响了教师教育质量和办学效益的提高。很明显已不适应现代社会对新一代教师的要求,必须进行改革。

现在的地方学院,从专业结构上看,既有师范专业,也有非师范专业;从层次结构上看,既有本科,也有专科。这种多样化的结构,需要多层次、多元化的人才培养模式与之相适应。既要为专科学生的进一步发展开辟新的渠道,也要为本科生的发展积极创造条件。因此,地方学院应创新教师教育专业人才培养模式 ,要求师资培养在保证数量前提下提高质量,现行“混编模式”将逐步转换到“大学+师范”的国际通行轨道上来。为此,笔者建议,地方学院在改变原有运行体系的条件下,应采取分步推进的策略,组建新的教师教育学院,兼有一定的行政管理职能。这种模式在定位上是二级学院,进行教师教育资源整合,对全校的教师教育进行统筹。成立教师教育学院有两种教师教育资源的整合模式:一是独立模式,即以后其它专业系不再招收师范生,师范生由教师教育学院统一招生,统一管理,这种模式实质是把原来的师专缩为一个教师教育学院,这是一种最为理想的整合模式;另一种是“X+1”或“2+2”模式,这种模式是师范生保留现有的招生模式,前X年(专科2年、本科2年或3年)进行本体专业的教育,最后1或2年转入教师教育学院接受专门的教师教育培训。在专科毕业生就业困难的情况下,许多专科学生学习的积极性不高,“3+2”模式对这些学生的学习动因起到激励作用。与此同时,学校还可以与其他有硕士点的院校联合试办“4+2”模式,或为其他院校输送攻读“4+2”教育专业硕士的学生。[6]基于以上对各种模式的分析,以及地方学院教师教育改革的目标定位,我们认为,在近期,地方学院可以先实行“3+1”模式改革的尝试,以积累经验;条件许可时,可同时试行“4+1”模式;待时机成熟时,应选择“4+2”模式。

(三)组建新的教师教育学院,整合教师教育资源的优势

教师教育资源整合后促进了以前分散的教育资源重新优化组合,拓宽了校内教育资源开发和利用的空间,带来了明显的效益。

1. 通过对教师教育资源的整合,可以实现对资源的合理配置,减少重复建设,避免资源闲置与浪费,使资源发挥更大效用,有利于这些地方学院教育质量的提高。

2. 学校整合全校教师教育资源,归并相关机构、人员以及权利和责任,将学校分散的教师教育资源和教师教育职能进行有效整合,提升学校整体的教师教育能力。学科教学教师与教育理论学科教师归并于统一组织,可以形成优势互补,彼此间可以生成更加有效的互相学习、

彼此合作和共同进步的效应；其次，全校教师教育职能的整合，有利于减少重复劳动，共享各种师范教育资源，有利于提升学校教师教育工作的效率和效益。

3. 有利于提高教师教育的管理水平。通过教师教育资源整合，师范生由相应的部门进行管理，一方面有利于这些新升格的院校发挥传统的专业优势；另一方面也利于各专业系集中力量去发展非师范专业。学校有专门的教师教育机构，可以有效协调全校的教师教育资源，将教师教育活动从学校其它教学活动中分离出来，自成系统，使教师继续教育和职前教师教育纳入统一的管理轨道。

教师教育资源整合模式的研究为地方学院教师教育资源整合的具体实施提供切实可行的方式和途径。各地可以根据自身的实际情况，认真调查、分析、论证，从而选出适合本地区发展的教师教育资源整合模式，使教育的发展适应社会的需求，实现教育规模和效益的共同增长。

参考文献

[1] 管培俊. 积极进取 锐意创新 推动教师教育和教师队伍建设迈上新台阶[J]. 中国教师，2005(5).

[2] 徐建中，等. 我国教育资源整合模式研究[J]. 黑龙江教育，2006(7).

[3] 王全林. 综合性学院发展师范教育的潜在优势与挑战[J]. 高等师范教育研究，2002(5).

[4] 麦茂生. 地方综合性学院发展教师教育的思考[J]. 广西梧州师范高等专科学校学报，2006(3).

[5] 武海顺. 高师院校教师教育改革的模式选择[N]. 光明日报，2007-01-02.

[6] 吴文燕. 地方院校教师教育改革与发展的几个问题[J]. 咸宁学院学报，2007(5).

拓宽阵地 整合课程

——关于“大学语文”课程内容设置的一个设想

陆 衡*

(钦州学院,广西 钦州 535000)

摘 要:教学内容设置混乱是多年来阻碍、制约大学语文发展的一个瓶颈。将口语训练与应用写作纳入大学语文课程体系是语文课程自身的要求,是社会发展的需要与受教者(学生)的期望,是对原有课程和教材的一种合理整合,能切实提高教学效率。作为一门独立学科,大学语文与经典赏析、应用写作、口语训练应构成一种属种关系。

关键词:大学语文;课程整合;经典赏析;口语训练;应用写作

基金项目:新世纪广西高等教育教学改革“十一五”第四批立项项目,项目编号为[2008(02)]。

Integrated Courses to Promote their Development

—On the assumption of the course setting of College Chinese

Lu Heng

(Qinzhou University, Qinzhou 535000, China)

Abstract: The confusion of teaching contents setting is one of the choke points to put off and restrict the development of College Chinese in the past years. Integrating oral training and practical writing with College Chinese courses system is the course' own requirements, the needs of social development and the expectations of students. A logical integration of existing courses and textbooks and it can effectively improve the teaching efficiency. As an independent course, College Chinese and classics appreciation, practical writing and oral training should

* 陆衡,钦州学院中文系教授,文学博士。

have proper inclusion relations.

Key words: College Chinese; course integration; classics appreciation; oral training; practical writing

以2006年9月《国家“十一五”时期文化发展规划纲要》的印发为界,学界关于《大学语文》课程的讨论可分为前后两个阶段。前阶段主要是争生存,谋求的是课程存在的合法性;后阶段主要为求发展,争取的是课程的合理发展。教学内容设置的优化是课程得以合理发展的前提与基础,而混乱恰是多年来阻碍、制约大学语文发展的一个瓶颈。且不谈各式教材中选文的五花八门,单是那些与应用写作、口语表达频频交叉、重叠的内容都已令广大师生不知所措了。为解决这一问题,笔者以为,大学语文应在经典赏析的基础上,将应用写作与口语训练纳入自身的课程体系。作为一门独立学科,大学语文与经典赏析、应用写作、口语训练应构成一种属种关系。

一、将口语训练与应用写作纳入大学语文课程体系是语文课程自身的要求

从概念的界定与历史沿革来看,听、说、读、写是中小学语文课程内容中紧密联系、不可或缺的四大内容。作为一门课程名称,“语文”出现于1949年。之前中学称“国文”,小学称“国语”。为什么要改为“语文”?叶圣陶先生认为:“平时说的话叫口头语言,写在纸面上叫书面语言。语就是口头语言,文就是书面语言。把口头语言和书面语言连在一起说,就叫做语文”[1]。1950年初中《实践语文》出版,编辑者的意图是:“说出来的是语言,写出来的是文章,文章依据语言。‘语’和‘文’是分不开的。语文教学应该包括听话、说话、阅读、写作四项。因此,这套课本不再用‘国文’或‘国语’的旧名称,改称‘语文课本’”[2]。2000年,与小学、初中一脉相承的高中语文,其培养目标被制定为“在初中的基础上,进一步提高学生正确理解和运用祖国语言文字的水平,使他们具有适应实际需要的现代文阅读能力、写作能力和口头交际能力,具有初步的文学鉴赏能力和阅读浅易文言文的能力;掌握语文学习的基本方法,养成自学语文的习惯,培养发现、探究解决问题的能力,为继续学习和终身发展打好基础”[3]。这些界说和阐释,规定了中小学语文课程既包括口头语言,又包括书面语言;既涉及文学语体,又涉及实用文体的属性。在文学性得以重拾与强调的今天,听说读写能力的培养仍然是中小学语文课程内容的重中之重。

从知识衔接与教学大纲来看,提高听说读写能力与培养人文素养是大学语文的两大教学目标。大学语文是中小学语文教育的必然延伸。与后者相比,前者所设置的课程内容理应更全面、更深入。当前,教育部高教司在其颁发的《大学语文教学大纲》(征求意见稿)中指出:“在全日制高校设置语文课程,其根本目的在于:充分发挥语文学科的人文性和基础性特点,适应当代人文科学与自然科学日益交叉的发展趋势,为我国的社会主义现代化建设培养具有全面素质的高质量人才”[4]。由此可见,尽管不同专业有着不尽相同的要求,但人文性与基础性的统一却是这门课程的基本特点。遗憾的是,在具体的实践当中,大学语文一直没有找准自己的定位。从1978年重新开设到20世纪90年代之前,我们只注重语文能力的提高;20世纪90年代中期之后,开始强调这是一门可以“培育大学生人文精神,营造大学里文化氛围的基础课

程”[5]。新世纪以来又主张以人文性替代工具性，要把大学语文改成“大学国文”或“大学人文”。2007年，陈洪提出了他的“大语文”观：大学语文要姓“语”，即以“语文”为立足点。这是我们从事这门课程教学及教学改革的基本点。如果改来改去，改得“语文”尽失，改掉了本体，就有违这门课程设置的初衷了。大学语文还要姓“大”，即相比于基础教育阶段的语文课，它是在更高层级意义上的语文素养和能力培养[6]。此观点显示了论者在这一问题上的高瞻远瞩，很快得到了学界的认可与支持。的确，既然人文性与基础性是大学语文的两大属性，那么它的课程设置就应根据教学大纲的要求，既注重人文精神的培育，又兼顾听说读写能力的提高，唯如此，才能为我国现代化建设培养具有全面素质的高质量人才。

二、将口语训练与应用写作纳入《大学语文》课程体系是社会发展的需要与受教者(学生)的期望

中华民族历来重视写作。在古代，人们把写作与建功立业相提并论，与治国安邦紧密相连。《左传·襄公二十四年》中提到“太上有立德，其次有立功，其次有立言，虽久不废，此之谓不朽”[7]。曹丕在他的《典论论文》中也说“盖文章，经国之大业，不朽之盛事”。[8]当前，在工业社会向信息社会过渡的过程中，写作越来越成为人们生活和工作最基本的能力。一个人如果既不善于表达，也不会写文章，那么他在这个世界上就会寸步难行。正因此，约翰·奈斯比特在《大趋势　改变我们生活的十个新方向》一书中指出：当今时代有五件最重要的事情是必须记住的，“我们比以往更需要具备基本的读写能力”[9]即为其中之一。国外许多大学都非常重视写作能力的培养，如哈佛大学文理学院规定大学毕业生，第一条要达到的标准就是“必须能够清晰而明白地写作”；普林斯顿大学要求本科毕业生必须“具有清楚的思维、谈吐、写作的能力”[10]。遗憾的是，这一点在国内并没有形成共识。尽管张志公先生早在20世纪80年代就指出“学会写现代社会常用到的多种文体，是要经过训练的，学生在学校里就应该接受这种训练。从未受到这种训练，到工作中才从头摸索，这在时间上是一种浪费”[11]，但不少论者却认为基本写作能力的培养是中学语文的教学任务，大学语文不应剩饭重炒，应把重点放在人文素养的提高上。实际上，这种想法是脱离实际的。写作虽然是中学语文教育的一个重头戏，但绝大部分的中学生在这六年中并没有得到系统的、专门的训练，尤其在应用写作这一个领域。更何况，大学语文面对的是非中文专业的学生，他们的写作能力普遍较差，有的甚至达不到基本写作的要求。曾经有一位美术系系主任向笔者抱怨，她的许多学生连请假条都不会写。为避免逐一纠错，她只好让秘书把请假条的格式放到系里的网页上供学生参照。更多的理工科学生向笔者坦诚自己不懂得填写开题报告、总结报告或科学论文。更为尴尬的是，还有不少的非中文专业院系领导向笔者提出：如果只能在“经典赏析”和“应用写作”中二择一，他们和学生们希望开设的是应用写作课。

与写作相比，口语训练的命运更令人担忧。虽然早在春秋战国时期，在孔子所设的四科当中，其中之一就是“言语科”，但传统语文教学却没有把它好好地继承下来。“不学诗，无以言”的思想很快就被“敏于行而慎于言，讷于言而敏于行”的教导所取代；再加上在长期的封建社会里，文言和口语分家的事实造成了读书人读与说的不一致；更兼科举以文章取士，白话学得好坏，无关紧要，社会自然而然地就形成了重写轻说的积弊。而在美国，由于人们坚信会演讲的人成功机会多两倍，因此，他们的母语教育要求“学生必须学会在不同领域内进行有效的听说

读写。所有的老师都必须适时适地地传授和加强与学生语言交流的技巧”[12]。演说能力的培养始于幼儿园;到了小学,老师鼓励和引导孩子们在课堂上独立地表达自己的思想;许多中学开设了演讲教育课,学生们以敢于和善于在公开场合讲话为荣。到了大学,学生们演讲能力培养的意识就更强烈了,Public Speaking(公众演说)一直都是最热门的选修课之一。受西方现代教育的影响,早在20世纪50年代末,张志公先生就大声疾呼:“对于语言教育重视不够,这是我们语文教学的主要缺点之一”[13],“要善于思考,善于说话,这是学习写作的根本”[14]。可惜这呼声并没有引起国人的响应。别说在大学,就是在中学也是一个被严重忽视的环节。结果我们培养出来的人才,一张口不是面红耳赤、手足无措;就是长篇大论、啰啰嗦嗦,令人不知所云。实际上,当今社会以说辞作为主要手段的工作越来越多,不仅政府官员、脱口秀或CEO们需要演讲能力,就是应聘求职者、商品推销员、乃至对上报告工作、向下布置任务的小组织者,都需要说话技巧。

面对社会发展的迫切需求、教育成品的能力残缺,我们与其坐视受教者的嗷嗷待哺,不如主动拓宽教学阵地,在课程设置的时候,旗帜鲜明地加上应用写作与口语训练这两门课。

三、将口语训练与应用写作纳入“大学语文”课程体系是对原有课程和教材的一种合理整合,能切实提高教学效率

口语训练与应用写作不是天兵天将,作为各自独立的课程,如演讲与口才、普通话口语训练、应用写作、公文写作等等,它们早已存在于大学课堂。但存在并不等于合理,尽管这两门课以培养受教者的说、写能力为教学目标,与大学语文的部分内容不吻而合,但它们却不能成为大学语文的麾下干将。原因很简单,当前,我国的许多大学,要么不开设大学语文,要么将之紧密相关的听说读写四个部分生硬分开,变为口语训练、大学语文(经典赏析)与公文写作三门课。具体的做法有两种:一是将口语训练、应用写作作为与大学语文(经典赏析)同等并列的两门课程来开设,口语直属于现代汉语教研室,写作则由写作或文艺理论教研室负责;二是让口语训练自立门户,将应用写作纳入大学语文体系。不过,加盟“大学语文”后的公文写作并不能与经典赏析平起平坐,过的是一种典型的寄人篱下的生活。这一点我们可以从教材内容的安排中得到印证。除了毛信德主编的《大学语文教程》包括文学与写作两卷外,更多的教材是以附录的形式向学生介绍公文格式以及写作注意事项,如袁智忠主编的《新编大学语文》、教育部高等教育司选编的《大学语文》、徐中玉和钱谷融主编的《大学语文》(自考本科用书)等等。其结果是,公文写作没有得到应有的重视甚至是有名无实。

针对这种现象,在去年教育部人事司与高等教育司承办的《大学语文》骨干教师高级研修班上,笔者曾建议将它们统一起来,作为联系紧密却又相对独立的三部分共同构建《大学语文》的课程内容。此议一出,毁誉参半。支持者觉得,将三门课同时收归《大学语文》,学生将是最大的受益者,他们既能得到人文素养的培育,又能接受全面、系统的语文能力的训练。反对者认为,课程合三为一、热闹风光的背后是任教者的自套枷锁。教学内容的增多与难度的加深自然会增加教师的负担,大学语文老师不是千手观音,要为大学生读、写、听、说能力的提高提供一条龙服务,实在是勉为其难。尤其是口语与写作训练,似应由专职老师承担。还有同行认为此举在理论上行得通,但实际操作却非常艰难,主要是涉及到的部门与人员太多,各种关系难以协调。再加上普通话水平等级考试已升格为国考,将之纳入大学语文课程体系绝非易事。

笔者坚持,大学语文既然是母语教育,就不应该只强调文字的美,却漠视应用写作的重要性、无视语音的纯正和流畅。口语训练、经典赏析与公文写作三门课,在目标上具有相同或相近的教育功能,在内容上具有内在的逻辑联系,但在具体的教学实践中,我们却让它们各自为战,呈散兵游勇之态。如此设置课程,不仅造成资源上的重复浪费,而且对学生的成长亦极为不利。针对大学语文各门课存在的割裂和对立问题,我们应在原有基础上加以整合、变革,创立综合性的课程文化,实现课程的新发展。至于整合所涉及到的课程结构与内容、课程资源与具体实施等各个方面的问题,虽是牵一发而动全身,但只要我们统一认识,坚定信念,一切从学生的成长出发,就不会有太大的困难。

综上所述,从求生存到谋发展,大学语文到了一个相对平静的修整期。为确保这门课程在下一阶段的合理发展,我们有必要回顾它的发展历史,重新认识语文教育本身的特点和规律。为切实解决大学生语文素养欠佳的问题,满足社会对大学生语文能力基本的需求,有必要对口语训练、经典赏析与公文写作进行整合处理,使之形成一个有价值有效率的整体。

参考文献

[1] 叶圣陶. 叶圣陶语文教育论集[M]. 北京:教育科学出版社,1980:138.

[2] 中央人民政府出版总署编审局. 初级中学语文课本第一册[M]. 北京:人民教育出版社,1950.

[3] 王柏勋,曹洪顺. 中学语文教学大纲 50 年的变迁[J]. 语文教学通讯,2000(18).

[4] 曾加荣. 谈谈大学语文的定位[J]. 四川教育学院学报,2006(9).

[5] 丁丁. 语文教育的根本是人文精神:访《大学语文》主编徐中玉[N]. 中国图书商报,2003-03-28.

[6] 陈洪. 在改革中加强"大学语文"课程教学[J]. 中国大学教学,2007(3).

[7] 左丘明. 左传・襄公二十四年[M]. 太原:山西古籍出版社,2006:268.

[8] 郭绍虞. 中国历代文论选[M]. 上海:上海古籍出版社,2001:61.

[9] 约翰・奈斯比特. 大趋势 改变我们生活的十个新方向[M]. 北京:中国社会科学出版社,1984:18.

[10] 韩水法. 人文学科与通才教育. http://www.edu.cn/20011023/3006262.shtml.

[11] 庄文中. 张志公语文教育论集[M]. 北京:人民教育出版社,1994:354.

[12] 雷实. 国外母语课程标准的基本理念[J]. 语文建设,北京:人民教育出版社,2001(10).

[13] 庄文中. 张志公语文教育论集[M]. 北京:人民教育出版社,1994:306.

[14] 庄文中. 张志公语文教育论集[M]. 北京:人民教育出版社,1994:314.

教师与高校课堂教学质量的提高

潘景丽*
（钦州学院，广西 钦州 535000）

摘 要：高校课堂教学质量影响着人才培养的质量。面对高校课堂教学中出现的不容乐观的现状，作为课堂教学的组织者和实施者的教师有着极大的影响。重视教师存在的问题，解决教师的问题，加强师资的培养是提高高校课堂教学质量的有效方法之一。

关键词：高校课堂；教学质量；教师；方法

Abstract：Teaching quality affects the cultivation of personnel. Facing the unsatisfied situation in the universities，teachers who organize the class have a great impact to the improvement of teaching quality. Paying more attention to the problems related to teachers，solving their problems and strengthening the training of them are the ways to improve teaching quality.

Key words：classes in the universities；teaching quality；teachers；ways

招生、教学和就业是高校办学的三大重要步骤。随着目前招生的规模日益扩大，就业的压力也日益明显。要求高校人才培养供需结合，提高教学质量，培养社会所需的合格和优秀人才的呼声日趋高涨。教育部部长周济也指出："高等教育要按照'巩固、深化、提高、发展'的八字方针，巩固成果，深化改革，提高质量，争取高等教育新的跨越式发展。"[1]高校课堂教学的质量如何，是关系到高等教育培养高素质创造性人才的大事。课堂教学质量是高等教育质量的主体组成部分，也是提高教育质量和保障高校可持续发展的关键。课堂教学质量的提高已经提到不可回避的日程上来了。因此，高校课堂教学质量的提高是势在必行、迫在眉睫。影响课堂质量的因素诸多，其中包括教学的定位、教学的管理、课程的设计、教材的选择、教学手段的使用和教师的课堂教学等。本文主要从教师对课堂质量影响的角度对高校课堂质量的问题进行分析并提出解决的途径。

一、高校课堂教学质量的现状

从一些调查数据得知，高校教学质量的问题不容乐观，学生的满意程度不高。根据清华大

* 潘景丽，钦州学院外语系副教授。研究方向为英语教学论。

学刘西拉教授的调查显示，对整个教学环节“认为‘很满意’和‘满意’的学生总和只有 5%；认为在大学苦读几年后，‘能学到一点点’和‘根本学不到’有用东西的学生总和占 79%”。[2] 据上海大学生发展报告的数据显示：大学生对教师课堂教学水平“很满意”的为 59.94%，学术水平满意为 53.53%[3]。早几年，有一则三所高校的专项调查资料表明，教学好的只占 5%，较好和一般总和的占 21%，而教学较差的比例却高达 74%[4]。

二、高校教师的主要存在问题

（一）上课态度不端正

有的教师的上课态度不端正，得过且过。有的教师课前没有认真备课，上课时忽悠学生，浪费课堂时间。有的教师上课随意性较大，东扯西拉，天南地北侃大山。有的教师甚至上课迟到，提前下课，教学纪律性较差。

（二）师资培养有待增强

随着招生规模的日益扩大，开办的专业增多与师资短缺的矛盾日渐突出。教师教学任务繁重，每天为日常教学工作疲于奔命，没有足够的时间和精力了解专业发展前沿，吸取新的知识营养，导致知识和观点滞后、专业水平不高和科研水平不强的状况。

（三）教学方法有待改进

在目前的大学课堂里，仍然有很多以教师为中心的课堂。课堂教学师生互动少，不能进行良好的教与学的双向课堂活动，学生的主体作用没有得到发挥。学生成为学习过程中的被动者，因此很容易缺乏学习的热情，逐渐丧失了好奇心、上进心和学习的动力。教学规律告诉我们，“教学过程不仅需要教师的活动，而且需要学生的活动。如果学生没有自己组织这些活动，教学最优化是不可思议的。”[5]有的教师上课仍然是传统的照本宣科，满堂灌，课堂教学沉闷，难以在课堂上激发学生学习的主动性和热情。有的教师没有与时俱进，根据社会需求调整讲课内容和方法，没有及时更新和补充新的内容，仍然沿用几年甚至是十几年前的教案。

（四）对学生的能力培养不足

党的十六届六中全会通过的《中共中央关于构建社会主义和谐社会若干重大问题的决定》中指出，要“保持高等院校招生合理增长，注重增强学生的实践能力、创造能力和就业能力、创业能力”。我们高校的人才培养要迎合社会的要求，课堂的教学也应该亦步亦趋。高校的课堂教学不仅要传授知识，更应该培养学生的各方面的能力，否则培养出来的人将很难成为社会需求的人才。

三、提高高校课堂教学质量的途径

学校作为管理方，应该建立机制监督、指导和评价教师的工作，提高教师的工作效能，为课堂教学质量的提高奠定有力的基础。教师作为教学的具体实施者，对于课堂教学质量的提高有着重要的作用。因此,学校应该重视教师的培养,建立一支教学水平和学术水平兼备,知识结构合理的教师队伍。通过解决教师的问题来解决课堂教学质量的一些问题。

(一)加强师德培养,教书育人

"学高为师,德高为范"。要提高教学质量,首先做好教师的思想工作,培养教师热爱教师岗位。高校里出现教师态度不端正,纪律性不强的问题,主要原因是教师对教师岗位的认识不够。教师对学生的影响是十分深远的。因此,作为一个教师,要明确自己肩负的时代责任,并把它当作终身的职责去努力做好。教师要严于律己,治学严谨,充分利用课堂时间,认真备课和上课。要以人为本,通过自己的教学,让学生掌握更多的知识和技能,把学生培养成为合格和优秀的人才。

(二)提高教师知识水平和能力,培养优秀人才

社会变化日新月异,作为知识传播者的教师必须与时俱进,丰富和更新知识,要精通所教课程的内容、性质和任务,要钻得深和讲得透,不能只是照本宣科,应付了事。如今的信息时代,要求教师不但要具备精深的本专业知识,而且还要有邻近其他学科的知识和具备教会学生学习的能力。要有整理、归纳和转化知识的能力,使知识产生更大的教学效用。要能发挥创造力,运用科学和先进的教育理念,运用为教学目的服务的多样化的教学活动方案。要能挖掘学生的潜能,发展学生的个性,促进学生的发展。还要求教师具备组织管理能力和增强人格魅力。社会发展快,学生的要求也是日益提高,如果教师对社会的发展和需求置之不理,就很难迎合学生的要求,要想学生积极参加课堂学习,提高教学质量就更难了。而且,目前培养人才,不仅要传授他们知识,而且还要培养他们的能力,因此,教师要及时转变观念,要有紧迫感,全面提高个人业务水平和素质才不至于被动和落后。

(三)改善教师的教学方法,创建有效课堂

作为教师,应该具备一定的教学法知识,要了解国外的教育教学理念、教学内容和教学方式等。但是教学的过程是动态的,不是一成不变的。若课堂教学一成不变,方式千篇一律,学生必定对课堂感到厌倦,失去学习的热情,教学质量不言而喻。因此,教师还应该灵活根据教学内容、教学对象、教学条件等的不同采取不同的教学方式。课前,教师要做好这些方面的调查,要充分尊重学生在教学中的主体地位,为学生的个性发展创造条件,组织有效的课堂。组织一个有效的课堂需要考虑多方因素,可采用的教学方法也很多,如:讨论式教学、案例教学、问题式教学、发现式教学等。教师在课堂上对学生进行引导,整合学生多种的学习方式,激发学生自主学习和探究的积极性,引导学生在学习过程中主动参与、乐于探究和勤于动手,可提高学生的能力,促进学生的发展,进行有效学习。

为了让课堂教学质量更高,教师应该充分利用课堂时间,有效地控制课堂,杜绝浪费时间的现象,如:应该避免跑题和聊天;避免花费大量时间用于重复已经学过的内容;避免花费大量的时间板书;避免课堂用语啰嗦等。在有限的课堂时间内,教师应该尽可能让学生接触和掌握足够的信息量,学到知识和得到锻炼。

(四)改进教师的教学手段,增加信息输入量

学生的满意程度主要体现在教师的教是否满足学生的学习需要,是否引起学生的学习兴

趣,激发学生的学习动机,使学生通过教师的教达到自己能学、想学、会学和坚持学的学习状态。[6]教师应该具备使用现代化教育手段的能力,并且在条件允许的情况下,在教学环节中恰当地使用现代教学手段,增加信息量,形象直观地呈现教学内容,提高学生的学习兴趣,切实提高教学质量。

(五)增强教师处理教材的能力,灵活使用

教材是教师教学的主要依据,是学生学习的主要对象。教学活动基本上是以教材为依据进行的有计划的活动。要提高课堂教学质量,教师就要具备处理教材的能力,精通教材和巧用教材。如:抓住教材最主要和最本质的教学内容,量体裁衣,根据教学对象对教材进行处理。要整体地科学地利用教材,提炼和拓展教材的内容,处理好教材更新和学生求知欲的矛盾,努力地使学生成为使用教材的主体,利用教材充分挖掘学生的潜能,培养学生的创新意识和探讨能力。

(六)教学和科研两手抓,教研互进

中国教育部部长周济教授在担任华中科技大学校长时曾说:"一个不搞教学的教师。算不上真正的教师;不能搞科研的教师,成不了第一流的教师;而不能将成果转化生产力的教师,跟不上时代的发展。"[7]科研可以让教师扩充知识面,拓宽学术视野;科研可以让教师更加有思想,把教师提高到更高的层次,而不是仅仅把教学工作当成是谋生的手段;科研可以使教师获得个人发展,形成专业发展的需求与意识,形成内在的动力。科研的过程,是不断地追求课堂教学新境界的过程。用科研成果不断地丰富和深化教学,使课堂更加有内涵,有风格和有个性,更加实用和鲜活。教学和科研两者的结合,对于课堂教学质量的提高也有着重要的作用。

(七)培养良好的师生关系,以身作则

教师的工作对象是人。因此,要提高课堂教学质量,教师就必须了解、热爱和尊重学生,了解学生的实际情况,因材施教,给学生充分的表现空间和发展空间,做好课堂的组织者和引导者。师生之间互敬互爱的良好关系能创造教书育人的有利环境,提高课堂教学质量。

(八)增加教师之间的交流,互帮互助

作为承担同样工作性质的教师们,应该通力合作,发挥集体的力量和智慧,互相交流教学经验,相互切磋,相互评价,相互激励,取长补短,通过"传、帮、带",以老带新,新老共进等方式和共同备课、听课和评课等方法共同应对教学中出现的各种问题,通过交流达到教学知识能力和学术水平的提高,从而促进高校课堂教学质量的提高。

教师作为课堂教学的组织者和实施者,在提高课堂教学质量这个工程中的位置举足轻重。只有重视教师存在的问题,解决教师的问题,才能更好地提高高校课堂教学质量,为社会培养优秀的人才。

参考文献

[1] 周济.创新发展思路,制订“211工程”“十五”建设计划[J].中国高等教育,2002.

[2] 朱九思.高等教育当前应当着重抓什么[J].北京大学教育评论, 2003 (1):60.

[3] 李玲.论高校师德的先进性[J].中国高等教育,2002(6).

[4] 文志传.当不了教授就别当教授[N].中国青年报,2002-11-6(8).

[5] 巴班斯塞.论教学过程的最优化[M].北京:教育科学出版社,1983.

[6] 肖川.论学习方式的变革[J].教育理论与实践,2003 (3):41.

[7] 陈志中.青山着意化为桥:记中国工程院院士、华中理工大学校长周济[J].中国高等教育,2000(3).

透过基础音乐教育现状看高师音乐教育改革

——以广西北部湾沿海地区基础音乐教育现状为例分析

曾美良* 莫世清**

（钦州学院，广西 钦州 535000）

摘 要：高等师范音乐教育的培养目标是为基础教育培养和输送合格的音乐教师，基于此，透过基础音乐教育现状中教师方面存在的问题更能看清高师音乐教育改革中人才培养方面存在的弊端。目前，基础音乐教育中教师方面存在专业技能单一、课堂教学方法欠缺、创造性开展教学的能力较低等问题，这些问题折射出高等师范学校为基础教育服务的观念不牢固，其课程设置、教学内容和教学方法与师范教育培养目标尚有距离。文章以广西北部湾沿海地区基础教育现状中教师方面存在的主要问题为例，进而分析高师音乐教育人才培养过程中需要解决的一些问题，并提出建设性意见。

关键词：基础音乐教育；高师；音乐教育改革

The View of Normal Music Education Reform from Current Situation of Basic Music Education

—The Example of Current Situations of Basic Music Education in Guangxi Beibu Gulf Coastal Areas

Zeng Mei-liang Mo Shi-qing

(Qinzhou University, Qinzhou 535000, China)

Abstract: The training objectives of normal music education is to cultivate and provide qualified music teachers for basic education. For this reason, with the view

* 曾美良，钦州学院音乐系讲师。

** 莫世清，钦州学院音乐系讲师。

of the teachers' problems in current situations of basic music education, the drawbacks in cultivating personnel of normal music education reform can be better seen. There are still some problems in basic music education such as teachers' single professional skill, shortage of classroom teaching methods and lack of creative teaching abilities, which reflect the concept of normal universities for basic education services being unreliable. There are still gaps between its curriculum, teaching contents, methods and the training objectives of normal education. Based on the example of the teachers' main problems in current situations of basic music education in Guangxi Beibu Gulf Coastal Areas, the article analyzes a number of issues needing to be resolved in cultivating personnel of normal music education and puts forward constructive comments.

Key words: basic music education; normal universities; music education reform

21 世纪初,我国开展了一轮学校音乐教育历史上规模最大、影响最深的基础音乐课程改革,基础音乐课程的课程目标、基本理念、课程内容、教学方法等方面发生了深刻的变化。在此背景下,为适应中小学音乐教育改革的发展,为基础音乐教育培养合格的音乐师资,教育部体卫教司于 2004 年 12 月颁布了《全国普通高等学校音乐学(教师教育)本科专业课程指导方案》(以下简称《课程方案》)。《课程方案》颁布和实施至今,我国高师音乐教育改革又过了几个年头,其改革成效如何?透过基础音乐教育现状中教师方面存在的一些问题,我们可以看到高师音乐教育在人才培养过程中亟待解决的一些问题。笔者在 2008 年 9 月至 2009 年 1 月期间曾经就广西北部湾沿海地区九年义务教育阶段的音乐教育现状开展过专门的调研工作,发现其中涉及教师方面存在的一些问题的主要成因在于高师音乐教育,换言之,高师音乐教育培养的人才不能完全胜任基础音乐教育工作。这种情况在全国来说还是比较普遍的,正如教育部体育卫生与艺术教育司司长杨贵仁在 2007 年全国普通高校音乐学(教师教育)会议上所指出的那样:高等师范学校为基础教育服务的观念尚不牢固,课程设置、教学内容和教学方法与师范教育培养目标尚有距离。笔者在此将以广西北部湾沿海地区基础教育现状中存在的主要问题为例,分析高师音乐教育人才培养过程中需要解决的问题,并提出建设性意见,以期抛砖引玉,希望有更多的高校音乐教育工作者关注中小学音乐师资的培养。

一、基础音乐教育中教师方面存在的问题及其所显露出的高师音乐教育中存在的问题

广西北部湾沿海地区包括钦州、北海、防城港三市,笔者采取分层抽样、问卷调查法、座谈会、访谈法等多种方法对沿海三市的部分学校展开调研,共计调查学校二十四所,二十四所学校覆盖城市、县城、乡镇、乡村各级。从调研的情况来看,基础音乐教育中教师方面存在一些问题,而其中某些问题究其成因在于高师音乐教育。

1. 音乐教师专业技能单一,无法完成中小学音乐课程中规定的四个领域的教学内容,问题折射出高师音乐教育专业必修课开设不够,培养的学生所掌握的音乐专业技能不够多样。

《全日制义务教育音乐课程标准》(以下简称《标准》)在教学领域分四个方面:感受与鉴赏、

表现、创造、音乐与相关文化。其中，感受与鉴赏主要形式是听赏(或鉴赏)音乐，主要表现形式包括演唱、演奏、综合性艺术表演、识读乐谱；创造的主要形式包括探索音乐与音乐、即兴创造、创作实践；音乐与相关文化主要活动形式是音乐与社会生活、音乐与姊妹艺术、音乐与艺术之外的其他学科的相关音乐活动。[1]教师要完成这四个教学领域的内容，意味着必须自身具备较高的音乐文化素质，掌握多样音乐专业技能技巧。我们在学生问卷中有一个问题是“你们的音乐课上课内容和形式有哪些”，该问题为多选题，设计的选项有唱歌、欣赏、歌表演或活动、创作、识谱、演奏等，关于这一问题，小学生选择“唱歌”的达 96.6%，选择“欣赏”的达 20.5%，其它选项的选择率较低；初中学生选择“唱歌”的达 93.5%，选择“欣赏”的达 39%，选择“识谱”的达 28.8%，其他选项的选择率较低。结果表明：小学、初中的音乐课内容都主要以唱歌为主，初中音乐课中欣赏和识谱的比例虽有所提高但其授课内容仍然不够全面，未能完全涉及《标准》规定的四个领域。令人诧异的是，无论是小学还是初中，北部湾沿海地区的“器乐”(或说“演奏”)内容几近空白。

音乐教师所掌握的专业技能单一，综合实践能力欠缺，使得小学、初中的“器乐”教学内容几乎成为空白，学校添置的一些乐器如竖笛、竹笛、吉他、小号、长号等因常年无人问津差不多处于“废弃”状态。音乐作为一门实践性很强的科目，要求参与者更多地参与实践活动，然而，多数音乐教师综合实践能力欠缺，他(她)们在学校时掌握的技能技巧多是偏向于单科，或唱、或跳、或弹(仅止于键盘乐器)，缺乏综合实践能力的锻炼，普通学校的音乐课更多的时候不是需要展现某项技术的“高、精、深”，而是要求技术技能方面的“全、正、质”，所谓“全”，要求教师掌握多门专业技术技巧，正是由于“全能型”教师的缺乏使得器乐教学成为义务教育阶段音乐教育中最薄弱的方面，也使得教师没有能力完成课程的四个领域的教学内容。

2. 中小学音乐教师的课堂教学方法欠缺，折射出高师音乐教育学生对中小学音乐教学法重视程度不够，实践程度不深。

学生问卷中有一个问题是“你的音乐老师常采用哪种方法进行教学?”这个问题是多选题，设计的选项有：讲授；一句一句教我们唱歌；结合游戏律动唱歌；讨论；让同学们即兴创作或即兴表演；启发同学们进行想象，鼓励同学们表达自己的看法。无论是小学还是初中“一句一句”教唱的这种听唱法是音乐教师采用得最多的方法，小学生选择“一句一句教我们唱歌”的人数达 78.2%，即使到了初中，选择该选项的人数也有 60.1%。此外，初中学生选择“讲授”的有 38.5%。“结合游戏律动唱歌”、“讨论”、“让同学们即兴创作或即兴表演”、“启发同学们进行想象，鼓励同学们表达自己的看法”这些选项的选择率很低，很显然，教师们在音乐课上采取的教学方法是比较呆板的，甚至有些模式化，缺乏“灵活性”和“创造性”。

教师在课堂中能否灵活运用教学方法以取得较好的教学效果达到预定的教学目标主要取决于教师对音乐课程教学法的学习掌握程度和教师所具备的音乐素质、所掌握的专业技术两方面的因素。有些教师对音乐教学方法知之甚少，在笔者借阅的部分教案中，关于“教学方法”要么是没有写这一栏，要么就是写得不对头，比如教学方法是“通过视听歌曲联想音乐描绘的意境，从中体会音乐的特点”；“大量有趣丰富的影音资料，错落有致地安排在自制的多媒体教学课件中，不仅为概念的讲解、举例提供了方便，而且更突出了知识的条理性，有效地突破重难点，增加教学密度，提高教学质量”，即使是专职音乐教师，他(她)们也难提出一些具体的教学方法，比如练习法、讨论法、探究法、谈话法等等。从这些情况来看，高校音乐教育专业学生对于中小学音乐教学法课程的学习和掌握程度是不够的，或者说不能学以致用，于是问题就显露在走上工作岗位之后。当然,我们也不能说高校音乐教育专业学生在理论上懂得了一些课程教学法知识就能熟练运用于教学当中了,作为音乐教师,既要懂得教育知识,还必须熟练掌握音乐基础理论知识和多项音乐专业基本技能技巧,如果音乐素养低,专业技术欠缺,即使了解了一些教育理论知识,也无法有效地运用教学方法开展课堂教学。事实上,我们相当一部分音乐教师的音乐素养和专业技术能力都还有待提高,其后果就是,即使他(她)想到采取什么方法来教学但却未必有那个能力来完成。

3. 中小学音乐教师创造性开展教学的能力较低,折射出高师音乐教育在开展实践活动方面缺乏有效性,对学生的创造能力和实践能力培养不够。

我国幅员辽阔、地广人多,长期以来,因为经济、文化、教育等多方面因素的综合影响,使得教育(包括音乐教育)水平的地区差异比较大,这种差异同样也体现在教育的外部环境方面,经济发达的地区早已按照《标准》和《学校艺术教育工作规程》、《全国学校艺术教育发展规划(2001～2010年)》的要求配备专门的音乐教室和相关的音乐教学设备,条件差的地区不仅没有专门的音乐教室,甚至连一些基本的音乐教育设备都还缺乏,面对这些条件的差异,需要音乐教师能因地制宜地创造性地开展教学。然而,就如王安国先生所指出的:音乐教师缺少自主开发地方和学校课程、创造性实施教学的能力。[2]笔者在调研中也发现,一些音乐教师习惯于将问题的原因归结在外部环境上,认为是没有专门的音乐教室,或者是教学条件差,或者是学生不重视音乐课的这些外部原因影响了音乐课的教学,甚至有教师说"阻碍我不能按照课改要求上音乐课的主要原因是因为没有专门的音乐教室",这些都体现出音乐教师创造性实施音乐教学的能力不强。诚然,教师的很多能力是在走上教学岗位之后逐步锻炼出来的,但我们不能否认的是,当这些教师刚从高师校门走出来时,他们的创新能力、实践能力就是非常弱的。

高师音乐教育专业对于学生创新精神、实践能力的培养方面存在教师本身的认识不足、参与活动的学生面窄、综合性活动缺乏等不足。教师在课堂教学中不注重理论联系实践,尤其是不突出师范性的实践教学,也不重视学生的课外音乐实践活动;课外活动差不多是专业尖子生的展现平台,学生的参与面窄;活动形式单一,综合性活动缺乏,创新性活动缺乏,种种原因导致所培养的学生创新实践能力不强。

二、对高师音乐教育改革的几点建议

1. 在专业必修模块中适当增加音乐表现类课程以适应基础音乐教学的需要。

《课程方案》对于音乐教育专业学生的培养规格提出了几方面的要求,其中一点是:系统掌握从事学校音乐教育所必备的音乐基础理论、基础知识和基本技能,具有较高的文化素养,较强的艺术表现能力和综合实践能力,能够胜任学校音乐课堂教学,指导课外活动,参与校园文化环境建设,并为终身学习打下坚实基础。具体来讲,这是对音乐专业知识、技能、能力方面的要求。王耀华先生在解读方案时更是指出,音乐教育专业学生应掌握多项音乐专业基本技能技巧。[3]基于此,在课程设置方面,《课程方案》规定的11门必修课中包含声乐、钢琴(含歌曲伴奏)、乐器演奏(中外乐器各一种)这几门表现类课程;专业任选课中又建议包含声乐、重唱与表演唱、钢琴(或手风琴、电子琴)、中外管弦乐器演奏等表现类课程。如果真正按照《课程方案》来实施,音乐教育专业学生就基本能做到在学习钢琴、声乐、舞蹈、艺术实践等课程的基础上,还能学习手风琴或电子琴,除此之外,再选修一到两种其他乐器。遗憾的是很多院校仍然沿用以前的课程设置,查阅一些学校的音乐教育专业课程计划表,我们在必修课模块仍然看到的音乐表现类课程是声乐、钢琴、舞蹈,限定选修课中的仍然是这几门课程加电子琴,任意选修课程中也涉及表现类课程,但任意选修课程中涉及表现类课程的实际开课情况并不理想。

分析表现类课程的开设不够多样或其实际开课情况不理想的原因有三:第一个原因是领导认识不足,为基础音乐教育服务意识不强,没有认识到开设多门专业技术课的必要性;第二个原因是学分的分配不尽合理,比如公共必修课占用学时和学分过多,势必会挤占专业必修课学时和学分,导致无法正常开设多门专业必修课(包括表现类课程);第三个原因是师资的缺乏,因为缺乏民乐、管弦乐等专业教师无法开设相关课程。要想解决相关问题,首先领导要认识到开设相关音乐表现类课程的必要性和重要性;其次要引进民乐和管弦乐教师以满足开设多门音乐专业课程的需要;再次要合理分配学分,科学进行课程设置,尽量在必修模块中增加音乐表现类课程。在高校音乐教育的改革过程中,也有少数院校已在调整旧的人才培养方案时做了一些调整,他们的一些举措可资我们借鉴和参考。比如,湖南师范大学将《器乐选修》调整为《基础器乐》必修课程,开课时间一年,这样,加上原来开设的《基础钢琴》、《基础声乐》、《舞蹈与形体》等必修课程,全面保证本科生在毕业时具备多项音乐基本技能技巧;再如,广西师范大学音乐学院专业必修中开设的声乐课中包含了重唱、表演唱,中外器乐课中包含了含重奏的声部练习,笔者以为这样的开课如能实施得当,不失为一种在人才培养过程中突出"师范性"的好方法。

2. 加教学实践课时,让学生在教学实践过程中灵活掌握和运用教学方法。

随着教育教学理念的更新,高校音乐教育专业也越来越重视对学生实践能力的培养,在学校的人才培养方案中关于实践环节是占了一定比例和学分的,然而我们仍然觉得对于教育实践的安排是不够科学的,多数学校将教育实习集中安排在最后一个学期,加上前七个学期较少针对教育见习和实习对学生进行培训或提供相应的实践锻炼机会,其教育实习质量欠佳,这样就造成学生在毕业前没有受到充分的关于中小学音乐教学的实践锻炼,没能掌握科学的教学方法,导致无法胜任音乐课教学工作。

笔者以为,教育教学实践活动应该贯穿于大学四年的全过程中,或者除了在第八学期安排相对比较集中和时间比较长的教育实习之外,从第二学期或者第二学年开始就应定期开展音乐教育专业学生的实践活动,而且其活动要突出其"师范"特点。很多师范院校也重视对学生实践能力的培养,但笔者看来,其"师范性"突出不够,很多实践活动比如声乐学习汇报会、钢琴学习汇报会、教学观摩会、文艺晚会等形式,这些形式提供给学生的表现方式就是演唱或演奏,很少开展结合性实践活动,或开展类似模拟中小学课堂教学的活动。实际上,开展这类活动是非常必要的,郭声健教授也指出:提高艺术师范学生的中小学课堂教学能力和课外艺术活动的组织能力,最有效的途径之一莫过于让他们自己在当学生的时候多参加和组织一些课外艺术活动,尽早地多体验一下中小学艺术教师这一角色。笔者工作所在的学校去年举办了一次"师范生教学技能竞赛",此次比赛分教学设计、课件制作、模拟课堂教学、板书设计等环节,参加比赛的音乐教育专业学生都普遍认为这样的比赛很锻炼人,尤其是模拟课堂教学的环节,在这当中要展现的不仅是音乐专业技能技巧,展现的还有作为一名"教师"在课堂上的语言表达能力、课堂组织能力、运用教学方法展开教学的能力等等,可以说,这种比赛比以往许多学校开展的"师范生五项全能比赛"更锻炼人,因为所谓全能比赛其实是在分开比单项即某专业技能,最后把几个单项加一块即为全能,这种脱离课堂实际的比赛应该是不能完全达到锻炼师范生的目的，所以我们提倡一种更接近教学的实践活动，那样才可以让学生在走出校门之前尽可能多地掌握一些音乐教学方法。

3. 开展丰富多彩的创造性活动，通过活动培养学生的创造能力。

锻炼学生的创造能力应该要将课内与课外结合起来，既要通过课内，尤其是通过音乐创造类课程培养学生的创造能力，也要通过课外一些有创造性的活动培养学生的创造能力。而我国高师音乐教育过去和现在一直都比较忽视对学生创造能力，动手能力的培养。目前主要开设的音乐创造类课程包括歌曲写作与改编、多声部音乐分析与习作、舞蹈编导基础等。从教学的实际情况来看，这类课程(除舞蹈编导外)纸上谈兵的为多，歌曲写作也好、多声部音乐分析与习作也好，都是在纸上做“文章”，缺乏实际表演，即缺乏将作品表现出来的实践能力的锻炼。此外，高师音乐教育的课外活动也很少考虑采取什么方式更能激发学生创造能力。

在中小学课堂教学中，对于创造领域的教学其实并不需要多么高超的作曲技巧、多么高水平的器乐编配或技术难度很高的音乐表演。因此，笔者认为，高师音乐教育的“歌曲写作与分析”、“和声”、“配器法”都不要一味地往“深”里学，而要多在课堂中让学生将自己创作的东西表现出来，多一点实践，着重对学生创造实践能力的培养。另一方面，可以开展一些展示学生创造能力的课外活动，比如像中央电视台少儿频道曾播出过的“奇思妙想”这类节目，给学生一个音乐主题和适当的一些材料，让他们设法用这些材料来即兴表现音乐；也可以设计一个活动，让学生提前根据主题设计自己的节目，自己搜集相关资料和材料，在活动中展现自我创造能力。如果高师音乐教育能够有意识且采取有效的方法开拓学生思维，锻炼他们的创造能力，那么他们在走上工作岗位后就能更好地应对各种不同的状况，在不同的条件下得心应手地开展音乐课教学工作。

参考文献

[1] 中华人民共和国教育部. 全日制义务教育音乐课程标准[M]. 北京：北京师范大学出版社，2002.

[2] 王安国. 我国学校音乐教育改革与发展对策研究[J]. 中央音乐学院学报，2004(4).

[3] 王耀华. 中小学音乐教育发展与高师音乐教育改革[J]. 音乐研究，2002(1).

[4] 郭声健. 艺术教育论[M]. 上海：上海教育出版社，1999：206.

论教师在特色校园文化建设中的作用
——以钦州学院校园文化建设为例

吴小玲*
（钦州学院，广西 钦州 535000）

摘　要：校园文化是学校师生在学校教育、管理、学习、生活等过程中创造的独具特色的文化，而教师是高校特色校园文化建设的主体力量和引导力量。广西北部湾文化有其独特的内涵与本质，建设具有广西北部湾特色的钦州学院校园文化是地方高校体现办学特色，服务地方经济发展的重要内容，钦州学院应充分发挥教师在特色校园文化建设中的作用，引领广西北部湾社会文化发展的方向。

关键词：校园文化；广西北部湾文化；钦州学院

On Teachers Role in the Construction of University Campus Characteristic Culture
—with the Example of Qinzhou University

Wu Xiao-ling
(Qinzhou University, Qinzhou 535000, China)

Abstract: Campus culture is formed in the process of education, administration, learning and living. Teachers are guiders in the construction of campus culture. Construction of university campus life with the characteristics of Beibu Gulf is a prsentation of Qinzhou University playing an active role in the development of Qinzhou. Teachers should act as guiders in the construction.

Key words: campus culture; Guangxi Beibu Gulf Culture; Qinzhou University

随着我国经济结构的战略性调整和高等教育大众化进程的推进，地方院校的发展面临着

* 吴小玲，钦州学院政经系副教授。

前所未有的发展机遇和严峻挑战,如何在激烈的竞争中发挥优势,将地方特色文化融入校园文化建设,形成自己的办学特色,以求得生存和发展,已成为地方高校关注的一个共同问题。教师作为校园中最稳定的群体,是校园文化建设中的主体力量和引导力量。具有广西北部湾特色的钦州学院校园文化的建设同样需要充分发挥教师的主体作用和引导作用。

一、高校校园文化的内涵

校园文化是以校园为空间,以高素质学生和教学研究型教师为主体、以课外科技活动为主要内容、以大众化活动为载体,以学习和研究人类文明为核心的物质文化、制度文化、精神文化相统一的具有时代特征的一种群体文化。校园文化是学校师生在学校教育、管理、学习、生活等过程中创造的独具特色的文化,它以潜在的、独具特色的方式熏陶、感染、规划并影响制约着学校师生的思想方式和行为方式,是学校精神文化的集中体现。校园文化的健康发展需要每个校园人的努力,尤其是广大教师,在校园文化建设中发挥着极其重要的作用。

二、教师在校园文化建设中的作用

邓小平同志曾指出:“一个学校能不能为社会主义建设培养合格的人才,培养德智体全面发展的、有社会主义觉悟的有文化的劳动者,关键在教师。”[1]教师是学校教育思想和教育目标的具体体现者和实施者,承担着培养人和教育人的重要职责,同时,也承担着校园文化建设的重任。

1. 教师培养人才的活动是校园文化建设的主要途径

教学活动是多种形式的师生互动过程,师生互动是校园文化形成的主要途径。在校园中,教师是最主要的教育者,担负着培养人才的责任,教师的职责一般可以概括为传统的“传道、授业、解惑”。但更重要的是,教师还要用其言传身教即用个人的思维方式、价值观念、高尚人格、敬业精神对学生产生潜移默化的影响。同时,作为校园里比较稳定的群体,教师的教学态度、价值观、思维方式乃至授课方式都会对一批又一批学生产生影响,从而铸就了整个学校的校风及学风;教师的教学科研水平的高低,基本上代表了一所学校的办学水平;教师本身素质的高低,决定了其所培养的学生素质的高低。可见,教师在校园文化建设中不但可以影响到整个学校深层价值观的形成,而且对校园精神文化建设也起着决定性的作用。教师是校园文化建设的主角,教师的身份规定了其作为校园文化建设主体的地位。

2. 教师的学术成果代表着校园文化建设的水平和声誉

大学教师在完成教学任务的同时,还要担负起学术研究的任务。教师的科研水平代表了一所学校的学术水平,教师的影响力决定着一所学校的声誉。因此,一所学校教师的数量和质量,基本上决定了一所高校的办学水平。原吉林大学校长匡亚明指出:“一所大学,没有教授,就不成其为大学,标志一所大学水平的是教授的数量和他们的学术水平。”

3. 教师对校园文化建设起着引导作用

教师是校园里与学生接触最多最密切的群体,熟悉学生的思想动态,他们承担着教书育人的责任和能力。对于处于成长阶段的学生来讲,教师的耐心教育和积极引导可以减少学生活动的盲目性;教师的精神风貌、道德修养、工作作风、言谈举止等为学生的文化选择及行为树立了榜样。教师作为国家各项教育方针和政策的代言人，传递着国家和社会对学生的要求和期望，为校园文化建设指明了方向，保证校园文化发展的正确方向。教师在学识修养、社会阅历等方面的文化优势，决定了他们在引领和主导校园文化建设中起着不可估量的作用。

三、广西北部湾文化的内涵特点

广西北部湾文化是中原的汉文化南迁、与来自广东、福建等地的粤文化和客家文化在播迁广西北部湾的过程中，因地理环境的不同、历史发展的差异等因素而与原始土著骆越文化相结合形成的一种区域性文化。它包括：

1. 精神文化层

广西北部湾的早期居民是骆越人，但从秦汉起，大批因戍军、屯田、逃难、流放、任官、经商等而迁来的汉民成为其居民的主要成分，儒家文化的影响在此不断加深。由于处于河、海、边交汇处的特殊生存环境，锻造了北部湾人民团结协助、勇于开拓的意识，使广西北部湾文化积淀了开放性、进取性、辐射性的特征。由于处于中华民族向海外拓展和维护自己生存领地的前哨地区，广西北部湾人民勤劳勇敢，不畏强敌，不怕牺牲，英雄辈出。广西北部湾文化的基本精神是以儒家传统文化为基础，以爱国主义为核心，不断推动自身发展的精神。

2. 制度文化层

制度文化层包括伦理道德和教育科技等方面。从秦朝迁移的“尝逋之人”、“赘婿”和“为士卒衣补”的妇女，到赵佗时“居南方长治之，甚有文理，中原人以故不耗减，粤人相攻击之俗益止，俱赖其力”[2](高帝纪)；从东汉任延教民铸田器，开垦荒田，改造婚姻制度，到锡光的“教民导夷，断以礼义”，“岭南华风始于二守颖”[3](汉纪三十八，章帝建初八年)，中原的社会风俗逐渐感染南方，“其流风遗韵，衣冠气习，薰陶渐染，故习渐变，而俗庶几中州”[4](卷九十二)；从孟尝的“合浦珠还”，到令狐熙“开设学校以教化其民”，宁氏家族开发钦州；从岳霖修建校舍，聘周去非为教，使钦州“士之众多也”到陶弼“重葺郡县，浚治壕堑，郡治愈固”，推广占城稻；从林希元到钦州推广屯田，劝农老人，教民耕织等[5]，至清代的朱椿“清正廉明”，治理海疆[6]，广西北部湾“人才出矣，财货通矣，中原之声教日近矣，遐陬之俗变矣”[7]。明清时期，随着大量外来人口的涌入，“昔日瘴乡，显而易见流人逐客不至”的广西北部湾，出现了“仕官、乐官其地，商贾愿出其地”[8]的趋势。

3. 器物文化层

广西北部湾的史前贝丘文化、百越土著文化、南方汉文化（含客家文化、疍家文化）、海上丝绸之路文化、南珠文化、坭兴陶文化、反侵略文化、京族文化、近代中西文化融合、现代革命文化、壮族文化等非常丰富，一大批历史文化遗址是广西北部湾文化特征的物化表现。

四、具有广西北部湾特色的钦州学院校园文化建设现状

1. 钦州学院是广西北部湾地区具有深厚文化底蕴的高等学府

（1）广西北部湾文化是钦州学院校园文化发展的重要源泉。钦州学院是目前广西北部湾唯一的公立普通本科高等院校。广西北部湾的人文精神，包括审美情趣、民风习俗、建筑习俗、环境风格等都深深地影响着学校。学院所处的区位对人们价值认同的影响，学院校园文化建

设渗透着广西北部湾的地域文化意识，包括传统特色、风俗习惯、历史知识等，是钦州学院作为北部湾高校的特色所在。

(2) 广西北部湾文化为钦州学院校园文化提供了丰富的教学、科研内容。地方高校必须依托于一定的区域并服务于其经济社会发展。长期以来，钦州学院利用广西北部湾的地域文化优势，扬长避短，及时调整专业设置和发展方向，形成依靠地方、面向地方、服务地方的格局，打造特色学科，发展优势产业，增强自我发展能力，在高校林立的状态中不断发展起来。

(3) 学院的校园文化、进步思想也在丰富着北部湾文化的内涵和精神家园。远至20世纪30～40年代，一批钦州师范的青年学生接受了马克思主义的影响，在广西北部湾开始了早期的革命活动；近30年来，钦州学院积极参与广西北部湾的教育、科研、文化活动，这不但体现在大学生们的社会活动中，更体现在成千上万的学院毕业生在各行各业的突出贡献，学院成为广西北部湾"文化人"的聚集地，其校园文化精神对当地社会具有一定的示范效应。

2. 钦州学院校园文化建设奠定了其在广西北部湾经济区的良好声誉

钦州学院一直高度重视校园文化的培育和拓展，努力提炼学校精神和办学理念，秉承地方文化的优良传统，弘扬民族精神，创造先进文化，提高人文素养，铸造特色校园文化。

钦州学院的发展史就是一部发奋图强，争生存、争发展的奋斗史。学校在艰难困苦中一次次走出困境，一次次走向新的辉煌，这是广西北部湾优良文化传统和学校在特殊环境下所凝练成的人文精神，它造就了一代又一代的莘莘学子，通过他们散发到社会，赋予了广西北部湾文化一定的新的时代意义。

钦州学院在长期办学过程中逐步形成了求真务实、笃学敏行的传统，正是广西北部湾文化精神中的进取性、开拓性精神的一再闪现。近年来，钦州学院积极通过打造五个品牌(临海工业、石油化工、海洋经济、东盟、北部湾经济)，加大专业结构的调整，融入广西北部湾的开放开发热潮；学院成立了北部湾人文研究中心，使广西北部湾历史文化研究从历史学、文化学走向了经济学、文学、艺术学、政治学、教育学等诸多领域，在地域经济和文化的结合上发挥地方高校的作用。此外，学院还依托学生社团，深入到农村、工厂企业、城镇社区等开展活动，参与社会服务，为广西北部湾良好文化氛围的形成起到了重要作用。

3. 钦州学院校园文化建设的不足

在校园文化建设中，学院比较重视浅层的校园文化建设，更深层次的校园文化建设仍重视不够。近年来，学校的物质基础、校园环境、图书资料、传播媒体、文化设施建设力度加大，校园文体活动和社会实践活动丰富多彩。但精神文化建设涉及面还不够宽，如对广西北部湾文化利用不够，没有形成具有地方特色的成熟的校园文化。同时，仍缺乏对广西北部湾文化不断进取、顽强拼搏精神的充分利用，以进一步改进目前的校风、教风和学风。此外，对地方优秀历史文化的学习和领会不够、结合不到位，各类活动所反映的精神内容不够集中，作用不够持久，特色仍不够鲜明，感染力还不够强。

五、发挥教师作用，建设具有广西北部湾特色的校园文化

随着广西北部湾的进一步开放开发，文化发展的层次必然会提升。面对新形势，作为钦州学院人的教师更应积极参与北部湾文化建设，努力建构有广西北部湾特色的符合时代要求的校园文化，不断提升校园文化建设的品质和知名度，为学生成才创造优越的文化氛围，让学院

以其独特的校园文化精神而成为北部湾文化的象征。

1. 发挥理论优势，弘扬先进文化，引领广西北部湾的先进文化

钦州学院现有教职员工700多人，聚集着一批长期从事人文社会科学教学与研究工作的教师，他们具有较为系统的马克思主义理论修养和丰厚的科技文化知识，应充分发挥理论优势，以邓小平理论、“三个代表”重要思想和科学发展观为指导思想，以健康向上、丰富多彩的思想政治与科技文化娱乐体育活动为载体，以树立正确的人生观、世界观、价值观为导向，弘扬主旋律，不断向社会辐射先进文化的理念，以引领广西北部湾的先进文化。

2. 转变观念，明确定位，培育优势学科和专业，形成特色

钦州学院牢固树立为区域经济社会发展服务的意识，服务广西、服务大西南、服务东盟，充分发挥广大教师的作用，大力进行专业结构的调整，已初见成效。学院开设了海洋类专业（港口物流、轮机工程、海洋科学等），实现了广西海洋类专业的新突破。开设了泰语专业，开设了北部湾历史文化概论、东南亚概况、东南亚历史文化、越南语、泰语等课程，与越南、泰国的有关高校合作办学，招收越南、泰国留学生，每年的5月都举办泰国文化周，校园文化进一步反映广西北部湾的知识经济、技术、文化等特色。今后，学院应进一步转变观念，树立接轨东盟，面向世界的思想，在全校完善地方性课程改革的力度，以促进学院特色校园文化的进一步形成。

3. 建设开放式校园，发挥校园文化资源优势，实现与社会文化相交融，促进北部湾文化的和谐发展

钦州学院是广西沿海地域优势文化资源最集中的地方，先进校园文化对社会文化的引领，可使社会上人们的价值观念、思维方式、行为等方面逐步趋同，推进社会文化的和谐发展。因此，学院要最大限度地发挥教师的主观能动性，利用现有的社会文化资源，通过与地方行业、经济的互动不断地塑造校园文化，实现校园文化与社会文化的互动，形成并强化自己的特色，最大限度地提高素质教育，培养符合时代发展和社会需要的人才。

4. 加强文化研究，推进广西北部湾文化发展

作为广西北部湾高等教育的重要载体，学院应成为推进广西北部湾文化发展的主力军。因此，要通过对广西北部湾历史文化的研究，挖掘历史文化底蕴，凝练人文精神，指导广西北部湾的发展；要加强对广西区重点学科建设基地——北部湾人文研究中心的建设，积极承接地方的决策咨询项目，参与政府主导的城市文化建设活动，帮助制定科学的文化发展战略和文化市场管理规则等，推动当地文化事业的发展，充分发挥学院在地域经济和文化研究方面的优势；要通过扩大对外文化交流活动，宣传北部湾文化，促进中国文化与东南亚文化、西方文化的交流与融合；要通过多元化办学模式、多层次、多途径的培养方式，造就更多适应北部湾文化事业和文化产业发展所需要的应用型高级人才。

5. 深入社会，扩大影响，活跃第二课堂，为地方经济社会发展服务

高校具有人才库、知识源的作用，钦州学院已发展为综合性的高等院校，为推动地方文化发展创造了条件。因此，应发挥教师的优势，通过发展继续教育，提高当地人民的素质；通过深入社区、农村、企业开展文化活动，普及文化知识，开阔人们的视野；要依托现有的研究团体，推动学术研究、科技实践活动向更高层次发展，建设具有浓厚校园文化氛围的校园环境，营造优秀的校园文化，为国家培养更多的全面发展、一专多能的高素质人才。

随着校园文化建设的深入，钦州学院必会以其应有的文化品位和文化形象影响广西北部湾区域文化的发展，以其具有高校品质的建筑形态与广西北部湾的人文背景相结合来构建校

园环境，使校园处处“流淌”着文化，使涉足校园的人能够感觉到以广西北部湾文化为背景的校园文化的悠久与厚重，引以为自豪，增强建设广西北部湾这一美好家园的信心。

参考文献

[1] 邓小平文选(第一卷)[M]. 北京：人民出版社，1985.

[2] 班固. 汉书[M]. 北京：中华书局，1982.

[3] 司马光. 资治通鉴[M]. 海口：海南国际新闻出版中心，诚成文化出版有限公司，1990.

[4] 阮元修，陈昌济，等. 广东通志[M]. 上海：古籍出版社，1990.

[5] 郦道元. 水经注(卷三六)温水条[M]. 北京：中华书局，1991.

[6] 范晔撰. 后汉书·任延传[M]. 北京：中华书局，1965.

社会转型期大学数学教学应加强数学建模环节

王远干*
（钦州学院，广西 钦州 535000）

摘 要：社会转型期对大学数学的教学提出了新要求，现行的大学数学教学面临诸多问题。文章从社会转型期对科学技术人才的数学素养要求入手，提出大学数学教学应加强数学建模环节。在大学数学的教学内容、教学手段及教学方法的改革上进行了研究，并从激发学生兴趣、实行多轨教学模式、开展课程建设和实施培训等方面进行了实践，收到了较为显著的效果。

关键词：社会转型；大学数学教学；数学建模；课程建设

To Promote Mathematical Modeling in College and University Maths Teaching upon the Social Transition Period

Wang Yuan-gan
（Qinzhou University, Qinzhou 535000, China）

Abstract: Social transition in China has now posed many new problems and requirements for college and university maths teaching. In accordance with the required maths qualities of scientific and technical personnels in this period, this paper proposes that mathematical modeling should be promoted in the teaching of mathematics in colleges and universities. We've carried out researches on the reform of college and university maths teaching in terms of teaching content, teaching aids and teaching methods. Notable good results have been attained in the practice of stimulating student's learning interests, implementating "multi-track" teaching mode, and in the development of curriculums and related trainings.

---

* 王远干，钦州学院数计系副教授。

Key words: social transition; mathematical teaching in colleges and universities; mathematical modeling; curriculum development

0 引言

社会转型是社会从较低社会发展形态向较高社会发展形态的转变过程，是一个社会各领域的开放与重新融合的过程，它为各类人才提供了更高的展现自我的平台，是对社会传统的、旧的社会发展体系的一种挑战[1]。社会转型时期，特别是社会经济的转型时期，对社会科学与技术的发展提出了新的要求。作为未来社会科技主流的在校大学生更是面临前所未有的挑战，要想在社会转型时期的激烈竞争中站稳脚跟，拥有一席之地，就必须要具备扎实的基础知识和过硬的专业技能。

在这一背景下，必然对高等学校的大学数学教学与改革提出了新的要求。数学作为大学教学中的重要基础课，在转型时期，对培养跨世纪的应用型人才具有重要作用，有效地改善数学的教学方法，提高教学效果，对培养人才的影响将是巨大的。传统的数学教学在强调理论系统性的同时存在知识陈旧，内容单调和理论脱离实际的缺陷，迫切需要加以改革。现行的大学数学教学模式存在一些问题，缺乏对学生数学应用能力的培养，阻碍了学生应用性思维和能力的发展[2]。如何改进和改善大学数学的教学效果是我们目前有待解决的问题。在大学数学教学过程中，贯以数学建模思想，可很好地提升学生应用数学方法和计算机工具分析、解决实际问题的能力，培养了学生的抽象思维和应变能力，锻炼拼搏、协作精神和主动探索和发现新知识的能力，提高了学生的创新意识，是大学数学教学与改革的出发点与突破口[3]。

多年来，我们面向信息时代，以培养具有综合素质的竞争性人才为目标，以数学建模教学为突破口，针对传统数学教学模式的弱点，为推动大学数学的教学内容、教学手段及教学方法的改革，进行了一系列的研究，在激发学生兴趣、实行多轨教学模式、课程建设和培训实施等方面取得了较为显著的成果。

1 目前大学数学教学中所存在的主要问题

大学的数学教学目前存在如下几个方面的问题[4]：(1) 我们已进入计算机革命时代，而高等数学等教材几十年来无多大变化，没有反映出时代的特点。(2) 教学方式变化不大，仍是传统的“老师上课、学生听课、记笔记、做习题、考试”。反馈信息少，师生相互交流更少，由于数学课程中很少有实验学时，使得数学课中利用计算机的机会相当少。(3) 教学的最终效果是学生“学以致用”，现在的教学过程基本上是“学”的过程，没有学生“用”数学知识的教学环节，“学”与“用”脱节问题相当严重。参加工作后的许多大学生反映，工作中运用大学所学知识的机会很少，真的是数学知识在工作中使用不上吗？显然不是，这正是由于数学教学缺乏用的环节，许多学生不知怎样用数学来解决实际问题。(4) 数学教学越来越形式化，重概念、定理、推导、证明，轻计算，轻数学方法的可行性分析，误差分析，使得学生觉得数学相当抽象，数学远离我们周围的世界，远离我们的日常生活。(5) 没有引导学生培养查阅数学书籍与文献以获取新的数学知识的能力。通过在大学数学的教学与学习中加强数学建模能力的培养与训练，可很好地解决上述问题，提高数学教学质量。

2. 加强数学建模能力培养，提高大学数学教学质量的方法与途径

2.1 推广建模内含，激发学习兴趣

数学建模就是将实际问题用数学语言描述并加以解决的过程，采用的手段就是建立数学模型，通过对数学模型的求解可以获得相应实际问题的解决方案，或对该问题的更深入了解[5]。大学数学的教学应结合数学建模的思想，给数学知识和数学的应用搭起桥梁。教师在给低年级学生传授数学知识的同时，就应授以数学建模思想，将数学建模带入基础数学的教学课堂，把数学与实际问题结合起来，使大多数学生在进入大学时就受到数学建模思想与方法的熏陶，领略数学的用武之地。同时也培养学生的创新兴趣和创新意识，激发学生应用数学理论与方法解决实际问题的激情。从而提高大学数学的教学效果和学生应用数学的能力，促进大学数学教学改革。

数学建模对初次接触它的学生来说，是一个新鲜事物，对其认识是肤浅和模糊的，特别是对非数学专业的学生尤其如此[6]。为提高数学建模课程的影响，扩大学生受益面，必须要做进一步的推广工作，激发广大学生的学习兴趣。可从如下三方面开展工作：

(1) 组建数学建模协会，通过学生社团介绍一些数学建模的基本知识和基本素材，进行初步的模型探讨，来感知数学建模的思想与方法，提升他们的兴趣，同时带动更多的学生，特别是非数学专业的学生参与到这项活动中来。

(2) 组织全校性的报告会，邀请校外专家和校内有经验的指导教师做全校性的数学建模报告，报告内容通常选取浅显的、不需要太深数学知识，同时又是社会关心的热点或有趣的问题。

(3) 通过其他各种渠道大力宣传数学建模，鼓励优秀学生参加数学建模活动。

上述活动的开展，推广了数学建模知识，体现了数学建模的意义，提高了学生的数学学习兴趣。

2.2 课程建设与教学模式改革

“数学建模”课程的开设，对大学生和数学教师综合素质的提高，以及数学课程的教学改革和研究都具有重要的意义。

现代工程技术人员所面临的都是实际问题，而非某种简化或抽象的数学形式[7]。学生及工程技术人员通常所处的困境是不能顺利地将以原始形式出现的实际问题转化为他们所熟悉的数学形式或数学模型。这正暴露了传统大学数学教学的一个严重薄弱环节。数学模型是实际课题、数学知识与计算机之间的桥梁。我们在数学建模教学中逐步摸索出了一套“多轨并行”的教学模式，从多轨上，我们将数学知识的学习与计算机教学通过案例分析有机地结合起来组织教学。而各种案例多数是数学与其他专业知识的交叉，具有很强的实际背景。其特点如下：

(1) 数学建模教学是数学知识与应用能力共同提高的最佳结合点。它有助于克服传统数学教学中知识与能力脱节的弊端。数学建模课程具有系统性强、联系实际的领域宽阔、实际案例的分析占有较大比重的特点。培养的学生来自几十个专业。在组织教学中，我们注意诱导学生应用数学的意识、兴趣和能力，这对提高学生运用数学知识与计算机解决问题的能力起到了积极作用。

(2) 在数学建模教学中及时引入新的数学方法和工具,如定性与定量相结合的层次分析法、统计法,还有能够处理非结构化问题的模糊数学和神经网络方法及数学软件包等。同时,我们还注意培养学生自我开拓的能力,使学生有效地接受不断涌现的新概念、新思想和新方法。

(3) 组织"综合训练"教学,实际上是向学生施行一项科研工作的模拟"飞行"训练,它也是学生毕业设计的重要补充[8]。如教师准备实际课件,学生要经过查阅资料、分析并合理假设、多方案选择建立模型,数值计算(使用软件包及编制程序)、检验并推广、撰写论文、排版打印等研究过程,从而使学生应具备的应用数学知识能力、用计算机处理计算的能力、系统思维能力与实践能力在"实战"中得以锻炼和提高。

(4) 认真贯彻国家教委提出的"重在参与,重在普及"的精神,组织校内竞赛,其目的是让更多的学生参与数模学习、参与竞争,亲身体验"一次参赛,终生受益"的效果,让学生普遍得到综合素质的提高。组织全国竞赛,有利于培养学生快速反应能力、创造性思维及竞争意识。

2.3 数学建模培训的实施

数学建模培训的目标是增强学生知识应用的能力,达到应用数学方法来解决实际问题,并让学生能够更好地参加全国数学建模竞赛。参培学生一般都具有一定的数学基础(学过"线性代数"、"高等数学"等课程),参加过"数学建模"课程的学习。培训主要根据数学学科的特点和数学建模要达到的能力目标,通过开设一些专题讲座,有针对性地提高学生应用数学知识解决实际问题的能力。

1. 数学建模培训的目标

经过多年的实践和探索,我们发现,学生通过参与数学建模培训[9],必须使自己具备如下几个方面的能力:

(1) 对数学学科有一个宏观的认识,了解数学学科特点和相关学科分类,一定程度上提高数学修养,提升宏观驾驭和应用数学的能力。

(2) 针对不同问题的背景,能够挖掘出问题的数学本质,能将实际问题转化为用数学语言和数学符号来描述(模型建立);能用已有的数学知识求解数学模型(模型求解);并能对求解后的模型结果进行实际解释和反馈(模型检验)。

(3) 具有较强的自学、领悟以及查阅和搜集资料的能力,在培训中要让学生具备通过自学和查阅资料来解决问题的能力。

(4) 数学建模过程是一个团队的集体行为,要求学生具有良好的心理素质和团队协作精神。

(5) 掌握常用数学软件(Matlab, Maple, Mathematica, Lingo 等)的使用技巧,并能熟练使用网络资料。

(6) 通过培训,提高自己的科技论文写作水平,达到数学建模的论文写作要求。

2. 数学建模培训体系的设计

紧密结合数学建模应具备的能力和培训目标,在培训过程中,采用有针对性的专题来提高学生各方面的能力[10]。通常培训分 3 个阶段进行专题训练。

(1) 对数学的学科分类、专业划分、课程设置、专业特点等问题进行泛讲,提高自身数学修养和宏观驾驭能力;介绍应用计算机网络资源查询文献和资料搜集的方法,让学生熟悉几个常用电子文献库的使用方法;介绍常用数学工具软件的功能、使用方法和编程技巧,让学生会熟练使用1～2个常用数学软件；介绍一些常见的数据分析和处理的方法，如：回归分析、相关分析、聚类分析、数据插值和拟合等，提高他们依据实际问题提取和分析处理数据的能力。并且在后续的专题选讲和模型培训过程中，结合具体内容将该过程不断加强和完善。

(2) 数学建模竞赛一般都是按连续和离散两个大的方向来设置两道赛题，在培训的过程中也应依据连续和离散两个大方向进行相关内容的专题知识讲座。

连续方向的赛题通常是用微分方程的方法来求解。相应的知识有：三类常见数学物理方程及其数值解法、微分方程的定性和稳定性理论、积分和微分的数值计算方法、排队论、对策论等。

离散方向的赛题主要是从运筹与优化的角度来考查。相应的知识有：组合数学、运筹学、图论、人工神经网络、遗传算法、层次分析法、计算机模拟等。

两大方向建模知识的讲解应结合具体的模型进行，连续问题可通过传染病模型、人口增长模型、位置定位模型等来讲解；离散方向可通过图论和网络流模型、优化选址问题模型、线性规划模型、多目标优化问题模型等来讲解。具体的例子可结合历年的竞赛题，讲解题目的整个建模与求解过程，使学生了解数学建模的问题分析、模型假设、模型建立、模型求解和模型检验过程。

当然两个方向的模型也不是孤立的，有的是相互交叉的复杂问题，所以最后也要对一些综合性的交叉问题进行分析和讨论。通过以上的培训学习，使学生从知识结构上达到建立模型和模型求解的能力要求。

(3) 最后阶段要进行两到三次模拟竞赛和实战训练，并完成最后参赛队伍的选拔。将培训学生按三人分组，选定一个模拟题目，安全按照数学建模竞赛的要求，在3天的时间里完成问题分析、模型建立和求解、论文写作等环节。每次模拟竞赛后，各位指导教师应针对各组存在的问题进行指导，提高他们分析和解决问题、建立数学模型的能力以及创新思维能力。同时，通过实战的磨合，培养和形成良好的心理素质和协作、协调能力以及科技论文写作能力。

数学建模和数学建模培训是一个长效的、繁杂的系统过程，在这期间不仅要对参训学生进行知识的传授，而且还要使学生在多方面的能力和素质得到培养和提高。

3 结束语

社会转型期需要大量基础扎实、专业技能过硬的应用型科学技术人才，在大学数学教学中开展“数学建模”课程建设和数学建模竞赛活动，有利于培养学生的学习能力、实践能力和创新精神，促进大学数学的教学与改革，增强学生应用已有知识解决实际问题的能力，提高毕业生就业竞争力。可为转型后社会提供大量的应用型科学技术人才储备，是一项值得开展、有意义的活动，是促进素质教育工作进一步推进，提升高等院校的数学教学质量的必备途径。

参考文献

[1] 李帅军. 社会转型时期教师创造素质的内涵与培养[J]. 教育理论与实践，1999(1)：19-22.

[2] 黄伟祥，刘雄. 数学建模对数学教学的促进作用[J]. 广东水利电力职业技术学院学报，2007(3).

[3] 姜启源. 数学模型[M]. 3版. 北京：高等教育出版社，2003.

[4] 胡菊华,方桂英.开展数学建模教学活动与大学数学教育改革[J].江西农业大学学报,2002(4).

[5] 张硕.论大学开展数学建模教育[J].数学的实践与认识,2002,32(1).

[6] 杨宁,袁俭,杨晗.大学生数学建模的教学组织和培训初探[J].西南交通大学学报,2004,5(2).

[7] 任善强,刘琼荪,龚劬,等.以数学建模教学为突破口,促进工科数学教学改革[J].工科数学,1998,14(2).

[8] 石玉强.大学生数学建模竞赛的教学组织和培训[J].琼州大学学报,2005,12(2).

[9] 王茂芝,徐文哲,郭科.数学建模培训课程体系设计探讨[J].数学教育学报,2005,14(1).

[10] 孙玉莉.数学建模与学生数学素质的培养[J].边疆经济与文化,2008,54(6).

社会转型时期高校计算机教学思路的探究

黎永壹*

（钦州学院，广西 钦州 535000）

摘　要：社会转型的到来对高校计算机教学提出了新的要求，使得高校计算机教育面临许多新问题。本文从社会转型对计算机人才培养的影响入手，分析目前高校计算机教学中存在的部分现象，根据信息时代的要求，从高校实际出发，本文重点提出了计算机教学思路在培养体系、专业课程设置、教学方法、考核方式和教师培养等方面的改革中要注意的几个关键问题，并给出了部分可行性实施方案。

关键词：社会转型；计算机教学；高校

Study on College and University Computer Teaching in the Period of Social Transition

Li Yong-yi

(Qinzhou College, Qinzhou 535000, China)

Abstract: Social transition in China has now posed many new problems and requirements for computer teaching in colleges and universities. This paper starts with the impacts that social transition brings about towards computer teaching, and then analyses the problems that currently exisits in college and university computer teaching. Based on the requirments of the information age and the reality of colleges and universities, this paper focuses on the reform of computer teaching concerning the following aspects: training system, development of curriculum, teaching methods, acessment, and teacher's training, and finally provides feasible plans for implementation.

Key words: social transition; computer teaching; colleges and universities

---

* 黎永壹，钦州学院数计系讲师。

0 引言

我国当前的社会转型是社会经济、政治、文化结构分化重组；递升跃迁的历史运动；是整个社会由僵滞走向变革、由封闭走向开放、由落后走向文明的现代化过程。在这场空前的社会变革过程中，新旧体制胶着、利益分化、价值取向多元、文化碰撞等各种矛盾日益凸现出来，并导致人们的生存意识转化，从过去取向转向未来取向，从稳定取向转向发展取向；从趋同取向转向多元自主取向，[1]这些转变对高校计算机教学提出了新的要求。

1 社会转型对计算机人才培养的影响

计算机人才培养是社会专业体系的重要组成部分，也是推动专业发展与专业化进程的基本手段。在全面建设小康社会的进程中，计算机人才培养遵循需求回应原则、专业化原则、素质教育原则[2]。

1.1 需求回应原则和经济全球化与教育国际化确定计算机人才的培养目标

社会需求作为人才培养的出发点和落脚点，要适应转型时期中国社会的不同需求，就要发展不同层次的专业教育，培养不同类型的人才，而计算机人才培养目标则随着经济发展和市场需求而变化，计算机方面的人才可分为三个层次：高层次指创造型、研发型人才，主要从事基础理论研究、系统软硬件开发、协议研发和高等教育等工作；低层次指技艺型人才，主要从事技术层次较低的规程化操作岗位等工作，需要掌握计算机基础知识及一个或几个工种的操作技艺；中层次是指应用型和技术型人才，具有扎实的基础知识，理论较全面，同时具有较强的实践能力。高校计算机教育人才培养要针对不同层次的市场需求，相应调整人才培养结构，主要以初级实用型人才培养为基础，为高级人才的培养输送资源，以中层次专业技术人才培养为主要目标。

1.2 专业化原则和科技信息网络化与学校教育教学的现代化决定计算机人才类型

计算机科学的研究是结合基础学科体现专业能力的过程，计算机科学与技术是对逻辑能力的应用，是理论和实践的结合体，体现了计算机的专业性；而作为现代科技信息的载体，计算机在政治、经济、军事、文化和教育等领域起到了重要的作用，而社会转型导致这些领域结构逐渐复杂，多元化日益明显，这就决定了我们培养理论结合实践的实用型计算机人才、培养具有扎实的基础知识和自学能力的可持续发展的计算机人才。

1.3 素质教育原则和社会文化价值多元化决定计算机人才培养的规模

社会各领域的分化重组交错复杂，服务于这些领域，计算机已经成为了社会的不可分割的一部分，因此计算机水平也是社会发展的综合体现。计算机专业人才培养的主要任务是为教育、医疗、司法、社会救助、社会管理、社会福利、基层社区等众多机构和领域培养和输送应用型专门人才，这就更加突出了计算机教学对综合素质教育的重要性，所以，要实现素质教育和提高社会的综合实力就必须不断扩大计算机人才的培养规模，全面发展计算机教育，不断加快社会信息化、数字化的进程。

2 高校计算机教学中存在的问题

2.1 传统教学模式影响计算机教学效果

传统的教学模式是以“教”为主，特点是教师灌输知识，学生被动机械地接受知识，书中文字与教师的讲解几乎完全一致，学生对答与书本或教师的讲解一致，学生是靠机械的重复进行学习。这种模式忽视了学生在学习中的主体性，片面强调灌输方式，在不同程度上压抑和阻碍了学生的个性发展，不能培养学生的扩散思维能力和创新能力。网络与信息技术的发展，使得新知识、新信息、新技术层出不穷，社会需要学习型、创新型、开放型的人才，所以传统教学模式在计算机教学和人才培养中不能起到良好的效果。由于计算机技术发展日新月异，计算机应用日益广泛，给高校计算机基础教育工作带来了机遇和挑战。

2.2 教学方案和人才培养模式单一

长期以来单一的教学方案和人才培养模式使计算机人才培养没有特色，近年来计算机专业在规模上蓬勃发展，给更多的学子创造了接受高等教育的机会，为社会输送了大批专业人才；但同时也存在着专业特色不明显以及教育质量需要提高等问题。随着计算机技术的进步与普及，“会计算机”已经不再是计算机专业学生独有的优势。在这种现实下，更需要调整培养规格和要求，使计算机专业的学生能有相对优势的知识结构。目前国内高校的教学内容都是由国家教学大纲来制定，应该说还是带有很强的计划经济的色彩。大学或学院要创办出自己的特色，就应当由学校制定自己的教学大纲，由教授制定授课的内容。教学大纲定死了，就不容易创办出自己的特色来。在课程设置上，必须紧密结合市场的经济需求，克服脱离实际的现象，同时还要避免因迎合市场而盲目追求最新的理论。

2.3 计算机教学改革不能与知识、人才需求等方面的变化同步

在目前计算机人才培养的过程中，师资力量缺乏成为比较普遍的现象。沿用着从多年前的“经验之谈”而沉淀下来的教材，内容的更新跟不上技术应用的进步。在实践环节方面，一直以来很多高校做得不够，达不到人才培养目标的要求，与用人单位要求差距较大。通常表现在学生专业实践的机会偏少，实践动手能力较差。

3 社会转型时期，随着经济、文化等多元化的转变，计算机教学的思路也应随之在培养体系、专业课程设置、教学方法、考核方式和教师培养等方面发生变化

3.1 培养体系的变化

改变当前以课程教学作为学生培养的主要形式，而赋予具体实践内容更大的比重，如给予实习环节更多的学分，使得学生扩展获取知识的方式。可以考虑采用的方法，一是协助和鼓励学生更多参与同学科相关的实习工作；二是教师在从事应用科研项目的过程中，可以安排本科学生进行参与；三是学校设立专门应用科研项目，面向本科学生进行招标，学生形成团队共同完成。

3.2 专业课程设置的变化

为了针对用人单位的需求，高校计算机专业课程设置可以包含几种类型：基础类课程。主

要包括两个方面：一是人文社科基础课，主要包括政治、英语等高校各专业均开设的人文类课程；二是为学习之后的专业课程而奠定的自然科学基础课，包括数学、物理学等方面的课程。专业核心课程，是指计算机专业的基础类课程，包括电路理论、模拟电子、数字逻辑、数据结构、计算机组成原理、操作系统等方面的课程；应用类型的课程，指用人单位实际需要计算机专业的学生掌握的技能，该课程可以根据当前用人单位的需求，划分为不同的大的类别，供计算机专业的学生根据自身的特点和今后愿意从事的发展方向，而进行自行的选择，如可将应用类型的课划分为基础理论深化、软件工程、控制与检测、计算机网络等不同的方向。以计算机网络为例，可以开设的课程包括 WEB 程序设计、分布式数据库、网络数据库编程、Internet 原理及应用等课程。交叉类课程，指计算机专业具体在某些行业当中应用的交叉类课程，例如讲授信息技术如何在金融行业中进行具体应用等类似的课程，根据不同的行业，将课程划分为不同的大类，以选修课的形式，供学生自我选择。讲座和其他选修课，请专家或学校老师自行开发，包括计算机的前沿方面的课程或者人文类的课程，学生可以自由选择，目的是开阔视野，提高修养。外部课程，由外部其他教育机构，如培训班和高校，提供更多的课程，学校将外部课程纳入自身的课程体系当中，即允许学生参加外部课程，经过审核，可以代替内部课程或冲抵学分。课堂内容的改变，更多采用实践内容。意味着课堂教学，特别是专业课程的学习中，讲授更多理论的具体运用，这需要教师不仅仅关注二手的实践资料，同时也要亲身实践。计算机专业和高校在开展好常规的教学之外，应开展各种类型的课外活动，如各种形式的校内竞赛等，并且组织各种学生社团，通过开展课外活动和学生社团的形式，培养学生各方面的综合能力。

3.3 教学方法的变化

首先，根据专业课程的变化，为各种类型的专业课程制定合理的教学大纲、教学目标。在构建教学计划时，应根据办学的层次、人才培养规格及学生的实际，详细设计和整合内容。在构建培养方案和培养计划时，应借鉴计算机发展较快国家的教育经验，根据自身办学层次、人才培养规格及学生实际进行课程体系、内容设计上的创新。特别要注重计算机专业课程和学校其他特色学科的结合，合理选用教材、规划培养目标，由此确定教学任务。比如海洋类专业是我院的特色专业，计算机网络类、数据库类等课程都与之关联，明确这些课程教学大纲和培养目标至关重要。

其次，将多媒体教室教学和网络教学相结合，一方面，利用多媒体教室给学生指明学习思路，学生访问"计算机文化基础"网站开展网上学习和网上讨论；另一方面，利用多媒体教室讲授课程可以弥补网络学习的不足，帮助学生掌握不容易理解的操作和知识。把教师的课堂讲解、演示和学生的自学、互学相结合，把学生的听课、完成作业和搞好课程设计相结合，扬长避短，达到"双赢"。而这二者之间联系的纽带就是上机实践，真正地将学到的知识变成实践中的能力。

再次，要改变传统的教学模式，将任务驱动和项目教学法相结合。项目教学法是一种教和学的模式，它集中关注于某一学科的中心概念和原则，旨在把学生融入有意义的任务完成的过程中，让学生积极地学习、自主地进行知识的建构，以现实的学生生成的知识和培养起来的能力为最高成就目标。项目学习可以成为概念的教与学所赖以存在的中心环节，而不仅仅是在努力学习过程之后进行的一种辅助性的充实。项目教学法是符合建构主义理论促进学生全面发展的科学教学方法。基于建构主义的教学法要求，在学习过程中，要以学生为中心，教师应起帮助者角色，利用情景、协作、会话等学习环境要素，充分发挥学生的主体性和创新精神，使学生有效地达到对当前所学知识的意义建构。[4]

3.4 考核方式的变化

计算机考试应该采用笔试考试与实践考试相结合的方式,注重考察学生的实际应用能力,解决问题能力和创新能力。实践考试应根据教材内容、实际环境,合理安排实践操作测试内容,可以结合课程设计、分组实验等多种形式组织学生动手操作,考察学生的实践操作能力。要将笔试考试和实践考试两部分成绩合并作为期末成绩,这样就调动了学生平时的学习和实践积极性。

3.5 教师培养的变化

计算机技术的更新速度是任何其他一门学科所没有的,这就要求从事计算机教学的教师自身须不断努力学习,进行继续教育,并且这是一项长期而必需的任务。计算机专业教师应该是既有教学经验,又具有从事软件项目研发、管理的产业背景、并掌握 IT 关键技术的人员,要让计算机教师及时掌握新技术,密切关注学生最感兴趣的内容,积极正面引导学生,防止网络中的不良因素对学生的负面影响。教师要在教学中发挥高效的主导作用,使学生能充分发挥学习的主动性。要重视专业教师的实际 IT 研发能力及工程素养的培养,重视开发软件的研究与实践。可以让教师脱产到 IT 企业工作一段时间,以了解 IT 行业的最新技术并将其带到教学中来。高校要大力推动和扶植学校创新成果的商品化、产业化,鼓励高校教师把产学研结合起来,这样既可以提高教师的科研水平,又可让学生直接参与实际的工程项目。此外,高等院校可聘用软件生产企业中具有教学能力的科技人员来校执教。

3.6 其他方面

社会转型时期,为适应社会多元化发展,除了注重计算机专业教学的变化,还应加强培养学生的批判精神、创新意识和协助能力。在教学实践中以爱心和高度的教学责任感培养教学敏感和教学机智,开动脑筋,集思广益,积极实践,及时发现问题和解决问题,不断总结和交流经验教训,促使感性认识向理性认识发展。教师还应致力于研究如何培养学生良好的道德品质与人格魅力。要不断完善自己的言行举止,严格要求,以身作则,以良好的品行影响和带动学生,从而以自己独具的人格魅力吸引学生,使学生乐于仿效。同时,用心观察学生的微小进步,将及时的正面激励与适当的点拨有机结合,使道德内化为学生主动和经常性的行为,使学生在知、行、意、信的相得益彰中走向道德自律,实现道德内化。坚持"教书育人"理念,实现真正的素质教育。

4 小结

本文首先介绍了社会转型的概念;根据人才培养的需求回应原则、专业化原则和素质教育原则阐述了社会转型对计算机人才培养的影响;针对目前高校计算机教学中存在的部分现象,分析其原因,本文认为计算机教学思路应该在培养体系、专业课程设置、教学方法、考核方式和教师培养等方面随着社会转型而转变,从我校实际出发,给出了部分可行性实施方案。在社会转型的环境下,探究计算机教学改革对发展计算机技术和素质教育具有促进作用,但是计算机教学思路的转变还需要更多的关注、分析、论证和实践。

参 考 文 献

[1] 范国睿.从时代需求到战略抉择:社会转型期的学校变革[J].教育发展研究,2008(1).

[2] 杨贵华,王瑞华.社会转型中的社会工作专业人才培养问题研究[J].集美大学学报,2006(04).

[3] 陈道蓄.社会需求与计算机专业的学科建设[J].计算机教育,2004(2):8-9.

[4] 蒋宗礼,王志英,李晓明,等.构建计算机科学与技术专业公共核心课程[J].中国大学教学,2007(11).

[5] 李锦.高等院校计算机教育现状与改革[J].大连教育学院学报,2007(01).

社会转型期成人教育的研究与发展

唐国丽*

（钦州学院，广西 钦州 535000）

摘 要：我国目前面临着前所未有的社会变革，成人教育在这社会转型期中也面临前所未有的发展挑战，存在无限的发展空间：1. 非学历教育和学历教育应均衡发展；2. 成人教育可为农村社会转型和劳动力转移服务；3. 向多元结构的城市社会成员延伸，提升建设者创业能力。成人教育要向开放式、服务型、多样化转变，以求更大的发展。

关键词：社会转型；成人教育；发展；研究

Study and Development of Adult Education in Social Transitional Period

Tang Guo-li

（Qinzhou university，Qinzhou 535000，China）

Abstract：Adult education has been faced with unprecedented challenges in the social transition period and possesses unlimited developing space since we have met with unprecedented social reform：1. non-degree education and academic education should be a balanced development；2. adult education can serve rural social transformation and labor force transfer；3. adult education should expand to city members of pluralistic structure to enhance builders entrepreneurial capacity and change to be open，service-oriented and diversified to further development.

Key words：social transition；adult education；development；study

* 唐国丽，钦州学院成人教育学院教师。

一、社会转型与成人教育

1. 社会转型的特征

在中国,"转型"概念是1992年以后开始流行的。我国目前正面临着前所未有的社会发展进程中社会系统的整体性变革,由传统的、整合型社会向现代的、分化型社会转变。具体表现为:从计划经济向社会主义市场经济、从农业社会向工业社会、从乡村社会向城镇社会、从封闭半封闭社会向开放社会、从同质的单一社会向异质的多样社会、从伦理社会向法理社会的转型。转型的具体表象也不再是以阶级斗争为主线的社会形态变更,而是随着社会主义市场经济体制的确立和不断完善,以经济管理形态变迁为主导的社会体制与机制转变,即由农业化社会向工业化社会转变,由计划经济社会向市场经济社会转型。从这个视野上看,"三大转变"是其最明显的特征:一是就业结构转变;二是城乡结构转变;三是社会阶层结构转变。

2. 成人教育的价值

教育是关乎国计民生和未来发展的大事,为经济社会转型计,为民族的未来发展计,我国成人教育都应该有革命性的变革。成人教育本质上是经济社会变革的产物。成人教育价值在整体上表现为,在社会转型的过程中,作为与社会经济发展联系最为紧密的教育类型,将积极回应社会转型的需求,审时度势、加快实现教育体制与管理机制的转变,卓有成效地发挥教育的先导性、基础性、战略性作用,推动教育转轨与社会转型的同步发展。成人教育价值在具体形态上表现为,顺应社会转型的历史潮流,建立以市场引导为主、政府宏观调控为辅的管理体制和运行机制,"以人为本",充分发挥社会公益职能,以培养造就一代社会新人为己任,以开展持续不断、有的放矢、卓有成效的社会教育服务为平台,加快推进"人"的不同群体与个体社会位置、角色、环境的转变,为社会转型提供源源不断的人才与人力资源支撑。目前,随着"三农"问题逐渐凸显,"新农村建设"逐步成为党和国家工作的重要内容,成人教育发展问题成为新时期建设的一个不容忽视的部分。新时期,面对社会的结构性转型与发展,成人教育应如何发展,成人教育如何发挥其在社会经济发展中的作用等相关问题逐渐成为学者们研究的关注点。为了适应当前这种社会转型,成人教育面临前所未有的发展挑战,也存在无限的发展空间。

二、成人教育在社会转型期的发展

1. 非学历教育和学历教育应均衡发展[1]

社会转型必然促使成人教育的功能发生转变。在剧烈的社会转型过程中,在今后一段时期内,成人教育仍然要依靠学历教育与非学历教育来求得发展,其教育的重点应该逐渐转向非学历教育。在1987年国务院转批的《国家教育委员会关于改革和发展成人教育的决定》中明确指出,"成人教育是我国教育的重要组成部分,在整体教育事业中,它与基础教育、职业教育、普通高等教育同等重要。"但在成人教育办学实践中,并没有真正作为一种新型教育形式推向社会,只是作为普通高等教育的一种补充形式,成为政府对受文革影响而耽误了高等教育的一代人所进行的学历补偿,尽管成人教育举办了函授、夜大学、业余制、全日制脱产等多种办学形式,但始终没有摆脱"知识补课、学历补偿教育"的窠臼。当高等教育进入大众化阶段以后,成人教育更多承载着继续教育、终身教育的使命,以及为产业结构调整,社会成员合理流动服务的功能。当今世界科学技术突飞猛进，人们必须不断地学习新知识，才能适应工作的需要。同时随着生活水平的不断改善，人们为了提高生活质量，学习各种知识的愿望也越来越强烈，学历提升已不再是学习的唯一目的。社会对各类技能培训的需求呈现出日益增长的趋势，成人教育以学历教育为主的格局在动摇。毋庸置疑，成人教育中学历和非学历教育均衡发展的趋势是客观的，成人教育只有适应客观发展的需要，学历和非学历教育均衡发展，实现教育功能创新，才能富有活力和生命力。总之，社会发展要求成人教育对原有的制度体系和运行模式进行调整和创新，以提供更系统、更到位的服务和贡献。当然，成人教育自身也将在这一过程中获得更为广阔的发展空间。

2. 成人教育可为农村社会转型和劳动力转移服务

目前我国乡村社会向城镇社会转变，城乡结构在发生着翻天覆地的转变。我国改革开放三十多年的实践表明，城市的发展需要大量的劳动力，大量的农民工已进入城市打工。但应该看到，这些农村劳动力的素质并非全是城市经济发展所需要的有知识、有技能的劳动力，大量的劳动力流入城市，有的由于找不到合适的工作又流回到农村，即便是留在城市也只是从事一些简单的技术含量低的工作。这些农村富余劳动力的转移并没有与城市实现产业的对接。结果是，一方面城市经济发展需要大量的有知识、有技能的劳动力；另一方面农村中却积压着大量的富余劳动力。随着社会科学技术的发展，原始的农业生产方式已经不能够满足农业科技化和农村工业化的社会发展需求，普通教育的唯一途径也同样不能够满足农村对于技术人才的需要。另外，随着近些年农村外出打工人员逐年增多，打工收入成为农民增收的一条重要途径。但伴随着社会生产方式的转变，社会对劳动力的需求开始逐渐从体力型劳动力向技术型劳动力转变，纯体力劳动已经不能够满足现代社会对劳动力的需要。有研究者指出，“农民工受教育的时间越长，他们的收入水平就越高，同时，那些在近五年内接受过培训的农民工比没有接受过培训的人的收入也要明显高出不少。”[2]因此，通过职业技术培训提高劳动力的文化知识技能、技术水平成为外出打工人员拓宽出路的迫切需要。农村社会的持续发展同样需要建立与普通教育相协调的农村职业教育、成人教育体系。为进城务工的农民提供岗位培训，提高他们的知识水平、专业技能和安全生产知识，让他们适应新的岗位，脱离贫困，逐渐达到小康生活水平。为其配置充分的教育资源，是成人教育面临的重要课题。

3. 向多元结构的城市社会成员延伸，提升建设者创业能力

城市社会成员在社会阶层之间的流动和分类最为活跃和剧烈。随着城市化进程的推进，大量农村和欠发达地区劳动人口涌入发达地区城市，城市新的建设者的加入，使社会阶层的发育出现许多新的变数。社会学研究对新的中间阶层作了划分和界定。他们大多是从劳动大军中分化出来的，包括工人阶级中的一部分，如高级技术人员等。不管出现什么变数，在城市中开展成人教育、继续教育等，对社会成员在阶层中的流动，一定能起到向上推动的作用。以吉登斯为代表的英国学者探讨了市场培育中的“封闭过程结构化”现象，指出：在“高阶层成员对低阶层成员的排斥手段中，生产资料所有权、教育与技术方面的资格证书和体力劳动的力量等都是中介型结构化的进入壁垒”。[3]向大多数社会成员提供成人教育资源，是成人教育机构的重要职能。而成人教育、各级各类的培训都将为大多数成员提供专业技术教育以及各专业的资格证书等，为进入新的职业领域提供“教育准入”，从而为社会弱势群体成员处境的改善提供平等的机会，鼓励社会成员“往高处走”，使社会阶层结构运动在中间阶层增多或两极化两者间选择前者，最终对“橄榄型”社会结构进行塑造和维护。

三、成人教育的转型

在我国全面建设小康社会时期,我国的成人教育机构必须转型,必须从传统型组织向学习型组织转变。学习型组织的特点是开放式、服务型、多样化。[4]

1. 开放式

我国从封闭半封闭社会向开放社会的转型必然彰显于成人教育的发展之中,这种彰显集中为成人教育应追求其发展的开放性。具体说来,首先,成人教育应以培养开放型人才为目标指向。其次,成人教育应向开放性模式发展,即成人教育应在办学体制、管理体制、教育对象方面改变,允许社会团体、其他社会组织及个人依法举办各种形式的成人教育。同时,我国成人教育应适度向境外开放,允许外籍团体或个人来我国投资办学、提供教育服务。此外,我国成人教育也可以拓展国外服务市场,在境外设立成人教育办学机构,开展成人教育培训等。在管理体制上,表现为我国进一步下放权利,赋予学校、企业、社区等更多的办学自主权。成人教育对象的开放是指成人教育应向全社会的成人开放,而不应在年龄、职业等方面做出种种限制,尤其是要保障残疾人等弱势群体受教育的基本权利。需要指出的是,教育对象的开放还指允许境外来华人员接受成人教育。最后,成人教育亦应注重形式上的开放性。例如,通过广播电视、网络等多种手段教学,以让更多的人更方便地接受教育。我们可以作这样的归纳:学习型社会的基本特征是"开放性"。[5]这个开放性是全方位的,一是向全社会开放;二是向国际开放。

2. 服务型

成人高等教育机构的基本任务不应该是学历教育和文凭教育,它的基本任务应是为社会承担教育服务,但自 20 世纪 80 年代以来,我国的成人高等教育主要是学历教育、文凭教育,生源的主体是应届高中毕业生。当前,我国成人高等教育机构应当把"服务"作为自己的核心办学理念之一。一是为社区服务,学校要自觉纳人社区经济、文化建设和社会进步中去,主动为社区服务,在服务中找到发挥自己优势的阵地。在服务中使学生增知识、长才干,有利于推动教学改革。二是为学习者服务,我们应当提出这样一个口号:"为学习者服务"。学习者是学习型社会的主体。要构建学习型社会,首要的一条就是要树立一切为了学习者的观念。[6]在当代,人们越来越清晰地认识到,无论你是文化程度不高的打工者,还是受过高等教育的白领阶层,如果没有不断学习和接受新知识的意识和行动,不能及时与迅速发展的社会相适应,都会被"时代列车"抛弃,因为,优胜劣汰的竞争法则对任何人都是无情的。人们需要不断地学习,而且这种学习是以自我为中心的,是高度自我主导的。以前是学校选择学生,学校占据主动。以后将是学习者选择学校,学习者占据主动。学习者将选择适合他需要的、能提供令他满意的教育服务的学校。我们的成人高等教育机构应当清楚地认识这种主客体的变化与换位。为学习者服务,就要以学习者为中心,为他们提供各种形式的教育服务,让他们通过不同形式的学习,不断获取新知识和新技能,不断改善心智模式,提高自身素质,适应生存需要,提高生活质量,实现人生价值。

3. 异质、多样性

在整个社会从同质、单一向异质、多样转型的过程中,成人教育也应寻求其异质、多样的发展态势。其一,成人教育应充分发挥其个体和社会功能,引导成人认同并适应这种异质、多样的社会生活,同时促进社会的多样化发展。比如,基于当前我国社会职业阶层的多样化,成人教育应有针对性地对不同职业阶层尤其是新兴职业阶层的成人开展教育培训。其二，成人教育应进一步向多层次、多序列、多形式发展。具体而言，在层次上，成人教育应包括成人扫盲教育、成人初等教育、成人中等教育、成人高等教育及大学后继续教育等文化层次，也应包括青壮年教育、中年人教育以及老年人教育等年龄层次上的全面多样。多序列主要包括：按教育对象的职业划分，成人教育应包括职工教育、农民教育、干部教育以及专业技术人员教育等方面；按功能划分，既包括岗位培训、职业资格证书教育等职业教育系统，也包括社会文化教育、休闲娱乐教育等非职业教育系统。成人教育的多形式发展是指成人教育从组织上应兼及函授教育、自学考试、广播电视以及回归教育等类型，从时间上则应全面包括脱产、半脱产、全业余等形式。一切以满足学习者需要为依归，只要是符合学习者需要的，对构建学习型社会有利的，就应当促其发展。这就是多样化理念。还有的就是办学主体的多样化。构建学习型社会，国家办学的高等教育机构应当发挥重要作用，但社会力量办学，还有私人办学对于构建学习型社会的贡献一样是不容置疑的。

在社会转型期中成人教育要求发展就要适应时代变化实施变革，才能在转型中使自身得到长足的发展。总之，社会发展要求成人教育对原有的制度体系和运行模式进行调整和创新，以提供更系统、更到位的服务和贡献。当然，成人教育自身也将在这一过程中获得更为广阔的发展空间。

参考文献

[1] 王亚敏. 论我国社会转型与成人教育功能创新[J]. 中国成人教育，2005(10).

[2] 王奋宇，赵延东. 流动民工的经济地位获得及决定因素[M]//李培林. 农民工：中国进城农民工的经济社会分析. 北京：社会科学文献出版社，2003：142.

[3] [澳]马尔可姆·沃特斯. 现代社会学理论[M]. 杨善华，等，译. 北京：华夏出版社，2000.

[4] 赵卿敏，易元祥. 学习型社会创建与成人高等教育发展转型[J]. 当代教育论坛，2004(9).

[5] 厉以宁. 社区教育·终身教育·学习社会[J]. 中国成人教育，2001(11)：5-7.

[6] 梁耀，李纶，刘智国. 成人教育在社会转型中面临的问题[J]. 中外企业家，2007(8).

中等程度英语学习者作文错误的简要分析及其对英语教学的启示

李祖君*

（钦州学院，广西 钦州 535000）

摘　要：错误是二语习得过程中无法避免的现象。错误分析则是改进二语的教、学以及二语习得研究的重要工具。基于对错误分析理论中前人研究成果的概括与归纳，本文进行了实证性的实验。此项研究遵循 Corder(1974)提出的错误分析步骤，但除去第五步，错误评估。研究发现，总体来看，中国中等程度英语学习者写作中所犯的错误主要来源于语际迁移和语内迁移的影响，而且语内迁移错误的比例大于语际迁移错误。最后，本文分析了对英语教学的启示，并尝试性地提出了意在减少犯错，改进英语教和学的建议和对策。

关键词：错误；错误分析；语内迁移错误；语际迁移错误

1　Introduction

1.1　Background of the Study

In the process of learning English, the learner inevitably makes various errors. Before 1960s, when the behaviouristic viewpoint of language learning was prevailing, learner errors were considered something undesirable and to be avoided, as errors were considered to be a wrong response to the stimulus, which should be corrected immediately after they were made. Unless corrected properly, the error became a habit and a wrong behavioural pattern would stick in learner's mind.

It was not until the late 1960s that people came to realize the importance of the errors made by a foreign language (FL) learner. Actually, an FL learner's errors tell us more than when he/she produces correct, error-free utterances. As soon as an error is made, we can look at its nature and try to work out why it was made. It is rather like the pain that may tell the doctor more than all the parts that do not hurt.

In the history of SLA research, Error Analysis (EA) was a successor which supplanted Contrastive Analysis (CA) in the 1970s. CA was based on Behaviourism psychologically and

* 李祖君，广西钦州学院外语系讲师。

Structurism in terms of linguistics. Contrastive Analysis had been interested in comparing two linguistic systems—the learner's L1 (mother tongue) and the target L2 in order to find out the similarities as well as differences between them. The underlying assumption of CA was that L2 learners transfer the habits of their L1 into the L2. The transfer could be divided into two types. One was positive transfer which occurred when the habits of the L1 were the same as those of the L2. At that time, the learner would transfer appropriate properties and be successful. That is to say, the learner would find that part easy to learn and use it correctly. The other kind of transfer was called negative transfer. It occurred whenever the habit of the native language differed from those of the target language. In this process, the learner would transfer inappropriate properties and learner errors would result. On this account, CA sought to predict the errors that learners make by identifying the linguistic differences between their L1 and the target language.

However, during the 1960s the Contrastive Analysis Hypothesis (CAH) was challenged by Mentalism. Besides, people found that many errors committed by the learners could not be accounted for in terms of CA. There appeared a growing skepticism about the plausibility of a behaviourist (i. e. habit formation) account of Second Language Acquisition which was the basement of Contrastive Analysis Hypothesis. Meanwhile many empirical studies of SLA failed to prove the Contrastive Analysis Hypothesis. On the contrary, many of these kinds of studies turned out to indicate that the Contrastive Analysis Hypothesis made the wrong predictions. For example, people found that sometimes the second language learners were successful and made little errors where the linguistic structure of their mother tongue differed from those in the target language. That was beyond the explanation of CAH.

As a result, the Contrastive Analysis Hypothesis was in a wane and lost favor with many researchers. The awareness that many errors made by the second language learners were not due to the negative transfer led to researchers focusing on errors themselves, rather than on comparing the similarities and divergences between L1 and L2. With the shift of interest, researchers began to study and analyze the errors themselves. The study of errors was carried out by means of Error Analysis (EA).

The era of Error Analysis came with the publication of a well-known article — *The Significance of Learner's Errors* which was written by Corder (1967). The shift from comparing two linguistic systems —the learner's L1 and the target L2 with a view to determining structural similarities and differences to focusing on the errors themselves was captured in Corder's article. Corder maintained that learners' errors were invaluable to the study of the language-learning process. According to him, if a teacher undertakes a systematic analysis, he will find how far towards the goal the learner has progressed and, consequently, what remains for him to learn. Errors came to be viewed as a reflection of L2 learners' mental knowledge of the second language: their interlanguage grammar (Selinker, 1972). Researchers therefore began to analyze corpora of second language errors in order to understand better the nature of interlanguage grammar.

Serving as an important instrument of research, Error Analysis was first prominent in the late 1960s. As being mentioned above, the wave of interest in learner errors started as a challenge to the Contrastive Analysis notion that errors were solely evidence of the first language interference. CA gave way to EA as this notion came to be challenged. In fact, Error Analysis was not a new development. As Sridhar pointed out, Error Analysis had a long tradition. However, before the early 1970s, Error Analysis consisted of little more than impressionistic collections of"common" errors and their linguistic classification. The goals of traditional Error Analysis were pedagogic, for errors provided information for teaching and for designing remedial lessons. But because of the absence of any theoretical framework for explaining the role played by errors in the process of Second Language Acquisition (SLA), there were no serious attempts to define "error" or to account for it in terms of psychology. Also as the enthusiasm for Contrastive Analysis grew, the interest in Error Analysis declined. In accordance with Behaviouristive learning theory, the prevention of errors (the goal of Contrastive Analysis) was more important than the identification of errors. It was not until the late 1960s that there was a resurgence of interest in Error Analysis. A series of articles by Corder (e. g. 1967, 1971, 1974, 1981) traced this resurgence and helped to give it direction. According to Corder (1974: 25), EA was instructive because it can be used in three ways : (1) to tell the teachers how much the learners have learnt, (2) to assist SLA researchers in piecing together a picture of language development, and (3) to enable learners to learn the rules of language through error correction. Besides, Corder (1981) also stated that there were two justifications for studying learners' errors: its relevance to language teaching and the study of the language acquisition process.

Since the late 1960s, Error Analysis had been a heated subject, becoming a recognized part of applied linguistics as well as a development owing much to the work of Corder's works, many works had focused on it concerning the classifications, the causes of the errors committed by the second language learners. In China, most researches into Error Analysis focused on the review or survey of it (Tang, 1995; Wu, 1998; Hong, 1998).

1.2 Aims of the Study

In spite of the intense interest in EA, there is still much disagreement concerning some particular subjects. For example, Duay and Burt (1973) find that only 3 per cent of errors committed by the second language learners are due to the cause of interference. But there are considerable discrepancies concerning the proportion of interlingual errors as well as intralingual errors. These discrepancies may result from different variables, such as age of the learners, degree of contrast between the first and second language, type of data collected and so on. Motivated by the desire to have a picture of the errors committed by Chinese intermediate EFL learners in written English, the present writer attempts to find out the percentage of interference errors as well as intralingual errors in the samples of compositions by some English majors in a college, meanwhile looking into the causes of the learners' errors, for I have been teaching English in a college for four years. As a teacher, I always want to seek the causes of the errors made by the students so that I can find ways to deal with them and help the students to progress towards the target language-English. Besides, the present writer assumes that Form Two students of English majors in the college perform significantly better in writing, committing fewer errors than Form One students do. By comparing their errors in writing statistically, the problem whether significant differences between their errors exist will be investigated. Meanwhile, some relatively detailed situations concerning errors in written English by Chinese EFL learners will be discussed. In view of the findings in the present study, some practical suggestions to minimize the occurrence of errors in the learners' written English as well as to better English teaching methods are to be put forward. The present study follows the procedure put forward by Corder (1974) as follows:

1) Collection of samples of learner language
2) Identification of errors
3) Description of errors
4) Explanation of errors
5) Evaluation of errors

Like many studies concerning EA, the present study does not include the fifth step. As Ellis (1994:48) points out that the evaluation of learner errors has generally been handled as a separate issue, with its own methods of enquiry. The present thesis focuses on the fourth step with a view to getting some enlightenment for English teaching, such as decreasing errors, improving teaching methods, better the English teaching materials and so on. The study will be meaningful since Error Analysis had long been a part of language pedagogy.

The result of the present study indicate: 1) On the whole, the errors committed by Chinese intermediate EFL learners in written English result from the influence of mother tongue and the target language itself; and other errors belong to unique errors which are hard to explain their sources; 2) The percentage of intralingual errors is larger than interlingual errors; 3) No significant differences between the errors in written English respectively made by Form One students and Form Two students have been found.

2 Methodology

2.1 Purposes of the Study

There are three goals in this study: 1) to probe the causes of the errors committed by the Chinese EFL learners in written English; 2) to look into the percentage of interlingual errors as well as intralingual errors in the samples of compositions by the Chinese EFL learners; 3) to prove that Form Two English majors are significantly better than Form One English majors in terms of the performance in written English.

In order to achieve these aims, an experiment is conducted. The experiment is a pilot one, which is carried out to obtain the data indicating the errors committed by the learners. In this experiment, some learners are required to write a composition.

2.2 Questions and Hypotheses

Four questions are raised for the experiment:

1) What are the possible causes of the errors committed by intermediate Chinese EFL learners?

2) Is the percentage of intralingual errors larger than that of interlingual errors?

3) Do Form One students make more errors than Form Two students do in written English?

4) Are Form One students more prone to mother tongue interference in written English, compared with the Form Two students?

From these questions, four hypotheses are derived as follows:

1) The influence of both mother and target language may result in the occurrence of errors committed by intermediate Chinese EFL learners in written English.

2) The percentage of intralingual errors is larger than that of interlingual errors.

3) Form One students make more errors than Form Two students do in written English.

4) Form One students are more prone to mother tongue interference in written English, compared with the Form Two students.

In hypothesis, the first step is to make null hypothesis. The next step is to go through a statistical process to see whether evidence can be found to support or reject the null hypothesis.

Null hypotheses:

1) The influence of mother tongue and the target language will not result in the occurrence of errors committed by intermediate Chinese EFL learners in written English.

2) The percentage of interlingual errors is larger than intralingual errors.

3) Form One students do not make more errors than Form Two students do in written English.

4) Form One students are not more prone to mother tongue interference in written English, compared with the Form Two students.

Alternative hypotheses:

1) The Chinese intermediate EFL learners committed errors in written English owing to the influence of both mother tongue and the target language.

2) The percentage of intralingual errors is larger than that of interlingual errors.

3) In writing, Form One students make more errors than Form Two students do.

4) In writing, compared with the Form Two students, Form One students are inclined to make more interlingual errors.

2.3 Subjects

The subjects in the present study are 40 English majors from Qinzhou University, being chosen randomly from two grades. They are divided into two groups. The first group consists of 20 Form One students. The other group is composed of 20 Form Two students. The 20 Form Two students were enrolled in Qinzhou Teachers College in 2006, while the 20 Form One students in 2007. All of them had received 6 ~ 8 years of formal English instruction in middle school. By the time they were assigned the composition, the 20 Form Two students had received instruction as English majors for about one year and two months, while the 20 Form One students only two months. By making a comparison between the errors in their language samples, we should find out some features.

It should be noted that these subjects are students from a college, instead of a university. It goes without saying that their English level is comparatively lower than that of other students from other parts of China, which may lead to the fact that maybe the conclusions of the present study lack generalization.

2.4 Material

All of the students are required to write a composition entitled"What Can I Learn in the College". Their compositions are used to be the samples for errors analysis.

2.5 Procedure of the Study

It is obvious that the second language learners make various errors in oral utterances and written utterances, as a result of different processing conditions involved. The present study focuses on the latter one. Before the study is carried out, the decision regarding the manner in which the samples are to be collected has to be made. It is acknowledged that natural samples are generally preferred. Considering that the present study focuses on the written samples, the present writer has to make a choice concerning the means of samples collection, i. e. composition or translation. In this study the samples of learner language are collected by means of composition instead of translation. Compared with translation, composition reflects the nature of the second language learner's language-Interlanguage more naturally and objectively.

In this experiment, the subjects were required to write a short composition of 160-200 words as mentioned in the part to Material. The composition had to be finished in class during the given time of 45 minutes. Students were encouraged to express their ideas freely. It was decided to elicit data in this way because it appeared to be a more natural way of elicitation of the learners' performance, since the subjects did not have enough time to think about the grammatical correctness.

Corder (1974) suggests five steps in EA research as follows:

1) Collection of a sample of learner language

2) Identification of errors

3) Description of errors

4) Explanation of errors

5) Evaluation of errors

The present study is carried out following the procedures mentioned above. The issue of collection of samples has been tackled. Now it is the turn of the second step: identification of errors. In the process of the study, the present writer finds it rather difficult to distinguish errors from mistakes. According to the theories of EA, an error should be a persistent deviation from the target language. However, the distinction between errors and mistakes is not easy to put into practice, considering that the samples used for analysis are compositions and the study is carried out cross-sectionally. The present writer tries his best to identify the errors in the samples, and he has to admit that the judgements lack objectivity sometimes. The errors identified are considered to be evident.

When it comes to the step of errors description, the study adopts surface strategy taxonomy put forward by Dulay, Burt, and Krashen (1982), although Ellis (1994:56) says, "surface strategy taxonomy does not represent mental processes." Because the present writer agrees that surface strategy taxonomy can indicate the cognitive process that underlie the learner's reconstruction of the L2 (see Ellis 1994:56).

Since one of the aims of the study is trying to probe the causes of the errors committed by the second language learners, the explanation of errors is highlighted. The errors will be classified into interlingual errors, intralingual errors and unique errors. Interlingual errors occur because of the interference of the learner's mother tongue. Intralingual errors are similar to those appear L1 acquisition. Unique errors refer to those errors that are neither interlingual nor intralingual. In the process of errors explanation, the numbers of interlingual errors and intralingual errors are calculated in order to find out the result of the hypothesis put forward in this thesis.

2.6 Procedure of Data-Analysis

The learners' evident, persistent grammatical errors in written English are to be analyzed by the first four steps in EA research. In order to make a comparison of the errors committed by Form One students, statistics was used, Unpaired Samples t-test being established. t-test instead of Z-test was adopted, for the samples in this experiment were not large enough.

3 Results and Discussion

As one of the aims of the present study is to investigate the relatively detailed situations, and probe into the causes of the errors committed by Chinese EFL learners, it is not suitable to manipulate the errors on scale. On the other hand, a comparison between the errors is made statistically. Therefore, the error analysis is both qualitative and quantitative.

3. 1 A Comparison of the Errors

Table 1 Unpaired Sample *t*-test for the Numbers of the Errors Committed by Chinese EFL Learners

	Mean	Standard Deviation	Standard Error Mean	$/t/$
The Numbers of Errors Committed by Form One Students	3. 8	2. 31	0. 52	0. 809
The Numbers of Errors Committed by Form Two Students	3. 25	2. 61	0. 60	

$df=20+20-1=39$, $t^{(39, 0.05)}=1.697$

The mean of the numbers of errors committed by Form One students is 3. 8, and that by Form Two students is 3. 25. As table 1 shows, the calculated value of $/t/$ is 0. 809, which is smaller than the critical value of 1. 697 at 0. 05 level. It indicates that there is no significant difference between the two groups. This result suggests that one of the null hypotheses which states that Form One students will not make more errors than Form Two students do can not be rejected.

Table 2 Unpaired Sample *t*-test for the Numbers of the Errors Committed by Chinese EFL learners

	Mean	Standard Deviation	Standard Error Mean	$/t/$
The Number of Interlingual Errors Committed by Form One Students	1. 25	1. 08	0. 25	1. 18
The Numbers of Interlingual Errors Committed by Form Two Students	0. 85	1. 09	0. 25	

$df=20+20-1=39$, $t^{(39, 0.05)}=1.697$

The mean of the numbers of interlingual errors committed by Form One students is 1. 25, and that by Form Two students is 0. 85. Table 2 demonstrates that the calculated value of $/t/$ is 1. 18, which is smaller than the critical value of 1. 697 at 0. 05 level. According to this result, one of the null hypotheses that Form One students are not more likely to turn to the help of mother tongue-Chinese in writing, compared with the Form Two student is acceptable.

In the present study, the numbers of errors are calculated, we have found that 20 Form One students commit 76 evident errors, while 20 Form Two students commit 64 evident errors. Furthermore, the present writer identifies 25 interlingual errors among the 76 errors by the 20 Form One students. That is to say about 33% errors are interlingual. On the other hand, about 27% i. e. 17 among 65 errors committed by the 20 Form Two students are interlingual. The result is in accordance with the mean percentage reported by other researchers, which is about 33 percent. (see Ellis 1985: 29)

Although the total number of errors and the number of interlingual errors committed by 20 Form One students, which are greater than that by Form Two students, *t*-tests of the errors show no significant difference between these errors. The result indicates three possibilities: one is that Form Two students have not made considerable enough progress in their writing performance. Another possibility is that Form One students are as varied as Form Two students in terms of English level, which lead to the similarity of Standard Deviation. The third possibility is that mother tongue influence exists in their writings, which is very hard to overcome even though the learners have reached a relatively high level.

Some researchers have found that the second language learners, especially the learners with a weak level are likely to depend on L1 thinking. Although the comparison of the errors committed respectively by Form One students and Form Two students show no significant difference, it should be pointed out that the result of the present study will not reject the statement"lower level learners are particularly prone to negative transfer." In fact Form One students and Form Two students are not significantly different in terms of English level. They should not be divided into two distinct groups such as beginners and intermediates, for they all seem to be regarded as intermediate learners.

Some errors made by the students are article errors. Article error is a special headache for most Chinese students, as there is no article feature in their mother tongue. The article errors suggest that the learner has no consciousness of using articles or has uncertainty and confusion with articles. Language teachers and researchers do not pay much attention to the error because they think it does not interfere with language learning and communication. In fact, it is a very serious problem for language learners, especially for us Chinese learners.

Some students tend to process the language on the basis of the native language, or direct translation, whose language inevitably was interfered by the native language. Therefore, it can be inferred that negative transfer from Chinese is another source of errors.

The result of the present study indicates that the percentage of intralingual errors is larger than that of interlingual errors. However, the precise percentages of these kinds of errors vary considerably from study to study.

Owing to a number of variables such as age of learners and learner level, many studies show considerable discrepancies concerning the percentage of interlingual errors and intralingual errors. For example, some researchers found that learners at an elementary level produced more transfer errors than learners at an intermediate or advanced level. Conversely, the occurrences of intralingual errors increased with the advancement of learner level.

The varieties of the proportion are also related to the task used to elicit samples of learner language. Some researchers found that different means of data collection result in the discrepancies as regards the numbers as well as types of errors. For instance, there are more errors reflecting L1 interference in translation task than other kinds of instruments. This thesis adopts the means of composition instead of translation, considering that composition reflects the nature of the second language learner's language-Interlanguage relatively more naturally and objectively than in translation. In another word, the learners can express their ideas more freely and spontaneously in compositions than translations which seem to be born with manipulative nature.

It should be noted that the present writer admits that the percentage of interlingual errors might be larger than that of intralingual errors when the data are elicited by means of translation or others.

As Ellis (1994:59) says, "It is not easy to distinguish transfer and intralingual errors, and even more difficult to identify the different types of intralingual errors that Richards describes". Some arguments regarding the explanation of errors as well as the classification of errors may arise. Where one researcher identifies the source of an error as intralingual, another researcher may identify the source of the same error as interlingual. The present writer realizes that it is inevitable that the explanations of some errors especially some lexical errors are not convincing and satisfactory enough because of the weakness in the methodological procedures of this thesis. But it is still personally believed that the results and conclusions submitted in the thesis should be tenable on the whole even though some flaws exist.

Some lexical errors occur in the samples. One of the explanations for wrong uses of these words is lack of enough attention to form. The learners who focus on meaning rather than form when they write are likely to make errors. They should be clear that meaning and form are of the same importance, and it is not right to neglect the correctness of form given that idea is conveyed. Accordingly they ought to pay at least equal attention to meaning and form when writing. Another explanation is that these kinds of errors occur because the learners are not familiar with the particular word and its usage. According to Cohen (1990) and Nation (1990) a foreign language learner has to master a particular word's connotation, denotation, its derivatives, syntactic features, semantic features and collocation etc in order to use it correctly.

4 Conclusion

4.1 A Summary of the Study

The thesis has made a general overview of the previous researchers related to EA, and conducted a qualitative and quantitative analysis of the errors committed by two groups of Chinese intermediate EFL learners.

After the experiment and discussion, some conclusions may be drawn.

1) On the whole, the errors committed by Chinese intermediate EFL learners in written English result from the interference from mother tongue as well as the target language, and other errors belong to unique errors which are hard to explain their causes.

2) The percentage of intralingual errors is larger than that of interlingual errors.

3) No significant differences between the errors respectively committed by Form One

students and Form Two students have been found.

4) Some errors resulting from ways of thinking in mother tongue are hard to be corrected.

5) Some grammar errors have to be corrected otherwise they may remain even after a long time.

6) Having not mastered enough vocabuaries may lead to making errors.

7) Some errors are made owing to the fact that the students are not familiar with the language rules.

8) It can be speculated that some of the persistent errors in the subjects' written English could be due to the fact that the teacher's written feedback concerning the errors fails to become input or intake.

9) Some stategies used by the students may be one of the reasons why the errors occur.

4.2 Implications of the Study

1) The present study reflects that interlingual errors resulting from the negative influence of mother tongue are hard to be diminished. Consequently, teachers must frequently remind their students that when they speak or write in English they must think in the target language so that they do not bring in the feature of their mother tongue.

2) Students should be aware of their errors, and the attention to errors of their own should be aroused. They should be instructed to establish an appropriate attitude towards making errors, which should neither be an indifferent one nor an unforgivable one.

3) The teacher should explain why certain constructions are ungrammatical.

4) The teacher should advise their students to persevere in studying English. There is no short cut to learning the language. When they are sufficiently exposed to the target language through the various language skills of reading and listening, the possibility of making errors is minimized.

5) Teachers should encourage students to speak in English with their fellow students in school or on campus and create an atmosphere in class, which is conductive to learning the language.

6) Teachers must inform students of exceptions to the rules as regards grammar, vocabulary and pronunciation.

7) Students should be advised to listen to good English from whatever available sources-radio, television, native speakers and so on.

8) Students should be advised to form the habit of reading. Francis Bacon says, "Reading makes a full man." Reading helps students to learn the correct spelling, enrich their vocabulary and internalize acceptable and appropriate sentence constructions. According to SLA theories by Krashen (1982), intake can not be guaranteed without enough input. Reading is a good way of getting intake. Besides, students should be required to practice writing often. Students should be encouraged to persevere in keeping diary or reading

reports.

9) Teachers should pay attention to the issue of input. Inside the class, teachers should try to provide genuine and grammitically accurate and comprehensible input. Tapes, records, films, and books including authentic materials should be arranged according to the levels of comprehensibility and student interest. Teachers should also encourage or assign students to obtain such input outside class.

10) The majority of teachers of English are non-native speakers, English is not our first language. Consequently, there is a likelihood of our going wrong in some aspects of the English language, which may result in the students' errors. Teachers should try to approximate to native speaker competence.

4.3 Limitations of the Study

1) The investigation I have conducted is based on the previous studies of other researchers, especially when the theoretical basis is concerned. In addition, I have used some of the methods other researchers have applied.

2) The samples of learner language are collected cross-sectionally instead of being collected longitudinally, thus making it difficult to identify accurately the different errors that learners produce at different stages of their development.

3) Maybe the samples collected in this study are not large enough. There are only 40 subjects in the study, therefore, the results of the study perhaps cannot totally be extened to all Chinese EFL learners.

4) In the process of the research, the present writer finds that it is rather difficult to point out the correct and exact sources of the errors, which lead to the result not convincing enough. As Ellis (1994: 59) says, "It is not easy to distinguish transfer and intralingual errors, and even more difficult to identify the different types of intralingual errors that Richards describes." Consequently, the research instruments such as interview and think-aloud should be adopted in order to investigate the source of errors more clearly.

5) Because of the weaknesses in the methodological procedures in the present study, some issues such as the evaluation of errors, induced errors, overt & covert errors and so on remain untouched. Researchers who are interested in this subject of EA may conduct further research on either the aspects I have preliminarily worked on or the issues which remain untouched in my study.

To summarize, viewing the students' errors, we come to the conclusion that language learning is more than a simple matter of habit-formation. Errors making is real reflection of the students' underlying grammatical system, from which we can infer their learning process. Besides, errors are necessary stages in the gradual acquisition of the target language and they may help language teachers reach a deeper understanding of language learning and adopt an appropriate attitude towards language teaching.

Reference

[1] COHEN A. D. Language Learning[M]. Boston: Heinle and Heinle Publisher, 1990.

[2] CORDER S. P. The significance of learner's errors. International Review of Applied Linguistics 5, 1967:161-70.

[3] CORDER S. P. Error Analysis and Interlanguage[M]. Oxford: Oxford University Press, 1981.

[4] DULAY H, Burt M. Should we teach children syntax? Language Learning 23, 1973:245-258

[5] ELLIS R. The Study of Second Language Acquisition[M]. Oxford: Oxford University Press, 1994;上海:上海外语教育出版社,1999.

[6] ELLIS ROD. Understanding Second Language Acquisition[M]. Oxford: Oxford University Press, 1985;上海外语教育出版社,1999.

[7] KRASHEN S. D. Principles and Practice in Second Language Acquisition[M]. Oxford: Pergamon Institute of English, 1982.

[8] NATION I. Teaching and Learning Vocabulary[M]. Boston: Heinlle and Heinle Publisher, 1990.

[9] 洪流.中介语错误探源[J].山东外语教学,1998(4):34-37.

[10] 唐承贤.差错分析综述[J].山东外语教学,1995(6):46-50.

[11] 武波.误差分析述评[J].外语与翻译,1998(2):23-28.

浅议英语阅读教学中的读中活动

吴飞燕*
（钦州学院，广西 钦州 535000）

摘 要：阅读教学在英语学习中起着不可替代的重要作用，而读中活动更是阅读教学中的重要环节。目前很多教师对大学英语阅读教学中读中活动存在理解上的误区。通过有效地组织读中活动及注意活动过程中的几个问题，最终达到真正提高学生阅读能力的目的。

关键词：英语阅读教学；读中活动；阅读能力

On While-reading Activities in English Reading Teaching

Wu Fei-yan
(Qinzhou University, Qinzhou 535000, China)

Abstract: Reading teaching plays an essential role in English learning and while-reading activity is an important part in reading teaching. Nowadays some teachers have misunderstanding in while-reading activity in college English reading teaching. By organizing while-reading activities effectively and paying attention to some attentive problems in it, we can achieve the goal of improving the students' reading ability in deed.

Key words: English reading teaching; while-reading activity; reading ability

语言的输入在英语学习中起到了很重要的作用。由于通过听这一途径来输入语言受到一定的限制，语言的输入更大程度上取决于课堂的教学以及学生广泛而有效的课外阅读。而高效阅读课堂教学是学生进行广泛而有效的课外阅读的前提，所以英语的阅读教学越来越受到

* 吴飞燕，钦州学院外语系教师。

大家关注。根据《英语教学法教程》[1]，阅读教学模式可概括为阅读课堂教学的三大活动：阅读前活动（pre-reading activities），阅读中活动（while-reading activities），阅读后活动（post-reading activities）。国内很多教育者对阅读前后的活动做了很多研究，但对于阅读中活动的研究仍较少，只是在一些文章里做简要的介绍。本文旨在探讨教师如何有效地组织阅读读中活动及活动过程中应该注意的几个问题，进而提高学生的阅读水平。

一、目前大学英语阅读读中活动的现状

由于受到传统教学以及大部分非英语专业大学生英语基础薄弱的影响，很多教师对英语阅读读中活动存在一些理解上的误区。读中活动是阅读教学活动中的重中之重，但这一阶段往往被许多教师忽视，他们认为此阶段只要让学生去读，读后做练习，最后由教师来核对答案即可。在读中活动中，部分阅读教师在阅读课堂中多是讲解课文，把课文从头到尾翻译一遍，或者让学生个别或集体读完每个段落后讲解语法点、词汇等。他们认为在课堂的有限时间里，让学生理解文章的中文意思和掌握词汇是教学的主要任务。而对于文章的文化知识、语言、结构等几乎不讲。于是整个课堂就变成了完完全全的中文翻译课或词汇语法课。课堂气氛沉闷，活动方式单一，几乎都是老师一个人在说话，缺乏师生和生生之间的互动，学生在课堂上应有的主体地位荡然无存。大多数学生缺乏英语学习的兴趣，在阅读课堂上只是被动听老师讲解，做笔记。甚至有些学生上课时注意力不集中，老师一提问就不知所措。他们不知道如何进行有效的阅读，无法很好地把握文章的大意。

而受到应试教育的影响，在四六级的指挥棒下，有些教师干脆直接让学生做练习，然后讲解答案，或是直接核对答案。把阅读课变成训练课、练习课。学生在阅读上没有任何乐趣可言，甚至有些学生对完答案后还是搞不清文章讲的是什么内容。久而久之，他们就会对阅读产生厌烦的心理。

因此，我们教师应该有效地组织阅读读中活动，活跃课堂气氛，提高学生阅读兴趣，促进阅读理解，提高学生的阅读能力。

二、如何有效地组织读中活动

（一）读中活动的目的及原则

读中活动的目的是帮助学生理解文章内容，结构以及作者的写作意图等。通过不同的活动形式组织学生进行阅读并完成相应的任务。在组织活动的过程中，应该遵循“以学生为主体，教师为主导”的原则，让学生积极主动地思考，真正参与到阅读活动当中来。教师课前要围绕中心主旨，精心设计一些指导性问题。以这些问题为契机，引导学生从整体到局部，从语篇到语句到词汇，逐步深入地阅读。

（二）读中活动的步骤

1. 第一次阅读

阅读的方法可分为三种：略读法、查读法和精读法。略读法，即跳过细节、不重要的描写与

例子，进行快速阅读，其目的是了解大意、主旨，大概了解体裁、结构和逻辑关系；查读法，又称寻读，用眼睛快速扫描，以最快速度找到所要的信息，使用这种方法，可先看一下问题，扫描，找到相关的词、句，找到后就不要往下读了，节省时间；精读法，先浏览全文，然后再根据短文后的问题，在特定区域仔细推敲，进行适当的推理和判断，从而选出正确答案。

这一阶段应该训练学生进行快速阅读（略读法：skimming；查读法：scanning[2]）的能力，所以要限定阅读的时间。阅读前提出阅读任务，但这些阅读任务必须具有概括性，有助于学生了解文章大意。如从三到四个选项里选出正确的标题或者文章的大意；确证他们读前的预测是否正确；把打乱顺序的事件或解说等重新排序；也可以让学生回答一些关于文章结构或文章基调方面的问题等等。需要注意的是教师必须指导学生正确而有效地进行略读和查读，而且读前必须让学生明确阅读的目的，清楚这一阶段他们应该运用快速阅读的方法进行阅读。

学生在规定时间完成相应的任务后，可以两人或小组进行讨论、对比，最后教师叫个别学生起来或者全班一起核对答案。

2. 第二次阅读

这一阶段教师围绕中心主旨，提出各种细节性问题，让学生获取有关 what，where，when，why，who，how 等基本事实。也可以让学生完成一些关于上下文的推理题等。下面列举一些具体的阅读活动：给文章的某些段落起小标题或给文章起标题，如果文章本来已有标题，也可以改标题[3]；把文章内容转换成表格、图表、流程图、图片等的形式或者填空所缺的内容[3]；根据文章内容判断所陈述内容的正误，回答跟意思有关的或推理方面的问题，概括段落大意等。让学生单独在规定的时间内完成相应的任务，在最后一两分钟的时候可以提醒学生，再次培养学生的时间观念，同时，有利于学生充分利用好时间。然后组织学生进行两人活动，教师在教室里走动关注学生动态并给予相应的帮助。最后教师就可以直接让全班或个别学生说出他们的答案及阐明理由。

3. 第三次阅读

这一阶段的阅读可以更多地关注文章更深层面的东西，例如一些个别的语言现象以及词汇、语法和句法等方面。如让学生了解、分析文章语言风格；分析和学习文章的文化背景知识；通过上下文、词缀、词根和学生已有知识猜测某些词汇的意思；分析文章中某些句子的结构，理解难句和长句；分析文章的结构、写作特点，把握行文的脉络；理解文章中的不同观点和态度等等。可以小组进行讨论或给每个小组分配相应的内容，最后由小组代表报告总结，教师可做补充说明。这样不仅有助于学生积极参与到相应的活动当中来，而且避免了教师一堂言的状况。

（三）读中活动组织形式的多样性

这一阶段能较好地体现出读中活动组织形式的多样性。教师应根据学生及课文内容的特点组织读中活动。如课文内容可以让学生自己阅读后同桌或小组交流意见。而对于文章内容篇幅较长，可以分成几个板块，让学生分组完成相应的任务后把自己所得到的信息告诉其他的小组。再如让学生独立完成相应的任务后，进行四人左右的小组活动。这样，他们经过小组讨论、对比后，不仅学会了自己分析、理解文章内容，而且培养了他们合作学习的精神。更重要的是，经过学生的讨论后，他们不会惧怕说出想法了，而教师也就不用花费大量宝贵的时间去讲解了，只需让学生来说即可。这真是一举多得！当然了，也可以在活动快要结束前的几分钟，走到组员当中告诉他们待会每个组都要选出一名代表来汇报他们总结出来的信息或者是他们认为最有价值的一个方面;或者让他们到其他小组去交流自己小组的观点或信息;或把他们所写的信息收上来后重新分配,让他们查看别人的信息等。另外,关于阅读的次数也是比较灵活的,教师可以根据阅读材料的内容及学生的真实情况设定阅读的次数及所要完成的任务。总之,读中活动组织形式的灵活性及多样性更有助于课堂活动的有效进行,学生也不易产生厌烦的心理。

三、读中活动应注意的几个问题

(一) 课堂时间的有限性

大学英语课堂的时间是非常有限的,用于阅读读中活动的时间更是少之又少。如何在有限的时间里有效完成相应的教学任务,大学英语教师责无旁贷。首先,课前一定要合理地选取教材。相对学生的知识水平及课堂的有效操作来说,文章的长度和难度要适中。

教师在上课前必须清楚了解教材内容及相关的背景知识,准备一切上课所需要的东西,并针对课文内容提出一些针对性的问题。教师在设置读中问题及任务时,必须充分考虑学生的语言和社会文化的真实水平。如学生进行第一次阅读要回答什么样的问题,完成怎样的任务,第二、第三次呢? 还必须设置好课堂教学活动,包括活动的组织形式是什么,如:individual work(个人活动), pair work(两人活动), group work(小组活动), whole class[4](全班活动)等;活动分几个步骤;每个步骤是什么,所需要的时间多少;给学生清楚明了的指令,一个活生生的例子或者示范远远比长篇大论的解说要好得多[4]。还要想象一下:学生将会有什么问题,犯些什么错误,教师需要给他们提供什么帮助、引导等。另外,在读中活动中,教师必须清楚自己的角色,做到游刃有余地控制整个课堂。

值得注意的是,把整排的座位变成几个小组,让学生围着坐,更有利于学生进行面对面的交流或进行小组讨论活动。也为学生在有限的时间内完成任务提供了保障。

(二) 关于快速阅读方法的训练

训练学生灵活运用各种阅读技巧进行阅读,而不是像很多学生那样看到一篇文章,就会从头到尾逐字逐段地去读。

快速阅读的主要目的是获取文章的主题思想。现行的部分阅读文章是分段撰写的,阅读的进程也应逐段进行。通常来讲,文章的第一段和最后一段是文章主题思想的阐明和总结,而每一段的段首尾句又往往是该段的主题思想和总结,这些值得我们特别关注。快速阅读的另一个目的是把握细节事实(detailed information),关键是要找到原文的出处。关于略读,指导学生理解文章标题,阅读首尾段,然后留意每段的段首句和段尾句。关于寻读,指导学生带着问题去寻找答案,根据问题的顺序位置及小标题等判断文章的什么地方能找到所需要的信息,尽可能快地扫视文章,直到所需的信息就出现在眼前。一旦确定所需的信息,就没必要继续往前阅读了。当然了,由于阅读的材料和难易程度不同,阅读的速度应是不均匀的;同样,由于阅读的目的不同,阅读的速度也应是不一样的。因此,在阅读过程中,要求有意识地变换阅读节奏以取得阅读的最大效度。教师可以通过让学生寻找主题句,拓展句或者其他的一些相关信息如:时间、地点和数据等来训练指导学生正确使用快速阅读的方法。

在阅读前教师可以明确要求学生几分钟的时间里完成相应的任务，时间一到，马上让学生合起课本并回答问题。这就避免了学生拖拖拉拉的习惯，让他们真正按要求去训练了，养成良好的时间概念。在各种英语考试的阅读中，学生反映出来较大的问题就是他们无法在规定的时间内完成相应的任务。如果我们平常注重这方面的训练，就可以从根本上解决这个问题。

(三) 培养学生良好的阅读习惯

为了保证读中活动的有效进行，教师应注重在这一阶段培养和训练学生养成良好的阅读习惯，纠正一些不良的阅读习惯。

1. 学会关注文中的信号词或关联词

这些词在句子中、句子之间或段落之间有起、承、转、合等作用。e. g. first of all, because, for example, in addition, on the contrary, however, if, in short, etc. ，这些词会暗示很多文章的信息：顺序，因果，列举，递进，对比，转折，条件，总结等，留意他们，有助于更好更快地理清文章的思路，大意及作者的观点和态度。

2. 学会猜测单词的意思

学生喜欢在阅读过程中一边读，一边查字典，遇到不懂的单词马上查字典。如果他们懂得一些猜测词义的技巧，就不用一看到新单词就马上查字典了。下面列举一些猜测词义的方法：

(1) 上下文语境法

上下文是指一个词或短语所在的句子，或其周围其他的句子。在阅读中，我们通常可以在这种上下文中找到猜测生词词义的线索。这些线索包括：文中给了该词的定义、同义词、相关信息(根据语义场知识)、例证、重述、比较、对比等，有时我们得对相关信息进行归纳。

(2) 构词法

利用构词法线索猜测生词的词义，如：复合词 (e. g. website)；混合词(由另外两个词的某个部分构，e. g. brunch: breakfast + lunch)；词根(因为词根能反映一个词的基本意义 e. g. spacious 的词根是 space)；前后缀(e. g. co-, un-, -tion, -tive, etc.)

3. 学会按意群阅读

意群是由许多词按一定语法结构组合而成共同表达一个完整意思的句子的基本单位。因为句子的整体意思是由各个意群相联系而成，所以在阅读时要抓住意群来获取句子所表达的主要信息。如：The man in / the brown coat / was reading a book. 这句话有十个单词，如果看一个单词想一个单词，速度会很慢且不易掌握整句话的意思。但如果按照上面的斜线稍作停顿，则只需"注视"四次即可完成，阅读速度明显提高，而且能很好地把握整句话的意思。

4. 读懂字里行间 (read between the lines) 及隐含的意思

事实上，并不是所有的语言都可以直接从字面及句法的表层结构翻译过来并表达作者的特定含义。看下面的例子：

John Henderson was driving home late last night from an exhausting business trip.

从这句话中，如果我们认真阅读并思考，就会推断出 John Henderson 可能刚刚结束了他的"business trip"；他一定很累了，因为旅途是令人疲惫不堪的(exhausting)；而且他一定很想回家，因为那么晚了他还开车回去。

在阅读过程中对相关信息进行推断有利于我们更好地理解文章内容。需要注意的是，要阅读并思考文中提供的信息，进行分析处理，弄清楚作者选词的用意。

5. 纠正不良的阅读习惯

学生出声、手指、心译及摇头的阅读习惯会明显减慢他们的阅读速度。实践证明，学生正常的默读速度是他们说话速度的两倍。而且，阅读的时候应用英语思维理解内容，而不是把英语翻译成中文来理解。回读也一样会减慢速度，其实重要的内容或者你所需要的信息通常在后面会有详细的阐述。

四、结语

英语阅读读中活动是整个阅读教学过程中的重要环节，大学英语教师应该在上课前根据上课材料的内容灵活设计好读中活动，以保证在课堂的有限时间内完成相应的任务。另外，在读中活动进行过程中，要注重培养学生良好的阅读习惯及阅读技巧的训练。本文在探讨有效组织读中活动的过程中，活动的设计方法还不够全面。本人将在以后的工作和实践中，加强相关理论的学习及应用。

参 考 文 献

[1] 王蔷. 英语教学法教程[M]. 北京：高等教育出版社，2000：117-135.

[2] BROWN H，DOUGLAS. Teaching by Principles：An Interactive Approach to Language Pedagory [M]. Beijing：Foreign Language Teaching and Research Press，2007：293.

[3] UR P. A Course in Language Teaching：Practice and Theory [M]. Cambridge：Cambridge University Press，2007：146.

[4] JIM SCRIVENER. Learning Teaching：A guidebook for English language teacher (second edition) [M]. Malaysia：Macmillan Education，2005：43-45.

[5] 马丽. 英语阅读课堂活动的设计. 科技教育创新[J]. 中国科技信息，2007(24).

[6] 丰玉芳. 培养英语阅读技巧 提高阅读理解能力[J]. 泰州职业技术学院学报，2008. 12.

[7] 冯远，周彬. 英语泛读课阅读前活动设计原则[J]. 乌鲁木齐成人教育学院学报，2008(3).

[8] 郭瑞华. 英语阅读前后活动设计的几种方法[J]. 教育实践与研究，2008(9).

[9] 刘明东，蒋学军. 试论大学英语阅读教学的三种活动[J]. 湖南第一师范学报，2005，12.

[10] 阮国艳. 英语阅读理论研究[J]. 赤峰学院学报，2009(5).

面向就业的学生管理模式初步研究

——以钦州学院为例

黎树式* 林俊良

(钦州学院,广西 钦州 535000)

摘　要:日益激烈的就业竞争,使传统的高校管理工作面临巨大的挑战,传统的学生管理模式已不能适应社会发展的要求。推动学生管理工作的观念转变、学生管理机构改革与完善、专业设置优化、社团组织优化、就业信息网络化、学生管理信息化,是实现新形势下的学生管理模式——面向就业的学生管理模式,提高高校的学生管理水平和大学生就业能力的现实需要。

关键词:就业;创业精神;学生管理模式

基金项目:广西自然科学基金重点项目(桂科自0832018Z);广西高校重点建设实验室;北部湾海洋保护与开发利用实验室;钦州学院校级项目(2009QB03,2007XJ03)。

Preliminary study on Employment-oriented Student management model

—Taking Qinzhou University for example

Li Shu-shi　Lin Jun-liang

(Qinzhou University, Qinzhou　535000, China)

Abstract: The more and more intense job competitions make that the traditional institution's management faces huge challenges. The traditional mode of students' management work has no longer adapted social development. Promoting the concept of students' management, reforming and perfecting students' management machine, optimizing the professions setting and communities' structure,

* 黎树式,钦州学院环经系讲师。

networking the employment information, informationizing students' management are types of management in new times, which can meet needs of employment, prove the students' management work and students' employability.

Key words: Employment; Entrepreneurship; Student management model

高校一直在履行社会赋予的职责——培养具有良好社会适应能力的高素质人才。近几年高等教育在高校扩招的过程中得到了迅速的发展,但随着大学毕业生的增多,社会环境的变化及当前金融危机的影响,就业形势异常严峻,给高校学生管理工作带来巨大压力和挑战。传统的学生管理模式在新形势下已不堪重负,必须探索新的学生管理模式,培养高素质的就业型人才以适应社会的变化与发展。

1　学生管理工作面临严峻形势

1.1　就业竞争日益激烈

2003 年是高校扩招的第一个毕业生高峰年,全国高校毕业生从 2002 年的 145 万猛增到 212 万人,2004 年再增 68 万,达 280 万人。到 2005 年,高校毕业生为 338 万。2009 年,高校毕业生人数竟是 2003 年的近 3 倍,如图 1 所示。

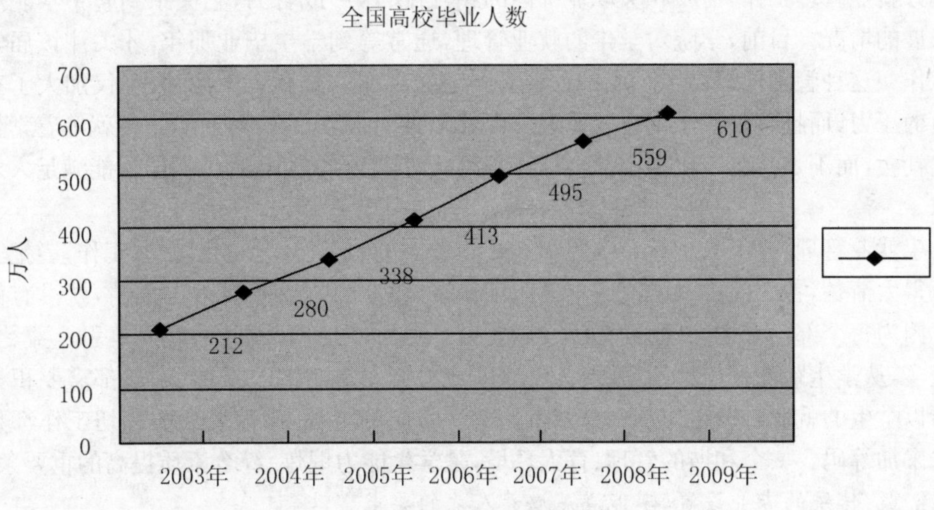

图 1　全国高校毕业人数[1]

据教育部统计,大学毕业生待业人数呈逐年增长态势:2001 年 34 万人,2002 年 37 万人,2003 年 52 万人,2004 年 69 万人,2005 年 79 万人,2006 年近百万[2],至 2009 年竟还有 250 万往届大学毕业生要找工作,大学生就业一年紧于一年。

1.2　社会对人才、专业要求更高

影响大学生就业重要因素之一即所学专业是否与社会需求相一致。用人单位对大学生的专业偏好比大学知名度更高,一些名牌大学里不适合市场的专业,学生就业不理想。他们在看重“专业”的同时，还对大学毕业生的“专长”很重视，有专长的复合型人才是用人单位竞相争聘的热点。他们要求人才除了基本的专业知识技能外，相关的行业知识、语言表达能力等也是要求达到标准。

2 传统的学生管理现状及存在问题

2.1 传统学生管理现状

长期以来，高校采取的学生管理模式是以行政和权利为中心，通过管理者对管理对象的控制和约束的形式，使高校朝着预定的目标和方向发展，进而实现学生管理的效率最大化。这里的效率最大化实际上是一种生产实践活动产品的数量最大化。由上到下控制导向的传统模式，通常是垂直、多层次职能化的组织结构，具有鲜明的等级特点[3]。

现代管理学奠基人彼得·杜拉克认为，“在大多数情况下，我们做的是正确的，只是没有效果。为什么会出现这种自相矛盾的情况？原因是时代变了，组织一直赖以为基础的假设不再符合现实了”[4]。

2.2 传统学生管理存在的主要问题

2.2.1 就业管理环境不协调，体制落后于社会发展

搞好就业管理工作，需要相关职业部门的相互配合，形成合力，它关系到整个学院和学生今后发展的情况。目前，学院对学生的就业管理，通常等到学生毕业那年，才关注该届学生的就业工作。这种管理模式已经形成一种较为固定的工作方式和思维活动，不仅加大了有关工作人员的压力，而且容易让学生在就业竞争中处于被动状态。快毕业了，学生就等着学校把他们推向社会，而不是自己希望走向社会、融入社会。传统的学生管理体制已不能满足人才培养的要求。

学生就业管理，并不只是就业部门和某些管理人员的工作，它是全院的“工作”。把工作范围划分得太清楚，各部门都只顾完成本部门工作，那本来可以做得更好的事情，就没有做到更好的。因为每个部门考虑问题都有欠缺性，要做到尽可能地面面俱到，就要集思广益、全员努力。其实，从学生踏入校门开始，就要为将来就业打好基础，知识、技能、素质都需要积累和提高。所以学生的就业管理工作从一开始就是整个学院的责任，学院开展的一切工作都是为学生的未来加筹码。一个和谐的管理、育人环境，是学生能力锻炼、综合素质提高的重要条件。

2.2.2 传统的专业设置，不能满足培养人才的要求

学院采用的是“顺向式”的传统专业课程定制法，往往从公共基础课程、专业基础课程再到专业课程和技能课程的顺序和角度制定修业年限内完成的课程学习[5]。弹性制的学分和课程选修制度还没有形成，学生只能按照课程安排的要求进行学习，缺乏自主性，没有选择权。

传统的课程定制法，适用于计划经济时代，却不适应知识经济迅速发展的今天。社会的变化发展是捉摸不定的，或许近年热门的专业，几年后市场又饱和转为冷门。没有弹性的课程设置，学生所学的知识和技能难以适应激烈的就业竞争。每所高校都有各自不同的环境氛围、地缘优势、师资队伍、教学条件和文化沉淀。钦州学院与广西同类高校一样，都是由师范高等专科学校升格而成，在专业课程设置方面都存在不足，需要在原有的基础上不断完善和提高，才

能满足学生和社会发展的要求。不同的是,学院有着独特的地缘优势和政策支持,发展机遇和空间很大。但由于多方面的原因,学院目前还没有立足自身优势真正打造出品牌特色专业。

2.2.3 社团组织缺乏活力,开展活动有待创新

为了全面了解钦州学院社团的概况,我们组织了本次调查活动。这次调查发放问卷150份,回收136份,有效问卷136份。问卷由64位社团干部、13位干事和59位普通成员进行填写,统计结果表明学院社团在运作中存在以下主要问题:(1) 学院社团数量多,但有的名不副实,需改善管理制度;(2) 社团开展活动形式单一,有待创新,普遍存在成员流失现象;(3) 社团活动经费不足,需要学院的大力支持;从问卷中还可以看出来,个人的能力素质在就业竞争中的重要性,且社团在这方面发挥着毋庸置疑的作用。

2.2.4 学生就业管理方式需改进

学院传统的就业教育主要是通过课堂、书本对学生进行就业政策宣传、就业信息传达和就业技能教育,信息交流手段较为单一,导致信息流通渠道不够畅通,政策、信息宣传不够及时、到位。学院就业网站招聘信息较长时间都得不到更新。在就业指导工作中,学院一般是让有经验的教师开设就业指导课,指导毕业生如何写简历、如何面试等一些务实性的技巧。

传统的就业工作管理模式使得毕业生择业自主权和用人单位的用人自主权不能得到有效地提高,毕业生和用人单位要花费大量的时间和精力参加全国各地各种类型的招聘会,并且还可能因为时间冲突,而错过了机会,使得毕业生和用人单位之间缺乏及时、充分和较为全面的信息交流。学生就业管理工作是一项头绪多、耗时长、动用人力多、政策性强的工作。利用网络,改革传统就业管理方式,能有效地促进就业管理工作的规范化、科学化和高效化建设。

3 面向就业的学生管理模式构建

面向就业的学生管理模式,不是字面上理解的如何就业、找工作,它是一种新的学生管理模式,在培养学生过程中结合社会的实际需求和未来发展趋势,从学生知识结构、能力锻炼、综合素质等多方面出发,把教学、教育的内容也纳入到就业管理过程中,促进和帮助学生的发展,使其适应社会的变化,并在激烈的就业竞争中赢得生存和更多的发展机会,是科学的且具前瞻性的学生管理模式。

3.1 观念的转变

3.1.1 转变学生的就业观念

在知识经济时代,大学生就业可以说是实力和综合素质的大比拼,面对如此激烈的就业竞争,大学生首先要转变传统的就业观念,以退为进,才能在竞争中生存和发展。一要转变进国有、集体企事业单位找“铁饭碗”的择业观;二要转变强调对口就业的传统就业观;三要转变只愿在当地就业的地域观[5];四要转变一就业就定终生的观念。

只有思想观念转变,行动才能改变。那些在计划经济时代大学生的传统就业观,已经不适合当今社会发展的要求,大学生需要认清当前的形势,树立新的择就业观。首先,明白凡是通过合法劳动取得收入即是就业;其次,相信中、小企业也有发展的潜力和机会,自主创业同样可以实现人生价值;再者,就业是一个不断学习、积累的过程,不可能一蹴而就。

3.1.2 转变学校对学生的评价观

学校里传统的学生评价观认为，好学生的标准是循规蹈矩、成绩优异、表现突出，而时逾常规、淘气的学生就很难得到认同。学校应改变这种评价观念，因为往往创造的源泉就来自那些调皮的学生，他们好奇心强，不喜欢按常规做事，甚至会做出与常人反思维的事情。通过建立新的学生品行标准，剖璞见玉，保护那些有见地的创造型学生，让他们的个性得到发展。通过支持和动员广大学生结合专业特色和自身兴趣爱好，设计创造出成果，给予奖励，激发学生的创造力。如校运会、社团向全院学生征集会徽，就给学生提供了很好的平台；又如：学校要订制、购买一批桌椅、路灯、垃圾桶等公用设施，其大小、形状及颜色都可由学生设计，这不仅可以满足学生的实际需求，而且还激发了学生的创造想象力，但学校很多时候都没有充分利用这些资源。

3.2 改革与完善学生管理机构

学院对学生管理工作的各项调整、改革，无疑都是为了完善学生管理工作机构，更好地为学生提供服务。

在学生就业管理工作必然涉及责权利的关系，为了充分调动各系的积极性、主动性和创造性，增强各系对学生就业工作的责任感，实现学院对管理学生就业工作层次和管理幅度的优化。横向上，各职能部门间边界模糊化，这并不是说不需要界限，事实上，某些边界是必要的，但如果彼此间没有相互渗透的部分，就业管理工作就难以做到全面和优化。就业办可向有关部门传达就业、目前学生就业状况、及在校学生应需提高哪方面能力等信息，相关部门相互协调，责无旁贷，为学生就业创造条件。纵向上，使原有的以职能部门为主体的管理模式转变为以各系管理为主体的管理模式。调整学院与各系及相关部门的责权利关系，赋予各系在就业指导工作中拥有对等的权利、责任和利益，使各系成为一个相对独立的责任、权利和利益实体，变权利集中为“重心下移”。学院可以定期召开就业工作会议，对各系工作及学生就业情况进行总体的把握，解决存在的问题，作出新的决策和方案。

总之，各系、各部门的相关工作都以“提高学生就业能力，指导学生就业”为目标，主动承担相应的责权利，做到“就业的好坏，匹夫有责”。

3.3 逆向思维，优化专业设置

以单一职业知识技能为出发点的传统课程显然不能适应社会新的要求。目前，美国职业群课程模式是将数种性质相近的职业视为一个职业群，分析该职业群所需的共同知识技能，对它们进行组合，作为课程编制的出发点和基础[6]。美国的这种课程设置模式，以经济发展和就业需求为主，培养学生的就业弹性和职业适应能力，从而实现学生终身职业生涯发展。在就业竞争激烈的今天是值得借鉴的。面向就业的管理模式，采用的也是逆向式的专业定制法，以社会对人才的实际需求为导向，设置实用专业。不仅要传授学生核心专业理论知识，还要培养学生的通用能力，做到“一专多能”，使学生能胜任至少两个相关的工作岗位。这不仅有利于学生未来职业生涯的发展和选择，而且也满足用人单位要求“复合型”的专长人才。

打造品牌特色专业，就要从自身的优势出发，立足现实，又高于现实。要让学生普遍在就业竞争中赢得优势，课程的设置要讲究科学性，既要有专业理论知识和知识技能，又要从北部湾的地理区位条件出发，根据北部湾发展过程中对人才的要求，增加相关课程，突出特色打造品牌。

3.4 优化社团组织,引导学生开展就业特性的活动

3.4.1 培养学生的创业精神,开展就业性的活动

如果学生在毕业后能自主创业,不但创造新的就业岗位,缓解就业压力,还能转变大学生的就业择业观,提高学生的就业竞争力。对于那些毕业后自主创业的学生,除了享受国家的扶持优惠政策外,学院应给予相应的奖励,因为自主创业也是一种"就业"。培养学生的创业精神,可以通过社团或以系、班级为单位,开展各种活动(社会实践、职业人生规划、创业设计等)。以兴趣或专业特性培养学生的创业精神,具体来说,社团组织属于"兴趣型"培养方式,系和班级为单位是具专业特性的培养方式,两种方式相得益彰,相互促进。目前,学院尚缺少这方面的平台,培养鼓励学生创业的工作还有待提高。

3.4.2 专业教师指导,财务经费支持

学生社团活动在注重培养人文知识和修养的同时,还需将科技精神与学术研究充实到学生社团的活动中去。相关知识的缺乏,可能使开展的活动对学生缺少吸引力。某些社团在开展活动的初期,通过得力的宣传,吸引大量学生参加,但时间一长,许多社团就丧失了吸引力,作用也逐渐下降,活动内容不丰富、不规范就是其中原因之一。所以不同社团不同时期开展的活动需要专业教师的指导,使学生社团保持生机与活力,真正能为提高学生综合素质服务。

缺乏经费,也是社团活动开展不顺的原因。单凭征收新会员有限的会费,是不能支持多项活动支出的,活动在一定层面上也受到限制。学校应鼓励学生社团走出校园,利用自身智力和文化优势,为企业的发展作贡献,得到企业经费支持的同时,社团活动的范围和层次也得到提高。减轻了学院的财务负担也使学生更多地了解和接触社会。除了拉赞助取得经费,学院以鼓励的形式给社团经费补助,也是可行的。

3.5 就业信息网络化,学生管理信息化

在信息网络化的今天,就业信息网络化的重要意义是能及时为学生提供招聘信息的同时,又为用人单位搜罗人才提供条件,适应了双向选择、自主择业为主要方式的就业制度改革。毕业生可以在网上迅速查询到大量符合自己求职要求的就业信息,根据用人单位运转状况和招聘情况,投放电子简历。这不仅省下印制自荐书的费用,更能使投放有方向性减少无的放矢的情况。用人单位不仅可以利用网络向毕业生全面地介绍本单位的具体情况,还可以通过高校就业网获悉应聘者的有关详细资料,更方便对人才的选用。

高校就业信息网可促进学校对学生管理信息化的实现。建立本校的就业信息网,拥有一个大型的数据库,存储关于毕业生资料、用人单位资料、单位需求、签约情况等各种类型的数据。学校利用这些资源,及时了解学生的就业状况,制定相应的就业指导政策,对数据库进行统计、分析、处理,实现就业部门对工作的横纵对比,及科学预测社会对人才的需求情况,调整人才培养的计划和要求。

在本校的就业网站上,不断完善服务系统。首先要杜绝虚假信息,提高就业信息的可靠性;其次增加有关应聘所需的技巧和方法、毕业生心理健康咨询与治疗及鼓励毕业生创业等板块;再者高校通过信息技术,对毕业生和用人单位信息进行保密,只对相关人员开放。当然,完善这个就业信息服务系统,需要一定的人力、物力,但一旦形成这个系统就可以方便毕业生找工作,也可减轻学校对学生就业管理的工作负担。

4 小结

在就业竞争激烈的今天,面向就业的学生管理模式是培养人才的科学模式。它是以培养能适应社会变化和发展的人才为目标,在不断调整中与时俱进。它只是一种方法和框架,构建的内容要具体问题具体分析。

参考文献

[1] 商江.浅谈严格控制普通高等学校招生规模[EB/OL]. http://dqddsj.blogcn.com/diary,811047.shtml,2006-08-25.

[2] 红网.大学毕业生待业人数[EB/OL]. http://news.sina.com.cn/o/2007-03-22/122811471630s.shtml,2007-03-22.

[3] 程勉中.现代大学管理机制[M].北京:人民出版社,2006:19-100.

[4] 彼德·杜拉克.巨变时代的管理[M].山西:经济出版社,1998:4.

[5] 李燕冰,俞励平.新形势下大学生创业意识和创业能力的培养[J].中山大学学报论丛,2005(6).

[6] 陈晶晶.面向就业的美国职业群课程模式探析[J].职业技术教育(科教版),2006,31(27).

浅论高校青年教师科研能力的培养

何光耀* 郭李芒**
（钦州学院，广西 钦州 535000）

摘　要：高校青年教师应该积极开展科学研究，在研究活动中不断锤炼和提高研究的能力；高校青年教师开展科学研究十分必要，是完成社会赋予高校职能的重要体现，是社会和教育事业发展的新要求，是高校科学研究创新梯队形成，实现学校可持续发展的重要条件，是教师自身专业发展的迫切需要；培养高校青年教师的科研能力要解决观念和意识问题、知识和方法问题、时间和精力问题、经费和条件问题以及政策和措施等问题；高校青年教师自身和高校都要从自己的角度出发做好工作，才能有效地促进青年教师的科研能力的形成和发展。

关键词：高校教师；科学研究；科研能力

On the Cultivation of Scientific Research Abilities of Young College Teachers

He Guang-yao　Guo LI-ren
(Qinzhou University, Qinzhou 535000, China)

Abstract: It is imperative for young college teachers to carry on scientific research, which helps to improve their competence, meet the new requirements of education, form groups of scientific and research, realize the sustainable development of college In order to cultivate the abilities of scientific research, a series of problems such as concepts, methods, policies and so on have to be solved by younth and college as well.

Key words: college teachers; scientific research; abilities of scientific research

* 何光耀，钦州学院科研处副处长。
** 郭李芒，钦州学院科研处处长。

科学研究是人们有目的、有计划、有系统地采用科学方法去认识自然和社会现象，探索真理，改造客观世界的过程[1]。它是一种创新性活动，对于推动高校的发展乃至国家的科学技术进步发挥着十分重要的作用。高校青年教师是高校教师队伍中年轻而富有朝气的新生力量，是高校可持续发展的主力军和基础，因此，高校青年教师应该积极开展科学研究，在研究活动中不断锤炼和提高科学研究的能力，促进高质量科学研究成果的产生，为学校的发展和国家的科学技术进步作出自己应有的贡献。

一、高校教师的科学研究能力及其构成

高校教师的科学研究能力就是指高校教师利用有关知识与工具进行科学课题研究的能力。这种能力主要表现在教师进行科学课题的研究过程中确定科研课题，设计实验方案，组织并实施实验研究，收集整理实验资料，进行科学分析，推出正确结论等活动的过程中。

高校教师的科学研究能力主要由以下几个方面的能力组成：

1. 发现问题的能力

发现问题是开展科学研究的第一步，教师善于从自己所从事专业的教育教学和研究实践中发现有价值的问题，这对于开展科学研究非常关键。

2. 预测设计的能力

教师在已有知识经验的基础上，根据相关信息的提示，预测问题的发展趋势，并把它设计为一定的研究课题，制定课题研究的目标、任务、内容以及开展研究的技术路线、方法和步骤等。

3. 实验操作的能力

为完成课题研究目标和任务，教师开展必要的科学实验、调查研究等工作，对于复杂的研究课题，科学实验、调查研究等往往需要反复多次地进行，才能获得真实可靠的数据和信息。

4. 信息筛选的能力

课题研究过程中，教师要懂得获取相关信息资料的途径与方法，要能够有效地判别所获得信息资料的真伪、有用或无用，还要恰当地对有用的信息资料进行整理分类等。信息筛选能力还涉及到对计算机的应用能力、专业外语的使用能力等方面。

5. 组织协调的能力

课题研究过程中，教师往往要和其他教师或研究人员合作开展研究工作，或者要和学校的教学、管理等部门以及社会上的各级各类部门、单位等打交道，因此，教师必须具备一定的合作、平衡、协调等组织能力。

6. 文字表达的能力

在科学研究活动中，要把科学研究的全过程以及取得的成果用文字完整地表述出来，从科研课题申请报告的撰写，科研计划的编制，到课题的开题论证，中期进展情况汇报，再到后期的结题报告、成果的鉴定推广，以及其中的论文写作，形成著作等，都需要教师具备较强的文字表述能力。

二、高校青年教师开展科学研究的必要性

1. 高校青年教师开展科学研究是完成社会赋予高校职能的重要体现

高等学校有三大职能，一是培养人才，二是发展科技，三是直接为社会服务。显然，开展科学研究，探索自然、社会发展的本质和规律，推动科学的发展和进步是社会赋予高等学校的重要职能之一。因此，每一位高校青年教师都应该努力学习，积极实践，不断提高自己开展科学研究的能力，为高校完成社会赋予的职能作出自己应有的贡献。

2. 高校青年教师开展科学研究是社会和教育事业发展的新要求

当今社会已经进入了以信息技术为先导的知识经济时代，科学技术的发展日新月异，国际竞争异常激烈。一个民族要兴发达旺，一个国家要繁荣富强，要在激烈的国际竞争中立于不败之地，必须紧紧抓住科学技术，要培养大批具有创新素质的人才。我们的教育应该努力培养学生的创新意识、创新精神和创新能力，而做到这一点的前提是教师应当比学生具有更强的创新精神和创造才能。教师的创新精神和创造才能离不开科学研究，只有不断探索、积极研究的教师，才可能具备创新精神和创造才能。

3. 高校青年教师开展科学研究是高校科学研究创新梯队形成，实现学校可持续发展的重要条件

高校科学研究创新群体由老、中、青年教师组成，是高校科学研究工作可持续发展的基础。如果老、中年教师积极开展科学研究，而青年教师袖手旁观的现象长期存在，则青年教师的专业水平和科学研究能力都无法提高，年龄结构合理的科学研究创新梯队就无法形成，学校师资队伍的建设就会出现人才短缺或青黄不接的现象。因此，青年教师开展科学研究是高校科学研究创新梯队形成、实现学校可持续发展的重要条件。

4. 高校青年教师开展科学研究是教师自身专业发展的迫切需要

科学研究是教学的基础，带动教学的发展，没有科学研究为支撑的教学，是没有生命力的教学[2]。实践证明，开展科学研究是教师更新专业知识的最佳途径和方法。高校的青年教师如果不开展科学研究，就很难了解和掌握本学科或专业发展的前沿动态与最新技术，就无法有效地改善和更新自身的知识结构，就会缺乏知识创新的源泉，就不可能保持高水平的教学，就不能成为一名好教师。随着时代的发展，他终将被学生所淘汰、被学校所淘汰，成为误人子弟，误人误己的人。因此，从教师专业发展的角度看，高校青年教师开展科学研究具有迫切性。

三、影响高校青年教师科学研究能力形成和发展的主要问题

1. 观念和意识问题

很多高校青年教师对开展科学研究的重要性缺少足够的认识，往往认为“教学是硬任务、科研是软指标”，认为只要把教学工作做好了就行，开展科学研究的意识比较淡薄；部分青年教师错误地认为，自己的知识经验不足，职称不高，很难真正开展科学研究，科学研究主要是那些高级职称的教授和专家们的事，与自己关系不大；有些青年教师认为，开展科学研究是一件繁杂艰苦的工作，需要投入大量的时间和精力，而且还不一定会取得成功，因而对开展科学研究产生畏惧心理，对科学研究工作敬而远之。个别青年教师甚至说：“如果不是为了评职称，我才

不去搞什么课题研究呢。”凡此种种，高校青年教师的科学研究观念和意识确实存在诸多问题。

2. 知识和方法问题

随着时代的发展，科学知识的更新速度不断加快。高校青年教师从学校毕业后，如果不及时学习进修，其所拥有的知识将在几年内过时。当前的现实是，一些高校特别是像我校一样的新建地方性本科院校，由于青年教师人数较多，教学任务繁重，加上学校安排的进修经费有限等原因，正常的离岗学习进修很难得到保证，这使得大部分青年教师的知识结构无法得到及时、系统的更新和完善，再加上一些青年教师对本专业学术动态、前沿信息等掌握不够，使得他们无法有效开展科学研究活动。另外，不少高校青年教师缺乏开展科学研究的基本知识和方法。尽管过去在读书期间学过一些相关的理论知识并受过一定的形式训练，但是在真正面对实际的科学研究工作时却感觉力不从心、无从下手。他们对科研课题如何选题、申报、评审、组织实施、结题验收等都不很了解，如果不能得到具有丰富研究经验的教师或研究人员的有效指导和学校科研管理等部门的大力帮助，他们就很难开展正常的科学研究活动。

3. 时间和精力问题

近年来，随着高等学校规模的快速扩大，很多高校的师资队伍建设跟不上形势发展的需要，导致师资力量紧张，一些高校特别是我校一类的新建地方性本科院校，青年教师已作为学校教学的主力军，承担了大部分教学任务；同时，也由于高校中的学生辅导员队伍建设滞后，使得部分青年教师在承担繁重的教学任务的同时还要兼任辅导员、班主任等学生管理工作。另一方面，随着现代计算机技术不断应用于教学实践，教学方式不断更新，采用计算机多媒体教学越来越普遍，这使得许多青年教师不得不花费大量的时间和精力制作教学课件。显然，繁重的教学和管理任务使得青年教师无暇顾及科学研究工作，制约了他们科学研究能力的形成和发展。

4. 经费和条件问题

近年来，高校规模的快速发展，很多高校特别是我校一类的新建地方性本科院校为了确保学校工作的正常进行，将大量资金投入到基本建设和基础设施上，科学研究方面的经费受到挤压。由于科研经费投入不足，学校的科研实验条件比较落后，无论是实验设备，还是图书资料等，都不能充分满足教师开展科学研究的需要。同时由于经费的限制，教师特别是青年教师外出参加学术交流的机会比较少，对学科发展的前沿动态了解不够。另外，像我校一类的新建的地方性本科院校，学校本身的师资力量还不够雄厚，在进行科学研究方面真正能起到榜样和示范作用的学术带头人与课题组织者还不多，未能大面积地引领青年教师开展科学研究工作。

5. 政策和措施问题

当前，对高校青年教师开展科学研究的约束和激励的机制不够合理和完善，青年教师开展科学研究的压力不大，动力不足，开展科学研究工作的积极性和主动性不高。青年教师一般职称较低，在课题申报时，容易受论资排辈的影响，如果没有特别的扶持政策，往往很难申报成功科研课题，特别是高级别的科研课题，这在一定程度上打击了青年教师开展科学研究的积极性；在课题研究的过程中，青年教师往往会遇到比有经验的中、老年教师更多的困难，如果不能及时得到学校科研及相关管理部门的大力支持和帮助，他们也容易半途而废或马虎应付了事，造成研究工作的停顿、失败或降低研究的质量和水平，这会使青年教师对开展科学研究产生恐惧和畏难心理，严重影响青年教师科学研究活动的顺利进行；课题研究结束，青年教师取得的研究成果往往因为质量和水平还不够高而很难引起学校的重视，对他们取得研究成果所给予的物质和精神奖励远远不够,影响了他们进一步开展研究的热情。

四、高校青年教师科学研究能力的培养

对高校青年教师科学研究能力的培养涉及高校青年教师自身和高校两个方面:

(一) 高校青年教师自身要做好的工作

1. 高校青年教师要自觉转变观念,树立和增强开展科学研究的意识和自觉性

高校青年教师要转变观念,把开展科学研究视为自己分内的工作,增强开展科学研究的自觉性和主动性;在把开展科学研究与个人的前途密切联系的同时,还要把它和学校发展以及社会的进步联系起来,增强开展科学研究的责任心;要深刻认识开展科学研究与教育教学工作的辩证关系,克服重教学轻科研的思想;要树立自信心,克服畏难情绪,积极尝试开展研究,不断积累研究经验,在研究实践中培养和提高自己的研究能力。

2. 高校青年教师要不断更新和完善专业知识结构,学习开展科学研究的基础知识和方法,主动借鉴他人的研究经验

高校青年教师要树立终身学习的观念,不断更新和完善专业知识结构,这是开展科学研究的前提。在此基础上,要主动地通过专业报刊、杂志、网络等多种途径搜集本专业及相关研究领域的前沿动态信息,结合自己教育教学实践的需要和实际,思考和确定研究的方向和课题。青年教师还要认真学习进行科研研究的基础知识和方法。首先是解决方法论问题,要自觉学习和掌握马克思主义的基本原理、唯物辩证法思想等,并以之指导研究工作;同时有必要学习一些关于系统科学、管理科学、心理学、逻辑学、写作、计算机和外语等方面的知识。对于常用的一些研究方法如调查法、观察法、实验法和行动研究法等则要认真学习研究,掌握该研究方法的适用范围、具体操作步骤、应该注意的问题等。青年教师还应该虚心向有丰富研究经验的老教师和研究人员学习、请教,借鉴他们开展研究的经验,尽量避免走弯路,节省时间和精力。

(二) 高校方面应该做好的工作

1. 学校领导要重视青年教师的科学研究工作

学校领导要深刻认识科学研究工作在学校发展中的地位和作用,要经常在不同的场合,通过多种途径,采取多种形式向广大青年教师宣讲开展科学研究的意义和重要性,讲清青年教师开展科学研究的必要性与可能性,使他们明确开展科学研究既是学校发展的要求,也是自我提高所必需的,帮助他们树立开展科学研究的责任心和自信心。

2. 学校要努力为青年教师开展科学研究创设必要的条件

(1) 学校领导要正确处理学校基本建设经费投入与科学研究经费投入的关系,在学校经费使用的安排上统筹兼顾,确保对科学研究工作的经费投入,并且随着学校的发展不断增加,使学校科学研究的软、硬环境和条件不断得到改善和提高,为青年教师开展科学研究奠定基础。

(2) 学校的科研管理部门要对青年教师进行科学研究的业务培训,定期或不定期邀请有关管理部门的领导和有经验的科研骨干,介绍科研政策、管理规定,讲授如何申报科研项目以及如何开展具体的研究工作等,使青年教师了解科研政策规定,掌握科研的方法和步骤,帮助

他们尽快走上科学研究的道路。

(3) 学校要把青年教师作为一个需要给予特别关怀和帮助的团体来对待，在制定科研管理政策和落实具体措施时，不能把青年教师和那些富于研究经验的中、老年教师放在同一起跑线上进行竞争，要建立倾向于青年教师的科研基金，为他们申报科研项目提供政策和经费上的支持，促使他们尽快成长，成为学校科学研究的中坚力量。

(4) 学校要为青年教师参加学术交流活动提供机会，采取"请进来和走出去"的方法，一方面邀请校外专家、学者到学校讲学、做学术报告和学术研讨，另一方面要积极选派和鼓励教师外出进修学习、参与合作科研项目研究、参加学术会议，尤其是要到知名高校、科研机构进行学术交流和开展合作研究，使青年教师在良好的学术环境中更新专业知识，开阔研究视野，从而提高科学研究工作的能力和成效[3]。

(5) 学校要注重师资队伍建设，要根据学校发展的要求做好师资队伍的发展规划，加强师资培养的计划性，同时做好师资的引进和吸收工作，使青年教师的教学和管理的工作量维持在一个比较恰当的水平，以确保他们有充足时间来开展科学研究活动。

3. 学校要建立约束与激励并举的科研管理机制，调动青年教师开展科学研究的积极性、主动性和创造性

学校要给具有职称的青年教师规定一定的科学研究工作任务，每年进行考核，把完成科学研究工作任务的好坏情况与其职务评聘、评优、晋升、获得科研资助等联系起来，对完成科学研究工作任务好的青年教师，优先给予聘任、晋升等，对不完成任务的，推迟聘任、晋升；对青年教师的学历提高进修或做访问学者等，学校要对其提出科研成果方面的要求，对不能完成一定质量和数量的论文的，可以考虑减少其进修费用报销的比例，以此形成一定的科学研究工作压力，激发其开展科学研究的动力；对于青年教师开展科学研究所取得的成果，学校要以制度化的形式给予精神上的表彰和物质上的奖励。

4. 学校要重视和加强科研团队和科研机构(基地)的建设，为青年教师开展科学研究搭建载体和平台

科研团队和科研机构(基地)是青年教师开展科学研究的载体和平台，青年教师加入到一定的科研团队和科研机构(基地)之中，能够得到学术带头人、课题负责人以及其他有经验的教师和研究人员的帮助和指导，这对推动他们积极开展科学研究有重要作用。因此，学校要重视和加强科研团队和科研机构(基地)的建设工作，切实落实有关学科、专业带头人及骨干教师之类的学术队伍建设制度；要根据教学和专业优势整合资源，建立相应的研究机构，并形成老中青相结合的科研团队。

参考文献

[1] 王素. 转变思想观念 促进教师科研能力的提高[J]. 新乡教育学院学报，2006(3):48-50.

[2] 张年国. 高校青年教师科研能力培养的问题及对策分析[J]. 当代教育论坛，2008(8):91-93.

[3] 余文盛，彭时敏. 新建本科院校教师科研能力发展路径探讨[J]. 继续教育研究，2008(2):71-74.

社会转型与英语师资教学技能改革
——以听力教学为例

黎茂昌*

(钦州学院,广西 钦州 535000)

摘 要:社会转型期对人才要求的改变,迫使教育模式的转型,教师教学技能的提高。然而尽管英语教师有着丰富的英语知识以及相关教学技能,但教学效果并不理想。究其原因,主要是课堂教学存在一些问题。因此,根据实施素质教育和转型期社会的实际需要,运用新的教学理念,改革英语教师教学技能,创新教学,从而培养出能听会说,能读善写,有特色的高素质人才。

关键词:英语教育专业;听力;教学技能

Social Transformation and Teaching Skills Reform of English Teachers
—Take Listening Teaching as Example

Li Mao-chang

(Qinzhou University, Qinzhou 535000, China)

Abstract: The changes of the requirements to the personnel in social transformation period reinforce the transformation of education model and improvement of teachers' teaching skills. However, although English teachers have a rich knowledge of English and related teaching skills, their teaching effectiveness is not satisfactory. The main reasons are that there are some problems in their classroom teaching. Therefore, according to the implementation of quality education and the actual social needs of the transformation period, the English teachers should reform their teaching skills with new teaching ideas and innovative

* 黎茂昌,钦州学院讲师,主要研究英语课程与教学论。

teaching, so as to cultivate characteristic high-quality persons who are able to listen, speak, read and write well in English.

Key words: social transformation; English teachers; teaching skills reform

随着当代社会由计划经济转型发展为市场经济,"应试教育"所培养的单一素质人才已经不能够适应社会潮流了,取而代之的是具有综合能力的高素质人才。为了培养出适应现在潮流的综合素质人才,教育也就与时俱进,由传统的应试教育转型为新型的素质教育。教育模式转型了,教育者的教学技能也要相应提高,英语教师也不例外,须通过课堂教学提高学生英语听说读写译的综合能力。然而,尽管英语教师有着丰富的英语知识以及相关教学技能,并按照课程标准要求进行课堂教学,但教学效果并不理想。中学生普遍认为最难也是最怕的是听力理解,上课过程中教师也花大量的时间和精力对学生进行听力理解训练,可学生听力水平提高不快,怕听力的仍然对听力感到恐惧。其中的主要原因之一是教师的听力教学技能达不到要求,在教学中存在一些问题。

一、英语教师听力教学中存在的问题

(一) 所选听力材料不当,内容偏难偏多

由于教学资源不足,难以找到合适的材料用来训练学生的听力,因此有些教师只要是找到一些与学生所学知识相关的内容就拿来训练学生的听力,没有顾及到学生现有的知识水平,或为了快速提高学生的听力,特地找些难度较大的听力材料训练学生的听力,从而造成听力材料过难过多的现象,以及学生害怕英语听力训练的不良后果。

(二) 听力训练时逐词逐句、词词句句过关

由于有些学生掌握的词汇和句式有限,没有形成一定的英语语感,所以当听一段英语对话或叙述时,即使会的单词也不一定能全听懂。因此在听力训练时,教师老担心学生听不懂。当训练学生听一个简单的句子时,学生听了一遍磁带之后,教师又一个词一个词慢速重复,又再让听一次磁带,以便他们对每个单词都清楚,这样才能了解句子的意思。听小短文也这样句句过关。岂不料养成了学生不良的听力习惯,以后每次听力也会词词句句过关,如果有个不重要的单词没听清楚,也认为自己不了解所听的内容。由此及彼,阅读时学生也会采用这种不良的方法进行阅读。

(三) 听力训练只是反复地、机械地做听力练习

在进行听力训练时,学生听一遍没有听懂,再让学生听一遍或两遍使他们能正确理解是很正常的,但如果学生听不懂时,总是反复地、机械地让学生多听,甚至"百听不厌",专注于所听的单词,而非听的过程[1]。如果某个听力材料学生听 2～3 遍还听不懂,就说明该材料超过了学生的能力限度,或者语言材料中包含的知识大多数是学生还不了解的。在这种情况下,即使再听多少遍也不一定有任何进展。

（四）听说分开

部分教师只是为教听力而训听力，在听力训练过程中只听不说，手做口不动。有时由于枯燥单调而使学生在听力训练时容易走神。而听的最终目的是说，只听不说最后也会使学生学成“哑巴英语”。

（五）听力训练一定要用录音机或多媒体进行

上课时，学生只要一看到教师放录音或者叫他们看多媒体播放的片子，就知道要进行听力训练了。因为教师往往会说上一句：Now, let's listen. 或者：Listen to the tape and fill in the blanks. 有些学生本来对听力就不感兴趣，看到录音机就想睡觉，或者由于画面太精彩，令学生只顾着看画面而忘记听里面对话的内容，从而达不到训练的目的。

（六）没有注意培养学生的听力技巧或良好的听力习惯

有些教师在给学生练习听力时，只听那些能听得懂的材料，一遇到听不大懂的内容就放弃，或马上告诉学生答案；有些教师在进行听力训练时，担心学生听不懂，就在听录音之前让学生读一遍录音原文，或者听一遍之后没听懂，就让学生阅读录音原文或边听边看原文。其实，这样做会大大降低听力材料的难度，降低训练效果，达不到听力训练的目的（一边听一边读的目的应该是纠音）。而且以后学生碰到听不懂的材料时，会急着找听力原文来阅读或者马上对答案。

二、英语教师听力教学技能改革

针对以上教学中出现的问题，改革教师英语听力教学技能。提醒他们在教学过程中避免出现以上现象，同时将教学理论与实际教学相结合，通过课堂教学提高学生听力技能，使他们的弱项变为强项。

（一）有积极向上的教学态度，有信心提高学生的听力水平

一个没有信心的教师会认为：“我的学生听力很差，如果我上课多说英语他们就会听不懂，所以我要多说中文以便他们能听懂我的意思。”可这样的后果是，学生在课堂很少听到英文，导致他们的英语听力越来越差。一个有信心的教师则这样想：“我的学生听力很差，因此我觉得他们需要更多的听力练习，因此我在课堂尽可能多说简单的英语，那样他们在课堂就能听到很多英语，所以他们的英语听力水平就得到提高。”后者的教学效果明显可知。因此，在听力训练和要求上应由易到难，循序渐进，帮助学生树立自信。在学习的起始阶段，可进行识别单词、词组和句子的听力训练，或用慢速英语听一些情节相似、语句大量重复的故事，并根据学生的需要作适当的重复。然后，逐步让学生听正常语速讲的各种对话与叙述，并将所听材料编成连线、判断、选择、排序、回答问题等多种练习形式。这样层层递进，使学生听力水平呈螺旋式上升。

（二）所选听力材料恰当，符合“二语习得”规律

美国语言学家 Krashen 在 20 世纪 80 年代初提出了著名且颇有争议的二语习得模式——

“监察模式”，主张“可理解输入”。Krashen 把当前的语言知识状态定义为 i+1。这里的 1 就是当前语言知识与下一阶段语言知识之间的距离。只有当学习者接触到属于 i+1 水平的语言材料，才能对学习者的语言发展产生积极作用。语言输入的作用就是激活大脑中的习得机制，而激活的条件就是恰当的可理解的语言输入。而习得语言以倾听策略为主。[2]因此，听力语料(内容、长度、难度)要以学生能听懂基本内容为前提，既要考虑到学生的现有语言能力，又要考虑到语料本身是否与教学对象的心理和生理发展水平相适应，有利于学生语言能力的进一步发展。语料的选编要立足于教材内容，根据教学目标和重点，对课文内容进行替换和改写，语料分为精听与泛听，或对课外语言材料进行必要的扩、缩、增、删，对语言表达方式进行科学地分解或合成处理，使之更接近学生的认知水平。

(三) 采用任务型听力训练，有的放矢

Skehan(2003)认为，在培养语言运用能力方面，任务型语言教学是目前最有效的途径。任务型语言教学就是指基于任务的一种教学途径，学生在教师的指导下开展各种各样的语言运用活动，在运用语言的过程之中接触语言、理解语言和学习语言。[3]在任务型听力训练中，学生一般都需要完成一个具体的任务。根据所设计的任务给学生播放听力材料，让学生带着目的去听并完成英语课堂任务，对于提高学生的听力水平可谓是一个行之有效的方法。

1. 在学生听材料之前，给他们布置相关的听力任务。这些任务可能是关于短文主题的，或者辨别对错的，学生带着听力任务去听思想不容易开小差，而且懂得听力的重点。如给学生听下列短文：

A bus came at the first stop and 14 people got on. At the next stop, 8 got off and 14 got on. Atthe next stop nobody was waiting, but 3 people got off. 6 people got off and 2 got on at the next stop. At the final stop everyone got off.

如果没有相关的问题，学生听的时候会觉得不知所云。但在给学生听之前首先给他们提出问题：How many bus stops were there? 那么学生即使只听一遍，他们也懂得根据问题而侧重听的内容。因此，把听力材料分为精听与泛听，让学生有的放矢。

2. 给出听力内容的关键词有助于学生的听力理解。给学生听配图小故事或短文时，如果听力材料中出现学生没学过的单词，先教学生一些重要的关键词(新单词)，以便减少听力障碍，帮助他们完成听力任务，如“Three Pigs”中的“Mr. Wolf, straw, wood, brick”。同时相关的背景介绍也能很好地引入或解释新单词。

3. 适当降低听力难度。听力内容过长时，学生会觉得很难听懂，难以完成听力任务。教师可以根据内容将其分为几个部分，中间设一定的停顿，以便学生有时间思考并且检查答案，同时将问题简单化，或把一个问题分成几个小问题。降低了难度，学生较容易完成听力任务。同一个内容，采取的方法不同，也会带来不同的教学效果。

(四) 设计多类型的听力活动，使学生动起来

非智力因素的利用，能激发学生的学习兴趣，从而达到教学目的。如可根据教学内容设计训练听力的游戏：“听与做”，即按照指令做动作，如“Siman said”等；“听与画”，让学生把听到的画出来，如画图、画表情等；“听与说”，将听到的内容重复出来，如传单词、句子、复述故事等；“听与写”，可以是听写单词、句子，或者找不同等；唱英文歌曲，如“Do-Re-Mi”；也可以创造情

景让学生进行对话练习,如"询问信息"等。

(五) 视听说结合

语言教学中的听,实质上是理解和吸收口头信息的交际能力。[4]语言的学习过程是一个有序的过程,表现为信息的输入和输出,即必须以一定量的信息输入为前提。一般说来,学生的理解能力往往高于他们的表达能力。听的过程中可以让学生大声跟着说、读,形成辨音能力,因此听的过程和说的过程往往交织在一起,形成一个轻松、活跃的氛围。学生喜欢看童话、动画、科幻等电视电影,因为这种活动本身吸引他们。因此,在教学中,教师可以选择、利用和课堂教学内容关系密切、水平相当的多媒体创设情境,引发学生直接兴趣,让学生观察、模仿、扮演,视听说结合。如教学"自我介绍"的表达形式,可以播放《音乐之声》中七个孩子出场时两次自我介绍的那一部分电影片断,通过让学生观看,模仿影片中自我介绍的语言、动作和表情,训练学生的听说能力。

(六) 培养学生良好的听力技巧和听力习惯

英语课程的任务是:"激发和培养学生英语学习的兴趣,使学生树立自信心,养成良好的学习习惯和形成有效的学习策略。"[5]因此,教师应培养学生良好的学习习惯,由他们的性格、动机、态度来决定他们的学习风格、学习策略、学习结果,而不是由教学制度、教学评估方式来决定。

1. 培养学生良好的听力技巧。(1) 在日常对话中,培养学生听的意识。如在两个学生对话结束之后,问别的学生相应的问题,使学生听英语时都下意识地去听。(2) 遇到学生听不懂的情况,从其他角度寻求解决方法。不要马上告诉学生答案,更不要让学生读原文。如听力材料过长时,可以根据问题在适当的地方停顿,提醒学生怎样抓住关键词来听,从而完成听力任务。(3) 培养学生猜词技巧。听力材料属于有声信息,让学生根据语气、语调、停顿来判断说话者想表达的意思。如学生听到"happy, angry, scare" 这三个词,scare 是学生刚接触的,但学生可以根据教师的表情猜出 scare 的意思。另外,说话者的语气、语调的变化还可以帮助学生把握说话内容的重点。(4) 适应各种听力题型。现在很多听力材料都采用选择题的形式,这种活动侧重检测听的结果,而非听的过程,因此并不是练习学生听力的有效方法。教师应该让学生尝试其他强调听的过程的练习活动,如一边听一边填空、做笔记或根据听的内容进行操作活动等。另外,知识的积累有利于扩大学生的知识面,如果所听材料为学生接触过的知识,那么他们就能正确理解听力内容。

2. 培养学生良好的听力习惯。(1) 使学生处于英语氛围中。教师上课时尽量使用课堂英语,让学生处于听英语的环境中,同时有意识地引导学生说英语,培养学生良好的听说习惯。(2) 下意识地听英语。看英文原声电影、卡通时,有意识地听里面人物的对话,而非看中文字幕。英文原声影片的对白,最能提高学生的听力,很多英语自学者也都是通过英文原声影片来提高自己的英文水平。(3) 专注于所听到的英语。在师生或生生面对面的谈话中,有的学生只注意自己怎么说,别人讲话时,他们仍然在思考下一步自己说什么,而不注意听别人怎么讲,错过了练习听的机会。因此,当别人说英语时,要专注地听。

教师良好的英语教学技能,能有效提高学生英语综合能力。教师应根据实施素质教育和转型期社会的实际需要,适应国家"科教兴国"、"人才强国"的发展战略,运用新的教学理念,全面进行教育教学改革，创新教学，从而培养出能听会说，能读善写、有特色的高素质人才。

参考文献

[1] 杨阳.英语教学法[M].北京：高等教育出版社，2005：22.

[2] 张国扬，朱亚夫.外语教育语言学[M].南宁：广西教育出版社，1996：125.

[3] 程晓堂，鲁子问，钟淑梅.任务型语言教学在英语教学中的应用[J].山东师范大学外国语学院学报，2007(6).

[4] 杭宝桐.中学英语教学法[M].上海：华东师范大学出版社，2006：79.

[5] 英语课程标准研制组.英语课程标准解读[M].北京：北京大学出版社，2002：36.

浅议新课改背景下民族地区高师院校化学专业师范生培养模式的改变

郑韵英*
（钦州学院，广西　钦州　535000）

摘　要：当前进行的基础教育课程改革以形成一个学习型的课程改革共同体，构建一个整体性、全方位的符合素质教育要求的基础教育课程体系为目标。这一改革对广大中小学教师素质和能力提出了全方位、实质性的新要求。本文结合当前我国民族地区的实际情况，探讨如何通过改变高师院校化学专业师范生的培养模式，以期能培养出适应基础教育课程改革的合格教师，为基础教育课程改革做出高师院校应有的贡献。

关键词：基础教育；课程改革；民族地区；高师；化学专业；师范生培养模式

On the Changes of Education Model of Normal Chemistry Majors of National Colleges in the Light of Displine Innovation

Zheng Yun-ying
(Qinzhou University, Qinzhou 535000, China)

Abstract: Aiming to construct a system of primary education curriculum which meet the needs of quality-oriented education, innovation is underway, which makes new requirements for the teachers in primary schools and middle schools. This paper probes into the changes of education model of normal chemistry majors of national colleges, aiming to make contribution to the innovation of primary education.

Key words: primary education; curriculum innovation; national region; normal

---

* 郑韵英，钦州学院生物与化学系教师。

college; major of chemistry; education model of normal majors

基础教育课程改革是我国整个基础教育改革的核心内容，广大中小学教师在课程改革中扮演着重要的角色。作为为中小学培养师资的高师院校应建立灵活开放、多样化的师范生培养模式，不断提高教师教育质量，这是教师教育适应社会经济发展与基础教育改革的必然要求和选择。当前，民族地区高师院校化学专业师范生的教师教育明显滞后于新课改，应结合基础教育课程改革的要求和高师院校自身的实际情况，积极主动地将自身的知识、科研优势融入基础教育改革中去，探索和实践高师院校化学专业师范生培养模式，以此推动我国民族地区基础教育改革的不断发展，进而从根本上促进自身发展定位的转型。

一、近年来我国基础教育课程改革的基本情况

1. 我国基础教育课程改革的实施情况

1998年12月24日，教育部发布了《面向21世纪教育振兴行动计划》；1999年6月，党中央国务院召开了改革开放以来的第三次全国教育工作会议，通过了《中共中央国务院关于深化教育改革全面推进素质教育的决定》(中发[1999]9号)；2001年5月29日，国务院发布了《国务院关于基础教育改革与发展的决定》(国发[2001]21号)，这些纲领性文件为我国基础教育课程改革指明了方向。课程集中反映了社会发展对教育的需求，体现着教育的价值取向，制约着教育的活动方式，直接影响着学生身心成长和整体教育质量的提高。因此，基础教育课程改革是实施素质教育的核心环节，加快构建符合素质教育要求的新基础教育课程体系成为基础教育深化改革和素质教育取得明显成效的主要目标之一。2001年6月8日教育部颁布了《基础教育课程改革纲要(试行)》，组织实施新一轮课程教材改革，与其配套的18种义务教育课程标准和相应教材也已于2001年9月起在全国27个省市的38个实验区进行课程改革实验，这标志着我国新一轮基础教育课程改革在经历了广泛的调研、考察、论证之后进入了实施阶段。2003年6月，相应的高中课程标准也由教育部颁布，新教材也逐步在编制和试用之中。国家计划用两三年的时间，初步形成新的课程教材体系，并用5年左右时间，在全国实行新课程，使用新教材。2005年秋季起，全国初中、小学的起始年级也全部进入课程改革；2006年，高中阶段也进行了课改实验。

2. 我国基础教育课程改革的目标

(1) 基础教育课程改革的总体目标

基础教育课程改革要以邓小平同志关于“教育要面向现代化，面向世界，面向未来”和江泽民同志“三个代表”重要思想为指导，全面贯彻党的教育方针，全面推进素质教育。

新课程的培养目标应体现时代要求。要使学生具有爱国主义、集体主义精神，热爱社会主义，继承和发扬中华民族的优秀传统和革命传统；具有社会主义民主法治意识，遵守国家法律和社会公德；逐步形成正确的世界观、人生观、价值观；具有社会责任感，努力为人民服务；具有初步的创新精神、实践能力、科学和人文素养以及环境意识；具有适应终身学习的基础知识、基本技能和方法；具有健壮的体魄和良好的心理素质，养成健康的审美情趣和生活方式，成为有理想、有道德、有文化、有纪律的一代新人。

(2) 基础教育课程改革的具体目标

国家教育部在2001年7月27日颁布的《基础教育课程改革纲要(试行)》中将基础教育课程改革的具体目标定为如下六点:一是改革传统课程过于注重知识传授的倾向,强调形成积极主动的学习态度,使获得基础知识与基本技能的过程同时成为学会学习和形成正确价值观的过程;二是改变课程结构过于强调学科本位、科目过多和缺乏整合的现状,整体设置九年一贯的课程门类和课时比例,并设置综合课程,以适应不同地区和学生发展的需求,体现课程结构的均衡性、综合性和选择性;三是改变课程内容"难、繁、偏、旧"和过于注重书本知识的现状,加强课程内容与学生生活以及现代社会和科学技术发展的联系,关注学生的学习兴趣和经验,精选终身学习必备的基础知识和技能;四是改变课程实施过于强调接受学习、死记硬背、机械训练的现状,倡导学生主动参与、乐于探究、勤于动手,培养学生搜集和处理信息的能力、获取新知识的能力、分析和解决问题的能力以及交流与合作的能力;五是改变课程评价过分强调甄别与选拔的功能,发挥评价促进学生发展、教师提高和改进教学实践的功能;六是改变课程过于集中的状况,实行国家、地方、学校三级课程管理,增强课程对地方、学校及学生的适应性。

二、基础教育课程改革对中小学教师的能力、素质提出了全新要求

正在进行的基础教育课程改革针对我国现行中小学课程门类过多、强调学科本位、课程内容缺乏整合、学生的课业负担过重等不足对课程结构进行了改革,其改革目标思路是对现行课程结构进行重大调整,减少学科门类,对具体科目之间的比重进行调整,在保留传统学科的同时,加强了旨在养成学生科学素养和实用技能学科的地位,使科学、综合实践等学科的比重上升[1]。例如在《高中化学课程标准》中明确指出:高中化学课程由若干课程模块构成,分为必修(2个模块)、选修(6个模块)两类。这些课程模块从不同的层面和视角建构内容体系,有关科学探究能力和情感态度与价值观等方面的目标在各模块中都有所体现。通过课程结构的调整体现出课程的均衡性、综合性、选择性。基础教育课程结构的改革对中小学教师的能力素质提出了更高的要求,主要体现在以下三个方面:

1. 开设综合课程,要求中小学教师具有更扎实的专业知识和更强的专业适应能力

当前进行的基础教育课程改革最重要的一大亮点就是设置综合课程,改变课程观念,改变中学一贯以来单一的"学科本位"状况,致力于形成一个分科课程和综合课程相互依存、相互联系的课程体系。综合课程的一大特点是横跨多个学科,如综合理科横跨数学、物理、化学、生物、地理等众多专业领域。综合课程的开设,要求在基础教育一线的中小学教师必须打破原有的学科壁垒,淡化学科界限,从单一的学科中走出来,不断拓宽自己的知识结构,只有这样才能完成综合课程的授课任务。

2. 开设综合实践活动课程和研究型课程,要求中小学教师要有较强的创新意识和创新能力

基础教育课程中设置综合实践活动课程的主要目的是最大限度地拓展学生的学习空间,强调学生通过实践,增强探究和创新意识;学习科学研究的方法,发展综合运用知识的能力;增进学校与社会的密切联系,培养学生的社会责任感;为学生生活经验的获得和社会实践能力的形成开辟渠道,为学生个性的发展创造空间。综合实践活动的设置,其根本目的就是要培养学生的创新精神和实践能力,这就要求教师本身首先要有较强的创新意识和创新能力,才能胜任综合实践活动课程的设计与指导。我国传统的中小学课程多为接受型课程,不重视课程的情

境性和问题性，不利于培养学生的探究精神和解决问题的能力。新一轮基础教育课程改革将研究型课程从小学阶段一直延续到高中阶段，为学生构建开放的学习环境，让学生通过更多渠道获取知识，并将学到的知识综合应用于实践，培养学生的创新精神和实践能力。它要求学生使用科学的思维方法并主动探索、发现和创新。

3. 开设选修课，要求中小学教师要具有自我发展能力

在基础教育阶段开设选修课的目的是为了促进学生个性的发展，拓宽学生的知识面，使学生在掌握基础课程的同时，也学习一定数量、不同程度、不同范围的学术课程以及相应的职业技术课程。《高中化学课程标准》中指出：高中化学选修课程是在必修课程基础上为满足学生的不同需要而设置的。选修课程旨在引导学生运用实验探究、调查访问、查阅资料、交流讨论等方式，进一步学习化学科学的基础知识、基本技能和研究方法，更深刻地了解化学与人类生活、科学技术进步和社会发展的关系，以提高化学科学素养，为具有不同潜能和特长的学生未来的发展打下良好基础。高中阶段的选修课程包括 6 个模块，每个模块 2 学分，所有学生至少应从中选择一个模块进行学习。由于选修课涵盖范围较大，中小学教师在大学期间学习的知识是远远不够的，因此就要求中小学教师要树立终身学习的观念，不断拓宽自己的知识视野，不断更新知识结构，善于运用新知识、新技术，发展自己的学术专长，从而能够开设出新的选修课程，满足学生对新知识的不断需求。

三、我国民族地区的教师教育滞后于新课改

由于各种因素的制约，作为中小学教师培养主体的高师院校不仅未能起到为基础教育改革保驾护航的作用，而且严重滞后于基础教育新课程改革的进程。综观我国的教师教育特别是民族地区的教师教育，造成教师教育严重滞后于新课改的原因概括起来主要有以下几个方面[2]：

1. 高师培养目标定位不当

长期以来，高师院校都强调要培养具有扎实功底的专业学科教师，在专业学科方面片面地向综合性大学看齐，而教育学科和人文学科的教学受到不同程度的削弱。

2. 高师在人才培养模式方面，师范特色未受到应有的重视

高师院校一直以来普遍重视专业理论知识的教学，而教育理论、教育实践环节的教学和师范生教师职业技能的培养和训练却得不到足够的重视。教育实践包括教育见习和教育实习。对教育见习，很多高师院校重视不够，特别是一些民族地区的高师院校的化学系，学生深入中学进行教育见习的机会和时间都很少，教育见习缺乏必要的指导。另外，教育实习时间太短，师范院校的教育实习时间一般为六周，每个实习生上课 4～6 节左右，实习生往往刚熟悉环境，刚刚摸到点教学的门道，实习就结束了，导致学生在毕业踏上工作岗位后，很难立即进入教师角色，需要一个较长的过渡和适应期。

3. 高师学科教学内容陈旧，跟不上科学技术和现代社会的发展步伐

目前我国师范院校的教学片面强调学科知识的系统性、完整性，教学内容偏重学科知识、陈旧落后、重复多、与中小学实际脱节、各知识点处于离散状态等问题，呈现“旧、窄、杂、空”现象，无法反映当今科学发展的最新成果，缺乏时代感。

4. 高师对学生的科学素质和人文素质教育重视不够

为使学生构建文理渗透的知识结构，不少高师院校采取了一定的措施，如开设了一些通识课程和选修课程，取得了一定的成效，但情况依然不容乐观，特别是民族地区的高师院校仍然得不到足够的重视。科学知识、科学方法、科学态度和科学精神对培养学生的创新精神意义重大，所以师范生的科学素质不高对其今后从事教师工作，影响非同一般。特别是教师的工作是陶冶人、塑造人的事业，师范生人文素质不高不仅影响其本人今后作为教师的形象和人格魅力，而且也会对中小学生有不良的影响。因此应该加强对高师学生的科学素质和人文素质教育。

四、适应新课改的高师化学系师范生培养模式的探讨

新一轮基础教育课程改革的实施，对高师院校的人才培养模式提出严峻挑战，改革高师院校的人才培养模式已迫在眉睫。民族地区的高师化学系，应结合基础教育课程改革对中学化学教师的要求，引领基础教育课程改革，改变师范生培养模式，为基础教育输送创新型、素质型的中学化学教师。

1. 充分认识高师院校引领基础教育课程的重要现实意义

引领的实质，就是理论对实践的指导，理论与实践之间的对话，理论与实践的紧密结合[3]。民族地区的高师化学系，要引领基础教育课程改革，最重要的就是要充分认识高师院校引领基础教育课程的重要现实意义[4]。首先，民族地区的高师化学系要着眼于对当前基础教育课程改革和高师院校教育教学基本状况及存在的问题进行分析和认识，找出高师院校与基础教育之间相互联系的途径，从而制订高师院校引领基础教育课程改革的策略。其次，要着眼于对“引领”内涵的把握，通过分析和研究，找出高师院校引领基础教育课程改革的基本特点，从而创造性地构建高师院校引领基础教育课程改革的模式。

2. 完善高师化学系课程体系，优化课程结构

当前我国高师院校在课程结构上以学科专业为中心设置课程，比例不协调，学科专业课程比重过大，选修课程比例低，教育专业课程比重偏低现象严重。这样的课程结构容易培养出知识面窄，职业知识技能缺乏，教育方法单一，教育教学缺乏创造性的教师。从教育部颁发的《全日制义务教育化学课程标准（实验稿）》和《高中化学课程标准》中我们看到中学化学课程中已出现了许多综合性课程、活动实践课程、研究性课程，学科型教师已不能适应当今的基础教育课程改革的需要。因此，高师院校应按照综合素质课、学科专业课、教育理论与技能课、实践能力培养课四大模块，重新构建高师课程体系。民族地区高师院校化学系要按照化学教育专业培养目标重新审视各门课程的地位与作用，确立化学教育专业的基础课和主干课、必修课和选修课，组建新的核心课程；对相关课程进行必要的调整、合并和重组，进一步优化课程结构；增加小型化、专题性课程，积极探索多样化、系列化的研究性课程，注意开设新课程，如适应基础教育改革的课程、体现本学科发展前沿的课程、适应信息社会发展的课程；加大教育理论与技能课的比重，构建合理的、科学的，由教育理论课、教育教学技能课和教育实践课三大课程模块构成的教育理论与技能课程体系；强化通识课程，构建学生宽厚的基础知识平台，为学生进一步深入学习打下坚实的基础；增大选修课的比例并由学生根据自己的学习兴趣和学习能力自主选择，拓宽学生的学术视野。

3. 改革高师化学系教学内容，增加教学内容的时代性和适应性

从目前的高师课程来看，有些课程内容脱离中学实际，抽象的、深奥的理论课程和缺乏实际应用价值的课程过多，而培养实际需要的理论知识和教师职业技能训练的课程则相对较少，甚至一些培养中学教师必备能力的课程并没有设置。有些课程设置，如选修课不是从学生需要或培养目标考虑，并不是由学生自主选择，而是从教师的研究方向或研究成果来设置课程，整个课程缺乏注重务实的内容。所以，高师院校化学系应根据职业素质培养的需要增加当前教育教学改革的新理论、新成果，遵循"新而实、少而精、博而通"的原则更新教学内容，在夯实基础的前提下，压缩专业课课时，合理筛选专业课的内容，通过专业课教学使学生掌握学科学习和研究的思想、方法，提高专业课的实际教学效果；更新陈旧落后的教学内容，紧密结合当代社会、经济和文化发展的实际，努力吸收现代科技的新思想、新观点、新成就，充分体现学科的前沿知识和研究成果；删减重复内容，突出重点，增加课程容量；突破课程体系的封闭性，加强综合课程，注重学科交叉、文理渗透和多学科的融合，实现相关课程内容交叉整合，使课程内容综合化和通识化。

4. 改进高师化学系教学方法和教学手段，实现课程实施方式的现代化

高师院校应改革传统的以教师为中心的教学方式，让学生积极主动地参与教学全过程。在教学中充分发挥学生的主体作用，倡导启发式、发现式、讨论式、研究式等教学方法，促使学生积极主动地学习，使学习过程变成学生不断提出问题、解决问题的探索过程，并能针对不同的教学内容，选择不同的学习方式。改革陈旧单一的教学手段，将教育观念的更新和教学手段的更新结合起来，将信息技术与学科教学有机结合起来，充分发挥信息技术的优势，为学生的学习和发展提供丰富多彩的教学环境和有力的学习工具。

5. 加大教学实践的力度，提高民族地区高师化学系师范生化学教学技能

高师院校化学专业师范生在校期间学习化学专业知识及教育教学理论，不等于他们已掌握了化学教学技能。师范生在校期间要形成合理完善的智能结构，需要实现两个飞跃（突变）[5]，第一个飞跃是指学生把学习的化学专业知识及教学理论通过实践（如试讲）转化为化学教学技能，第二个"飞跃"是指学生把所掌握的有关化学专业知识及教学技能通过教学实践活动（如到中学参加教育见习、实习，到化工厂进行工业见习）再转化为教学能力。

(1) 加强实验技能训练，提高师范生实验操作能力

学好和掌握实验技能是化学教师的职业性素质，化学教师除了必须具备一般教师所需掌握的一般教学技能外，还必须具备娴熟、规范的实验操作技能，因此高师院校特别是民族地区高师院校化学系应该在教学计划中加强实践环节，加强实验教学，把化学教学技能训练程序化、系列化，开设系列必修课与选修课，并建立和完善化学实验微格教学实验室。

(2) 增加见习活动，确保教育实习质量

由于民族地区的经济文化和基础教育发展相对滞后，高师院校在生源竞争中始终处于弱势地位，特别是国家实施高校扩大招生的政策后，招生规模不断扩大，民族地区高师院校招收到的大学新生中分数较低、基础较差的学生也越来越多，生源总体质量相对以往有所下降。所以，民族地区高师院校化学系应该突破化学课程分科界限，有计划地安排、组织学生到化工厂进行综合性工业见习[6]，观察化工生产实际流程，运用所学的化学理论知识和教育理论知识分析见习活动中的所见所闻，让学生能够理论联系实际，提高运用知识解决实际问题的能力。

教育实习对师范生毕业从师任教起着举足轻重的作用，为了切实抓好教育实习，提高教育实习的质量，民族地区高师院校化学系应从以下几方面着手：一是增加教育见习的机会和时

间，把教育见习的时间分散到各个学期，保证每个学期都有 1 周以上的时间让学生结合该学期开设的教育理论课程到中学进行教育见习，巩固所学的教育理论知识；二是延长教育实习时间，最少也要达到其他国家的平均水平即 10～12 周；三是拓宽教育实习内容，让学生有更多的机会认识和参与实习学校的教学与管理，真正将教育实习落到实处，对学生进行一次职前的全方位训练；四是加强高师院校与中学的交流与合作，在中学建立教育实习基地，为师范生深入中学教学一线进行学习和交流创造便利条件。

6. 加强对师范生进行化学教学和科研能力培养的力度

高等师范院校化学专业教学必须充分体现“在教学中研究，在研究中教学”和“教学与科研并重”的思想，采取多种措施提高师范生的化学教学和科研能力。一是通过让学生参与课题研究，使学生更清楚地了解本学科的发展趋势，明确科研的发展方向，学会如何确定课题、如何论证课题、如何申报课题、如何制定教学实验计划、如何进行具体的教学实验活动、如何结题、如何撰写各种类型的科研论文等，鼓励他们亲身经历教学科研的全过程，并关注中小学化学教与学的热点问题，特别是结合中学化学新课程实施过程出现的问题进行有针对性的研究。广西高等教育学会化学专业委员会每年举办的“广西高校化学化工类论文及设计竞赛”就是一个很好的实践平台，很多化学专业的高师生在参与竞赛的过程中，科研能力得到了很大的提高，为他们毕业后在中学教学一线从事教育研究打下扎实的基础。二是通过指导学生广泛阅读有关化学教学理论和教学研究方法的论著来增长化学教学理论知识，以利于今后毕业后直接用于化学教学实践。三是通过与中小学建立化学教育教学合作伙伴的方式（如在中学建立教育教学实习基地），为解决中学化学教学过程中某些“理论与实践脱节”问题而有针对性进行教学研究活动。

五、结语

基础教育的发展有赖于高质量的师资，而高师教育的主要培养目标就是为中小学提供合格的师资。民族地区高师院校化学系应该根据当前基础教育课程改革和自身教育教学的实际状况，有针对性地推广和实施高师院校引领基础教育课程改革的策略，才能适应基础教育飞速发展的需要，为基础教育输送高质量的新型师资，为实施素质教育、发展基础教育做出更大的贡献，同时也从根本上促进自身发展定位的转型。

参考文献

[1] 梁梅.高师教育应对基础教育课程改革的策略思考[J].学术论坛，2004(3).
[2] 蒋家安.新课程背景下的师范院校教学改革[J].桂林师范高等专科学校学报，2004(3).
[3] 余文森.论以校为本的教学研究[J].教育研究，2003(4).
[4] 沈小碚.关于高师院校引领基础教育课程改革的一些思考[J].中国教育学刊，2004(1).
[5] 饶志明.论新型中学化学教师培养模式的构建[J].漳州师范学院学报(自然科学版)，2001,14(2).
[6] 莫国炜.高师化学系工业见习的新构想[J].广西高教研究，2000(2).

论高校体育教师如何应对社会转型的挑战

马小清*
（钦州学院，广西 钦州 535000）

摘　要：随着高校体育课程改革的深入，在体育教学中出现的新问题不断困扰着体育教育工作者，而探索和进行体育教学改革是体育教学重现生命力的必由之路。为此，高校体育教师要更新教学理念，变换社会角色，调整教学策略，不断加强自身的知识素养和提高教学实践能力，积极应对新课程的挑战。

关键词：高校体育教学；应对挑战；社会转型；教师角色

Discussion on How College Physical Teachers Respond to the Challenge of Social Transformation

Ma Xiao-qing
(Qinzhou University, Qinzhou 535000, China)

Abstract: Along with the deepening of college physical curriculum reform, the physical educators are plagued frequently by new issues appearing in physical teaching. Exploration of physical teaching reform is the only way to reproduce its vitality. So, college physical teachers should update teaching philosophy, transform their social roles, adjust teaching strategies, and continually improve their knowledge and teaching practice to respond to the challenges of the new curriculum.

Key words: college physical education; respond to challenge; social transformation; teacher's role

* 马小清，钦州学院体育系副教授。

1 前言

《中国教育改革发展纲要》指出:"谁掌握了21世纪的教育,谁就能在21世纪的国际竞争中处于战略主动地位"。在世界性教育改革浪潮滚滚而来的今天,为中华民族培养具有崇高人格、富有创新能力,可持续发展的一代新人,已成为一个极为重要的课题摆在了每一位教育工作者的面前。新的体育课程改革已经进行了七、八年,教学内容不断更新,教学手段层出不穷,但这似乎仅限于理论上和局部的修修改改,旧的教育体系仍然主宰着高校体育课程教学的全过程。随着社会的发展,愈演愈烈的人才竞争对传统的教育理念、教学方法、教师所扮演的角色诸方面发起了全新的挑战。在这样的时代背景下,广大的高校体育教育工作者如何找准自己的位置,扮演好自己的角色,是一个值得研究的重要课题。

2 传统的体育课教学对体育教师的影响

2.1 课的形式单一,缺乏实用性

在传统的体育教学中,教学仍以运动技术教学为主,重形式轻效果,重技术轻理论,教学形式单一、教学内容单调重复,缺乏实用性,严重束缚了体育教师和学生的积极性、创造性的发挥。日复一日,年复一年,这种重形轻实的教学现象,进一步导致了学生轻视体育课,对体育教学产生了厌烦,甚至产生抵触的心理情绪,同时也挫伤了体育教师的积极性,从而使体育教学陷入一定的恶性循环中。

2.2 重视教师指导,忽视学生能力的培养

体育教学是由教师的教和学生的学共同参与的双边活动过程。在这过程中,教师的教为主导,学生的学为主体,两者缺一不可。然而,目前的体育教学中大多数进行的是以教师为中心,学生处于被动从属地位的教学。教者发令,学者强应,身顺而心违,丧失了体育课应有的健身、娱乐成分,导致学生害怕体育课,由此造成"多数学生喜欢体育而不喜欢体育课"的现象。这种重教轻能,是不能达到系统地发展学生能力和培养学生终身体育意识的目的的。

2.3 重视教学结果,忽视过程性的发展

传统的体育教学对教学的评价基本上局限于学生体能和运动技能的终结性结果,忽视了对学生的学习态度、学习过程、习惯养成、情感、合作等能力方面的考虑,这种重结果轻过程发展的方法对学生来说是很不公平的,因为学生无论在体能、技能、兴趣、个性等方面都存在很大差异。这种重结果、轻过程的教学排斥了学生的思维和个性,把教学过程庸俗化到无需智慧努力,只听讲和记忆就能掌握知识的那种程度,于是便有了掌握知识却不思考知识、评判知识、创新知识的"好学生",这实际上是对学生智慧的扼杀、个性的摧残。

3 社会转型期体育教师的角色

3.1 变“教学控制管理者”为“适应社会发展的引路人”

21世纪是科学精神与人文精神交融统一的新世纪，是开拓创新的新世纪，是可持续发展的新世纪。随着社会生活节奏的加快和人才竞争的加剧，当今社会客观上要求青年大学生既要有强烈的爱国之志、报国之情，又要有很强的社会适应能力，在与他人的交往和互动中，正确协调好多方面的人际关系，积极学习和体验多种社会角色，个体社会化进程中必须面对难以预测的挫折和磨难。适应社会的过程实质上是一个个体不断社会化的过程，新时代所要求的社会适应赋予了学校体育更高的人文价值。传统的教学控制和全程的教学管理淡化、埋没了体育教学在提高学生社会适应力方面本应起到的巨大作用，阻碍和扼杀了学生强烈的进取心、能动的创造力和乐于接受新事物的渴望。因此，实现提高学生社会适应力的引路人的角色转变，把学生培养成为高质量、高素质的现代人才是每位高校教师义不容辞的职责。因此，体育教师在平时的体育课堂教学中，通过群体环境的身体练习来有效地促进学生团队精神、集体观念、价值观念的有效形成，利用形式多样、科学有效的方法来为学生的人际交往提供广阔的发展空间；通过形式多样的体育比赛和游戏练习来培养学生团结协作，全力竞争的心理品质，并使学生积极学习和体验多种社会角色，提高抗挫折能力，有效地积累自己的生活经验，利用体育活动特殊的规则效应有效规范、调整自己的行为方式和规则方式以及规则约束下的合理与人竞争和协同的心理素质。

3.2 变“传统封闭的教书匠”为“研究开放型的名师”

作为一名培养人、教育人的高校体育教师，必须具有对社会高度的责任感、高尚的服务和奉献精神、对本职工作以及培养新一代大学生的热情和激情。如果仅仅停留在“春蚕”、“人梯”和“蜡烛”的层面上，还远远不能满足日新月异的社会变革对高标准、高质量的竞争型人才的召唤和渴求。长期形成的传统封闭、学科封锁、画地为牢、知识结构老化使很多的体育教师落后于知识经济、信息化时代对体育教师的客观要求，使体育教师在社会发展和社会改革中的首创精神和重要作用难以体现。开拓创新的新时代，体育教师可持续发展的能力缺乏、底气不足的现象已日益凸显；崭新的时代期待和呼唤着能与国际教育接轨的研究开放型的名师。因此我们必须广泛地开展与国外教育机构、学校的国际学术交流、教师互访、合作科研、联合办学，积极引进和利用国外教育教学的先进经验、先进教材、先进的教学方法和教改经验等教育资源，及时捕捉和利用现代信息技术为教育教学提供优质服务，这已经成为当今世界教育与改革的新潮流。这就对传统封闭的教书匠角色发起了前所未有的冲击与挑战。因此，广大的高校体育教师必须重新审视自己所处的角色位置，全力调整好自己的心态，以饱满的热情、顽强的进取精神积极主动地投入到全球化教育改革的大潮中去。

3.3 变“知识技能的传递者”为“终身体育的促进者”

随着现代科学技术的迅猛发展，人们的生活和生产方式发生了质的变化，现代体育所带给人们的绝不仅仅是紧张之余的片刻松弛、闲暇之余的消遣娱乐，而是对一个现代人的体质提出了更高的要求。在现代生活节奏加快、工作高度紧张的环境中,旺盛的精力和强壮的体魄无疑是大学生进行社会主义现代化建设的物质基础和必要保证。现代学校体育所凸现出来的更多的是人生价值和生命价值的自我实现,没有一个健康的人类,当今社会一切物质文明的进步和发展必然成为空中楼阁。因此,实现当代大学生在校期间的体育锻炼和步入社会后的强身健体、终身体育的良性接轨,应当是一项利在当代,功在千秋的宏伟战略目标。这在客观和主观上要求广大高校体育教师大胆突破传统的体育教学观念,突破自身传统的体育知识和技能传递者角色身份,并积极向学生终身体育的促进者转轨。在平时的体育课堂教学中,充分发挥体育教师的主观能动性,把富有趣味性、娱乐性、竞赛性、激励性、实用性、富有时代特点和民族特色、在社会上广泛流行并有条件开展的可以满足学生体育需要的运动项目、不失时机地引入到体育课堂教学中来,振奋学生的体育学习热情;对运动竞技项目的规则和相关的体育考核办法进行大胆地改造,立足于学生的后天努力,使全体学生得到展示自己能力和才华的机会,使学生得以快乐地学习并获得成功的体验,从而有效地内化为学生积极参与体育锻炼的推动力;有目的、有计划地经常举办体育健身方法讲座,有意识地指导学生社团举办各种体育竞赛,向学生开放各种体育场馆并安排有特长的体育教师进行专门运动技术、技能和锻炼方法的指导;积极开展如篮球、排球、乒乓球、汽排球和武术等多种易于开展、难度不大、实用性强的运动项目选修课。多渠道、全方位地加大对学生科学锻炼身体方法的传播力度。使学生熟练掌握一、二项在校期间能够经常锻炼身体并延续到社会的终身体育运动项目,让健康陪伴他们步入人生生活的全过程。高校体育教师应努力使自己成为大学生终身体育锻炼的促进者和导航员,这是“以人为本,服务社会”的长远效益目标对高校体育教师的更高要求。

4 社会转型期高校体育教师的培养模式

4.1 体育教师的知识构建

4.1.1 更新课程理念,优化知识结构

高校体育是学校体育的最后阶段,是国民体育的基础,又是全民健身的中间环节、终身体育的桥梁和纽带,是培养全面发展直接适应社会的人才,强调教育结果的阶段。随着高等教育的全面推进,素质教育和培养创新人才的改革不断深入,转变教育观念更新知识结构,提高教学质量是体育教师的关键。体育教师通过丰富的文化知识,精深的专业理论和技术技能知识,通晓学科的基本结构和内在联系,创造必要的条件和氛围,主动积极地引导、调动学生的情感认知,以体育课程改革为中心,强调“身、心、社”三维健康观,确立教学目标,设立教学手段、教学策略方法,课程内外一体化的教学模式,使学生在体育锻炼中获得“学会了”的愉快、“增长了”的喜悦、“成功了”的兴奋,既增长知识发展能力,产生充实感,又磨炼了性格,锻炼了意志,增进学生的心理健康,使学生各方面都得到和谐的发展。所以,体育教师必须更新课程理念,对学生的影响不能局限于体育学科本身,而应是全方位的知识结构。

4.1.2 广泛积累经验,拓宽知识层面

体育教师既要有渊博的知识,又要积累丰富的经验,要以学科特点和学生的认识规律为依据,围绕培养厚基础、宽口径、高素质、强能力、广适应的人才为目标,对原有课程重新设计、更新构建,加强学科之间的内在联系,拓宽课程知识覆盖面,这样才能提高教师的课程教学质量

与效果，进一步满足和激发学生的求知欲，达到人才培养的目标定位。

4.2 体育教师的能力构建

4.2.1 自我学习能力

在科学技术飞速发展、高校信息化的今天，科技创新能力已经成为国际经济竞争和综合国力提高的制高点，成为一个国家和民族兴衰成败的关键所在，这将我们带入一个需要终身学习和自我学习的时代，同时也是高等院校立足科技舞台的坚实基础。社会转型阶段体育课程目标体系的改革需要体育教师不断拓展自己的知识领域。首先要成为学习者，善于学习，提高自我学习能力，了解教育改革的趋势，将自己从事的教学改革符合社会发展趋势，学习现代化的科技教学知识，掌握科技教学手段，深入了解体育教育创新的新领域、新方向、新成果，特别是随着现代体育、余暇体育、快乐体育的不断涌现，体育知识的不断更新，体育教师必须根据社会的发展，学生的兴趣爱好，充分调动学生的学习积极性，主动吸收有关体育与健康知识，不断提高自己的自我学习能力，以适应现代教育的发展需要，胜任新课程教学中的现代科技教学。

4.2.2 创新能力

21 世纪社会的发展呼唤创新型人才，学生创新意识和创新精神的培养乃至创新素质和创新能力的提高都与教师有着密切的关系。教师没有创造性，就很难培养出适应未来社会发展需要的创造性人才。体育教师因其教学方式的特殊性，教学有着广阔的创新空间，其创新的教学方法、教学形式对学生的影响是巨大的。因此，体育教师要充分利用体育课程的各种形式、内容、方法等方面的特殊性，培养和发展学生的创新意识和创新能力。体育教师要突破学科专业的界限，将相关的具有联系的内容融合为跨学科的综合性课程形式，这就需要体育教师富有创造力，只有这样才能打破体育教育过程中的单一和呆板，开展富有创造性的工作。另一方面，开发创造力是体育教师自身发展的内在需要，是发展能力的核心和动力目标，是高层次发展的要求，它具有自我创新、自我开发、自我实现的意义。

4.2.3 教学科研能力

教学科研能力是高校体育教师必须具备的条件之一。是体育教师由“单纯教学型”向“科研学者型”转变的必由之路，要想提高教学训练的质量和效果，使教学改革朝着纵深方向发展，获得更多更有价值的成果，有待于教师科研理论水平和实际工作能力的提高，这也是建设一支适应教育改革的高质量体育师资队伍的需要。

4.3 体育教师的素质构建

4.3.1 树立正确的人生观、价值观

社会转型期的体育教师首先要具有正确的人生观、价值观。政治素质在体育教师的素质结构中起着决定性作用，只有端正思想认识，树立正确的、科学的、合乎时代要求的教育观、价值观，才能获得持久的生命力，全身心地投入到教育事业中。

4.3.2 全面提高自身综合素质

体育教育改革新的学科体系建立，如何适应社会转型期的基本要求，实施素质教育，有利于学生身心完善、全面发展，体育教师的基本素质将决定其教学效果并对学生身心发展有直接和间接影响。全面提高教师的综合素质，是社会发展的需要，是社会转型期体育教育改革的趋势。同时，良好的职业道德是教师培养、塑造合格人才的核心，只有具备高度的事业心和责任

感，才能爱岗敬业，教书育人。教学中能以渊博的知识、高尚的道德、光明磊落的行为感染学生，做学生的楷模，成为学生的良师益友；能始终保持积极乐观的态度，不断完善自我，适应现代社会的发展。

5 结束语

高校体育经过多年的不断探索，已经取得了一定的成绩。随着社会的不断发展，社会给高校体育带来机遇的同时也带来了新的挑战，传统的高校体育教学已经不能适应日益发展的社会主义市场经济体制的要求，社会体育的蓬勃发展，体育教育的多元化功能以及教学形式的灵活多变冲击着传统的体育观、价值观，向体育教师提出了更严峻的挑战。

参考文献

[1] 于晓东，等. 关于体育课程中健康教育的几点思考[J]. 体育教学，2008(2).
[2] 吴键. 体育课程与教学改革的反思与困惑[J]. 体育教学，2008(10).
[3] 程杰出. 我国高校体育教学现状及改革设想[J]. 上海体育学院学报，1999(3).
[4] 徐元君，等. 体育课改方案的新走向[J]. 体育学刊，2002(5).
[5] 余文森. 教师教育课程改革的探索[J]. 教育评论，2007(5).
[6] 章克，傅晓军. 谈基于课程或课程群的教学团队建设[J]. 中国大学教学，2007(12).

识字教学中教师的汉字素养：问题、成因与对策

李永妃*

（钦州学院，广西　钦州　535000）

摘　要：当前识字教学中教师的汉字素养不高，其中字义方面的理论素养最低。主要原因是在传统小学教师教育的汉字教学、知识教学缺乏深度。小教专业应转变“词本位”为“字本位”观念，增补汉字宏观系统知识，加强语素的教学，增设汉字学、新课标解读和小学语文教材导读课程。

关键词：教师教育；小教专业；汉字素养；识字教学

识字教学是小学语文教学的重要组成部分，主要集中在小学低年级段。就我国大多数地区而言，小学教学以分科教学为主，有些教师甚至还固定在低、中、高的某个学段。所以，识字教学中教师的汉字素养，主要指小学语文教师所应具备的汉字学科素养。基于对小学语文教学的长期观察，本文试图对小学识字教学中教师在汉字素养方面存在的问题进行归纳，在此基础之上，分析成因，并对小教专业（综合文科）的部分课程的整改提出自己的应对之策。

一、识字教学中教师汉字素养存在的主要问题

（一）字音素养方面

1. 方音知识缺失

以汉语为母语学习普通话，就是由汉语方言向普通话过渡。其标准程度就是方音向普通话靠拢的程度。识字教学的教师应掌握所在教学地区方言的特点，以及与普通话的一一对应关系，具备方音辨正能力。这是识字教学的教师在汉字字音方面的职业素养。是否具备这方面的素养，决定其教学是否具有针对性。而现实是，小学一线教师方音素养普遍缺失，字音辨正能力不强。表现为，对所在教学地区汉语拼音教学的重难点不清，教学平均用力，只教标准音，对比辨别能力差，无力纠正学生的语音偏误，甚至存在盲点音，导致遗留问题较多，此其一。其二，在识字教学中，某个字音是否成为所在课时的重难点，举棋不定。其三，在农村小学低年级段，语言转换是学生要克服的主要困难，但是教师往往指导乏术，甚至没有指导意识，只能顺其自然。

2. 形声字的声符素养缺失

* 李永妃，钦州学院初等教育系副主任，副教授。主要研究语文课程与教学论。

汉字80%以上是形声字，所以掌握形声字的构字规律具有普遍意义。尽管形声字的表音功能已经弱化，但还是存在众多的全表音声符、半表音声符和部件音声符。识字教学的教师平时应注意收集积累，在教学中加以运用，但目前总体上表现得很无为。当然，关于形声字声符表音的规律，新课标也还是认识不足，已出版的12套教材中也没有得到体现[1]。此为题外话。

(二) 字形素养方面

1. 只顾笔画、笔顺和部件，对部首的功能认识不足

关于字形，有些教师只顾笔画、笔顺、部件，不顾其他。只教笔画、笔顺和部件，在低年级段当然可以，但在整个识字教学过程中只教这些，就成为大问题了。

汉字的构字是从字元，到字族。部首在汉字整个字集中起到提纲挈领的作用。如部首“页”与“头”有关，带出的字单在《现代汉语通用字表》里就有40多个。虽说部首现今的主要功能是检字，但它仍有极强的表意性和构字功能，往往教一个字元，带动一个字族。小学要求教识3000字，涉及的部首180个。教师如能充分利用，则可以简驭繁，帮助学生理解和识记各部首系统中众多的字，成倍提高识字效率。例如，“壴”(zhù)就有一个小系统，作义符，它和“支”(手持棍)构成“鼓”(敲鼓)，与“加”(声符)构成“嘉”(美好)，与“彡”(象征鼓声)构成“彭”(鼓声，后来写成“嘭”)；在“厨”中则做声符。遗憾的是，多数教师对部首未能予以重视，未能以部首带动字族的教学。

2. 部分部首含义理解偏误

有些教师从事小学语文教学十几年，甚至几十年，但对部分部首表示的含义仍是云里雾里。譬如，不知“阝”(左耳朵)是“阜”的变体，以其为偏旁的汉字与山丘、壁障、阶梯、楼台等有关，而“阝”(右耳朵)是“邑”的变体，以其为偏旁的汉字多与城镇、地域有关；不知“罒”是“网”的变体；不知“月”部的字主要与肌肉有关，与月亮有关只是少量字；不知“王”只与玉石有关，与“王”根本无关；不明白表示颜色的字何以以“纟”为部首；把“灬”理解为四点水，把“⺗”解释为小字底多一点，等等。

(三) 字义素养方面

1. 字义理解表浅化

识字教学中的字义，是指字在生活语境中的具体含义，包含字所代表的概念所反映的自然、社会和人文知识。但是，部分教师的教学，在随课文识字中只局限于课文语境的意义，在集中识字中只局限于现今使用的主要意义，而不涉及次要含义或本义、比喻义。由此引发的是学生写错字，用错字。譬如，不跟学生交代清楚我国古代丝绸业发达，颜色多跟染丝有关，凡是跟颜色有关的字均从“纟”(丝线)，所以学生容易写错表示颜色的字；不跟学生交代清楚“初”的本义是用剪刀裁剪衣服的开始，所以学生对“初”的左边是“衤”还是“礻”，印象不深；没有告诉学生“启”由本义“打开门”虚化泛指“打开”，“缄”由本义“捆扎箱子”引申为“封住信封”，所以学生才在明信片上写“×××启”和“×××缄”。

汉字本身蕴含着丰富的文化信息。如能运用汉字科学教学，当能从中潜移默化传播中华文化，进行文学教育，富有情趣。教学生字时，应把字词的比喻义、象征义或双关义、联想义教给学生。比如，狐狸的狡猾，鸽子的儒雅，鹰的强硬，变色龙的适应，松竹梅的高洁，等等。这是字词的文学意蕴，带有深刻的民族文化烙印，字典词典上查不到，教材不给出，课标不作要求，

全凭教师自行把握，却又是一句话即可轻易交代清楚。倘若教师能教，那么，学生语感就日渐见强，不至于对“那人像条狗”之类的话搭茬儿说“狗很可爱啊”，令人语塞。很遗憾，关于汉字的文化信息，在识字教学中大多是遗失的。相比而言，在汉字音形义之中，教师们在字义尤其是汉字所蕴含的文化信息方面的素养是最低的。

2. 缺乏构字知识，随意拆解汉字

(1) 根据习惯分析字义，造成形义脱节

譬如“章”，教师习惯将其拆分为“立”和“早”。许慎《说文解字》却说“乐竟为一章，从音从十。十，数之终也。”“音”为“音乐”，“十”有“终止之意”。又譬如，将“喜”分解成“十、豆、口”，解释为“十豆落入口”。可这个字却是“壴”(音 zhù)和“口”的合体。“壴”是象形字，像架设着的一面鼓，上面是装饰，中间是一面鼓，下面是鼓架。“壴、口”合体，就是以鼓乐和笑口表示“喜”义。再譬如，“颖”、“腾”，教师们习惯将其拆分为左右结构，实际上“颖”是“禾”和“顷”的合体，“腾”是“联”和“马”的合体。

(2) 按照现代生活分析字义，造成形义脱节

譬如，把“富”拆分为“一家一口人一亩田”。看似既说明了字形，又合乎字义，很有道理，其实是望文生义，支离了字的结构。“富”其实是个会意字，上下结构，上从“宀”，意思是房屋，下从“畐(fù)”意思是是酒器，同时兼表音，合起来表示“家中有酒”。这个字造出来的当时表示的意义是家中有酒，才算富，因为酒是用粮食酿造的，当粮食多得吃不完有富余之时才用于酿酒。

(3) 重形轻义，拆解汉字随意性大

字形教学是识字教学的难点。教师们为了让学生记住字形，编制了许多歌谣、字谜等韵语，以增强教学的形象性和趣味性。这本来无可厚非。但是有些教师过分地强调字形，不顾字义，造成重形轻义，因形害义的后果。譬如，将“怕”拆解为“因为害怕，脸都吓白了”，将“浊”拆解为“水里有小虫”，将“蚕”拆解为“造福于人类的天虫”。

(四) 语素素养方面

让学生用所学的生字组词，是字义教学最常用也是最有效的手段。生字组词，其实就是语素构词。但由于汉字与语素关系复杂，所以识字教学中总是问题不断，纰漏丛生。

1. 误拆多音节语素

作为单纯词，连绵词中的音节(汉字)，合则有义，分则无义，本身并不具备独立的语素意义和构词能力。譬如，“乒乓、蜻蜓、吉普、巧克力、奥林匹克”中任何一个音节(汉字)，教学生字时教师总是将其拆成一个个的汉字来先后出示，而不是整体呈现。更荒唐的是，还要求学生用这些汉字来组词。究其原因，是因教师不了解多音节语素造成的。当然也有一些无义音节(汉字)明显已语素化，构词能力较强，譬如，“蝶、蛛”，另当别论。

2. 常用多语素义汉字的部分含义缺失

汉字与语素的关系复杂，表现之一就是一个汉字可以有几个不同的语素意义。譬如，“副”这个字就可以代表三个语素：“副①”，表示第二的，次级的意思，如“副手”、“副食”；“副②”，表示相称，如“名不副实”；“副③”，表示某种事物的计量单位，如“一副手套”、“一副担架”。这类汉字在不同的复合词中有不同的意义和作用。学生在生字组词中感觉难度不大，但如倒过来要求在词中辨析字义难度就大，教师也有同感。

3. 语素构词理论缺失

有些语素构词之后,语素义与词义差别很大,词义往往不是语素义的简单相加,譬如"下课、买单、眼球、阳光、露马脚"等,这类词是使用引申、借代、比喻、象征、双关、关联或联想或利用语用场合差异构成的,可教师们往往说不清楚。

4. 混淆不同功能的同形语素

(1) 混淆外来音节语素化的语素和汉语固有的同形语素

譬如,"吧"是一个音译外来词音节,后来逐渐语素化,成为一个构词能力极强的名词性词缀。喜爱新鲜事物的年轻学生容易接受这一类新词,故而在给语气词和象声词语素"吧"组词时组成"酒吧、网吧、氧吧、吧台"等,拒斥汉语固有的同形语素。对此,教师往往是无话可说。

(2) 混淆语法功能不同的同形语素

汉语的语素既有意义的不同,也有功能的不同。语素的构词功能和语素意义密切相关。例如,集中识字"把、的、和、以、从、在、吗、呢"。从教材给出的语境看,这些字均是虚语素。可是教师很容易忽略这类语素的非构词性而要求学生组词。于是,学生也就将其当成同形实语素来对待。无疑,这是有违教材编写的初衷的。

还有另一种情况,就是由于汉语的词缀多是由词根逐步虚化而来,当虚化了的词缀在语义、功能上脱离母体词根以后,仍用同一汉字来记录,这样就形成了词根词缀同形的情况。由于词根、词缀的不同参与,语素构词就形成了复合词与派生词的不同,所以要对同形词根、词缀语素加以区别。但是部分教师未能予以区别。譬如,将"莲子、赤子、长子"等中的"子"与"桃子、桌子、帘子"等中的"子"相混,将"舌头、磁头、桥头"等中的"头"与"石头、跟头、兆头"等中的"头"相混。

二、识字教学中教师汉字素养部分缺失的成因

现代经济体制要求社会个体合模化工作,个性化生存。教育同时承担人的社会化和个性化职能。教育就是要通过较长一段时间的培养,使受教育者具备适应现代经济体制的思维习惯和生活方式。对于教育来说,人在社会化的同时个性化,建构个体精神世界才是最根本的东西。课程的核心要素是知识。知识是激起学生终身发展的愿望并要求学生以多种方式学习并获得人生意义的信息。[2]因此课程知识的教学突破"外在于人的精神"的知识—能力思维范式,着眼于"知识与人的相遇"[3]的生动情景。

具体到语文课程,就是要在"语文知识教学和个体自由精神的内在关联"中确立人本主义的语文知识观。[4]在教学中突破语言符号表征的层面,深入到语言的形式和意义领域,实现深度教学,[5]帮助学生实现个体整体素养的提升。与其他学科相比,语文课程的人文性更为突出。语文课程要借助语文学科帮助学生建立起他们的精神家园。要将学习语文知识和形成语文能力的过程,变成同时也是个体建构精神世界的过程。在学习语文知识,形成语文技能,发展语文能力的同时,也是在接受汉民族文化传统熏陶,形成思维方式,建构个体精神世界。可具体到汉字教学,现实与上述教学理想存在着差距:

(一) 汉字教学只停留在符号表征层面,未能实现深度教学

传统小学教师教育汉字教学只停留在符号表征层面,未能深入到形式和意义领域。主要体现为:由于对汉字基本理论缺乏深刻的认识,教学内容主要局限在3500个常用汉字的音形

义的范围内。在音形义中又仅仅重视音和形的教学,本应是教学重点的义,却得不到到应有的重视,此其一。其二,包括汉字孳生繁衍规律、汉字效用递减律、汉字音形义关联、汉字区别性和节约性高度统一等一系列汉字构字规律在内的整个汉字宏观系统知识,却付之阙如。其三,语素在识字教学中地位非常重要,但却因其概念抽象而被拒斥,成为致命的薄弱点。这样,学生得到的知识是零碎的、不成系统的、浮于表层的。学生只知其一,不知其二,当然生成不了一个完整的汉字学概念,当然就难以内化,难以转识成智,在之后的识字教学中缺乏肥沃的汉字学土壤。

(二) 教学用时严重不足,教学的过程属性缺失

受印欧系语言的影响,目前我国汉语母语教学实行的是“词本位”教学,以词为基本语法单位,把汉字作为单纯的书写符号,使其附庸于词汇教学。目前高师现代汉语教材的多个版本,内容包括现代汉语及其书写符号、语音、语汇、语法、语用。把汉字仅当作现代汉语的书写符号。以笔者所在的钦州学院的高师现代汉语课程计划为例,“汉字”就仅作为现代汉语的书写符号来教学,内容包括汉字的性质和作用、现行汉字的形体和构造、现行汉字的规范化和现代化,仅用 4 个课时,约占现代汉语课程课时总量 99 个课时的 4%。时间的仓促,导致教学蜻蜓点水,教与学都无法充分展开,知识缺乏个体化的过程。知识无法与学生相遇、相识、相知,学生无暇体悟、构建、生成,无法将公共的知识内化为个体的知识。

识字教学的教师汉字素养不高的主要原因是课程知识观的问题,表现为汉字知识教学深度不够。

三、小教专业汉字教学应采取的课程整改对策

(一) 变“词本位”观念为“字本位”观念

识字教学是小学语文教学的重要内容之一。汉字学是小教专业最重要的专业基础知识。小教专业的汉字学知识的教学,倘若再如传统现代汉语课程那样设置和实施,所培养的小学师资汉字学科素养储备肯定不够,将来难以担当识字教学的重任。汉字是用于整体转写言语音节的书面汉语的基本单位。[6]汉字、音节、语素三位一体。(吕叔湘,1964)对汉字性质和特点的澄清,目的在于扭转识字教学师资培养主体的思想观念,在今后的学科课程整合中有所举措,变“词本位”观念为“字本位”观念,重视汉字学的课程建设。

(二) 增补汉字宏观系统知识

汉字宏观系统知识主要指孳生繁衍规律、效用递减律、音形义关联、区别性和节约性高度统一。汉字宏观系统知识的教学,旨在帮助学生搭建汉字学的基本理论框架。传统小教专业现代汉语的汉字部分,教学内容只局限在汉字微观系统的范围内,即局限在 3500 个常用汉字的音形义的范围内,汉字宏观系统知识几乎付之阙如。小教专业的学生如果只有 3500 个常用汉字的音形义方面的零散不成体系的汉字微观系统知识,缺乏汉字宏观系统理论知识作支撑,是很难成就高水平的识字教学师资的。

普通话水平等级测试的铺开,注重字音的训练,更加剧了这种状况。在这样的课程设置下

培养出来的师资,当然不可能创造性地发挥汉字宏观系统知识在识字教学中的威力。新课标对以上汉字构字规律认识仍然不足,已出版的12套小语教材,同样未能得到体现。[7]此为题外话。

字元,字族,常用字,能产度,实词,虚词,具体,抽象,构成生字表生成的基本原则。核心是能产度和频度。两数平均,便是生字表的编写依据。汉字“因义构形”,“因形表意”,“形”“义”密切相关。识字教学遵循这个原理,才不至于随意拆解汉字,“因形害义”。识字教学教师如能深刻认识汉字区别性和节约性高度统一,就能高度重视汉字的生成元素——24个基本笔画和120个部件的教学。

汉字宏观系统知识的增补,就是要引导学生读懂隐藏在生字表背后的字频和孳生繁衍规律,生成字理、笔画、部件、部首等概念。

(三)重视语素的教学

汉字语素一体。一个汉字对应一个语素的情况有上万种之多。但是,汉字与语素并非一对一的关系:同一汉字有多个不同意义的语素,不同的汉字表示同一语素,一个汉字包含两个语素,有的汉字不表示任何语素,多个汉字合起来表示一个语素。所以说汉字与语素关系是复杂的。

众所周知,有上万之多的汉字是一个汉字对应一个语素,而大部分的语素可以单独成词。尽管现在还不知道确切数字,也不知道具体是哪些语素可以单独成词,但是,可以肯定的是,能单独成词的语素毕竟占大多数。所以,字的教学,其实就是语素的教学,就是词汇教学。汉语的教学,可以用“字”的教学取代拼音文字中的“语素”的教学。[8]

语素地位尽管重要,但因概念抽象,故而多数时候是避而不教。传统中师以及现今的小教专业的现代汉语课程,语素教学的内容就仅仅是语素是汉语最小的单位,语素是词的下一层级语言单位,至于汉字与语素是什么关系,则避而不教。同时,语素的教学与词的教学糊在一起,没有专用的课时。语素是小教专业汉字教学内容中的短板。小学一线教师在生字组词和词义辨析方面暴露出来的问题表明,今后语素理论的内容亟待充实,包括常用实语素的认知在内。

(四)整合相关课程

小教专业应以识字教学师资的汉字学科素养需求为依据,从现有的古代汉语、现代汉语课程中选取内容要素,构建成对识字教学能起实际支撑作用的汉字学课程。这应是今后小教专业的专业基础课程建设的一个着力点。同时,增加语文新课标解读和小学语文教材导读两门课程,以便让学生更好地把握新课标,理解教材的编写意图。语文新课标解读和小学语文教材导读,宜作为小教专业核心课程小学语文教育学的配套选修课来开设。

参考文献

[1][7] 雷实.语文课程标准实验教科书识字教材的发展与问题探讨[J].课程·教材,教法.2009(5).

[2] 郭元祥.新课程背景下课程知识观的转向[J].全球教育展望,2005(2).

[3] 郭元祥.知识与人的相遇[J].华中师范大学博导讲坛,2008(5).

[4] 谌安荣.语文知识教学与个体精神自由[J].语文学习,2007(2).

[5] 郭元祥.知识的性质、结构域深度教学[J].课程·教材·教法,2009(11).

[6][8] 吕必松.说“字”[J].汉字文化,2009(1).

问题表征对问题解决影响的教学实践

李燕清*
（钦州学院，广西　钦州　535000）

摘　要：解决数学问题是数学学习的核心，是体现学生数学能力的重要标志，是数学教学的重要任务。表征问题是解决问题的关键，决定着解决问题的方向和成败，不同的表征产生不同的解决方法，注意语言互译、利用熟知图式、多角度表征、合理调节表征都有利于问题的解决。

关键词：问题表征；问题解决；教学实践

Teaching Practice on How Problem Understanding Affects Solution

Li Yanqing
（Qinzhou University Qinzhou，Guangxi 535000，China）

Abstract：How to solve problems is the center of learning the main task of teaching and an important symbol of students aptitude for mathematics. Understanding determines problem solution，for it guides the way to success or failure. Diffent understanding produces different solution. Understanding correctly，taking advantage of familiar methods and formula analysing problem from different points of view and regulating understanding reasonably are beneficial to problem solution.

Key words：problem understanding；problem solution；teching practice

“问题是数学的心脏”。因此，问题解决成为数学教学的重要任务，学生是否能解决不同的问题是数学能力高低的标志之一。现代心理学认为，正确的问题表征是解决问题的必要条件，

* 李燕清，广西钦州学院初等教育系讲师，主要从事数学教育和研究。

不同的表征会产生不同的解决方法。所谓问题表征是指解题者通过审题,认识和了解问题的结构,通过联想,激活头脑中与之相关的知识经验,从而形成对所要解决问题的一种完整的印象。问题表征分为问题字面理解和问题深层理解两个层面,问题的字面理解是指解题者能用自己的话重新表述问题,把问题中的每一陈述转换成解题者内部的心理表征。问题的深层次理解是指在问题表层理解的基础上,进一步把问题的每一陈述综合成条件、目标统一的心理表征[1]。虽然如何表征问题才有利于问题解决没有固定模式,但问题的表征对问题的解决存在着必然的联系。因此,在教学实践中,研究问题表征对问题解决的影响是十分必要的。

1 注意语言互译,进入问题空间

数学语言分为文字语言、符号语言和图形语言,是人们进行数学思维和交流的工具。文字语言通俗易懂,便于理解和思维,符号语言简洁明了,图形语言直观形象。数学问题都是通过这三种语言表达的。从现代认知心理学的角度来看,问题解决者对问题的表征也就是形成问题空间,对同一个问题,不同的解题者会形成不同的问题空间;即使是同一个问题,同一个解题者在不同的时间也会有不同的问题空间。问题空间的形成很大程度上取决于解题者的语言互译能力,这种语言互译能力,是解题者将外部信息转化为内部信息去实现的,也就是必须将问题的各种信息转化为内部表征,才能形成问题空间。

在问题表征过程中,导致建构出错误的或者不完整的问题空间的因素包括:信息遗漏、信息误解、喻隐干扰(问题信息中潜在的歧义使被试困惑或误导被试的解题思想)等[2]。在解决实际问题中,不能形成正确的问题空间往往是由背景障碍所引发的,对背景的生疏感、模糊感、神秘感、主要是由于缺乏实际的感受,不能将问题正确表征成容易理解、容易表达的语言。例如,不了解“增长率”、“纯利”;“单循环制”、“淘汰赛”;“增长了”、“增长到”等。这些都会影响到问题的表征,因此在教学中要时刻强化学生的联想意识,调动他们平常留心观察、发现数学应用问题背景的积极性,把日常生活中的各种情景摄入大脑中,对物理、化学、生物、地理等各个学科中的有关问题赋予数学的思考,这样就能大大缩短学生与购物、投资、管理、设计、环境、资源、气象、天文、航海、信息技术等背景的距离,进一步正确理解题意从而正确地表征问题。通过对书面考试的仔细分析后得出,学生在考核中的失败往往不是由于未能掌握相关的算法,而是语言上的困难,包括语义结构、词汇和数学的符号等,从而,在数学教学中我们就不应只关注学生对算法的掌握,而应更加重视“理解”和“转换”(后者即指由问题的词语转向适当算法的选择)[3]。能克服不利于建构问题空间的因素产生,采用恰当的数学语言表达问题,是正确表征问题的关键,是正确理解问题的第一步。在错误的或者不完整的问题空间中搜索不可能求得问题的正确解[4]。因此,在教学中应注意文字语言、符号语言和图形语言三者之间相互表征的能力培养,从而在表征转换的过程中使对问题的理解更准确和深化,以便形成正确的问题空间。

2 调用熟知图式,作为切入点

数学问题解决是解题者在自己的长时记忆中提取问题解决图式用于新问题情境的过程。图式理论认为,知识图式是表征储存在记忆中的一般概念的网状资料结构,其基本活动方式是自下而上的资料驱动加工和自上而下的概念驱动加工，其中心作用在于构建对于某个事件、某客体、或某种情形的解析。问题图式包括个体已有的与新问题有关的知识基础、解题决策和解题经验。图式具有激活、预测和引导的功能，有利于问题的迅速表征和解决。在解决问题时，若把一个命题的条件或结论转化成熟知的图式表征，就能在解题的指导思想上体现得较深刻，而在方法论意义上使其应用更为广泛。从认知心理学的角度来看，问题的关键认知因素是能否对问题进行恰当表征，能否实现模式迁移，能否有效执行自我监控。问题的表征意义是为了使问题得到解决，而问题的解决受熟知图式的影响，因此，表征某一问题时，都是尽可能向熟知的图式接近，在教学实践中已充分证明了这一点。虽然图式的运用可以顺利地解析数学活动，但是如何在适当的教材课程中正确运用图式、并以图式作为数学问题思考的工具，则着实考验教学者的智慧与学习者的学习能力。有些数学关系如果能用图式表征，赋给它一定的几何意义，其结果便显而易见。

例如，设 $A(x_1,y_1)$，$B(x_2,y_2)$两点在抛物线 $y=2x^2$ 上，l 是 AB 的垂直平分线，当且仅当 x_1+x_2取何值时，直线 l 经过抛物线的焦点 F？

若按抛物线的概念来表征，则可解为：

$F\in l\Leftrightarrow|FA|=|FB|\Leftrightarrow$ A、B 两点到抛物线的距离相等，$y_1\geqslant0$，$y_2\geqslant0$，y_1、y_2不同时为 0，上述条件等价于 $y_1=y_2\Leftrightarrow x_1^2=x_2^2\Leftrightarrow(x_1+x_2)(x_1-x_2)=0$，因为 $x_1\neq x_2$，所以上述条件等价于 $x_1+x_2=0$。

若按线段垂直平分线的性质表征，则可解为：

依题意知，$F\left(0,\frac{1}{8}\right)$，$\mathrm{A}(x_1,2x_1^2)$，$\mathrm{B}(x_2,2x_2^2)$ $(x_1\neq x_2)$。

l 是 AB 的垂直平分线

$$\begin{aligned}|FA|=|FB|&=\sqrt{x_1^2+\left(2x_1^2-\frac{1}{8}\right)^2}\\&=\sqrt{x_2^2+\left(2x_2^2-\frac{1}{8}\right)^2}\Leftrightarrow 4x_1^4+\frac{1}{2}x_1^2\\&=4x_2^4+\frac{1}{2}x_2^2\Leftrightarrow(8x_1^2+8x_2^2+1)(x_1+x_2)(x_1-x_2)=0\end{aligned}$$

因为 $x_1\neq x_2$，所以上式等价于 $x_1+x_2=0$。

若按向量来表征，则可解为：

依题意知，$F\left(0,\frac{1}{8}\right)$，$A(x_1,2x_1^2)$，$B(x_2,2x_2^2)$，其中，$x_1\neq x_2$，$AB$ 的中点 $M\left(\frac{x_1+x_2}{2},x_1^2+x_2^2\right)$，$l$ 是 AB 的垂直平分线$\Leftrightarrow\overrightarrow{FM}\cdot\overrightarrow{FB}=0\Leftrightarrow\left(\frac{x_1+x_2}{2},x_1^2+x_2^2-\frac{1}{8}\right)(x_2-x_1^2,x_2^2-2x_1^2)=0\Leftrightarrow(x_2-x_1)(x_1+x_2)\left(2x_1^2+2x_2^2+\frac{1}{4}\right)=0$，因为 $x_1\neq x_2$，所以上式等价于 $x_1+x_2=0$。

可见，向熟知的图式进行问题表征，就会找到解决问题的突破口。因此，在教学中要培养学生敏锐的观察力，通过训练来强化数学结构图式的应用，并把积累的经验在头脑中形成“集成块”，提高表征的速度和质量，将所提供的材料或既定的信息序列进行重新组合或转化，形成大量有意义的结构图式，以便更快地找到表征问题的切入点。

3 多角度表征,寻找最佳方案

在问题表征过程中,如果对问题进行合理地等价描述,就可以选择最有利于问题解决的方向进行表征,从而可以优化解题过程,得到问题解决的最佳方案。问题表征形式一般包括数式表征、示意图表征、列表表征等,在数式表征中,应力求做到科学、准确、通识,因为正确的问题表征往往是“数”认识的成果表征,若能将问题的数字、符号、算式、关系等写出来,则可以减轻记忆的负担,若利用已有信息做层次关系分析逐步进行数式表征,问题就会变得清晰明了;在解决比较复杂的问题时,画出示意图形是表征问题十分有效的方法,当数学问题中数量关系所包含的规律比较隐蔽、不容易理解时,应当恰当地画出示意图。这种表征方法可以使复杂的问题简单化;列表表征可以清楚地呈现信息间的关系或规律,往往可以缩短理解的时间,有利于发现解决问题的结果和方向。问题解决者确定以什么方式来解决问题,一方面取决于他自身的相关知识和经验,另一方面取决于他如何表征问题。

例如,已知两点 $M\left(1,\frac{5}{4}\right)$,$N\left(-4,-\frac{5}{4}\right)$并给出下面曲线方程:

(1) $4x+2y-1=0$;(2) $x^2+y^2=3$;(3) $\frac{x^2}{2}+y^2=1$;(4) $\frac{x^2}{2}-y^2=1$。这些方程的曲线上存在点 P,能满足 $|MP|=|NP|$ 的是__________。

审题对“在满足 $|MP|=|NP|$”这一信息,可有(1) 曲线上存在点 P 到 MN 的距离相等;(2) 曲线上有一点 P 在线段 MN 的垂直平分线上;(3) 线段 MN 的垂直平分线与曲线相交等三种不同的表征。可见,表征(3)的运算最小,最有利于问题的解决。

4 合理调节表征,培养思维能力

我们知道,问题表征分为问题的字面理解和问题的深层理解两个层面,而问题的深层理解包括识别问题类型,以及区分问题中的有关信息和无关信息。在解决问题中,具有共同结构的一类问题或具有相同解法的一类问题称为一种模式,当解题者接触到数学问题以后,能将该问题归类,使得与自己认知结构中的某种书模式相匹配的过程。认知心理学研究表明,模式识别过程是感觉信息与长时记忆中的有关信息进行比较,再决定它与哪个信息有着最佳匹配的过程,可见在表征问题时,头脑中经历了直觉选择与搭配的思维过程,这个过程对培养一个人的直觉思维是非常必要的。

在教学实践中,我们发现思维能力好的学生在表征一些问题时,总努力寻找一个特殊情况表征,这是从共性中找个性,从那些不具体的、抽象的数学问题的普遍性中抓住其本质,进而把这一结果放大,从而筛选出适宜问题普遍解决的表征,因此,我们必须利用这一有利时机进行培养学生思维的深刻性。

当一个问题的某一种表征不利于或不能使问题得到解决时,解题者就应该有意识地改变表征问题的方式。在解决问题的过程中,随着信息的积累,可以从不适宜的表征过渡到适宜的表征。对于思维能力好、问题意识强的学生来说,一旦发现了问题,就会产生解决问题的需要和内驱力,产生一种心理上的不平衡,激起强烈的求知欲和好奇心,进行积极自主地思维,从而表征问题，直到解决问题。

“思维是可以通过专门的训练教会的”[5]。在教学实践中我们发现，大多数学生在表征问题的过程中，往往只顺着事物发展过程去思考，注重由因到果的思维习惯，不注重变换方式，不及时调节表征，对那些不具体的抽象的数学问题常常抓不住其本质，转化为已知的数学模型或过程分析去解决。当原来的表征不奏效时，就应该换一个角度思考问题，有意识地改变表征问题的方式，这是培养学生思维能力的有利时机。

总之，在问题解决过程中，问题表征是至关重要的一步，决定着问题解决的方向和成败，在教学中应引起足够的重视，这样才有利于问题解决，有利于学生数学素质的全面提高。

参考文献

[1] 喻平. 数学教育心理学[J]. 南宁：广西教育出版社，2004：238.
[2] 傅小兰，何海东. 问题表征的一项研究[J]. 心理学报，1995，2.
[3] 郑毓信. 语言与数学教育[J]. 数学教育学报，2000，3.
[4] 傅小兰，何海东. 问题表征的一项研究[J]. 心理学报，1995，2.
[5] 郅庭瑾. 为思维而教[J]. 教育研究，2007，2.

适应基础教育改革需求,凸显地方特色,建设科学实用的课程体系

——试论小学教育文科方向汉语类课程教学改革*

施日梅

(钦州学院,广西 钦州 535000)

摘 要:汉语类课程是小学教育专业文科方向的骨干课程,根据其专业特点及培养目标,应整合为"一主一修几选"的课程体系,其中应注重方言和汉字的教学。

关键词:小学教育;文科方向;汉语类课程

一、关于小学教育专业文科方向培养目标定位问题

小学教育专业是我国高等教育新兴的重要专业之一[1],纳入高校教育体系仅有十年的时间,它是为了适应我国基础教育的发展需求而设置的专业,目标是培养高素质、高学历的小学师资。

由于小学教育专业脱胎于中师教育,纳入高等教育体系的时间不长,从事小学教育教学和研究的人员大多数为中师原班的人马,新纳入高等教育体系的小学教育专业还未能从更高的高度审视小学教育,对于该专业的性质、专业的定位还有很多争议,甚至专业的名称还处于争议当中。

上海师范大学惠中教授2003年指出小学教育专业是我国高等教育专业体系中一个以培养高素质新型教师的综合性专业[1],它既不同于中等师范教育,也应区别于高等教育中的教育类专业或学科教育,其专业特征一是以社会需求为导向,二是具有很大的学科综合性。

惠中从战略高度界定了小学教育专业的性质、地位,根据惠中等人见解,我们认为小学教育专业具备有以下几个方面的特点:

1. 职业导向明显,小学教育专业培养的是适应21世纪基础教育改革和发展需要的小学教师。2001年国家教育部颁布《全国义务教育课程标准(实验稿)》,新一轮的教育教学改革已全面铺开,新课改对教师提出了新的要求,直接影响到高师教育教学,尤其影响到小学教育专业。小学教育专业应以基础教育改革导向调整课程体系和教学计划。

2. 小学教育具有基础性、综合性的鲜明特征,使得小学教育专业成为复合型的专业,不是学科与教育学简单的拼凑,而是学科知识与教育学有机的融合。

---

* 本文为新世纪高等教育教学改革工程项目小学教育课程整合研究(编号为2008B021)阶段性研究成果之一。

3. 小学教育应凸显地方特色。

由于基础教育具有基础性,同时我们也认为,小学教育专业应面向地方,为地方培养合格的人才,特别是培养农村基础教育急需的师资力量。我国是农业大国,农村人口7.27亿,农村人口占全国总人口的58.24%[2]。农村基础教育水平关系到国民素质提升问题。但目前,据周昆[3],农村基础教育状况不容乐观。农村教师编制少,数量不足;流失严重,队伍老龄化;提高农村师资建设水平已迫在眉睫。2007年1月1日颁布的《2007年教育部工作要点》把教师队伍建设特别是提高农村师资水平放在更加突出的战略位置。

作为地方高校,应直接服务于地方的经济建设和文化建设。作为以教学为主的地方高师院校[4],在课程设置方面应该结合本地区经济和文化的特点,突出地方特色,体现办学层次,为地方尤其是广大农村输送合格的基础教育师资。小学教育专业是培养基础教育师资的主阵地,应为地方输送基础教育的师资力量,它的设置应根据地方经济发展水平和文化特色以及文化水平,为地方培养应用型人才。

二、小学教育专业文科方向课程设置的特点

小学教育专业文科方向是小学教育专业重要的专业方向,目标是培养合格的高素质的小学语文师资。

课程的设置与教学手段及教学方法的选用取决于课程培养目标,课程培养目标是课程设置的指南针。小学教育专业文科方向的课程应根据小学教育专业培养目标进行设置。汉语类课程是小学教育文科方向的骨干课程,它的设置是否合理对能否培养合格的小学语文师资起着决定性的作用。

尽管高等教育面向基础教育培养师资,但教师职前培养与现实需要还存在诸多的问题,杨四海指出[5],目前的高师教师职前培养的目标不适应基础教育的需要;教师职前培养体制不科学;教师职前培养课程体系和结构不合理;教师职前培养的方法和手段陈旧落后;教师职前培养对学生从教能力培养不够;等等。

自从2005年钦州学院开设小学教育专业文科方向以来,已经毕业了三届毕业生,为社会输送了人才,在专业建设上也取得了重大的成绩。但回顾反思,由于专业开设时间不长,还不能形成自己独特的办学特色,在课程建设上还有许多的不足。以汉语言类课程为例,在课程设置上有以下特点:

1. 仿照汉语言文学专业,缺乏专业特色

汉语类课程由几大块构成:基础理论类,包括现代汉语、古代汉语、语言学概论;应用语言类,包括教师口语和普通话测试与培训。课程的设置未能根据小学教育特点设置课程,开课与汉语言文学专业雷同,甚至教材也选用普通师专的教材。

2. 学科之间缺乏整合,内容交叉重复

每门学科都强调系统性和完整性,各自为政,学科之间内容缺乏整合。如现代汉语讲造字法,古代汉语也讲造字法;现代汉语讲语音学理论,教师口语和普通话测试与培训也介绍语音知识,在内容上交叉重复,在课程总体设置上缺乏系统性。

3. 教学与实际需求脱节

主要指两个方面:① 不能适应基础教育改革的需求,现行的小学教育与基础教育实际脱

节，职前教育和职后需求衔接不上，毕业生初上岗无所适从。② 课程设置缺乏地域文化特征，缺乏针对性。

4. 教学方法和教学手段陈旧，缺乏现代色彩

尽管多媒体已经广泛运用于教学，但由于条件的限制，汉语类课程一般还采用"黑板＋粉笔"的教学手段，不能把现代技术运用于教学当中。

三、小学教育专业文科方向汉语类课程改革的思考

鉴于以上，我们认为小学教育文科方向汉语类课程应根据专业特点、社会的需求和地方文化特点作出调整：

（一）处理好学术性和师范性的关系，确定汉语类课程的教学目标

杜威(Dewey)提出一个人要成为合格的教师标准[6]：第一条件需要追溯到他对教材具有理智的准备，他应当有超前的丰富知识，他的知识必须比教科书上的原理，或任何固定的教材计划更为广博。学科知识是成为合格教师的前提条件，汉语类课程的设置使得未来的小学教师掌握语言基本理论和知识，为日后的教学工作奠定基础。如何定位小学教育文科方向语言类课程的目标是一个值得探讨的问题，职业的特点对他们的语言能力提出双重的要求：一方面他们自身应具备良好的语言能力和素养；另一方面，他们必须具备科学的语言教学能力，即能够对他们未来的学生在听、说、读、写方面进行有效的指导。

专科教育人才培养的目标是适应社会和经济的需要，培养应用型的专门人才，要求面向直接的具体工作，理论教学上以"够用为度"。小学教育专业应定位于"综合发展，学有所长"，汉语类课程设置的目的即要求学生掌握语言学基本的理论知识、原理，学会运用基本理论知识解决实际问题。对于学术上前沿的、有争议的领域不应出现在小学教育领域里；对于在未来的教学中不太用得着的知识，应减少出现，或者从小学教师的未来发展的角度做个抛砖引玉的介绍。如古代汉语中语法部分在小学教学中不直接运用的知识，可作简单的介绍，而与小学教学密切相关的知识应重点学习，如汉字部分。（下文述）

（二）适应基础教育改革的需求和地方语言文化的特点，建设"一主一修几选"的课程体系

根据小学教育"综合发展，学有所长"的特点，加强职前教育和职后的衔接，使学生尽快适应教学工作，我们认为有必要对现有的汉语课程体系进行整合，将"汉语类"课程设置"一主一修几选"的课程体系。

1. 整合现有的汉语类课程，形成以基础知识、基础理论为主的汉语基础课

"一主"指的是把现代汉语、古代汉语、语言学概论、教师口语等几门课整合成"汉语基础"课，成为主打课程，主要介绍汉语的语音、词汇、语法、文字、修辞的基本知识、原理，以提高学生的语言的素养及语言运用能力。

"一修"指的是把教师口语、普通话测试与培训、教学语言儿童化整合成"应用汉语"课，成为小学教育专业必修课，主要提高学生表达的口语技巧、技能。

"几选"指的是根据实际需要增开几门选修课。

2. 根据地方语言特点，开设方言课程

(1) 低年级教学对象的需要

与前几次相比较，新的课程标准非常注重小学生的口语训练。语文新课标规定口语交际教学：第一阶段(1～2 年级)学讲普通话，逐渐养成讲普通话的习惯；第二阶段(3～4 年级)能用普通话交谈。阅读教学也要求在第一阶段学习用普通话正确、流利、有感情地朗读课文。这一要求对经济、文化落后的农村方言地区的低年级学生似乎太高。以钦州地区为例，钦州地区是多民族多方言地区，方言(语言)复杂，有粤方言、客家方言、闽方言及壮语等少数民族语言，尽管广播、电视已很普及，当地推普工作的力度近几年得到了加强，但农村地区学龄前儿童的普通话水平还近乎零，据毕业生反馈，偏僻地区学龄前儿童几乎听不懂普通话。这里面有诸多原因，如方言与共同语差距大，文化发展相对落后，幼教师资水平低下，学生家长的认识等因素。

小学专业面向全区乃至全国招生，学生就业也流向各个地区，特别是农村地区。这些毕业生因为受过正规的师范教育，年富力强，语音标准，大多数被安排低年级教学。低年级教学就面临如何转变学生由用方言思维向普通话思维、培养学生用普通话进行口语交际的问题，如果教师不懂本地方言(语言)，与学生沟通交流就会成为障碍。首先，能和学生交流是教师执行教学任务的首要条件；其次，在教学中，能根据当地方言特点采取具有针对性的教学方法能提高学生学习的效率。

(2) 信息输入的需求

当今的时代是网络的时代，网络需要简便、快捷的信息输入方法。拼音输入法以其不用记忆字根、易学、易记的特点深受广大青年的喜爱。但拼音输入法需要语音标准，克服方言的干扰，能提高拼音输入法输入率，了解方言与共同语的对应关系更能提高拼音输入法的准确率。

3. 建设汉字理论和汉字教学理论相结合的汉字学

识字是阅读、写作的基础，新的语文课程标准提出小学阶段识字教学的总目标：培植热爱祖国语言文字的情感；认识 3000 个左右常用字，其中 2500 个会写；掌握字的形、音、义以及三者之间的联系，并能在语文实践中正确使用。所谓的“认识”，一般来说指“四会”：会读、会写、会讲、会用。但是，汉字教学还应提倡了解字的本义、引申义，从而提高读、写、用的能力，避免出现错别字[7]。汉字教学历史悠久，汉字学确立已有两千多年的历史，早在周朝就有人提出汉字教学理论，一直到现在，汉字教学成为对外汉语教学研究重要领域之一。王宁[8]提出汉字学应包括四个方面的内容。黄宇鸿[9]等提出完全有必要把汉字学从现代汉语和古代汉语分离出来，重新整合优化教学内容，构建有别于历史汉字学和现代汉字学的新型高师汉字学课程体系。同时，在汉字学课程构建和教学改革中，主要突出系统性、针对性、时代性、实践性和通用性，结合当前基础教育中汉字教学和汉字在计算机应用的实际，改革汉字的教学内容和教学手段，提高学生的汉字教学水平和实际运用能力，以适应信息时代的需求。

根据小学教育特点，我们认为汉字教学应从几个方面建设：

(1) 汉字的基本理论知识

包括汉字的起源及形成、汉字的性质、汉字音形义的关系、“六书”理论，汉字发展过程中的主要变化，现代汉字的特点等，用以提高未来小学语文教师的文字素养。

特别需要提出的是，小学教育汉字学理论要强调汉字音、形、义之间的联系。新华字典收字 8000 多个，汉语音节只有只有四百多个，汉语同音字很多。佟乐泉[10]指称，心理学研究表明人们的言语理解是通过语音信号或语音形式建立语义的过程，儿童通过字音和一个个字义对应起来，初学者更依赖字音。实际学习中，小学生特别是低年级学生在运用汉字时有使用同音字代替本字的现象，特别对用形近音同的字很难区分，如“近”和“进”、“记”和“纪”、“作”和“做”、“娃”和“蛙”等。用同音字来代替是因为没有掌握字形与字义、字音之间的关系。这里还包括字形与字的本义、字形与字的引申义之间的关系。段玉裁曾经说过：“凡字有本义，有引申、假借之余义焉。守其本义，而弃其余义者，其失也固；习其余义，而忘其本义，其失也蔽。”引申义由本义引申而来，引申义与本义有着千丝万缕的联系，引申义还与字形有一定的联系，由于汉字的讹变，现代汉字的象形意味减弱，字形与字义联系不明显。如果掌握了字形与本义、引申义的联系，用以指导学生识字，无疑可以降低学生因同音而产生的错别字现象。

(2) 汉字和汉文化的关系

汉字作为语素文字，是形音义的统一体，它在自身的结构中包含着丰富的文化因素。从字形里体现出来的构字理据，反映了汉民族悠久的文化特征。如“逆”的本字“屰”甲骨文写作“ⱽ”，为倒人形，示人自外入之状，体现了先民以直观为主的思维模式。能掌握相关的理论知识，在授课时适当地讲解，可以激发小学生热爱祖国语言文字之情。

(3) 儿童识字的认知心理

布鲁纳认为：“知识是我们给经验的规律性事实以意义和结构而组成的一个模式”，学科结构指的是人们根据某种观念、方法对已有知识进行整理和组织的形式表现为某一知识的基本逻辑、基本原理。认知结构是个体在学习和经验的基础上形成的关于事物规律的认识模式。布鲁纳的结构主义教学揭示了学科结构和认知结构的关系，为我们教学提供理论指导。

儿童心理学认为，儿童语言的习得遵循独特的规律，在识字上也表现出不同于成年人的特点。学龄儿童感知特点以整体轮廓感知占优势；在记忆方面，低年级自觉性差，善于记忆韵律化的材料，擅长形象化记忆，对记忆材料以视觉为主。

刘鸣、冯海志研究指出[11]，小学生在习得汉字的七种笔画后，学习者对字形的认识往往不再是以独立的笔画，而是以笔画组成的偏旁部首来进行相关的加工。韩布新也指出[12]，随着儿童感知觉的成熟，偏旁部首作为汉字的基本结构单位，称为记忆组块，在心理词典成为不同汉字的联结点。

吴世雄研究结果[13]，情节性记忆遵循这样的过程：感觉记忆—短时记忆—长时记忆，在这过程中，每一个阶段信息的传递伴随着大量信息的丢失，而心理学实验也表明：与受试实际经历过的情节相联系的知识一般比较容易进入受试者的长时记忆，并保存下来。

科学的识字教学方法的确定必须建立在两个互相依存的关系上：一个是对一种文字体系本身即学科结构的认识；一个是对认知者认知过程的认识。这两方面认识越深，识字方法就越符合客观规律。一方面掌握汉字的基本理论；另一方面掌握儿童认知心理特征，把两方面整合形成科学的实用的汉字学课程。

据此，我们认为小学教育汉字学应本着“务实、适需、与时俱进”的精神构建科学、实用的汉字学课程。

参考文献

[1] 惠中. 高等教育体系中小学教育专业的思考[J]. 高等师范教育研究，2003(3).

[2] http://www.stars.gov.cn/tjcj/ndsj/2005/indexch.htm.

[3] 周昆.我国村小教师队伍现存问题与对策研究[D].西南大学硕士论文,2008.
[4] 韩冰清.农村教师专业化与地方高师课程改革[J].黄冈师范学院学报,2008(1).
[5] 杨四海.教师职前培养与现实需要的对接研究[J].教育探索,2007(1).
[6] [美]约翰·杜威.经验与教育[C].姜文闵,译.北京:人民教育出版社,1991.
[7] 张亮.我国识字教学的反思[D].苏州大学硕士论文,2003.
[8] 王宁.汉字构形学讲座[M].上海:上海教育出版社,2000.
[9] 黄宇鸿,陆善采.新世纪高师汉字学教学内容与研究方法的思考[J].钦州高等师范学校学报,2004(6).
[10] 佟乐泉.小学识字教学研究[M].广州:广东教育出版社,1999.
[11] 刘鸣,冯海志.汉字信息编码特征与教材教法[J].华南师范大学学报,1998(2).
[12] 韩布新.汉字识别中部件的频率效应[J].心理科学,1998(3).
[13] 吴世雄.认知心理学的记忆原理对汉字教学的启迪[J].语言教学与研究,1998(4).

加强实验室全面建设　迎接本科教学评估

张艳军*
（钦州学院，广西　钦州　535000）

摘　要：根据教育部《高等学校基础课教学实验室评估办法》和《高等学校基础课教学实验室评估标准》开展实验室评估是全面推动实验室建设、提高实验教学质量与教学水平的有效措施。以评估为契机，在实验教学实践环节中不断探索实验室建设、实验教学改革和实验室管理的有效途径。

关键词：实验室建设；实验教学；管理

All-round Development of Laboratories to Meet the Assessment of University Teaching

Zhang Yan-jun
(Qinzhou University, Qinzhou 535000, China)

Abstract: Availing the opportunity of assessment of universtiy teaching by ministry of education, all-round development, innovation and management of laboratories should be carried out guided by the methods and criteria of university laboratories assessment.

Key words: development of laboratories; lab teaching; management

在党的十七大报告中胡锦涛总书记明确指出：科技自主创新是一个国家综合实力的核心，而科技创新的关键是人才培养。目前高校都把实验室看成是一个培养创新人才的基地，一个展示高校办学水平的窗口。搞好实验室建设与管理，是提高实验教学质量、教学水平、培养合格人才的根本保证和有效措施。从某种意义上说，一个学校实验室的建设和实验教学水平，体现一个学校的教学、科研和管理水平。因此，我们要以评估为契机，从实际出发，统筹规划，合

* 张艳军，钦州学院生物与化学系教师。

理设置，力争做到建筑设施、仪器设备、师资队伍与教学管理全面协调发展。切实加强实验室人、财、物等方面的管理，重视师资队伍建设与培养，提高实验教学水平，扩大实验教学投资效益，真正达到以评促教、以评促改、以评促建、以评促管、评建管改相结合，为高校培养出高素质科技创新人才。

1 实验室基础设施建设合理规划

以国家教育部《高等学校实验室工作规程》和《基础课教学实验室评估标准》为指导思想建设实验室。对实验室建设要有清晰的建设思路，明确的近期、中期和远期建设规划和规范化管理措施。具体包括：

(1) 学校对实验室的建设规划、资金投入；

(2) 实验室基本情况，包括实验室名称、房号、面积、功能等；

(3) 购置新仪器设备时，加强可行性和必要性的论证，把有限的经费合理调配，提高仪器利用率。

2 学科建设与实验教学改革

明确专业设置目标，要培养什么样的人才，然后利用什么样的方式来培养。通过制定学科建设与人才培养的需求相结合来规划，实验课程开设的环节必须紧扣专业的特点。

组织专业教师对相应学科的实验课程，按实验教学大纲进行统一规划，体现专业学科的特点。实验课程的设置应突出以下特点：(1) 合理调节基本操作实验、综合性实验和设计性实验的比重。在强化基本实验技能训练的基础上，进行综合性实验，指导学生观察、记录实验结果，整理实验数据，提出问题，引导学生进行科学思维，提高学生综合素质，为进行设计性、创新性实验教学改革研究与培养一专多能创新人才创造有利条件。(2) 在实验教学中，确定学生的主体地位，教师的主导作用。采用“课前认真预习思考与主动参与相结合”、“强调重点、突出难点与自主完成相结合”等教学方法，鼓励学生创新，充分发挥学生的积极性、主动性及创造性，创建一个以专业技术教育、创新能力教育与综合素质教育和谐统一的新实验教学模式，使实验室实践教学的功能得到充分发挥。(3) 充分资源共享，高校各专业实验室之间、高校与高校，高校与企业之间大型设备共享。如我校生化系的石油化工专业，部分专业实验课程的开设，可利用我市进出口检验检疫局的国家石油化工重点实验室的设备资源。

3 实验室规范化管理

3.1 规章制度建立

“不以规矩不能成方圆”。实验室为实验教学和科研提供了场所，实验室的管理也离不开各种规章制度，健全和完善各项规章制度有利于实验室建设和管理，也是协调各方面工作的依据。其中制度主要针对仪器设备、药品的管理和实验室的人员(包括上实验课或做实验的教师、学生及准备实验仪器药品的人员)管理两个大模块。仪器设备方面：例如“仪器设备管理制度"、"低值易耗品管理制度"、"仪器设备损坏、丢失赔偿制度"等；人员的管理方面："学生实验室安全制度"、"学生实验守则"、"实验技术人员岗位责任制"等。把各种规章制度制成板报，悬挂上墙。

3.2 档案建立

实验室档案管理在高校教学评估中是一个重点项目，实验室的一些数据是教师科研和教学工作的体现。主要可以从以下两个方面来看：

3.2.1 人员管理档案

实验室人员在实验室的工作及实验结果被记录并保存，成为实验室人员业务管理档案。涉及到教师的主要有：(1) 实验教学准备工作和组织工作的记录。首先对实验室人员合理分工，指定专人负责某一门课程或某一个专业实验室。实验人员在学生实验之前，进行相关仪器的调试准备情况，并且对一些复杂实验进行预实验，或者对于一些创新性实验进行改进和优化；(2) 实验室使用记录。要求教师每次上课要做详细的记录，包括授课的班级，授课的主要内容，仪器设备的完好情况与使用情况，本次课程的实验结论等；(3) 实验室科研记录。要求参与实验的人员认真记录每次实验的过程与结果，并得出实验结论；(4) 学期教学计划与实验项目完成表。要求教师每学期期初时按教学计划的要求逐条填写本学期的授课班级、班级人数、每节课的授课内容与学时安排，期末时按教学完成表填写教学任务完成情况。涉及到学生的主要有：(1) 实训作业。对于学生每次实验或实训后的作业要求存档；(2) 学生培训。主要针对学生开展一些实验室活动，如学生参加实践技能竞赛，实验理论竞赛的成果等。涉及实验室日常管理人员的主要有：(1) 岗位工作日志。要求管理人员每天认真填写个人实际工作内容；(2) 实验室安全排查记录。要求实验室管理人员定期填写实验室的设备完好情况、实验室使用情况及防火、防盗等安全隐患排查工作。

3.2.2 仪器设备档案

实验室所涉及的物品包括实验室的主体、实验室内的仪器设备及其配套设施、实验需要的低值易耗物品等。这些物品的采购，使用、维修等要一一记录并保存。主要包含有以下几方面：(1) 仪器设备账目管理。要求实验室内的所有设备必须登记上账，并注明购置日期及购置批次；(2) 大型仪器设备使用记录。大型仪器的使用说明，操作程序，制作成板，供广大师生使用仪器时参考。对大型精密仪器，有专人负责管理，每次调试或使用均有详细、规范的记录；(3) 仪器设备维修记录。要求专业维修人员对设备进行维修时需认真填写设备的名称、损坏部位、维修过程及更换部件等。设备管理及维修到位，帐、物、卡齐全，准确无误，定期保养、定期检查，保证设备的完好率及使用率。此外，物品管理档案还包括低值易耗物品的申报与领取，入出库账目等。

3.3 实验室人员队伍建设

作为实验室主体的实验技术人员承担着实验教学、科研以及实验室的建设和日常管理等多项任务，他们的思想状况、业务水平、专业技能等综合素质如何直接关系到实验教学、科研和管理水平的高低。加强队伍建设，主要从以下几方面着手：(1) 抓思想素质。就是要求实验教学人员具有爱岗敬业的职业精神和严谨、科学的工作态度。同时也应具备较强的服务意识、团队精神。(2) 抓技术素质。实验教学人员要求具备扎实的专业知识、较强的动手能力和创新意识。可以通过引进高学历人才参与实验室管理工作，同时重视实验教学人员的业务培训，采取定期培训、岗位辅导培训、送住高校深造等多种形式，不断更新提高实验教学人员的知识与技能。(3) 完善业绩奖励竞争机制。由于实验室人员工作性质特殊，应给予实验技术人员良好的工作环境和待遇，对实验技术人员的工作实行有偿服务，多劳多得，提高实验人员的待遇等。从实际出发制定评审标准，如设立实验教学评优奖、实验技术成果奖、实验室管理先进奖等。

4 展望

"双基实验室"评估是创建一个建设现代化、标准化，管理规范化、科学化、效益化实验教学中心的必由之路。借此，我们将按照评估的要求进行实验室建设、改革实验教学、提高实验教学质量、人才培养质量，为培养新世纪高素质创新型人才服务，使我校的办学水平再上一个新的台阶。

参考文献

[1] 卢常伟，李岩，刘陵顺. 实验技术人员综合素质培养的研究[J]. 实验技术与管理，2008，25(4).
[2] 陈洁. 加强高校实验室建设与管理的思考[J]. 玉林师范学院学报(自然科学版)，2008，29(5).
[3] 张远方. 高校实验室队伍建设的探讨[J]. 实验技术与管理，2008，25(6).
[4] 黎中良. 新办本科高校实验技术队伍建设的研究[J]. 中国现代教育装备，2006(11).
[5] 刘世钰. 高校大型仪器设备管理与利用的对策浅析[J]. 中国现代教育装备，2007(3).
[6] 郑兴福，陈大鹏. 深化实验室改革为培养人才服务[J]. 实验室研究与探索，2005，24(12).

化学工程与工艺专业核心课程体系建设

张　雪*

（钦州学院，广西　钦州　535000）

摘　要：本文从如何培养服务于北部湾经济社会发展的优秀复合型石化技术人才角度出发，结合专业教学改革，探讨了以石油化工和精细化工为培养方向的化学工程与工艺专业学科核心课程体系的构建及优化问题。指出必须建立一套结合区域特色经济、强调过程开发和工程实践能力培养的核心课程体系，从而培养熟悉地方经济特色、具备一定化学工程设计能力的地方急需的复合型石化技术人才。

关键词：化学工程；核心课程；优化

Abstract: This paper discussed the construction and optimization of core curriculum on chemical engineering and technology oriented petroleum and fine chemicals based on cultivating complexed petroleum technicians and engineers for Beibu Gulf economic and social development with teaching reform. In conclusion, a suit of core curriculum which adapts to local econmic development and emphasizes on training students' ability of process development and engineering practice should be established. By this means, the complexed petroleum technicians and engineers which are up on local economy and get a certain chemical engineering design ability for Beibu Gulf economy could be brought up.

Key words: chemical engineering; core curriculum; optimization

近年来，随着北部湾区域经济的逐渐升温，越来越多的大型企业入驻钦州，尤其是中石油广西石化千万吨炼油项目的建设，为钦州的发展提供了一个千载难逢的好机会。钦州学院作为北部湾沿海唯一一所高校，理应担负起为地方培养优秀工程人才的责任。2007年，钦州学院生化系设置了化学工程与工艺专业，分设石油化工和精细化工两个方向，旨在培养北部湾石油化工人才。在近两年的教学实践中，笔者不断思考如何培养能更好地适应北部湾区域经济发展的化学工程人才，有了一些体会，作为化学工程与工艺专业教学讨论的开始，希望起到抛砖引玉之效。

* 张雪，男，湖北荆州人，钦州学院生化系教师。研究方向：石油化工，催化。

一、核心课程体系的构建

1. 核心课程体系构建的原则

钦州学院开设化学工程与工艺专业有良好的机遇,同时也有多方面的挑战。在机遇方面,中石油广西石化千万吨炼油项目作为一个产业龙头,带动了整个北部湾化工行业蓬勃发展,为钦州学院化工专业学生提供了大量的就业机会,为钦州学院的发展提供了强有力的动力;但是另一方面,国内多所知名大学如天津大学、中国石油大学、华东理工大学、浙江大学等早就开设有同样的专业,区内也有几所大学,如广西大学、广西工学院等设置了相同的专业,毫无疑问,这些大学办学的实力远在钦州学院之上,这给钦州学院化学工程与工艺专业办学带来了多方面的挑战。要办好钦州学院化学工程与工艺专业,贯彻学院打造五大品牌专业的精神,需要从紧密联系北部湾区域经济建设方面着眼,努力办出具有石化特色的化学工程与工艺专业,重点建立一套紧密结合石化下游产业链、注重过程开发和工程实践能力培养的核心课程体系。在核心课程设置方面,确立夯实专业基础、强化工程意识、注重实验技能、拓宽专业口径,注重石化特色的原则。

2. 核心课程体系的内容与相互关系

所谓化工过程,主要包含分离过程和反应过程。与这两种过程紧密相关的一系列化工类课程共同构成了化工类课程的核心。按照"门数适宜,重点突出,相互支撑,形成一体"的要求,选择化工热力学、分离工程、传递原理、反应工程和化工工艺学等5门理论课以及与这5门理论课相关的化工专业实验课作为核心课程,建设具有石化特色化学工程与工艺专业的核心课程体系,全力打造化学工程与工艺这一品牌专业。

在这5门理论课程中,分离工程和反应工程分别研究各类分离过程和反应过程,它们构成了化工过程课程最核心的部分。其中,化工热力学是化工过程研究、开发和设计的理论基础,是化学工程的重要分支,与化学反应工程、分离工程关系密切。化工热力学的核心价值在于研究过程进行的方向和限度,为分离过程和反应过程提供相平衡、反应平衡数据,并对化工过程进行热力学分析[1]。反应工程是与工程实际紧密联系的课程之一,它广泛地将化工热力学、化学动力学、流体力学、传热、传质以及生产工艺、环境保护、经济学等方面的理论知识和经验综合于工业反应器的结构和操作参数的设计和优化中[2]。分离工程是化工专业基础课程,讲述的是如何将混合物进行分离与提纯的学科。作为专门研究分离方法的分离工程课程对学生工程素养的培养有很重要的作用。该课程阐明了化工分离过程的本质规律,重点研究分离方法的工业化途径,设备设计放大效应,最优分离路线的工业化及最优操作条件。在选择具体分离方法时,不仅要考虑技术上的可行性、经济上的合理性,而且要考虑能耗、环保、设备放大和开发成本等诸多问题[3]。传递原理旨在研究化工动量、热量及质量(俗称三传)的传递现象,用一种统一的观点来处理三种传递现象,并研究动量、热量和质量传递之间的类似性,是研究分离机理、分离效率和宏观反应动力学的基础理论,同时也是反应器放大研究的基础理论之一。与化工热力学不同,传递原理是一门探讨传递速率的课程,它对过程开发、过程设计、生产操作、优化控制及过程机理研究都有重要的使用意义[4]。化工工艺学重在工艺过程的分析,即在特定条件下,进行分离过程、反应过程的比较选择、整合优化。化工工艺学是大学基础化学、化工热力学、化工动力学、反应工程、分离工程等专业基础课和专业课的综合运用。化工热力学和传递原理旨在加强专业基础，化工专业实验、反应工程和分离工程重在强化工程意识，化工工艺学拓展了专业适应面，可以突出石化特色。

二、核心课程体系的优化

为了保障以上核心课程体系的顺利实施，建议结合钦州学院化学工程与工艺现有的教学计划，从以下几个方面作出适当的调整。

1. 加强数理基础教学力度，适度拓展

新世纪的工程人才必须有熟练应用数学、科学与工程等知识的能力，有进行设计、实验分析与数据处理的能力。在两年的教学实践中，学生普遍反映数理基础不够扎实，一些数学问题不知所云，比如热力学计算中要应用迭代法求解状态方程、精馏过程计算、反应工程中的偏微分方程求解等，问题大都源于数学基础较薄弱。因此建议加开线性代数、运筹学、概率论与数理统计、数值计算、C 程序语言、数学物理方法，流体力学等数理和计算机基础课程。多所兄弟院校早就开设了这些基础课程。线性代数和运筹学的开设可以解决反应器设计过程的优化问题；概率论与数理统计是实验数据处理和理解反应工程中一些基本概念的基础；数值计算和 C 程序语言两门课程是工科学生重要的基础课程，加开这两门课程也是落实我校化学工程与工艺专业培养计划中对学生计算机水平的要求，对学生就业能力的提高有好处；数学物理方法和流体力学是传递工程等课程的基础，加开这两门课程可以大大提高学生工程数学能力，为就业和进一步深造打下坚实的数理基础。考虑到 Matlab 在科学和工程计算领域的突出作用，建议开设 Matlab 在化工中的应用的相关课程[5]。

现将原钦州学院化学工程与工艺专业待调整课程列于表 1，加开课程（括号中注明课时）和调整后的课程列于表 2。

表 1　化学工程与工艺专业待调整课程表

	第一学期	第二学期	第三学期	第四学期	第五学期	第六学期
化学化工类				化工原理（34 学时）	化工原理（34 学时）	
			化学反应工程（51 学时）			
				化工热力学（34 学时）	化工热力学（34 学时）	
				计算机模拟与仿真（17 学时）	计算机模拟与仿真（17 学时）	计算机模拟与仿真（17 学时）

表 2　化学工程与工艺专业调整后课程表

	第一学期	第二学期	第三学期	第四学期	第五学期	第六学期
数学类	线性代数（40 学时）	数值计算（40 学时）	概率论与数理统计（40 学时）			
		运筹学（40 学时）	数学物理方法（40 学时）			
物理类				流体力学（40 学时）		
化学化工类					传递原理（60 学时）	
			化工热力学（34 学时）	化工热力学（34 学时）		
			化工原理（34 学时）	化工原理（34 学时）		
					化学反应工程（51 学时）	
计算机类		C 语言（60 学时）（暑期上机）			Matlab 在化工中的应用（40 学时）	
机械类		化工制图（40 学时）				
电子类				电工学（40 学时）（暑期实验）		
经济类						技术经济（40 学时）

化工热力学和化工原理是反应工程的基础，故将化工热力学从第四、五学期调整至第三、四学期；化工原理和反应工程两门课程共同构成了化学工程最核心的部分，将化工原理从第四、五学期调整至第二、三学期，反应工程从第三学期调整至第五学期，也是考虑到化工原理是反应工程的基础。同时，将计算机模拟与仿真删去，将其中的知识分散到加开的 Matlab 在化工中的应用和数值计算这两门课程中。

从表 2 中还可以看出，加开的课程中，突出了数理课程的基础，同时适度地拓展经济和计算机相关的课程，也增加了化工制图和电工学等实践性较强的课程，这对培养学生的工程实践能力是必不可少的。

2. 整合化工专业实验

为了整合学院教学资源，最大限度地利用现有的教学设备，建议从各门化学工程与工艺核心课程的专业实验中选出一些经典的、与石化行业紧密相关的进行重新编排，单独设置一门大学化工基础实验课程，分成 3 个学期展开教学。另外，考虑到传统的化工专业实验教材以单一验证实验为主，无法满足新世纪综合素质人才培养的要求，可将化工实验按由浅入深的原则划分成验证型实验、设计型实验和综合型实验 3 个层次。尽量精简验证型实验，增加设计型实验和综合型实验。可以从教师的一些科研项目中选出一部分让学生参与,将这些项目设计成设计型或综合型实验,这样,通过学生亲身体验科研过程,培养了正确的科研习惯,为学生的就业和进一步深造打下良好基础。

3. 加强多媒体教学

随着计算机众多领域广泛而深入的应用,掌握必要的计算机应用知识是相当必要的。一方面,由于现在石化企业的生产是高度自动化的,一些问题通过传统的教学形式很难向学生解释清楚,多媒体技术可有效增加信息的传递;另一方面,采用多媒体教学的教学形式,通过多媒体仿真实验,可以减少不必要的实验投入,减少人力物力,在保质保量的前提下降低教学成本。要将课堂教学和多媒体教学结合起来,既发挥课堂教学有利于教师与学生间面对面交流的作用,也让多媒体教学进入学生的学习中。

参考文献

[1] 陈钟秀,顾飞燕,胡望月. 化工热力学[M]. 北京:化学工业出版社,2001:1-3.
[2] 张濂,许知美,袁向前. 化学反应工程[M]. 北京:华东理工大学出版社,2007:1-6.
[3] 陈洪钫, 刘家祺. 化工分离过程[M]. 北京:化学工业出版社,1995:1-5.
[4] 陈晋南. 传递过程原理[M]. 北京:化学工业出版社,2004:1-2.
[5] 郭惠霞. 化工过程计算中 Matlab 的应用[J]. 计算机与应用化学,2007,(1).

后　记

一年一度的教师教育盛会，第三届教师教育国际研讨会暨全国教师教育学会师范院校协作委员会第二届学术年会于2009年10月23日至25日，在南国的热土——钦州学院隆重召开。会议围绕着“社会转型与教师教育改革”这一主题展开了友好而又热烈的讨论。来自美国、澳大利亚、泰国、越南、韩国等国家的教师教育专家、学者以及全国教师教育学会师范院校协作委员会各理事单位、国内各师范院校代表等共200多人参加了会议，会议共收到论文52篇。

一届盛会，一次分享学术智慧的盛宴；一本文集，承载着同仁们研究成果和教师教育的梦想。本届研讨会的论文集主编分别为全国教师教育学会师范学院协作委员会会长、安庆师范学院原院长（现任安徽行政学院常务副院长）汪青松教授，全国教师教育学会师范学院协作委员会副会长、钦州学院副院长徐书业教授，安庆师范学院副院长张群教授；副主编分别为全国教师教育学会师范学院协作委员会秘书长、安庆师范学院教育学院院长曹长德教授，全国教师教育学会师范学院协作委员会副秘书长、钦州学院公共教育部主任梁庆副教授，钦州学院院长办公室包琼就主任。

感谢全国教师教育课程资源专家委员会秘书长王宏凯先生，从百忙中拨冗为本书作序；感谢中国科学技术大学出版社为本书出版所做的卓有成效的工作；感谢各位代表提供了高质量的论文并在编辑过程中给予了配合与支持；尤其要感谢安庆师范学院与钦州学院为本书出版提供了经费支持。

由于我们水平有限，疏漏在所难免，欢迎大家批评指正。

编　者

2010年5月